OUR
(unlikely)
FATHERS

The Signers of the Texas
Declaration of Independence

LOUIS WILTZ KEMP

Edited by Michelle M. Haas

Copano Bay Press
2014

Originally published in 1944 under the title *The Signers of the Texas Declaration of Independence.*

Table of Contents

Publisher's Note

"Am I not a queer conglomerate—a sweet-scented mixture indeed!" Such was the opinion of legendary Texas cowboy author Charlie Siringo of his peculiar roots. And such is a very apt description of the men chronicled in this book. A Quebecer, a Scot, an Englishman, an Irishman, some Yankees, some Southern gents, a couple of Tejanos... listening to the duelling accents alone would have been well worth the price of admission. Some had led the quiet lives of family men. Others were known for drunkenness, noted for bravery, celebrated for military acumen and one was notorious for castrating a couple of guys back in his home state. Five signers resided on land that was technically in Arkansas. Two fathers who lost sons at the Alamo saddled up next to the father of the man who had burned their bodies. A couple of signers had been "permanently" tossed out of Texas after their participation in the Fredonian Rebellion. Is that not a queer conglomeration?

Low on provisions, in the cold, away from their homes and families, with the looming threat of Santa Anna kicking in the door, 59 individuals created an independent Texas. Despite all of the diversity and adversity, they managed to get it done. In the wake of their deliberations and pen strokes was born the storied Republic and the state that would define western expansion and reshape the United States.

In this book, Mr. Kemp serves up each signer to us so that we might place each, in our mind's eye, in that rented building in Washington. He tells us where they came from, how they got here and where they ended up. We *need* to know these men because they're the men who made us Texans!

In his preface to the first edition, included here, Kemp advises that "unusually voluminous footnotes" were necessary to document his refutation of points made by historians who came before him. No exaggeration there! His original notes are here, but presented as chapter notes, as I'm inclined to think that our readership might find page-long footnotes inhibitive to the experience of leisurely reading. But do peruse the chapter notes. They contain interesting letters, documents and statements about and by our Fathers and are worth reading in their own right.

The genealogist should be advised that none of the genealogy provided by Kemp has been revised in this edition. Some of it is outdated. The digital age has taken genealogy to a new level that I'm sure was unimaginable when Kemp was writing.

This book is lovingly dedicated to the men and women who continue to keep the history and spirit of Texas alive. The legacy of our unlikely Fathers would be lost were it not for your efforts. And I'd be out of a job. Mark, you give me new perspectives on history and the people who made it, allowing me to do my best each time and to keep learning. It is never boring.

To my favorite Lieutenant, I offer gratitude for the support you provided during my last big project. It was a monumental task for me and your daily positive attitude was an indispensable help. I thank you.

Michelle M. Haas, Managing Editor
-*Windy Hill*

Author's Preface

$\mathcal{T}$his volume proposes to accomplish two objects: first, to present brief, accurate biographical sketches of the signers of the Texas Declaration of Independence, and second, to correct traditional errors associated with the signing of that historic document.

Despite abundant evidence to the contrary, many well informed people believe the Declaration was signed by 58 instead of 59 men and that the building in which the document was adopted was a blacksmith shop gratuitously donated by Noah T. Byars instead of a house rented by Byars and his business partner, Peter M. Mercer, to a committee of townsmen, who, in turn, tendered its use, free of all cost, to the Convention. Many are also of the opinion that the signers were colonists who had lived in Texas for many years, when, as a matter of fact, only ten of them were in Texas on January 1, 1830, six years previous to the Declaration. Fifteen arrived in 1835, when it was generally known in the United States that war between Texas and Mexico was inevitable. March 2 is rightly celebrated as Independence Day, for it was on that day the Declaration was adopted, but the document was not signed until the following day.

Numerous persons whom I name in footnotes contributed significant materials to this study, and I am deeply grateful to them. I wish particularly to thank four whose assistance was substantial. Miss Harriet Smither, Archivist of the Texas State Library, and Miss Winnie Allen, Archivist of the University of Texas Library, made available the collections in their care. Mr. Bascom Giles, Commissioner of the General Land Office, permitted access to land cer-

OUR (unlikely) FATHERS

tificate files. Mr. Andrew Forest Muir, graduate student of
The Rice Institute and later fellow of the University of Texas, read the manuscript and made invaluable suggestions.

LOUIS WILTZ KEMP
March 2, 1944

iv

A Bibliographic Note

*T*his monograph is the result of years of personal research, the author's early conviction being that the impulses and events leading up to and influencing the signing of the Texas Declaration of Independence were not thoroughly understood. Unusually voluminous footnotes are essential. These are used to confirm the author's conclusions, as well as to apprehend for the reader such analogy or disagreement as may merit consideration.

Twenty-five authorities in particular are quoted often enough to justify, for practical brevity, the use of a key instead of a repetition of bibliographical detail. These keywords and the sources they indicate are:

BARKER: AUSTIN
Eugene C. Barker (ed.), *The Austin Papers* (Washington: Government Printing Office; Austin: The University of Texas, 1820-1926), 3 vols.

BARKER: MINUTES
Eugene C. Barker (ed.), "Minutes of the Ayuntamiento of San Felipe de Austin, 1828-1832" in *Southwestern Historical Quarterly*, XXI-XXIV.

BARKER & WILLIAMS
Amelia W. Williams and Eugene C. Barker (eds.), *The Writings of Sam Houston, 1813-1863* (Austin: The University of Texas, 1938-1943), 8 vols.

BINKLEY
William C. Binkley (ed.), *Official Correspondence of the Texan Revolution, 1835-1836* (New York & London: D. Appleton Century, c. 1936), 2 vols.

BROWN
John Henry Brown, *History of Texas from 1685 to 1892* (St. Louis: L. B. Daniell, c. 1893), 2 vols.

COMP. M. S. R.
Comptroller's Military Service Records: (MSS. in Archives, Texas State Library, Austin).

CRANE
William Carey Crane, *Life and Select Literary Remains of Sam Houston of Texas* (Philadelphia: J. B. Lippincott & Co., 1884), 2 vols. in 1.

CROCKET
George Louis Crocket, *Two Centuries in East Texas...* (Dallas: The Southwest Press, c. 1932).

DIXON
Sam Houston Dixon, *The Men Who Made Texas Free...* (Houston: Texas Historical Publishing, c. 1924).

FULMORE
Z. T. Fulmore, *The History and Geography of Texas as Told in County Names* (Austin: E. L. Steck, c. 1915).

GAMMEL
H. P. N. Gammel (ed.), *The Laws of Texas, 1822-1897* (Austin: Gammel Book Company, 1898), 10 vols.

GARRISON
George P. Garrison (ed.), *Diplomatic Correspondence of the Republic of Texas* (Washington: Government Printing Office, 1938-1911), 3 vols.

GOODRICH
Benjamin B. Goodrich's list of signers published in the *Telegraph & Texas Register* (Houston), August 3, 1842.

Bibliographic Note

GRAY
A. C. Gray (ed.), *From Virginia to Texas, 1835, Diary of Col. Wm. F. Gray...* (Houston: Gray, Dillaye & Co., 1909).

JAMES
Marquis James, *The Raven, a Biography of Sam Houston* (Indianapolis: Bobbs-Merrill, c. 1929).

KIDD
J. C. Kidd (comp.), *History of Holland Lodge No. 1, Ancient Free and Accepted Masons...* (Houston: Holland Lodge, c. 1920).

LINDLEY
E. R. Lindley (comp.), *Members of the Legislature of the State of Texas from 1846 to 1939* (Austin: State of Texas, 1939).

RETURNS
Convention Election Returns: (MSS. in Archives of Texas State Library: Austin).

SPAN. ARCH.
Spanish Archives: (MSS. in General Land Office: Austin).

THRALL
Homer S. Thrall, *A Pictorial History of Texas...* (St. Louis: N. D. Thompson & Co., 1879).

WADE
Houston Wade (comp.), *Masonic Dictionary, Republic of Texas* (LaGrange: *LaGrange Journal*, 1935).

WHARTON
Clarence R. Wharton, *History of Fort Bend County* (San Antonio: Naylor, 1939).

WINKLER
Ernest William Winkler (ed.), *Secret Journals of the Senate, Republic of Texas, 1836-1845* (Austin: Texas Library & Historical Commission, 1911).

WOOTEN
Dudley G. Wooten (ed.), *A Comprehensive History of Texas, 1685 to 1897* (Dallas: William G. Scarff, 1898), 2 vols.

YOAKUM
Henderson Yoakum, *...History of Texas...*(New York: Redfield, 1855), 2 vols.

San Felipe, Washington,
The Hall and the Document

*T*he General Council of the Provisional Government of Texas, on December 12, 1835, issued notice for an election to be held on February 1, 1836, to select delegates to a convention to be held at Washington beginning March 1. The notice stipulated that the municipalities of Bexar, Brazoria, Nacogdoches, San Augustine, and Washington each should elect four delegates; Liberty, Austin, and Mina each three; Goliad, Gonzales, Harrisburg, Jackson, Jasper, Jefferson, Matagorda, Refugio, San Patricio, Tenehaw, Guadalupe Victoria, and Viesca each two; and the citizens of Pecan Point, two.[1] Three days later the Council carved Sabine out of San Augustine, designated two delegates to be elected from the new municipality, and reduced to three the number of delegates from San Augustine.[2] On December 27, the Council changed the name of Viesca to Milam,[3] and, on January 11, 1836, changed that of Tenehaw to Shelby.[4] In addition, on the last date, it organized Colorado Municipality, with the privilege of returning two delegates.[5]

Due to conditions existing at San Felipe de Austin while the Consultation, and later the General Council of the Provisional Government, was in session there in 1835, the newly laid out town of Washington was chosen as the meeting place of the Constitutional Convention.

Authority for establishing San Felipe was given to Stephen F. Austin, July 26, 1823, by Luciano Garcia, Governor of Coahuila and Texas, who also named the town.[6] It was surveyed in the following year as the capital of Austin's Colony. As time passed, it be came the unofficial capital of Anglo-American Texas. There the conventions of 1832 and

1833 were held, and in 1835 it was chosen as the meeting place of the Consultation. From all accounts, the town was not attractive and did not improve with age.

Noah Smithwick described the town as he found it in 1828:

> Twenty-five or perhaps thirty log cabins strung along the west bank of the Brazos River was all there was of it, while the human population of all ages and colors could not have exceeded 200. Men were largely in the majority, coming from every state in the Union, and every walk of life.
>
> There seeming to be a good opening for my trade [blacksmithing] in San Felipe, I bought a set of tools from George Huff on the San Bernard and set up business in the parent colony in the year 1828. In the absence of a more comprehensive view, a pen picture of the old town may not be uninteresting. The buildings all being of unhewn logs with clapboard roofs, presented few distinguishing features. Stephen F. Austin had established his headquarters something like half a mile back from the river on the west bank of a little creek—Palmito—that ran into the Brazos just above the main village...[7]
>
> The alcalde's office was in a large double log house standing back some distance from the main thoroughfare almost immediately in the rear of the Whiteside Hotel, which building it much resembled. By whom it was built, or for what purpose, I do not remember, but my impression is that it was designed for a hotel. The walls of hewn logs were roofed in and abandoned at that stage. It was here the ayuntamiento held its sittings, and this windowless, floorless pen, through the unchinked cracks of which the wild winds wandered and whistled at will, was presumably the Faneuil Hall of Texas.[8]

That San Felipe had deteriorated after Smithwick left it in 1831 is indicated by the entry in Col. William Fairfax Gray's diary of February 16, 1836:

2

San Felipe is a wretched, decaying looking place. Five stores of small assortments, two mean taverns, and twenty or thirty scattering and mean looking houses, very little paint visible. No appearance of industry, or thrift or improvements of any kind.[9]

The Consultation met at San Felipe on October 16, 1835,[10] and adjourned on November 14, to meet March 1, 1836.[11]

The accommodations in San Felipe were poor, and, on November 17, 1835, on motion of Sam Houston, the General Council voted eight to six to move to Washington,[12] a town laid out in the spring of 1835. Upon the motion of Don Carlos Barrett the Council resolved that an express be sent immediately to Washington to inform the citizens there to be prepared for the reception of the Provisional Government and to notify the army and the citizens generally of the removal.[13] Gov. Henry Smith, however, vetoed the resolution on November 20, giving as his reasons the lack, in Washington, of a printing press,[14] essential to government business, and the failure of the Council to make "the necessary arrangements for our comfortable location at Washington."[15]

The Council remained in San Felipe, but, their discomforts and inconveniences increased instead of diminished. On November 24, the president of the Council directed the sergeant-at-arms "to cause the noise which annoyed and interrupted the Council to cease." The sergeant reported that "Mr. Urbane[16] refused to desist from interrupting the Council"; whereupon the president issued a warrant for Urban's arrest. Urban appeared and apologized.[17]

According to J. J. Linn, the Council, sitting in a house belonging to Urban, had two complaints against their landlord. The first was the smoky stove in the council room that forced the members periodically to seek fresh air outdoors. The other was the noise made by Urban in operating a steel corn mill located at or near his house but a few yards away. To the complaints, Urban replied that he knew of no means of procuring bread for his family and boarders other than by grinding his own grain, but if his boarders, most of whom apparently were members of the Council, had no objection to the lack of bread, he presumed he and his family could also stand the deprivation. As for the smoke, Urban suggested that the Council could remedy that by removing the stove. He ended his defense by stating that he was permitting the Council to use his building without charge, but that if the members did not like their quarters, they could go elsewhere.[18]

In a resolution approved December 10, 1835, by James W. Robinson (who signed himself lieutenant governor and ex-officio president of the General Council), but vetoed by Gov. Henry Smith and passed over his veto December 13, the General Council called for a convention to be held at Washington beginning March 1, 1836.[19]

4

The Council was unable to muster a quorum after January 17, 1836. On February 16 the few members present passed a resolution that the Council adjourn to meet at Washington, February 22. This was done, and meetings were held daily until March 11, when the Council adjourned *sine die*. No quorum had been present since January 17.[20]

The town of Washington is situated on the west side of the Brazos River, opposite the mouth of the Navasota. It was surveyed on the Andrew Robinson grant. Robinson, one of the "old three hundred" of Austin's colonists, on July 8, 1824, received title to two leagues and one labor of land which he surveyed in present Brazoria, Washington, and Waller Counties. He selected for his home a site near which Washington was later built, and there he conducted a ferry. His daughter, Patsy, was married to John W. Hall. On May 20, 1831, Robinson gave 640 acres of land to Mr. and Mrs. Hall, in consideration of their promise to take care of him in his old age.[21]

On March 24, 1835, John W. Hall, Asa Hoxey, Thomas Gray, and the firm of Miller & Somervell (composed of James B. Miller and Alexander Somervell) organized the Washington Townsite Company. In organizing the enterprise Hall sold one-fourth of the land to Hoxey, one-fourth to Thomas Gray, and one-fourth to Miller & Somervell. There were three lots on the one-fourth of the land reserved by Hall.[22]

That no time was lost in surveying the town is vouched for in a statement made by Dr. Hoxey, November 15, 1837: "Washington was laid out as a Town in the spring of 1835."[23] The progress it had made by July 18 is indicated by the number of votes, 58, cast in an election there on that date to elect a sheriff and other officers for the jurisdiction of Washington.[24] In the *Telegraph and Texas Register*, Hall advertised that lots would be sold to the highest bidders on January 8, 1836. "From the known healthiness of the situation, the facilities afforded for building by the near neighborhood of timber, etc., and the strong probability, if not certainty that Washington will be the future capital of Texas, the lots in that town offer great inducement to purchasers."[25]

The manner in which the town of Washington impressed Col. Gray is recorded in his diary, February 13, 1836:

> We stopt at a house, called a tavern, kept by a man named [John] Lot[t], which was the only place in the city at which we could get fodder for our horses. It was a frame house, consisting of only one room, about forty by twenty feet, with a large fire place at each end, a shed at the back, in which the table was spread. It was a frame house, covered with clapboards, a wretchedly made establishment, and a blackguard, rowdy set lounging about. The host's wife and children, and about thirty lodgers, all slept in the same apartment, some in beds, some on cots, but the greater part on the floor. The supper consisted of fried pork and coarse

corn bread and miserable coffee. I was fortunately lodged on a good cot with a decent Tennessean named Kimball [H. S. Kimble], who is looking for land, but says the state of anarchy is such that he is afraid to buy and is waiting to see the course of things after the meeting of the Convention. Was introduced to Dr. Goodrich, a physician of the place, and a member-elect of the new Convention, a strenuous Independence man.[26]

On the following morning he recorded:

A clear and cold morning. Rose early, took a wretched breakfast of the same coarse and dirty materials that we had last night. —Left Washington at 10 o'clock. Glad to get out of so disgusting a place. It is laid out in the woods; about a dozen wretched cabins or shanties constitute the city; not one decent house in it, and only one well defined street, which consists of an opening cut out of the woods. The stumps still standing. A rare place to hold a national convention in. They will have to leave it promptly to avoid starvation.[27]

On March 1, 1836, the day designated for the opening of the Convention, 44 delegates assembled: Badgett, Thomas Barnett, Blount, Bunton, Byrom, Caldwell, Childress, Clark, Coleman, Collinsworth, Conrad, Crawford, Ellis, Everitt, John Fisher, Gaines, Gazley, Goodrich, Grimes, Hamilton, Hardeman, Houston, Lacey, LeGrand, McKinney, Menefee, Mottley, Navarro, Parmer, Penington, Potter, Power, Robertson, Ruiz, Scates, Stewart, Smyth, Stapp, Swisher, Thomas, Turner, Waller, West, and Zavala.[28] Seven additional delegates took their seats on the next day: George W. Barnett, Brigham, Latimer, Menard, Roberts, Rusk, and Taylor.[29] The Convention seated Hardin on March 3;[30] Bower on March 4;[31] S. Rhoads Fisher, Woods, and Maverick on March 6;[32] Moore on March 7;[33] Carson on March 10;[34] and Briscoe on March 11.[35]

At the first session on March 1, James Collinsworth acted as temporary chairman and Willis A. Faris[36] as secretary pro tem.[37] The Convention immediately examined the credentials of its members. Upon the completion of this, it turned to the election of permanent officers and designated Richard Ellis, president; H. S. Kimble,[38] secretary; E. M. Pease,[39] assistant secretary; John A. Hueser,[40] doorkeeper; Thomas S. Saul,[41] engrossing clerk, and Isham Parmer,[42] sergeant-at-arms. On the following day Faris was elected reporter of the proceedings. Pease served until the afternoon of March 2, when he was replaced by F. W. Jackson.[43] The chair appointed George C. Childress, James Gaines, Edward Conrad, Collin McKinney, and Bailey Hardeman a committee to draft a Declaration of Independence, with Childress as chairman.[44] There is no evidence to indicate the authorship of the Declaration, but it is generally assumed that Childress was the principal author.

On March 2, the committee submitted a draft. The Convention resolved itself into a committee of the whole, and, after a rhetorical speech by Houston, who moved the draft be accepted, engrossed, and signed, the Convention turned the document over to the engrossing clerks with instructions to make an original and five copies, one copy to be sent to each Bexar, Goliad, Nacogdoches, Brazoria, and San Felipe. The Convention also directed the printers at San Felipe to run off 1,000 copies in handbill form.[45] Later, "a copy of the Declaration having been made in a fair hand, an attempt was made to read it, preparatory to signing it, but it was found so full of errors that it was recommitted to the committee that reported it for correction and engrossment."[46]

That the delegates did not begin signing the Declaration until March 3 may be adduced from several data of evidence. At the close of the session of March 2, there were 51 delegates present. On the following day it is recorded

7

that "Mr. A. B. Hardin, from the Municipality of Liberty, appeared, produced his credentials and took his seat as a member of the Convention."[47] Had the delegates who were present on March 2 signed the document on that date, signatures of those who arrived on subsequent dates would appear beneath theirs. Inasmuch as the signatures of Bunton, Gazley, Coleman, Robertson, and others who answered the roll call on March 2 follow that of Hardin's, it seems reasonable to assume that they signed the document after Hardin had signed it.

Then, too, in the minutes of the Convention mention is made of the date on which each man signed after March 3. For instance, it is recorded on March 7, "Messrs S. Rhodes Fisher, John W. Moore, John W. Bowers and Samuel A. Maverick, being absent at the adoption of the Declaration of Independence, asked and obtained leave to sign the same."[48] On March 10: "Mr. Samuel P. Carson, from Red River, appeared, produced his credentials and took his seat, and asked and obtained leave to sign the declaration of independence." On March 11: "The original Declaration of Independence was produced by the secretary and signed by James B. Woods and A. Briscoe." Had the document been signed on March 2, it is reasonable to believe that a similar record would have been kept of him who signed on March 3. Hardin arrived on March 3, and no mention is made of his having signed the document, just as there is no mention of the signing of the 51 members who were present on March 2.

This evidence, though circumstantial, amply proves that the Declaration was signed on March 3. Fortunately, there is also positive evidence. Gray, on March 3, wrote in his ubiquitous diary: "The convention met at 9 o'clock. Some new members appeared and took their seats; some, contested elections were decided. The engrossed Declaration was read and signed by all the members present."[49]

8

Of the 59 men who signed the Texas Declaration of Independence, two, Francisco Ruiz and Jose Antonio Navarro, were native Texans and life-long residents. Fifty-seven of the signers, then, had moved into Texas. James Gaines had resided on the Sabine since 1812, alternately claiming Texas and Louisiana as his home. He owned and operated a ferry on the Sabine, and his residence at the time he signed the Declaration of Independence was on the west bank of the river. Had the Revolution in Texas failed he could have built a house on the east bank and continued to operate his ferry.

Thomas Barnett came to Texas in 1823 and was the only member of the "old three hundred" of Austin's first colony who signed the Declaration. Augustine B. Hardin arrived in Texas in 1825. John S. Roberts was an officer in the "Fredonian" army in 1826 and was compelled by the Mexicans to flee across the Sabine. He returned to Nacogdoches, however, in 1827. James Power and Charles S. Taylor came in 1828, and Thomas J. Gazley in 1829. On January 1, 1830, there were resident in Texas but ten of the 59 who, six years later, signed the Declaration.

On April 6, 1830, Anastacio Bustamente, president of Mexico, signed a decree which in effect prohibited further immigration to Texas of United States citizens. This law was a fundamental cause of the Texan Revolution. Simultaneously with its promulgation Gen. Manuel de Mier y Teran was instructed to proceed to Texas with a sufficient force to carry its provisions into effect. Col. Jose de las Piedras was stationed at Nacogdoches with 350 men; Col. John Davis Bradburn at Anahuac with 150; Col. Domingo de Ugartechea established a fort at Velasco; Lieut. Col. Francisco Ruiz (who later signed the Texas Declaration of Independence) built and garrisoned Fort Tenoxtitlan on the Brazos, the site of which is in present Burleson County; and Col. Peter Ellis Bean, with a small force, occupied

9

Fort Teran on the Neches. These and other military posts were manned by convicts, vagabonds, and the worst class of men in Mexico, "contact with whom was contamination and whose bearing was insolent and outrageous."[50] There were additional complaints. "Titles to land were denied to a great number of settlers already domiciled, and incoming emigrants, from the United States were ordered to quit the country on their arrival."[51]

While it is true that the decree was interpreted to exempt immigrants who desired to settle in Austin's and De Witt's Colonies until the contracts between the empresarios and the Mexican government had been fulfilled, this was not the intent of the law. It was an evasion suggested by Austin and accepted by Teran.[52] The immigrants who entered Texas with certificates issued by Austin were few compared to the hundreds who evaded Mexican authorities and entered without passports.

Ten signers—Asa Brigham, John S. D. Byrom, S. Rhoads Fisher, William Menefee, John W. Moore, Sterling C. Robertson, Elijah Stapp, Charles B. Stewart, George W. Smyth, and James B. Woods—immigrated to Texas in 1830, and, of these, probably not more than three arrived before April 6, when the Mexican Congress closed Texas to American immigration.

During the year 1831 Collin McKinney, who had settled in Arkansas in 1824, moved to what is now Bowie County, Texas, thinking he was in Miller County, Arkansas. At no time did he receive land from the Mexican government. Five other signers moved to Texas in 1831: Mathew Caldwell, William D. Lacey, William B. Scates, Edwin Waller, and Claiborne West.

During the year 1831 the Anglo-American population in Texas continued to increase.[53] In that year, William H. Wharton of Nashville, Tennessee, came to Texas to make his home. He early began to organize a "war party" in which he was joined by Edwin Waller, William B. Travis, Henry Smith, Robert M. Williamson, and others. This party, greatly in the minority as compared with the peace party headed by Austin, was well organized, and its forces were augmented as immigrants continued to arrive from the United States.

While the Texans resented the presence of Mexican soldiers stationed at the numerous forts, there were no open breaks with Mexico until June, 1832.[54] A battle at Anahuac was narrowly averted in June. An important battle at Velasco followed on June 26, and a minor battle at Nacogdoches was fought on August 2; both of which were won by the Texans.

On October 1, 1832, the Texans held a convention at San Felipe which petitioned the Mexican government to repeal the obnoxious decree of April 6, 1830, to separate Texas from Coahuila, and to make other reforms. During the year 1832 three signers came to Texas: Robert M. Coleman, John Fisher, and Michel B. Menard.

A second convention was held at San Felipe beginning April 1, 1833, of which William H. Wharton, leader of the "war party," was elected president. Separate statehood in the Mexican union was advocated, and a constitution for such a state was adopted. Stephen F. Austin, Dr. James B. Miller, and Erasmo Seguin were appointed members of a committee to present a memorial to the Mexican government asking for separate statehood and for the repeal of the decree of 1830. Only Austin made the trip to Mexico. He succeeded, November 21, 1833, in having the decree repealed,[55] but he was arrested on his return trip home. On October 16, 1833, he had written a letter to the Ayuntamiento of Bexar, recommending that all the municipalities of Texas unite in organizing a state. The letter was transmitted by the Ayuntamiento to Gomez Farias, vice-president of the Republic of Mexico, who, consider-

11

ing it treasonable, ordered Austin imprisoned. In 1833, five signers—Andrew Briscoe, John W. Bunton, Sam Houston, Albert H. Latimer, and James G. Swisher—immigrated to Texas.

The law of April 6, 1830, having been repealed, Anglo-Americans, after November 21, 1833, could legally enter Texas. Peace prevailed during the year 1834, because Austin was held in Mexico as a hostage for the good behavior of Texas. That war was inevitable was known generally in the United States, as it was in Texas and Mexico. This fact did not prevent eight signers from entering Texas in 1834: George W. Barnett, Richard Ellis, Stephen H. Everitt, Benjamin B. Goodrich, Robert Hamilton, Edwin O. LeGrand, Sydney O. Penington, and John Turner.

Austin was released from prison in July, 1835, and arrived in Texas early in September. Prior to this the Texans had learned that General Cos, with an additional force, was to march to Bexar "to overrun and disarm the country, to drive out all Americans who had come into Texas since 1830, and to punish those who had trampled upon Mexican authority."[56]

Cos with 500 troops landed at Matagorda about the middle of September and proceeded to Bexar. The revolutionists recruited an army and organized a provisional government. Bexar was captured December 10, and all Mexican soldiers were driven from Texas. In 1835, fifteen signers—Jesse B. Badgett, Stephen W. Blount, John W. Bower, William Clark, Jr., James Collinsworth, Edward Conrad, William C. Crawford, Bailey Hardeman, Samuel A. Maverick, Junius W. Mottley, Martin Parmer, Robert Potter, Thomas J. Rusk, David Thomas, and Lorenzo de Zavala came to Texas to fight for rights that, as citizens of the United States, they already enjoyed. Badgett, Conrad, Maverick, Mottley, and Thomas arrived with guns on their shoulders. Zavala, a former Mexican diplomat, arrived with the avowed purpose of fanning the fires of revolution. Those who arrived late in 1835, with the exception of Zavala never had the opportunity or misfortune to live under the rule of which they complained in the Declaration of Independence.

Strange as it may seem, two of the signers of the Texas Declaration of Independence did not arrive in Texas until 1836. These were George C. Childress, believed by many to have been the author of the document, and the brilliant Samuel P. Carson, who could have voted in North Carolina, Arkansas and Texas.

Virginia was the birthplace of twelve signers, two more than were born in any other state. North Carolina gave birth to ten, Tennessee to nine, Kentucky to six, and Georgia to four. Four were born British subjects, one in each England, Ireland, Scotland, and Canada. South Carolina and Pennsylvania each furnished three. Three were natives of Mexico, two of whom were born in Texas. New York was the birthplace of two signers, and Massachusetts, Mississippi, and New Jersey of one each.

Although twelve signers were born in Virginia, only one, John Fisher, removed directly from there to Texas. Of the 57 who moved to Texas, thirteen were residents of Tennessee; eight of Alabama; seven of Louisiana; five of Arkansas; four each of Kentucky and Missouri; three of Georgia; two each of Pennsylvania, New York, North Carolina, Mississippi, and Mexico; and one each of Illinois and Virginia.

According to tradition,[57] the Constitutional Convention at Washington-on-the-Brazos met in a blacksmith shop belonging to Noah T. Byars,[58] a Baptist, who tendered the use of the building free of all charges. Such, however, was not the case. The building was not a blacksmith shop. Byars, who owned half interest in it, was a gunsmith and not a blacksmith, and his shop was not in the building. Byars did not magnanimously offer the building free of charge. He and his business partner, Peter M. Mercer,[59] rented the building, for three months beginning March 1, 1836, at $170, to a committee of Washington merchants who tendered the building free of charge to the Convention. While the government had made no agreement with Byars for the building, when the committee failed to pay the rent, Byars tried to collect it from the government. Byars and Mercer, both of whom arrived in Texas in the summer of 1835, were associated together as "Merchants and partners"[60] in what, from the number of deeds made, appears to have been a real estate business.

To encourage the General Council of the Provisional Government to designate Washington as the meeting place for the Constitutional Convention, a group of businessmen in the new town promised to furnish a convention hall free of cost; accordingly John W. Hall, John Lott, John G. Caldwell, John C. Neal, G. P. Patrick, J. W. Wood, R. R. Peebles, Moses T. Martin, Robert J. Clow, and Dr. William P. Smith, rented a building from Byars & Mercer. The original contract is of interest:

Washington 18th Feby 1836

We the subscribers do hereby bind and obligate ourselves to pay to Messrs Byers & Mercer, the sum of One Hundred and Seventy Dollars, being in consideration of the rent of the house owned by them, on Main Street for the term of 3 months to commence on the 1st day of March next—Said Byers & Mercer are to have the house in complete order & repair for use of the members of the convention to meet in March next—for which purpose Said building is rented by us.

Hall & Lott	Wood & Peebles
John G. Caldwell	S. R. Roberts
John C. Neal	Martin Clow & Co.
G. P. Patrick	William P. Smith[61]

That the owners did not have time to put the house in "complete order & repair" is indicated by a diary entry made March 1, 1836, by Col. Gray:

> Yesterday was a warm day, and at bed time I found it necessary to throw off some clothes. In the night the wind sprung up from the north and blew a gale, accompanied by lightning, thunder and rain and hail, and it became very cold. In the morning the thermometer was down to 33 degrees, and everybody shivering and exclaiming against the cold. This is the second regular norther that I have experienced.
>
> Notwithstanding the cold, the members of the Convention, to the number of ...., met today in an unfinished house, without doors or windows. In lieu of glass, cotton cloth was stretched across the windows, which partially excluded the cold wind.[62]

The building in which the Convention was held was probably situated on the corner of Main and Ferry Streets on lot 7, block 12, owned by Byars & Mercer. On March 14, 1837, this firm sold to Robert and William Moffat for $100 a tract fifty feet square out of the northeast corner of lot 7, block 12.[63] On September 18, 1837, they sold to Joseph L. Hood and William H. Steel for $1,000 the south end of lot 7, block 12, fronting 100 feet on Ferry Street and 50 feet on Main Street.[64] Hood and Steel, on July 18, 1838, sold the lot to Thomas Woodleif for $2,000.[65]

The Convention adjourned on March 17, and most of the inhabitants of Washington joined the Runaway Scrape, not returning until victory at San Jacinto. When the men who had rented the building from Byars & Mercer returned home, Byars presented them with a bill for the full rent of three months. For some reason—whether indifference or the fact that the building was used but seventeen days, it is impossible to determine—Hall and his associates failed to pay the bill. Byars tiled suit but recovered nothing. On December 20, 1849, from Navarro County, he addressed two petitions to the Third Legislature, one of which reads:

> Your petitioner would Respectfully represent to your Honrable boddy that in the Early part of 1836 he Rented a House to the Provisional Government of Texas for the term of 3 months at $56.00 fifty Six dollars per month, for the Use Of the Convention at the time our Declaration of Independence was made and Your petitioner would further represent that he Once applyed to the Government of Texas for his pay and they referred him to the Individuals that rented the house accordingly he brought suit against those individuals, but some being dead and some moved away he never had obtained one cent. That Your Honorable boddy May favourably Consider this claim and grant Your petitioner the sum of $168.00 he as in duty bound will Ever Pray.[66]

Since Mercer made no attempt to collect his share of the rent, it is assumed that he either sold his interest in the account to Byars or preferred to forget it.

At the time that he was associated with Mercer, Byars conducted a gunsmith business, but not in the building in which the Convention was held. On November 20, 1835, he repaired arms for the First Company of Texas Volunteers from New Orleans and on December 20, those of the Louisville Company of Volunteers. For these services he received payment.[67] In February, 1836, he was appointed armorer in the Texas Army and served as such one month. Congress was willing to pay him for this service at the rate paid to soldiers, plus twenty cents per day. This did not meet with his approval, however, and he was given permission to withdraw his petition. From his home at Society Hill in Navarro County, on December 17, 1849, he addressed a petition to the State Legislature, reciting the above facts and requesting that he be granted either $250 or 640 acres of land:

To the Honorable the Senate and House of Representatives of the State of Texas in the Legislator Assembled

Your petitioner would Respectfully represent to Your Honorable boddy That in February 1836 he was appointed by The Provisional Government of Texas as Armorer to the forces then in the servis of this Country; and in order to serve his country to the full extent of his ability he left his Journeyman and one apprentice in his shop in Washington, he paying there board himself at the tavern, and instructing them to work on the arms of Every person going to the field without charge while Your petitioner repaired himself To the field and performed the servises of Armorer there Until his health failed him So much that he was compelled to return but still carried on his shop in Washington until he had repaired the rise of 500 stand of Arms, which was at the least calculation worth $250. Your petitioner presented his act Once to the Honl Congress in Houston at a time when Our government was in Stratened circumstances—and the committee on Claims and accounts reported a bill for his relief allowing him a soldiers pay and 20 cts per day; and Your petitioner respectfully asked the withdrawal of the bill which was granted and he has never as yet received one cent. Your petitioner therefore would respectfully ask the $250 or the grant of 640 acres of land which has been granted to Each soldier that fought a battle with the arms that he himself repaired at his Own Expence.

That Your Honorable boddy will favourably consider his claim Your petitioner as in duty bound Will Ever Pray &c[68]

17

On January 23, 1850, the committee of claims and accounts rejected both petitions for lack of evidence.[69]

After the signing of the original Declaration of Independence on March 3, five copies were despatched to designated towns. None of them have been preserved. The handbills printed at San Felipe, one of which is to be found in the Archives of the Texas State Library, contain the names of but 50 of the 52 who signed the original on

March 3. The names of George C. Childress and Sterling C. Robertson, of Milam Municipality, were omitted.

The original Declaration of Independence was deposited with the United States Department of State in Washington, D. C, by William H. Wharton. On the back of the document someone wrote in ink: "Left at the Department of State May 28, 1836, by Mr. Wharton. The original." When, and by whom, the notation was made is not recorded. The author believes that Wharton left the document with the State Department subsequent to November 18, 1836, when President Houston appointed him minister plenipotentiary to the United States. It is true that he was in Washington on May 28, but there is no evidence, other than the notation, that he left the Declaration with the State Department at that time. Wharton, Stephen F. Austin, and Dr. Branch T. Archer had been away from Texas since December 26, 1835, when they left for the United States as agents for the Provisional Government of Texas. For Wharton to have had in his possession the original Declaration of Independence he would have had to receive it from the hands of either George C. Childress or Robert Hamilton, who on March 19, 1836, had been commissioned by President David G. Burnet and his cabinet to go to Washington and to endeavor to have the United States government recognize the independence of the new Republic of Texas.[70] They arrived at their destination about May 21 and lost no time in the performance of their duties. They evidently had with them one of the handbills of the Declaration printed by the *Telegraph and Texas Register* at San Felipe and containing the names of but 50 of the signers.

For propaganda purposes Hamilton and Childress published a 24 page pamphlet entitled *Constitution of The Republic of Texas: To Which is Prefixed The Declaration of Independence, Made In Convention, March 2, 1836.*[71] The booklet began with the salutation:

18

TO THE PUBLIC

The undersigned, Plenipotentiaries from the Republic of Texas to the United States of America, respectfully present to the American People the unanimous DECLARATION OF INDEPENDENCE made by the People of Texas in General Convention, on the 2nd day of March, 1836; and, also, the CONSTITUTION framed by the same body.

ROBERT HAMILTON
GEO. C. CHILDRESS
Washington City, May 22, 1836.

Had Hamilton and Childress the original Declaration of Independence in their possession when they published the booklet, no doubt they would have reproduced it instead of the printed copy, the list of signatures attached to which was incomplete and in accurate.

On March 27, 1836, the Republic recalled its agents, Wharton, Austin, and Archer, who returned to their homes. Austin became secretary of state of the Republic, and, on November 18, Houston appointed Wharton minister plenipotentiary to the United States. His most important duty was to seek the admittance of Texas into the Union. Failing in this he was to urge the recognition of Texas as an independent nation.[72] When Wharton left Texas for Washington, he carried with him the Declaration of Independence. The author believes this was the original document. Austin, on November 22, wrote to Wharton at Velasco:

I send you a tin case containing your credentials and instructions as minister plenipotentiary to the United States of America. It contains your commission, a letter of credence to the Secretary of State of the United States, and office copies of them—your general instructions, your private and special instructions, and Documents relative to the organization of the Govt. of Texas. I also send you a file of the Texas Telegraph, please to acknowledge the receipt of

19

them to file in this department. You already have the Declaration of Independence and the constitution.[73]

Wharton promptly replied and stated that he would "lose no time in repairing to the court of Washington."[74] He arrived at the national capital, December 19 and immediately communicated with Secretary of State John Forsyth.[75]

On March 5, 1837, Wharton wrote James Pinckney Henderson, who had been named secretary of state after Austin's death:

> I have at length the happiness to inform you that President Jackson has closed his political career by admitting our country into the great family of nations. On Friday [March 3] night last, at near 12 o'clock, he consumated the recognition of the Senate and the diplomatic appropriation bill of the lower House, by nominating a Mr. Labranche [La Branche] of Louisiana, charge d'affaires near the Republic of Texas. He also sent for General [Memucan] Hunt and myself and requested the pleasure of a glass of wine, and stated that Mr. Forsyth would see us officially on Monday. I close this brief communication on account of my intention to write at large after this interview with Mr. Forsyth. I repeat my desire to return home.[76]

If, as the author assumes, Wharton, while minister plenipotentiary, left the Texas Declaration of Independence with Secretary of State John Forsyth, it was fortunate that he did so, for had Wharton attempted to return it to Texas, it would have been destroyed or seized by the Mexican government. Shortly after the recognition of the Republic of Texas by the United States, Wharton left for home. On April 10, 1837, he boarded the *Invincible*, of the Texas Navy. Off the coast of Texas, almost in sight of his Eagle Island plantation in Brazoria County, the *Invincible* was captured by the Mexican brigs of war *Vencedor del Alamo* and *Libertador*.[77] Wharton and the other passengers were carried prisoners to Matamoros. Before he was thus captured, Wharton, who carried important dispatches addressed to the Republic of Texas, destroyed some of the papers. The Mexicans captured the remaining ones. The Texas Declaration of Independence would have met one of the two fates.

At Washington, D. C, in March, 1896, Seth Shepard,[78] native Texan and associate justice of the Court of Appeals for the District of Columbia, wrote the introduction to *A Comprehensive History of Texas*, edited by Dudley G. Wooten and published by William G. Scarff, of Dallas. Two months later, in May, 1896, William Hallett Phillips told Shepard that he had seen in the office of the United States Secretary of State a document that appeared to be the Texas Declaration of Independence. On June 1, Secretary of State Richard Olney wrote Shepard that inasmuch as the Declaration was the property of Texas, he would deliver it upon presentation of a receipt from the governor. Shepard wrote Gov. Charles A. Culberson on June 3, and Culberson replied on June 11 with the receipt. On an undesignated day Shepard presented the receipt and received the Declaration, which he forwarded to Culberson.[79] Shepard called Scarff's attention to the Declaration and Scarff reproduced it for his book. On October 9, he wrote Mrs. Adele Lubbock Looscan:

21

> I send you by today's mail a facsimile of the original Declaration of Independence. I am informed that it has been generally understood that the Declaration of Independence was destroyed when the Capitol at Austin was burned. Recently Hon. Seth Shepard, in hunting through the Archives in the State Department at Washington for some data for this [Scarff's] history, ran across the original Declaration of Independence of the Republic of Texas. It had been sent to Washington for examination when the annexation question was under discussion and was filed away there and never

returned. I had a facsimile of the original made, signatures and all. I think it will be a taking feature. By the proofs which I send you, you will readily see that the engraver has done a splendid job on it. It will appear in the book exactly as it does on the proof sheets sent you. After you have examined it please return to me. You might keep it a day to show to any of your friends who are interested in the work. It cost me $100.00 to reproduce it. I think it will prove a paying investment. Don't you?[80]

Unfortunately, and for some yet unexplained reason, a complete facsimile of the Declaration does not appear in Scarff's (generally called Wooten's) *Comprehensive History*. By some circumstance, either the deficiency of the reproducing lens or negligence of the photoengraver, the Scarff-Wooten reproduction, perfect in other respects, omits the name of Asa Brigham, the last and right-most signature on the first page of signatures. Because of this mistake, and the failure of regional historians to disclose sources, the belief that 58 instead of 59 men signed the Declaration of Independence arose and persevered.

On February 19, 1929, Senators Walter C. Woodward, Julien C. Hyer, and Pink L. Parish submitted Senate Concurrent Resolution No. 29 authorizing the transfer of the Declaration of Independence from the Secretary of State to the State Board of Control in order that it might be displayed in a niche to the left of the elevator on the first floor of the State Capitol. The Senate immediately adopted the resolution, and the House of Representatives adopted it the next day.[81]

The niche in which the Declaration is displayed was unveiled March 2, 1930.[82] Mrs. Jane Y. McCallum was Secretary of State at that time, and Claude D. Teer was chairman of the State Board of Control. The custody of the document has since been transferred to the Texas State Library.

Signers

JESSE B. BADGETT
of
BEXAR MUNICIPALITY

*J*esse B. Badgett is the most obscure of the signers of the Texas Declaration of Independence. Even less would have been known of him had it not been for Dr. Goodrich's recording the ages and nativities of the delegates. To Goodrich, Badgett gave his age as 29, stated that he was born in North Carolina and that he had emigrated to Texas from Arkansas.[1] He was born, therefore, in about 1807. Except for his services in the Texas Revolution, this is about all that is known of him.

With his brother William,[2] Badgett left Little Rock, Arkansas, for Texas in November, 1835. At Nacogdoches on November 15, they enlisted in the Army of Texas. The approximate date of their arrival is indicated by a letter written on December 10 by Joseph W. Hicks and M. Hawkins at San Felipe to the General Council of the Provisional Government of Texas:

> ...we the subscribers volunteers in the cause of Texas now on our way to San Antonio respectfully represent,—that we have been informed by Messrs Jesse & W Badget, known to judge [T. J.] Chambers as men of truth, and verily believe, that there are one hundred and twenty men, volunteers in the same just cause in which we have embarked, who left Natchitoches, Louisiana on or about the first day of December;—that under the impression that the provisional government of Texas, has provided the means of forwarding volunteers they are unprovided for further than Nacogdoches and cannot come on further unless the Honorable Council shall see proper to meet them there through an agent with the means of defraying their expenses to the Army.[3]

Jesse B. Badgett joined the command of Colonel Travis at the Alamo. The exact date is uncertain, but he was certainly there as early as February 1.

At the conventions of 1832 and 1833, and at the Consultation of 1835, the District of Bexar was not represented, probably because it was inhabited almost entirely by Mexicans whose loyalty to Texas was uncertain. On November 11, 1835, however, the Consultation resolved "that people in the department of Bexar, and all other parts of Texas, not represented in this body, be invited forthwith to send delegates to the council, and also to the convention to sit on the first day of March next."[4] Governor Henry Smith vetoed the bill on December 12, on the ground that the Mexicans at Bexar had not joined in the Revolution.[5] The bill was passed over the veto on December 13.[6]

On February 1, 1836, the Mexican population elected Jose Antonio Navarro, Francisco Ruiz, Juan N. Seguin, and Miguel Arciniega as delegates.[7] Upon the order of Lieut. Col. James C. Neill, on the same day the soldiers stationed at the Alamo held an election of their own. Capt. W. C. M. Baker, Samuel B. Blair, and William B. Blazeby were judges and Eliel Melton, clerk. Samuel A. Maverick received 103 votes; Badgett, 100; and James Butler Bonham and John M. Hays, one each, the last two receiving the votes of J. H. Nash.[8]

Most of the soldiers in the Alamo having but recently arrived in Texas, the civil population of San Antonio questioned their right to vote. Therefore, when Badgett left for the Convention, he carried with him a petition, signed by the officers stationed at the Alamo, urging that he and Maverick be seated as two of the delegates from Bexar:

> A memorial of the Undersigned Officers in and over the Army Stationed at Bexar, to the President and members of the Convention of Texas to be held at Washington on the 1st day of March next, respectfully showed that:

JESSE B. BADGETT

Whereas, it is evident as well from the Resolution of the Consultation which provides for the calling of a Convention of all Texas, as from the clear equity of the case, that an equal representation of all persons & interests was aimed at and intended: and whereas the volunteer and regular soldiers in the actual service of the country, are by the same Consultation, declared to be citizens and raised to the right of suffrage; and whereas it is but right on the grounds of population, and appears, from the early date of the aforesaid Resolution, to be intended, that the resident Mexican Citizens of Bexar should have four representatives in the Convention; and whereas our officers perceived that impediments were put in the way of our men voting, such as requiring an oath of actual citizenship in this Municipality before the vote would be taken; and furthermore they wished to prevent any, the least, breach in the good understanding which has so happily existed between the Citizens and our garrison, and whereas no facilities and insufficient time was afforded to such individuals in the army as live in a certain Municipality, to send their votes, and at the same time a large portion of this army, whilst they possess the declared right of voting for members of this Convention, do not yet possess any local habitation whatsoever; And whereas it is of great importance that this army should have representatives in the Convention who understand their wants and their wishes, and are participants of their feelings; and of importance also to all Texas, since she would proceed with less hesitation on any great measures whilst having the voice of all; and whereas if the army here would so far neglect their interests and their duty, as not to send members of their own choice, it is evident the wants of the Army and the necessity of maintaining & supplying this important garrison in a manner required by the public safety, might be forcibly reasonably urged on the attention of the Government—inasmuch as the members sent from their municipality, though they have the best intentions, are yet unable, from difference of language & habits, to represent the Anglo American and Army interest: and whereas the reasonableness as well as the particular advantage of such a representation has gained the hearty good wishes of the Mexicans as well as the Americans at this place; And whereas by general wish, under the influence of these powerful reasons, an order was issued to three respectable gentlemen, who are Captains, in this service, to hold an election for two members to the Convention, the Certificate of whom, with the return of the votes taken, is transmitted with this memorial; and whereas on the election being held at the time and in the manner prescribed by law, and in strict conformity with common usage, it appeared on summing up the votes, as the result of the election that, by a vote which was almost unanimous, Samuel A. Maverick and Jesse B. Badgett, Esquires, were elected as members of the Convention. Therefore, for these and other good reasons it is the united petition of ourselves and of the army under our command that the said Samuel A. Maverick and the said Jesse B. Badgett shall receive seats as members of your honorable body and be admitted to full participation in all the rights, powers, privileges and immunities enjoyed by the other members: all of which, your memorialists very respectfully submit to the President and members of your honorable body, & will ever pray.

J. C. Neill, Lt. Coln. Comd. Bexar
R. White, Capt of the Bejar Guards
Wm. A. Irwin, 1st Lieut
Wm. R. Carey, Capt of the Artillery
W. C. It Baker, Capt
Saml C. Blair, Capt
Geo. Evans, Mast Ord
Wm. Blazeby, Captain of the Orleans Greys
W. Barret Travis, Lt. Col of Cavalry
James Bowie
G. B. Jameson
E. Melton, 2nd Q. M.
Almeron Dickinson, Lt.
W. H. Patton, Capt.[9]

On February 14, Colonel Neill gave Badgett an honorable discharge, to permit him to attend the Convention.[10] He left for Washington on or shortly after February 17.[11] On March 1, the Convention without debate seated him along with Navarro and Ruiz.[12] Seguin and Arciniega did not attend, and Maverick did not arrive until March 6.

At Washington, Badgett, Navarro, Lorenzo de Zavala, and Ruiz occupied a room at a boarding house with William Fairfax Gray. On March 9, Gray wrote in his diary:

> Weather warm and fine. I have made a bargain with [Samuel] Heath, the carpenter, for his shop. He is to put a good floor in it, and rent it for $25 until 1st of April. Zavala, Navarro, Ruis, Badgett and myself are to occupy it and divide the cost equally. We shall then be retired and comparatively comfortable.[13]

Shortly after the adjournment of the convention Badgett returned to Arkansas, reaching Little Rock on April 10. His account of the revolution in Texas was printed in the *Arkansas Gazette*, Little Rock, April 12:[14]

LATEST FROM TEXAS-DIRECT

Mr. Jesse B. Badgett, who was one of a small party who left Little Rock, for Texas, last fall, and who was a member of the late convention at Washington, the Seat of Government of Texas, returned to this place, on Sunday evening last, direct from that country, and has communicated to us the following highly interesting war news from the theater of war.

San Antonio, as heretofore stated, was taken by storm, by a overwhelming force, commanded by Gen. Santa Anna, in person, early on the morning of the 6th ult. The whole force of Col. Travis, at its capture, was only 183 men, (14 of whom were on the sick list, and unable to take part in the battle). They were ALL SLAIN. The siege lasted 14 days and nights, and, from the best information that could be obtained from a Mexican deserter, the Mexican loss during the siege amounted to 881 killed and about 700 wounded. The deserter reported, that, at 11 o'clock on the night of the 5th ult. the Mexicans formed, to the number of 3,400 infantry, led by Santa Anna, in person, and, at between 3 and 4 o'clock on the next morning at a signal given by throwing up rockets from the town, the attack was simultaneously made on all sides of the garrison. The besieged considered their small number were well prepared for the assault—every man being provided with at least a brace of pistols and 4 or 5 rifles and muskets, all loaded, besides knives—and poured in a most deadly fire on the assailants, with cannon and small arms. The struggle, for a short period was most desperate, but the garrison could not long sustain the attack of so overwhelming a force. About half an hour before sunrise, on the morning of the 6th, the gallant spirits who had so bravely defended the post, and killed and wounded more than 5 times their own number, were numbered with the dead—and Santa Anna, surrounded by his life-guards, made his triumphant entry into the fort. In this assault, the Mexican loss was said to be 521 killed, and nearly the same number wounded.

28

Col. Travis was killed within the first hour of the storming of the garrison, having first killed, with his own hand, Gen. Moro, who led the storming party, by running him through with his sword. On his fall, the command of the Texians devolved on Adj't Maj. J. J. Baugh, who fell in the course of an hour or two, when the command devolved on Col. David Crockett, who likewise soon fell.

The following names of such of the officers who fell in defending San Antonio, as are recollected by Mr. Badgett:

Col. W. B. Travis, Commandant; Col. James Bowie, Col. David Crockett, Maj. Green B. Jamison (formerly of Ky.), Capts. Baugh, of Va., Blair, formerly of Conway county, A. T. Cory of La., Baker of Mississippi, Blasby of the New Orleans Grays, J. G. Washington of Tenn., Harrison of Tenn., Forsyth of N. York, Jones, J. K. Mable of Gonzales; Lieuts. Dickinson and Evans, Sergt. Maj. Williamson from Philadelphia, Dr. Mitcherson of Va., Surgeon Pollard.

JESSE B. BADGETT

The previous report of the death of Col. Jesse Benton, is incorrect. Mr. Badgett saw him near Nacogdoches, about the 25th, on his way to Jonesborough, Miller county, in this Territory, where a volunteer company was organising, and with whom he intended marching for the seat of the war.

On the 11th of March, Santa Anna marched from San Antonio, with 3,000 men, for Laborde (Goliad) which post was defended by Col. Fanning, with about 800 men, with plenty of provisions and ammunition, and who said he could defend his position against any force the Mexicans could bring against him.

On the 12th, Gen. Almonte and Col. Ball (an American) left San Antonio for Gonzales, with 2,000 men, but, after marching 27 miles, to the Sea Willow River; changed their direction, and bent their course toward Laborde, to assist Santa Anna in reducing that post. From the Sea Willow, they sent Mrs. Dickinson, the widow of Lieut. Dickinson, who was killed in the storming of San Antonio, with her child (who was not killed, as previously reported) and servant, to Gen. Houston's camp at Goliad; and at the same time Gen. Almonte sent his servant to Gen. Houston, with Gen. Santa Anna's proclamation, offering an amnesty to the inhabitants and Texian troops, provided that it yield submission, and give up their arms, to the Mexican authorities. Gen. Houston detained the servant, and sent to the Mexican Commander, by a Spaniard, a copy of the Declaration of Independence recently agreed at Washington.

Mr. Badgett left Washington (Seat of Government) on the 18th of March, and, on the next day, arrived at General Houston's camp, at Beason's Crossing of the Colorado, 90 miles this side of San Antonio, to which point Gen. H. had fallen back from Gonzales, which he burnt before abandoning it. Gen. H. was fortifying his camp, had about 2,900 men, and reinforcements were arriving daily. Mr. B. thinks there is no doubt he had a force of at least 4,000 men, in a few days after he left his camp.

On the 20th, Mr. Badgett left General Houston's camp, on the Colorado, and, on the next day, reached Washington, where the Convention was still in session, but adjourned on the following day, 22nd, after forming a Constitution for the Republic of Texas.

An express returned to General Houston's camp, on the 19th, from the vicinity of Col. Fannin's post, which was besieged by Santa Anna, but the express waited part of a day and night without being able to gain admission—during which period a heavy cannonade was kept up by both parties. The result had not transpired when Mr. B. left.

On his return from General Houston's camp, Mr. Badgett says the road was literally crowded with volunteers, and thinks he passed at least 1,000 men before he reached the Sabine—all hurrying to join their brethren in arms on the frontier. Mr. Badgett reached Natchitoches on the 30th, at which time no information had been received there of a second battle having been fought, and the Mexicans defeated with the loss of 800 or 1,000 men, as mentioned in our summary of Texians news on our first page. He thinks there is no foundation in the report, which reached us via Natchez.

The report of the death of his brother, Mr. William Badgett, which gives us pleasure to state, is incorrect. He left him with the forces of Gen. Houston, on the Colorado. He, however, we regret to state, confirms the report of the death of Mr. Charles E. Rice and Mr. Nathaniel Dannis. They were of the party of Col. Johnson, who were cut off (except J. and one other) at San Patricio, by a large party of Mexican troops, who promised to spare their lives on condition of their surrendering and, on their giving up their arms, commenced a indiscriminate massacre of them. This occurred a short time previous to the fall of San Antonio.

Although San Antonio has fallen, and its gallant defenders been put to the sword, Mr. Badgett thinks the prospects for the deliverance of Texas from the domination of Santa Anna, not the less flattering on that account. Instead of its dishearting the prospect, they seem to be inspired with new courage, and are rushing to the rescue of their country in such numbers as to give strong hopes of their ultimate success. They make urgent appeals for succor from their brethren in the United States, and we hear from New Orleans, Natchez and other places on the Mississippi, that great exertions are making to raise volunteers, and it is not improbable that a large portion of the volunteers, who are returning flushed with victory over the savage hordes of Florida, will proceed immediately to Texas, to defend the people of the country from the no less savage vassals of Santa Anna. God Speed their success to them.

GEORGE WASHINGTON BARNETT
of
WASHINGTON MUNICIPALITY

George Washington Barnett was born in South Carolina, December 12, 1793, a son of William and Margaret Barnett. His father was sheriff of Lancaster District, now Lancaster County, in 1793.[1] The early education of George probably began at the Waxhaw Academy of which William Richardson was the founder and principal for many years. It was a classical school where Latin and Greek were taught for the first time in South Carolina.[2] After George completed his medical preparation, probably under the direction of a preceptor, he began the practice of his profession in Williamson County, Tennessee, where on July 6, 1820, he was married to Eliza Patton. In 1823 he moved to Mississippi where he continued the practice of medicine. On January 1, 1834, he arrived in Texas to make it his future home.[3] He settled in Washington Municipality in that part now embraced in Burleson County. Later in the year 1834 he purchased a farm near the present city of Brenham, Washington County, and resumed the practice of medicine.

On July 20, 1835, Dr. Barnett was chosen captain of one of the four volunteer companies commanded by Colonel John H. Moore, organized to attack the Tehuacanas at the spring of that name now in Limestone County.[4]

Dr. Barnett joined Capt. James G. Swisher's "Washington Company," October 8; was elected second lieutenant, October 27; and was discharged December 22, 1835.[5] He participated in the capture of San Antonio, December 10, 1835.[6]

James Hass, election judge of Washington Municipality, reported to the Constitutional Convention that on February 1, Dr. Barnett, Dr. Benjamin B. Goodrich, James G. Swisher, and Jesse Grimes had been elected to represent Washington at the convention. The number of votes polled was not stated.[7] Dr. Barnett was seated in the convention March 1.[8]

John M. Swisher, son of James G. Swisher, in his *Memoirs* tells of the activities of his father and Dr. Barnett following the adjournment of the convention on March 17. He wrote:

> After the adjournment of the convention at Washington, Dr. G. W. Barnett and several other members had joined the army with a view of participating in the expected battle on the Colorado. When General Houston made up his mind to retreat, he gave them permission to leave the army to seek a place of safety for their families. My father Dr. Barnett, Captain [Horatio] Chriesman and many other families of the neighborhood then commenced their 'runaway scrape,' as it was called, in company. They had reached Beaumont in Jefferson county, before they heard of the battle of San Jacinto, when owing to the condition of their teams, they found it impossible to return to their homes. They therefore concluded to move up to San Augustine and spend the summer. Fortunately for them General Gaines of the United States army having concluded to occupy Nacogdoches with a portion of his troops, gave employment to their teams, in

transporting supplies at remunerative rates, thus enabling them to keep down expenses.[9]

Additional information concerning Dr. Barnett's and Captain Swisher's, movements is given in an affidavit by Dr. Barnett, May 24, 1837:

Republic of Texas
Washington County

Personally appeared before me James G. Swisher one of the acting Justices of the peace in and for said County, G. W. Barnett of the County aforesaid, who being sworn as to his indebtedness to the Republic of Texas saith, that about the 18th of April 1836 he the said Barnett in company with J. P. Cole was in The Town of Harrisburg, that Col Thomas then acting Secretary at War said he wished we had a waggon load of the flour captured at Sea for our famelies; seeing the Enemy had passed the River Brassos at foart bend & he feared it would have to be burned. The said Barnett saith he got of the aforesaid flour one hundred and sixty pounds or thereabout, & ten pounds of Coffee from Col Thomas; which was entered in a book in the Secretaries office. That he has received neither horses mules, armes, nor any other article of value from the said Republic, save one Mule which was entered by Esqr Moody in the month of March 1836 as Auditor under the provisional government as an extinguishment of his the said Barnetts services at San antone, leaving a balance in favour of the Republic of seven dollars as will appear by refferance to his Discharge now in file in the said Secretaries Office and farthermore he saith not.[10]

Dr. Barnett enrolled in Capt. William W. Hill's company of rangers. July 3, and served until October 3, 1836.[11] He was elected from the district composed of Washington County to the Senate of the Second Congress of the Republic.[12] In the Senate of the Third,[13] Fourth,[14] Fifth[15] and Sixth[16] Congress he represented the district composed of Washington

33

and Montgomery Counties, and in the Seventh Congress his district was composed of Washington, Montgomery and Brazos Counties.[17] In all, he served from September 25, 1837, to January 16, 1843.

Dr. Barnett moved to Gonzales County in 1846. In October, 1848, two bands of marauding Lipans left their camps in the State of Coahuila, Mexico, and entered Texas. On October 8, fifteen miles west of Gonzales, one of the bands killed Dr. Barnett, while he was hunting deer. Regarding his death Wilbarger wrote:

> ...Near the settlements on the Sandies in the western part of the county they encountered Doctor George Barnett, who was out deer hunting, and finally succeeded in killing him, though it was evident he had made a determined resistance. It appears he had only been wounded at first, and afterwards that he had taken his position in some thick brush, from which the Indians were unable to dislodge him, and there subsequently died from the effects of the wound he had received. It was evident the Indians had retreated before he died, as otherwise they would have scalped him and taken his gun. He had apparently been dead about two days when his body was found.[18]

The other band killed a Mr. Lockhart and a young man by the name of Vivian. The latter band crossed from the west to the east side of the San Antonio River and joined forces with the first band.

Dr. Barnett's remains were buried in the old cemetery in Gonzales, where in 1936 the Commission of Control for Texas Centennial Celebrations had a monument erected in his honor. He was a member of the Cumberland Presbyterian Church.

Dr. Barnett was married July 6, 1820, to Eliza Patton, daughter of Isaac and Ann Patton. She was born July 3, 1802, and died November 21, 1872. She is buried in a marked

34

grave in the Barnett family cemetery in Wrightsboro, Gonzales County, Texas.

Children of Dr. and Mrs. Barnett were: Rebecca P., who married Frederick Browder Gentry; James A., who was married to Martha T. Elder; William L., who was married to Elizabeth Walker; Margaret Ann, who was married to J. D. McCaughan; Isaac Patton, who was married to Margaret Forbes; and John W. Barnett, who was married to Alice Benham.

Some of the surviving grandchildren of Dr. George W. Barnett in 1942 were: Miss Ella Barnett, 912 Aganier Avenue, San Antonio; George W. Barnett, Karnes City; Robert Lee Barnett, Karnes City; Mrs. Lavenia Ellis, Gonzales County; Mrs, Emma Snell, Ballinger; Mrs. Alice Evans, San Marcos; Thomas D. McCaughan, San Marcos; Mrs. Emma Barnett Tomlinson, Fred Collin, George Barnett and Harvey Barnett, all of whom reside at R. F. D. No. 5, Box 63, Georgetown; Henry P. Barnett, Huffman, Harris County; Mary Barnett Cummings, Humble; Mrs. James Ward, 3720 Bell Avenue, Houston; J. W. Barnett, Knox City; Mrs. Ollie Shockley Moore, San Angelo; George A. Shockley, Santa Anna; Mrs. Ora Cathey, Hamilton; Frederick E. Shockley, Cisco; Frederick Gentry, Pecos; Stroud Gentry, Pecos; Mrs. "Bud" Rodgers, Shamrock; Mrs. J. E. Secrest, Hamilton; Mrs. W. J. Murphy, 125 Park Road, Burlingame, California; and Mrs. J. E. Moore, Hamilton, Texas.

THOMAS BARNETT
of
AUSTIN MUNICIPALITY

*T*homas Barnett was born January 18, 1798,[1] in Logan County, Kentucky. There he was reared and educated. He moved to Livingston County, Kentucky, and served as sheriff in 1821 and 1822.[2] In 1823, he, a single man, came to Texas as one of Austin's "Old Three Hundred."[3]

At an election held for officers of the newly created Ayuntamiento of San Felipe de Austin, Barnett was elected *comisario* and *sindico* of the district of Victoria. Since Mexican law forbade one's holding more than one office and Barnett had received more votes for *comisario* than for *sindico*, on February 10, 1828, he was declared elected *comisario*.[4] On December 13-14, 1829, he was elected alcalde of San Felipe de Austin, defeating Stephen Richardson by a vote of 270 to 83,[5] and served until Francis W. Johnson was elected on December 12-13, 1830.[6]

Barnett represented Austin Municipality at the Consultation held at San Felipe de Austin, November 3-14.[7] On November 18, 1835, the General Council of the Provisional Government elected him a supernumerary member.[8]

The returns of the election held in Austin Municipality, February 1, 1836, to select three delegates to the Constitutional Convention are not in the Texas State Library as those of most of the other municipalities are. Colonel Gray who attended the convention as a spectator stated in his diary that Dr. Charles B. Stewart, Barnett, and Randal Jones were elected from Austin.[9] Stewart was seated on March 1, Barnett on the following day[10] and Jones did not attend.

President Houston, on December 20, 1836, appointed Barnett chief justice of Austin County.[11] He represented

Fort Bend County in the House of Representatives of the Third[12] and Fourth[13] Congresses of the Republic. He died at his home in Fort Bend County, September 20, 1843, and is buried in a marked grave in the Barnett family cemetery eight miles from Richmond.

Sometime between July 10, 1824, and March 28, 1826, Barnett was married to Mrs. Nancy Spencer, widow of William S. Spencer who was killed by Indians early in 1824.[14] The census of Austin's colony, taken March 28, 1826, shows that the Barnetts had one child and two slaves.[15] Regarding his marriage, Barnett, on June 15, 1831, wrote to Stephen F. Austin:

> I have recently understood that yourself and Padre [Michael] Muldoon will shortly pay a visit to the Fort Settlement where the neighbourhood will assemble for the purpose of marriages, christening. Owing to the extreme indisposition of myself and helpless situation of my family it will be inconvenient for me to attend. I have therefore to request you, and through you the Rev. Father Muldoon to call at my house on your way down to the end that the marriage contract betwixt myself and wife may be consummated and my children christened.
>
> I request also that you will have the goodness to inform me on what particular day it will be convenient for you to be at my house.[16]

The Barnetts had six children: (1) A daughter, John Mary, was born in 1826 and died in 1879. She was married to William S. Jones, who was born in Virginia in 1810 and died in 1895. Thomas A. Wheat, of Liberty, Texas, is a descendant of this union. (2) William Barnett was born in 1827 and (3) John in 1829. (4) Elizabeth probably died in childhood, for the 1850 census does not list her.[17] (5) Sarah Catherina, born in 1835, was married to J. Foster Dyer. Lottie Dyer, a daughter of this union, married John M. Moore. Mr. and Mrs. Moore's children were: R. E. Moore, deceased; J. P.

D. Moore; John M. Moore, Jr., Richmond; Ivy Moore, who married a Mr. Morrison; and Etta Mae Moore, who married a Mr. Little of San Antonio. (6) James Barnett was born in 1842. In 1845, Mrs. Thomas Barnett, aged 43, married Thomas M. Gray, who was born in about 1807. Of this union, Robert M. Gray was born in 1847.[18]

Thos Barnett

STEPHEN WILLIAM BLOUNT
of
SAN AUGUSTINE MUNICIPALITY

38

Stephen William Blount was born in Burke County, Georgia, February 13, 1808, son of Stephen William and Elizabeth (Winn) Blount.[1] Little is recorded of his early life. In Texas he was referred to as "Colonel" on the assumption that he was the Stephen W. Blount who was made a Colonel of the Eighth Regiment, Georgia Militia, May 14, 1834, by Gov. Wilson Lumpkin.[2]

Of his coming to Texas, Crocket wrote:

> ...[Colonel Blount] while on a business trip to Montgomery, Alabama,...met Captain Archibald Hotchkiss of Nacogdoches, who gave him such a glowing description of Texas that he resolved to migrate thither. On his arrival at Alexandria he learned from some wagoners that there was a famine of salt meat in San Augustine. Finding a quantity of bacon in Alexandria he loaded a wagon with it and sold it in San Augustine at a small profit, thus giving evidence on his first arrival of the business enterprise and public spirit which were marked characteristics of his whole life.[3]

Blount arrived in Texas in August, 1835,[4] and settled in San Augustine. He, Edwin O. LeGrand, and Martin Parmer were elected on February 1, 1836, to represent San Augustine Municipality at the Constitutional Convention.[5] Blount took his seat in the Convention on March 1.[6]

After the adjournment of the Convention on March 17, Blount returned to San Augustine and, on April 1, enlisted in Capt. William D. Ratcliff's company, although his name does not appear on Captain Ratcliff's rolls.[7]

> En route to join the main army a disagreement arose between Captain Ratcliff and some of his men and as a result the company was disbanded. Captain Ratcliff, Philip Walker, Joseph Burns, William B. Richards, John B. Border, John P. Ryan, Colonel Blount continued their march and reached the battlefield on the day following the battle [of San Jacinto].[8]

A short while later, Capt. Leonard H. Mabbitt organized a company. All of the men named in the above quotation joined it, and Blount was elected orderly sergeant.[9]

Blount was the first county clerk of San Augustine County.[10] On January 4, 1841, he was defeated for re-election by John Pelham Border. From 1846 to 1849 he was postmaster at San Augustine.[11] He was a delegate to the 1850 State Democratic Convention in Waco and to the national convention in Cincinnati in 1876.[12] During the War Between the States he served the Confederacy as fiscal agent. He was a charter member of Redland Lodge No. 3, A. F. & A. M., at San Augustine, and of the Texas Veterans Association organized at Houston, May 13, 1873. While serving as first vice-president of this latter organization he died February 7, 1890.[13]

Sometime after February 1, 1838, Colonel Blount was married to Mrs. Mary (Landon) Lacy, daughter of David T. Landon.[14] Mrs. Blount was born in Vermont, January 12, 1812, and died September 5, 1891. Mr. and Mrs. Blount are buried in marked graves in the cemetery at San Augustine.

The Commission of Control for Texas Centennial Celebrations in 1936 placed a marker at Colonel Blount's home in San Augustine which was built in 1837.

Colonel and Mrs. Blount had six children: Jennie Elizabeth, who married Dr. A. C. Holmes; Thomas William, who married Mary E. Rather; Mary Landon, who married James E. Thomas; Edward Augustus, who married Itasca Simms; Stephen William, Jr., who married Mary Price; and Emma Eugenia, who married Robert Shindler.

Surviving grandchildren in 1942 were: John Franklin Blount, Thomas William Blount, Lamar Blount, San Augustine; R. Percy Blount, Edward S. Blount, and Wiliford G. Blount, Nacogdoches; A. Clarence Holmes, 1616 Washington Street, Waco; Mrs. Mamie E. Graham, Graham; Mrs. Mary L. Acker, Mrs. Willie L. Ingraham, 1700 Western Avenue, Fort Worth; Stephen W. Blount, San Antonio; Mrs. Emma E. Huffer, Huntsville; Miss Minnie C. Kinsel, Whittenberg; Mrs. Emma Blount Johnson, Hot Springs, Arkansas; Hubert F. Blount, Oklahoma City, Oklahoma; Dr. Stephen L. Blount, St. Louis, Missouri; S. Seymour Thomas, 323 N. Rosemont, La Crescenta, Los Angeles, California; Mrs. Emma E. Bassett, Portland, Oregon; Mrs. Mary L. Raymond, 15 Federal Road, Madison, New Jersey.

40

JOHN WHITE BOWER
of
SAN PATRICIO MUNICIPALITY[1]

*J*ohn White Bower was born in Talbotton, Talbot County, Georgia, December 7, 1808, son of Isaac and Frances Ann (Cuthbert) Bower.[2] In 1819, with his parents, he moved to Arkansas Territory. Sometime between May 2 and November 28, 1835, he came to Texas.[3]

On the latter date, Lewis Ayres presented to the General Council of the Provisional Government, certificates of election for Bower, John McMullen, and himself as delegates from San Patricio Municipality to the Consultation which had adjourned November 14. Bower and McMullen did not appear.[4] On January 16, 1836, and again on February 14,[5] the Consultation, which after January 17 had no quorum, requested Bower to attend, but there is no evidence that he complied.[6]

Approximately 63 electors voted at James McGloin's house in the town of San Patricio, on February 1, 1836, to elect two delegates to represent San Patricio Municipality in the Constitutional Convention. McGloin, Benjamin Odium, and Capt. Thomas K. Pearson were election judges and Festus Doyle secretary. Unable to agree on the number of votes cast for the candidates, the judges sent two sets of returns into the Convention. One showed that John Turner had received 38 votes; John McMullen, 31; Bower, 30; John F. Hefferman, 28; and John Carroll, 2. Accompanying this return was a statement, made February 5 by James McGloin, that Turner was one of the elected delegates. The other tabulation showed that Turner had received 33 votes; McMullen, 27; Bower, 26; Hefferman, 24; and Carroll, 1.[7]

Bower contested McMullen's right to a seat in the Convention. The dispute was submitted to the committee on privileges and election, composed of Stephen H. Everitt, chairman, E. O. LeGrand, and Charles B. Stewart. LeGrand favored McMullen, while Everitt and Stewart favored Bower. On March 4, the majority reported:

> ...that the Honl. John Turner came before the said committee and attested that his constituents instructed him to protest against Mr. McMullen being received as a member of this Convention; that the grounds on which the protest was founded was that many volunteers, who desired to vote on the day of election; that he heard four say that they intended to vote for Mr. Bower and he is clearly of the opinion that many others would have voted for Mr. Bower. Your committee differ in opinion, and respectfully desire the sense of the house to be taken.
>
> Your committee [the majority] is fully of opinion that Mr. Bower should be invited to take a seat in this house.[8]

Bower was seated March 4,[9] and on March 7 he signed the Declaration of Independence.[10]

There are few records of Bower following the adjournment of the Convention. On April 1, at Harrisburg, Maj. L. Smith impressed from him for the army one saddle, one bridle, and two blankets, valued at $35.[11] Bower was a member of the House of Representatives from Refugio County in the Sixth and Seventh Congresses, November 1, 1841, to January 16, 1843. On October 4, 1843, he was elected chief justice of Refugio County and was reelected in 1847.[12] He died January 13, 1850,[13] and is buried near the San Antonio River in Refugio County on land belonging, in 1942, to his grandson, James F. Power. In 1936 the Commission of Control for Texas Centennial Celebrations erected a monument at Bower's grave.

In 1838, Bower was married to Bridget O'Brien, daughter of Thomas and Elizabeth (Power) O'Brien.[14] After Bower's death, Mrs. Bower was married to Michael Whelan. Mrs. Whelan died in about 1863.

The Bowers had but one child, Frances Elizabeth Bower, who was married at Copano, June 21, 1866, to James Power, Jr., son of the empresario. Their children were: Mary Frances, who married Lewis Jane Woodworth of Refugio; Agnes Elizabeth, who married John P. Shelly; and James P. Power, Vidauri, Texas.

John W. Bower

ASA BRIGHAM[1]
of
BRAZORIA MUNICIPALITY

*A*sa Brigham was born in Massachusetts in about 1790 and came to Texas from Louisiana.[2] A farmer with his forty-one year old wife, Elizabeth S., and two sons, he arrived in April, 1830.[3]

The Ayuntamiento of San Felipe de Austin announced December 19, 1830, that in the elections held December 12 and 13 Brigham had been elected *sindico procurador* for the precinct of Victoria (Brazoria).[4] At the elections held December 11 and 12, 1831, he was elected *comisario* for the same precinct.[5]

The First Convention of Texas at San Felipe on October 5, 1832, created a Central Committee and subcommittees of Safety and Vigilance in the established districts. On the following day, Brigham was elected treasurer of the District of Victoria (Brazoria).[6]

In February, 1836, Brigham was a merchant in Brazoria and was junior warden of Holland Lodge No. 36, A. F. & A.

M. at that place,[7] He was a charter member of the Grand Lodge of Texas, organized at Houston, December 20, 1837.[8]

Approximately 397 votes were cast in the elections held in the Municipality of Brazoria February 1, 1836, to select four delegates to the Constitutional Convention.[9]

At a box unnamed, George B. McKinstry was the president, and E. Hodges, the secretary. Walter C. White received 5 votes; Peter W. Grayson, 5; C. D. Sayre, 5; and Edmund Andrews, 5. All of the voters expressed themselves in favor of independence.

At Brazoria, Anson Jones was the president, Gerren Hines and Hector McNeill judges, and James A. Priest and Stephen M. Hale secretaries. James Collinsworth led with 82 votes; Asa Brigham next with 69; John S. D. Byrom, 65; Edwin Waller, 64; Charles D. Sayre, 25; J. G. McNeel, 25; Captain T. F. L. Parrott, 4; John Sweeny, 3; Benjamin C. Franklin, 3; and Dr. Anson Jones, 2.

44

William Harris was the president of election at Chocolate Bayou and S. T. Angier and Alexander Edgar judges, and Stephen Richardson secretary. There Edmund Andrews received 10 votes; Thomas F. McKinney, 9; Charles D. Sayre, 8; Warren D. C. Hall, 7; Brigham, 5; Collinsworth, 2; Dr. Anson Jones, 2; Edwin Waller, 1; Parrott, 1; Dr. J. A. E. Phelps, 1.

At the box in the "Precinct East of the Brazos," E. Caples was the president, Jesse Strother and Soloman C. Page tellers, and Samuel Gillett secretary. Brigham received 8 votes; Sayre, 7; P. D. McNeel, 7; Andrews, 5; and Byrom, 2.

M. C. Patton was the president at the Columbia box, A. W. Breedlove teller and George W. Poe secretary. The vote: Byrom, 45; Waller, 42; Collinsworth, 37; Brigham, 35; Sayre, 19; Grayson, 17; J. D. Patton, 9; J. Greenville McNeel, 7; James F. Perry, 5; Franklin, 4; Parrott, 2; Jones, 1; P. D. McNeel, 1; John Dinsmore, 1; A. G. McNeel, 1; and John Sweeny, 1. Thirty-four of the voters expressed themselves in favor of independence, 17 for the constitution of 1824, and 12 "doubtful."

At Velasco, Francis J. Hoskins was judge, Mandred Wood clerk, William S. Fisher and J. C. Hoskins tellers. The returns are of exceptional interest. In making them, the officials listed the names of the 88 men who voted. At least 47 of these had been in Texas less than five days. They had been recruited in New Orleans for the Army of Texas by Captain Amasa Turner and had arrived at Velasco, January 28, 1836, aboard the schooner *Pennsylvania*. Fifty of the voters later participated in the Battle of San Jacinto.[10] Each of the 88 men voted for James Collinsworth, John S. D. Byrom, Edwin Waller, and Asa Brigham. The report showed that at least 158 other men had voted by proxy, but their names were not listed. The total votes cast were distributed as follows: Waller, 246; Collinsworth, 245; Brigham, 244; and Byrom, 238.

Following are the total number of votes received by the candidates in Brazoria Municipality: Asa Brigham, 430; James Collinsworth, 369; Edwin Waller, 354; John S. D. Byrom, 350; Chas. D. Sayre, 64; Peter W. Grayson, 46; J. Greenville McNeel, 40; Edmund Andrews, 20; Thomas F. McKinney, 9; J. D. Patton, 9; T. F. L. Parrott, 7; Benjamin C. Franklin, 7; W. D. C. Hall, 7; Dr. Phelps, 7; Walter C. White, 5; Anson Jones, 5; James F. Perry, 5; John Sweeny, 4; P. D. McNeel, 1; and John Dinsmore, 1. By receiving 430 votes Brigham received more votes than were cast for any other delegate elected to the convention.

Colonel Gray at San Felipe February 18, 1836, met Brigham en route to Washington:

Introduced to Asa Brigham, a delegate from Columbia. He is called here a *cornstalk* lawyer, which is explained to be equal to a *quack* physician.[11]

Brigham was seated on March 2[12] and remained at the Convention until at least March 16.[13]

45

Brigham was appointed auditor of the Republic by David G. Burnet, President *ad interim*. On December 20, 1836, President Houston named him treasurer of the Republic.[14] President Lamar reappointed him to that office, January 16, 1839.[15] On February 16 of that year he was sworn in as one of the aldermen of the city of Houston and held that office at the same time he held the office of treasurer of the Republic.

Due to ill health Brigham was unable to devote his full time to the affairs of the treasurer's office and left its management largely in the hands of his chief clerk, his brother-in-law, W. Henry H. Johnson. The manner in which Johnson administered affairs caused criticism, and President Lamar requested that he be discharged. Brigham refusing to acquiesce, President Lamar, on April 12, 1840, removed Brigham from office. President Houston, however, reappointed him treasurer, December 23, 1841.[16] In 1842 he was mayor of the city of Austin.

Mrs. Brigham having died, Brigham, on July 8, 1839, was married to Mrs. Ann (Johnson) Mather,[17] widow of Elijah Mather, who died in the winter of 1836-37. She was a sister of W. Henry H. Johnson and Rebecca Johnson. Rebecca was the second wife of Rev. John Wurts Cloud. Cloud was the first Episcopal priest in Texas.[18]

Brigham had at least three children: Samuel B., Benjamin Rice, and a daughter. Benjamin was mortally wounded in the Battle of San Jacinto. In reference to him, Brigham on November 5, 1838, wrote to President Lamar:

> Pardon me My Dear Sir, for this intrusion, when I reflect upon the many kindnesses my Familey have received at your hands, particularly on one occasion, the last attention given to my late and beloved son...I cannot find words that will convey to you my feelings, on that subject, or to express to you the gratitude which I owe.[19]

Brigham died in the town of Washington, Washington County, July 2, 1844. Samuel B. Brigham of Brazoria was appointed administrator of his estate, November 25, 1844.[20] On February 24, 1845, Mrs. Brigham was awarded Brigham's house and furniture on lot 11, block 57, of Austin. On February 29, 1852, the estate was closed, one half going to Mrs. Brigham, one fourth to Susannah Richeson [sic], and one fourth to Samuel B. Brigham.[21]

A daughter of Asa Brigham, born in Texas, was married to Edwin Richardson. Judge John Hancock, in November, 1855, was married to Miss Susan E. Richardson, who was a native Texan, and the granddaughter of Asa Brigham.[22] Mrs. Hancock was living in Travis County in 1880 and was at that time the only surviving member of the Brigham family.

In 1936 the Commission of Control for Texas Centennial Celebrations erected a monument at the grave of Asa Brigham in the old cemetery in the town of Washington, Texas.

47

Asa Brigham

ANDREW BRISCOE
of
HARRISBURG MUNICIPALITY

Andrew Briscoe, the eldest of Parmenas and Polly (Montgomery) Briscoe's twelve children, was born November 25, 1810, in Adams County, Mississippi.[1] He received his education at Clinton Academy in Hinds County, Mississippi,[2] and studied law under Gen. John A. Quitman at Jackson in 1831. He came to Texas in 1833.[3] In 1834 he began a mercantile business in Anahuac.[4] With DeWitt

Our (unlikely) Fathers

Clinton Harris, later his brother-in-law, he ran afoul of Mexican troops in June, 1835—a scene described by Harris in a letter dated at Harrisburg, August 17, to friends in New York:

> On the 10th of June I went to Anahuac (about fifty miles from Harrisburg) to purchase some goods of a Mr. Briscoe; after purchasing my goods, I was informed that I could not remove them from town until I got a gefe from the custom house; this I determined not to do, if I could avoid it. The evening previous to my intended departure there were several guards placed around Mr. Briscoe's store, to see that nothing was removed. About eight o'clock a young man came in the store and asked Briscoe for a box to put ballast in; this Mr. Briscoe gave him, and he placed it on a wheelbarrow filled with brick and started for the beach; after he had left the store I observed to Mr. Briscoe that we could not ascertain whether my goods would be stopped or not. Shortly after, we heard the young man calling for Mr. Smith the interpreter.
>
> Mr. Briscoe and I then walked up to the young man, and found that he had been stopped by the guard. Mr. Smith soon came up and informed the guard of the contents of the box; this appeared to satisfy him, and the box was taken to the beach, Mr. Briscoe and I going with the young man. After the box was put in the boat and we were about returning, ten or twelve Mexican soldiers came on us and ordered us to stand. Mr. Briscoe and I were taken prisoners. As we were ascending the bank a young man named William Smith came down the hill, and when within ten feet of us was shot down, the ball passing through the right breast; (he is recovering). Mr. Briscoe and I were then put in the calaboose, where I remained until next day at 11 o'clock, when I was liberated, Briscoe still being detained. I immediately came to Harrisburg and made statements of the facts, which were sent to San Felipe, and on the 24th of June an order came from San Felipe for the Mexicans to be disarmed, which was done on the 27th.[5]

William Barret Travis raised a company, went to Anahuac, and sent the Mexican troops packing to Goliad.[6]

During the latter part of 1835, Briscoe moved to Harrisburg, which, with a steam saw mill, was more thriving than Anahuac. During the Revolution, he rendered distinguished service to Texas. At the storming of Bexar, December 5 to 10, 1835, he was in command of the Liberty Volunteers.[7] The General Council, on November 28, appointed him captain of a regiment of artillery.[8]

On February 1, 1836, Lorenzo de Zavala and Briscoe were elected to represent Harrisburg Municipality at the Constitutional Convention.[9] Inasmuch as Briscoe was in the United States a few days before the Convention opened on March 1, and it was not known when he would return home, John W. Moore, who had received the third largest number of votes, was seated in his stead. Briscoe reached Washington from Nacogdoches on March 10. The following day:

> Mr. Palmer moved that A. Q. [sic] Briscoe, from the municipality of Harrisburg, he invited to take a seat in the convention. And the question being put by the chair, it was declared in the affirmative...[10]

On motion of Samuel P. Carson:

> The original Declaration of Independence was produced by the secretary, and signed by James B. Woods and A. Briscoe...[11]

Briscoe left the convention hall on March 17 and rejoined the army. According to an affidavit made by Lyman F. Rounds, a San Jacinto veteran, Briscoe, on April 18, assumed command of a company of regulars when its captain, Henry Teal, contracted measles.[12] As captain, Briscoe commanded the company at San Jacinto.[13]

After the Revolution, he bought a stock of goods in New Orleans and opened a store at Lynchburg.[14] On December

20, 1836, President Houston appointed him chief justice—the first—of Harrisburg County.[15] He resigned, effective May 7, 1839, to become agent of the Harrisburg Rail Road and Trading Company,[16] which started construction on a line from Harrisburg to the Brazos River. The project failed, but the survey of the road was later adopted by the Buffalo Bayou, Brazos and Colorado Railroad, which is today a part of the Southern Pacific System. Briscoe reentered politics and was elected alderman of Harrisburg, October 26, 1842.[17] On August 30, 1845, he was elected justice of the peace of Beat No. 5 of Harris County.[18]

Briscoe was twice married, first to Miss Elizabeth House, who evidently died before Briscoe came to Texas.[19] He then married Mary Jane Harris, daughter of John Richardson and Jane (Birdsall) Harris, in Houston, August 17, 1837.[20] Harris was the original proprietor of the town of Harrisburg. This town and Harris County were named for him.

50

> Five children were born to the Briscoes, one of whom died in infancy. When the eldest arrived at an age to require school advantages, his father decided to remove to New Orleans and engage in a banking business, and so in the spring of 1849, the move was made, but scarcely had the enterprise begun when its head and founder was taken sick and died on the 4th day of October. Gen. Parmenas Briscoe being present at the deathbed of his son, closed up the business and took the young widow and her children to his plantation home in Claiborne County, Mississippi, and the remains of Capt. Andrew Briscoe were laid to rest in the old family burying ground.[21]

Briscoe signed his will at Harrisburg, May 3, 1848. At that time he was evidently at odds with his brothers-in-law, for he specified that no one by the name of Harris should ever have anything to do with his estate.[22]

Briscoe County, when created August 21, 1876, was named "in honor of Andrew Briscoe, who commanded a company at the battle of Concepcion, in 1835."[23] The remains of Captain Briscoe were exhumed by order of the State of Texas and, on February 27, 1937, reinterred in the State cemetery at Austin. An appropriate monument was erected at his new grave.

Mrs. Mary Jane Briscoe was born August 17, 1819, and died March 8, 1903. She is buried in a marked grave in Glenwood Cemetery, Houston. She was prominent in the Daughters of the Republic of Texas, which was organized in her home, November 6, 1891, and served as first vice-president from the organization until her death.

Children of Mr. and Mrs. Briscoe, all deceased, were: Parmenas, who died unmarried; Andrew Birdsall, who married Annie F. Payne; Jessie Wade, who married Milton G. Howe; and Adele Lubbock, who married Maj. Michael Looscan. In 1942 among other surviving grandchildren of Mr. and Mrs. Briscoe were: Mrs. G. B. West, San Antonio; Birdsall P. Briscoe, Houston; Payne Briscoe, Hebbronville; and Mrs. T. M. Winsor, Scottsdale, Arizona.

51

JOHN WHEELER BUNTON
of
MINA MUNICIPALITY

*J*ohn Wheeler Bunton was born in Sumner County, Tennessee, February 22, 1807, son of Joseph Robert and Phoebe (Desha) Bunton. Graduating from a college in Kentucky he studied law in Gallatin, Tennessee.[1] In 1833[2] he came to Texas and settled at San Felipe, moving later to Mina (Bastrop).

Bunton was first sergeant from September 28 to Decem-

ber 27, 1835, when the company was disbanded, of Capt.
Robert M. Coleman's Company of Mina Volunteers.[3] For
the storming of Bexar, December 5 to 10, 1835, he was transferred to Capt. John York's Company.[4] On the day he was
honorably discharged from the army he was elected secretary of the Committee of Safety of Mina Municipality.[5]

Bunton, Thomas J. Gazley, and Robert M. Coleman
were the delegates representing Mina Municipality at the
Constitutional Convention.[6] Bunton was seated at the
Convention on March 1, 1836.[7] Leaving the Convention at
its adjournment he returned to Mina, where on March 28
he rejoined the army.[8] At the Battle of San Jacinto he served
in Capt. Jesse Billingsley's Company of Mina Volunteers.[9]

From October 3 to December 21, 1836, Bunton represented Bastrop County in the House of Representatives of
the First Congress of the Republic.[10] He did not, however,
attend the adjourned session which met in Houston from
May 1 to June 13, 1837. In the spring of 1837 he returned to
Tennessee and in Gallatin married Mary Howell, daughter of John Howell.[11] The Buntons remained in Tennessee
until April when they set out for Texas. At New Orleans
they boarded the *Julius Caesar*, carrying a cargo valued at
$30,000. As the vessel neared the Texas coast, on April 12, it
was captured by the Mexicans and taken into Matamoros
where the Buntons and other passengers were imprisoned.
The *Independence*, with William H. Wharton aboard, and
the *Champion* were also seized. Of the capture of these vessels, *The Telegraph and Texas Register* on June 24, 1837, said:

> The Honorable John W. Bunton and lady, having recent-
> ly arrived from Matamoras, via New Orleans, Mr. Bunton
> states that the *Champion* has been condemned by the Mex-
> icans as a piratical vessel, the *Julius Caesar* has also been
> condemned though not as a piratical craft. The officers of
> the *Independence* are not ill treated, but the crew are kept in
> close confinement. Captain Wheelwright has nearly recov-

52

ered. General Filisola made a proposition for the exchange of Prisoners just before Mr. B. left. This was "that all the Mexicans prisoners now in Texas should be released in exchange for the Texas Captives now in Mexico; the Texan government defraying the expenses of removing these captives to Matamoros." Colonel Wharton spurned the offer with indignation, considering it an insult upon the national character; the ratio of the Texan captives being to the Mexicans as one to ten or twelve.

At about this time, Bunton moved to Austin County, for he represented that county in the House of Representatives of the Third Congress, November 5, 1838, to November 11, 1839.[12] In 1840 he returned to Bastrop County and settled on a farm on Cedar Creek. In 1857 he removed to Hays County near Mountain City, where he engaged in large scale cattle ranching. A member of the Texas Veterans Association, he died August 24, 1879,[13] and was buried beside his wife in the Robinson cemetery near Mountain City. The State of Texas had their remains exhumed and on March 2, 1932, reinterred in the State cemetery at Austin with a joint monument at their new graves.

Mrs. Bunton was born in Gallatin, Tennessee, February 22, 1816, and died September 16, 1862. Both she and her husband were members of the Christian Church.[14]

Children of Mr. and Mrs. Bunton were: Elizabeth Howell, who married Dr. W. A. Oatman; Joseph Howell; Thomas Howell, who died unmarried; Desha; William Howell; and James Howell Bunton, who was never married. Surviving grandchildren in 1942 were: DeFla Bunton, Thomas Wilmot Bunton, and Desha Bunton, all of Hays County; John Ashley Bunton, Rio Frio; William Manlove Bunton, Laguna; John Bunton Oatman, Corpus Christi; and Mrs. Mary Oatman Wright, San Antonio.

OUR (unlikely) FATHERS

JOHN SMITH DAVENPORT BYROM
of
BRAZORIA MUNICIPALITY

John Smith Davenport Byrom was born in about 1798,[1] in Hancock County, Georgia, son of Henry and Catherine Smith (Davenport) Byrom. At the death of his father in 1806, his uncle, John Byrom, became his guardian. He moved with his uncle to Jasper County, Georgia, and there on March 17, 1818, was married to Nancy Fitzpatrick, who was born October 2, 1804, in Green County, Georgia. He later moved to Heard County, Georgia, and still later to Florida. Mr. and Mrs. Byrom were divorced, and Mrs. Byrom located near her brother, Jackson Fitzpatrick, in Gordon County, where she died August 3, 1877. She is buried in the Pine Chapel Cemetery. Byrom was next married to Mary Anne Knott. In 1830 he came to Texas and settled in what is now Brazoria County.[2]

Byrom participated in the Battle of Velasco, June 26, 1832.[3] In 1835 he represented Columbia (Brazoria) Municipality at the Consultation held at San Felipe de Austin.[4] On November 26, 1835, the General Council of the Provisional Government appointed Byrom, Matthew Patton, and James O'Connor commissioners for organizing the militia in Brazoria Municipality.[5] Byrom, James Collinsworth, Edwin Waller, and Asa Brigham represented Brazoria Municipality at the Constitutional Convention.[6] Byrom was seated March 1.[7] There is no evidence that he joined the Texas army after the adjournment of the convention, March 17.

Byrom was made an Entered Apprentice by Holland Lodge No. 36, A. F. & A. M. of Brazoria, in February, 1836, while he was sheriff of Brazoria Municipality, but he died before receiving the other two degrees.[8]

JOHN S. D. BYROM

Severely ill and realizing the proximity of death, on July 7, 1837, Byrom dictated his will and sent for a number of his friends—F. M. Nash, Henry Mackie, E. A. Gallagher, M. C. Patton, Parker D. Wallace, J. G. Welschmeyer, and B. T. Norman—to witness his signature. He died July 10 and on July 31 the will was opened for probate before Judge George B. McKinstry who appointed Henry P. Brewster and John A. Wharton executors of the estate, which was valued at $18,848.43.[9]

By his second wife, Mary Anne Knott, Byrom had two children, Susan Anne and James Wooten Byrom. On February 19, 1839, Mrs. Byrom was married to William Natt,[10] and on January 4, 1843, to John Frederick Hanson.[11]

Children of Byrom by his first marriage were Mary, Henry Clay, and William Hardwick Crawford Byrom. Mary Byrom, first child born to John S. D. Byrom, died before the year 1814 and is buried on the plantation owned by S. B. Byrom four miles north east of Hillsborough, Jasper County, Georgia.

Henry Clay Byrom, second child of John S. D. Byrom by his first wife, was born December 15, 1818, and died December 21, 1849. He was twice married but died childless.

William H. C. Byrom, third child of John S. D. Byrom, was born October 2, 1825, and died August 2, 1853. He is buried at Pine Chapel Cemetery, Gordon County, Georgia. He was married to Julia Harvey Fite. Their children were John Smith Davenport, Nancy Victoria, and William Henry Crawford Byrom.

S. B. Byrom, in a letter dated October 10, 1939, to the author, listed as some of the surviving great grandchildren of John S. D. Byrom: Mrs. Henry Compton, Monroe, Walton County, Georgia; Mrs. J. K. Hunt, Wilmington County, Delaware; Alex Mayfield Byrom, Ft. Lauderdale, Florida; Mrs. Rufus Thames, Milton, Florida; William Clinton By-

55

rom, Milton, Florida; and Mrs. Tom G. Curtis, Canton, Georgia.

The Commission of Control for Texas Centennial Celebrations erected a monument at John S. D. Byrom's grave in the cemetery at West Columbia in 1936.

MATHEW CALDWELL
of
GONZALES MUNICIPALITY

Mathew Caldwell was born in Kentucky in about 1798[1] and came to Texas from Missouri in 1831.[2]

On November 30, 1835, the General Council of the Provisional Government of Texas received a report from William Pettus, contractor for the Volunteer Army, in which he stated that he had appointed Caldwell subcontractor.[3] Apparently while serving in this capacity, he was "assaulted, beat and severely wounded" by Joseph P. Laller. The General Council of the Provisional Government of January 3, 1836, offered a reward of $150 for the arrest of Laller.[4]

On February 1, 1836, Caldwell and John Fisher were elected delegates from Gonzales Municipality to the Constitutional Convention.[5] On March 1 they were seated in the convention.[6]

On March 2, the Convention adopted William C. Crawford's motion that a committee of three be appointed by the president to procure couriers to send expresses to the army, "...whereupon the President appointed Messrs. Crawford, Lacy [sic] and Caldwell, said committee."

Believing it of vital importance that this convention know correctly the true situation of our enemy on the frontier, and also the condition of our army, they would recommend the convention to accept the services of Major Caldwell, who purposes to start this day to the frontier.[7]

The report was adopted, and Caldwell set out, not to return before the adjournment of the convention.

On January 15, 1839, President Lamar named Caldwell captain "of the company of Rangers to be raised under a special law for the defense of Goliad."[8] The senate promptly confirmed the nomination. On March 23 of the same year, Caldwell became captain of a company in the First Regiment of Infantry.[9] He was wounded at the Council House Fight with the Comanches in San Antonio, March 19, 1840.[10] At the Battle of Plum Creek on August 12, 1840, he headed a company,[11] and as captain of Company D bore a full share of suffering in the ill-fated Santa Fe Expedition in 1841-2.[12] Released from the Mexican dungeon in which the Santa Fe prisoners were incarcerated, he hastened to the relief of San Antonio. On September 18, 1842, following the capture on September 11 of San Antonio by Gen. Adrian Woll, Caldwell with the rank of colonel, commanding a force of about 200, met and defeated Woll's superior force at Salado Creek. Of this engagement, Caldwell reported:

Sunday, September 17 [18], 7 o'clock, p.m. at the Salado, two miles above the old crossing. We commenced fighting at eleven o'clock today. A hot fire was kept up till about one hour by the sun, when the army retreated, bearing off their dead on the ground, and very many dead and wounded were taken from the field by their friends. We have a glorious band of Texan patriots, among whom ten only were wounded, and not one killed. The enemy are all round me, on every side; but I fear them not. I will hold my position till I hear from reinforcements. Come and help me—it is the most favorable opportunity I have ever seen. There are eleven hundred of the enemy. I can whip them on my own ground without any help, but I cannot take prisoners. Why don't you come?...Huzza! huzza for Texas![13]

Colonel Caldwell died at his home in Gonzales, December 28, 1842,[14] and was buried on December 30 with a military funeral, of which C. C. Colley was marshal and commander of infantry. At the grave, D. C. Vanderlip delivered the oration, saying in part:

> ...when the events of the present day become matters of history—when the present generation are in their graves and other men occupy our places, posterity will read, with wonder and admiration, that the gallant Caldwell with a handful of undisciplined volunteers, fearlessly took a position in immediate neighborhood of a disciplined army of the enemy of more than six times his own number, checked their progress and encountered their attacks, and compelled them to return from the field and the country, and then saved the destruction of our capitol.

The act creating Caldwell County, Texas, approved March 6, 1848, does not state for whom the county was named.[15] Thrall, in 1879, said that it was named for Matthew [sic] Caldwell.[16] In 1930, the State of Texas erected a monument at Caldwell's grave in the old cemetery at Gonzales.

Caldwell twice married. In Washington County, on May 17, 1837, he was married to Mrs. H. Morrison.[17] After her death, he was married to Mrs. Lily Lawley.

The names of three of Caldwell's children are known: Martha married Isham D. Davis; Ann married Johnson Baker Ellison; and Curtis died before reaching maturity. Mr. and Mrs. Davis had two children, Thomas Jefferson Davis, who was residing at Iola, Texas, in 1942, and Mrs. D. A. Darby.

SAMUEL PRICE CARSON
of
PECAN POINT AND VICINITY

Samuel Price Carson was born in Pleasant Gardens, Burke County, North Carolina, January 22, 1798,[1] son of Col. John Carson[2] and his second wife, Mary Moffitt McDowell, daughter of Col. George Moffitt and widow of Gen. Joseph McDowell.

> He [Samuel Price Carson], like his father was a Democrat, and was young, handsome, eloquent, magnetic, blessed with a charming voice, delighting in all the pleasures and opportunities of a healthful, vigorous physique. He was educated at the "Old Field Schools" of the neighborhood till he reached his nineteenth year, when he was taken into the family of his half brother, Joseph M. Carson, where he was taught grammar and directed in a course of reading with an eye to political advancement; and before he was 22 years of age he represented the county of Burke in the legislature, defeating his kinsman James R. McDowell for that place... Even when a boy he was a great favorite not only with people of his own walk in life, but was worshipped by the negroes on his father's plantation. His mother was a Methodist and young Samuel was a great favorite at camp meetings where his deep-toned and harmonious voice led in their congregational singing. He was also popular with the ladies.[3]

Carson was a member of the State Senate, 1822-24. In 1824 and again in 1826 he defeated Dr. Robert Frank Vance for the position of representative to the United States Congress. In the campaign of the latter year, Dr. Vance, in a speech at Morgantown, spoke disparagingly of Carson's father:

> The Bible tells us that because the fathers have eaten sour grapes, their sons' teeth have been on edge.—My father never ate sour grapes and my competitor's father did—In the

time of the Revolutionary War my father, Col. Vance, stood up to the fight, while my competitor's father, Col. Carson, skulked, and took British protection.[4]

In answer to an ill-natured and abusive letter, Dr. Vance wrote to Col. John Carson:

> I can have no altercation with a man of your age; and, if I have aggrieved you, you certainly have some of your chivalrous sons that will protect you from the insult.[5]

Samuel Price Carson resented the insult to his father and challenged Dr. Vance.

> This challenge had been written by Carson at Pleasant Gardens and was dated September 12, 1827, taken to Jonesboro, Tenn., and sent from there in order to avoid a violation of the law of North Carolina regarding dueling; for he states in the challenge: "I will do no act in violation of the laws of my State; but as you have boasted that you had flung the gauntlet before me, which in point of fact is not true; for, in the language of chivalry, to fling the gauntlet is to challenge—to throw down the iron glove;—but, if you are serious, make good your boast; throw your gauntlet upon neutral ground; then, if not accepted, boast your victory."[6]

The duel was fought three weeks later at Saluda Gap, South Carolina, on the Greenville turnpike just across the line from North Carolina. Gen. Franklin Patton was Dr. Vance's second and Dr. George Phillips his surgeon. Gen. Alney Burgin and Warren Davis were seconds for Carson and Dr. Shufin his surgeon.

> The distance was ten paces and the firing was to be done between the words "Fire, One, Two, Three," with rising or falling pistols. Vance chose the rising and Carson the falling mode; and at the word "Fire," Carson sent a ball entirely through Vance's body, entering one and a half inches above the point of the hip and lodging in the skin of the opposite side. It does not appear that Vance fired at all. Vance

60

died the next day, thirty-two hours after having received his wound, at a hotel on the road, probably Davis'.

When he saw that Vance had been wounded Carson expressed a wish to speak to him, but was led away; and before his death Vance expressed regret that Carson had not been permitted to speak with him, and stated that he had "not the least unkind feeling for him."—The result of this duel is said to have embittered his [Carson's] life.[7]

Carson served in Congress from March 4, 1825, to March 3, 1833. He was defeated for re-election in 1833, his support of John C. Calhoun's nullification meeting with his constituents' disapproval. In 1834 he was again elected to the state senate.

On April 18, 1835, Carson purchased "one thousand acres more or less" on the west side of Red River "between what is called Cedar Bend [later called Hemphill Bend] which land was improved by L. G. Clawson." Twelve days later he bought from Andrew Hemphill for $3,750 a tract "believed to contain two and three hundred acres of Prairie Land."[8] This land and 84 slaves he sold December 8, to James A. Bass for $107,000.[9] On January 2, 1836, Carson purchased from Alexander Bole a tract situated west of Big Bayou and a little north of west from Fisher's Prairie with improvements.[10] All of these lands were situated in La Fayette (Lafayette) County, but some is now in Miller County. None of it was or is in Texas, although part is near the Arkansas-Texas line.

While in Arkansas, Carson was elected delegate from Burke County, N.C., to the North Carolina Constitutional Convention. His views on religion expressed at this convention were entirely consistent with those he voiced five months later at the Texas convention. In North Carolina he spoke against a proposed constitutional clause prohibiting Roman Catholics from holding office.[11] In Texas he favored religious freedom for Protestants as well as for Catholics.

61

Carson, Richard Ellis, Collin McKinney, Robert Hamilton, and Albert H. Latimer represented "Pecan Point and Vicinity" at the Constitutional Convention.[12] All had claimed citizenship in Arkansas Territory, but later treaties put their homes, except Carson's and possibly Hamilton's, in Texas. Carson reached the convention March 10 and during the afternoon of that day signed the Declaration of Independence.[13] Of his activities, Gray wrote in his diary, March 11:

> Mr. Carson has at once taken a prominent part in the business of the house. He has made a good impression, and much is expected of him. He is not yet forty years of age, but is in bad health, and looks much older. He and Potter are the only two members of the body who have ever been in Congress (except Gen. Houston, who is now in the Army), and their experience in public business gives them an ascendency over the rest of the body. The President is losing ground. He made a good impression at first, but by his partiality and weakness and great conceit he has forfeited the respect of the body, and a laxity of order begins to be apparent.[14]

During the early hours of March 17, David G. Burnet and Carson were nominated for president *ad interim* of the Republic of Texas. Burnet received 29 votes and Carson 23.[15] Carson was elected secretary of state,[16] holding this office until April 1, 1836, when President Burnet at Harrisburg addressed him:

> The infirm state of your health renders it necessary for you to repose from the fatigues of office and the suggestion of your physician that a change of climate would probably conduce to your restoration, I have submitted to the gentlemen associated with us in the government the propriety of your proceeding forthwith to the United States and there employing your valuable time in the service of Texas. Cabinet fully concur with me in the expediency of your temporary absence from us.

You will please repair as fast as circumstances will permit to Washington City and there unite your exertions with those of our *mother* country, and you will take in charge a general supervision of all the interests and concerns of Texas in that country.

You are fully apprised of our wants—they are numerous— as the means at present in our power of gratifying them are limited. Your exertions may be valuable employed in procuring aid of all sorts—fiscal aid is all important at this crisis.

Your absence will be too sensibly felt not to be deeply regretted—and I beg you will make it as little irksome as possible, not only by frequent communications, but by shortening the period of it as much as a prudent regard to your health and the ulterior objects of your visit will permit. An acting Secretary of State will be appointed ad interim—but the department will await the return of its most esteemed incumbent with impatient solicitude. Wishing you a pleasant trip, the speedy restoration of your health and an early return to us. I commend you to the protection of that God who cared for the oppressed.[17]

Burnet then appointed Bailey Hardeman acting secretary,[18] On May 23, Burnet at Velasco wrote Carson:

We have not had the pleasure of hearing from you since your arrival in the United States.

Since you left many events of a deep & stirring interest have occurred among us. You have before now, heard of the most prominent, notwithstanding the signal defeat of our external enemies our condition is by no means an enviable one, we are embarrassed on all hands and perplexed with many difficulties. Great patience and fortitude are necessary to enable us to bear up under the adverse circumstances that press upon us—but I hope that patience and that fortitude will be exercised.

After your departure, the department of State was for a time virtually vacant. At present its duties are ably discharged by Col. Collinsworth, a gentleman of high character, and efficiency. But he talks of declining and we are much at loss to replace him. One difficulty grows out of an aversion on the part of gentlemen to officiate only as acting Secretary—to fill an office, that is only vacant by the temporary absence of the proper incumbent.

I therefore suggest to you the propriety and indeed the necessity of your immediate return, or that you resign your office to enable us to procure the best talents of the country, in that important Department.[19]

Because of slowness in mail delivery, as late as July 3, Carson signed himself secretary of state.[20] He read in a New York newspaper a proclamation issued by Burnet on June 10 that Toby & Brother of New Orleans and R. F. Triplett were the only authorized agents of Texas in the United States. In disgust Carson returned to Arkansas. On November 28, at Douglas Place, Pulaski County, he wrote President Houston:

I take leave to lay before your Excellency (not knowing who may compose your Cabinet) a brief statement of the manner in which I fulfilled the mission upon which I was despatched by the Govt. 'ad Interim' of Texas under a commission bearing date 1st April last [1836].

...From thence [Natchitoches, Louisiana] I proceeded to my residence on upper Red River where I had left my family. The great exposure to which I had been subjected in my journey brought on a severe attack of 'typhoid pneumonia' or 'influenza' which confined me ten days. So soon as I was able to proceed on my journey to Washington City which place I was not able to reach until the 22 June. This detention was caused principally by my very feeble state of health which compelled me to delay at various points to recruit my strength. At Louisville, Ky. I had a very violent attack which confined me for some days. Mrs. Carson would not consent after my sickness at home to be separated from me in consequence of my debilitated situation, and therefore accompanied me through out my travel.

Meeting with Messrs Hamilton and Childress on my arrival at Washington City we adopted such plans and measures for the furtherance of the objects which we were charged, as seemed most expedient at the moment—Under the authority granted to the Executive Govt. to obtain a loan of money to supply the wants of the Army etc. Robert Hamilton Esqr. was thought by the cabinet to be the most suitable person to effect that object in part. He was therefore commissioned by the President on the 2d day of April last. His commission was confided to me for delivery to Mr. Hamilton, which I bore and delivered to him at Washington City.

Mr. Hamilton set out shortly after to Philadelphia on his mission at which place I joined him immediately after the rise of Congress.

To detail the course we pursued, the conversation we held with Gentlemen upon Exchanges etc. would be useless—sufficient to say that we had no understanding with *large capitalists* at that place, that we should proceed to New York, create a Govt. stock at such a rate of interest as we might think advisable and put them into market there and they (the capitalists of Philadelphia) assured us that they would take liberally at whatever we could start our stocks or bonds in New York.

Upon this Mr. Hamilton and myself proceeded to New York, sounded the money market and were arranging our plans of operations when to our surprise and astonishment there appeared in the Gazettes of New York the following proclamation extracted from the New Orleans papers...

To judge our feelings and decided upon our deep mortification could only be done by persons placed in similar situations. But great as our chagrin we deemed it better for the cause of Texas to bear it in silence—had we taken any other course we should have been compelled to give a *flat contradiction* to the President and publish in the public prints the authority under which we acted and had presumed to borrow money upon—but we preferred submitting to the injury, rather than bring the authorities of the Republic into disrepute in the only country from which could expect aid, and in which our dissentions at home, had been sufficiently magnified and done sufficient injury. I also thought and hoped that the omission of the name of Mr. Hamilton, as one of the Govt. Agents to obtain money, in the Proclamation of the President was a mere inadvertence of 'Casus ommissis' which would be rectified immediately but in this I have been disappointed and Mr. Hamilton and myself remain to this day under the odious light of having attempted to obtain money without authority from the Govt. which we profess to be serving. And this the more extraordinary as the commission of Mr. Hamilton is not only signed by President Burnet in his official capacity but every word of the Commission is also in his own handwriting...

From New York Mr. Hamilton and myself returned to Washington City when we met with Cols. Collinsworth and Grayson who seemed to be charged with all the duties necessary to be discharged for the benefit of the Republic.

To them I stated my determination of proceeding to the White Sulphur Springs of Virginia for the restoration of my health. Since which time I have been attending to my health and had hoped that I was restored, till a recent attack has thrown me quick back and I am barely able to make this communication.[21]

Carson expended a sizeable portion of his personal fortune in behalf of Texas. At New Orleans on March 23, 1837, he was so pinched he mortgaged for $10,000 a number of his plantation Negroes.[22]

On page 791 of the *Biographical Directory of the American Congress, 1774-1927*, it is stated that Samuel P. Carson died at Hot Springs, Arkansas, November 2, 1838, and was buried there in the U. S. Government Cemetery. The Houston *Telegraph* of January 19, 1839, announced: "Died recently at the Warm Springs in Arkansas, the Hon. Samuel P. Carson."

The author has been unable to locate his grave.[23] Carson signed his will January 1, 1838:

SAMUEL P. CARSON

I Samuel P. Carson formerly of North Carolina Now of Texas or State of Arkansas as the case may be do make, ordain & constitute this my last will & Testament.

First my will is that all my just debts should be paid— 2nd that all property real, personal & mixed after the payment of my debts I give and bequeath to my beloved wife Catherine for & during her natural life and widdowhood; should she marry, my will is that one fourth of my estate be set apart by my Executors for her comfort & support over which however her husband is to have no controle.

Should she never marry she is authorized to keep possession of every part of my estate till her death provided neither of the Children marry, But should either of them marry Previous to the death of Mrs. Carson my wish is that she should aportion them off as to her discretion may seem fit; at her death it is my will that two thirds of my whole estate go to my Daughter Racheal Rebecca & one third to my maternal Daughter Emily Carson. For the details of my wishes with regard to the disposition of my property in the event one or both of my children dying without issue I refer my Executors to a will which I made in the year 1835 & left in the hands of Genl Waddy Thompson of South Carolina assuming however the distribution set fourth in this will with regard to the children should they live and have issue. In the event of Mrs. Carson's marrying I wish three fourths of my estate mortgaged sold or assigned for the benefit of my Legetees & at the death of Mrs. Carson the fourth set apart for her support to be divided as aforesaid.

I wish my trusty servant Eli his wife Mary & her children to go to my Daughter Racheal Rebecca at a fair estimate in the division of my estate. My Old and Trusty faithful servant George or George Cathy I leave to the protection of my wife & children & leave him as free as the Laws will permit after my death.

In conclusion I nominate and appoint my friend Robert Hamilton Esqr, Col. Thos W. Williamson & Jess H. Hall Executors of this my last will & Testament

In Testimony whereof I have hereunto set my hand and

seal this first day of January, 1838. Done at Shreveport, Louisiana. In presents of Angus McNeil, James P. Pickett and B. Jenkins.

Samuel P. Carson (Seal)[24]

On August 26, 1856, Mrs. Carson received her husband's headright of one league and one labor.[25] Carson County, Texas, when created August 21, 1876, was named "in honor of Samuel P. Carson, Secretary of State under the Republic."[26]

Carson was married to Catherine Wilson, who was born in 1810 in Burke County, North Carolina, daughter of James and Rebecca Wilson. She died in 1882 in Salisbury, North Carolina. Mr. and Mrs. Carson had a daughter, Racheal Rebecca, and an adopted daughter, Emily.

Racheal Rebecca Carson married Dr. McDowel Whitson of Talladega, Alabama. Charles Whitson and Mrs. Emmie Baker, children of this union, were living in Talladega in 1942.

Emily Carson, the daughter of Carson's brother Logan, was married to P. J. Sinclair. In May, 1942, Mr. and Mrs. Sinclair were residing in Chapel Hill, North Carolina. A son, Dr. James A. Sinclair, lives in Asheville, North Carolina.

68

GEORGE CAMPBELL CHILDRESS
of
MILAM MUNICIPALITY

George Campbell Childress was a son of John and Elizabeth (Robertson) Childress. His mother was a sister of Sterling C. Robertson, a signer of the Texas Declaration of Independence. Of Childress, J. K. Greer in his "Committee on the Texas Declaration of Independence,"[1] said:

> [He] was born in Nashville, [Tennessee] January 8, 1804. Very little is known of his youth. In temperament, however, he was of an earnest disposition and subject to occasional fits of melancholy which at times made his behavior rather violent.[2] Yet all the evidence that has been ascertained indicates that his temperament was never other than admirable from adulthood to the time of his death.
>
> He studied law and was admitted to the Davidson County Bar in 1828.[3] Six years later, on September 22, 1834, he became one of the editors of *The Nashville Banner and Nashville Advertiser*, Nashville's daily paper, published by Hunt, Tardiff & Co. He continued in the editorial chair until November 9, 1835, when he was succeeded by Allen A. Hall, afterwards editor of the *Daily News*.[4] At the time that Childress began his editorship, the paper was reduced from a daily to a tri-weekly because "three years had convinced the publishers that a daily paper would not pay in Nashville."

Probably no one, while residing in the United States, did more for the cause of Texas than did Childress. He was doubtless the instigator of the several mass meetings held in Nashville to raise funds to finance the revolution and to enlist volunteers for the Texas army.

The Nashville Republican of November 19, 1835, devoted a great deal of space in reporting the proceeding on the meeting of the 17th which was described as being "large and enthusiastic" and which had been called "to take into consideration the situation of Texas." At this meeting "an eloquent address was delivered by George C. Childress, Esq. A number of persons enrolled their names as volunteers, and a considerable amount was subscribed on the spot to aid in equipping them and defraying their expenses...Since the meeting, we have been told that one gentleman alone, with that public spirit and princely liberality for which he is so well known, had made an individual donation to the cause of five thousand dollars,[5] appointed the chairman of the meeting—Mr. Geo. Childress, Esq.—his agent to tender it to the acting public authorities in Texas. Another meeting will be held this evening at the Court House on the same subject."[6] *The New Orleans Courier* of December 8 printed Childress's address in full.

From a letter written by Samuel Swartwout, a noted speculator of his time, it appears that one of the motives that induced Childress to come to Texas was to acquire, in co-operation with Swartwout, large holdings of lands:

70

New York Monday 7th Dec 1835

My dear Sir,

On the 8th, of November I read, a letter from Mr. Childress on the subject of our land speculation in Texas, and yesterday I read, a Nashville paper containing an account of the proceedings of a meeting in that city of the 21st ult, at which Mr. Childress was chairman. I really supposed from the anxiety expressed by Mr. C. & yourself, that he would have been in Texas by the 20th of November. Do press his departure, as every day's delay diminishes his prospects of procuring the lands—Companies are forming here to proceed direct to the Red River & take up the lands already belted upon the clearing out principle, and I am invited to become interested. It would be most distressing & mortifying to have others reap the benefit of our planning, entered into by them two months after the departure of Mr. Childress. Let him go, therefore, as soon as possible.

I am now more than ever satisfied that he can get the best lands and make the best bargains on Red River above the raft. There are two or 300 families settled there and they, being so far from the seat of war, will be found at home, ready for him. Let him go there first, by all means—Let him, also, take care to avoid those places which have been inundated this season. But, for God's sake, send him off & let his first landing be on Red River.

Again, my good friend, you must write to me, as must Mr. Childress. Do not let me be a month or two without information—Let me hear from you by return mail.

Very Truly Yours,
Saml. Swartwout[7]

The letter reached Nashville while Childress was en route to Texas and he never saw it. He arrived on Red River December 13, 1835,[8] and since he did not reach Robertson's Colony, his destination, until January 9, 1836,[9] it is not unreasonable to assume that he spent some time inspecting lands in the Red River area.

The claim that Childress made Nashville, Texas, the site of which is in Milam County, his home during his brief residence in this state before being sent as a delegate to the Convention at Washington, Texas, on March 1, has generally been accepted as true by students of Texas history, but the evidence at hand tends to prove otherwise. Rev. Z. N. Morrell stated that he and his five friends who had left Mississippi on horse back to visit Texas had arrived at the "Falls of the Brazos" (Milam) on December 27, 1835. "Here we found only one family. There was close by, the camp of about forty Tennesseans. They were all out on Little River, hunting lands."[10] The one 'family' most likely consisted of Captain Robertson, his son, E. S. C. Robertson, and William H. Steele, commissioner for the colony. The campers had been recently recruited by Captain Robertson in Tennessee. On December 18 Robertson petitioned the provisional government for authority to issue land titles to the immigrants. He stated that fifteen families had arrived with him on December 6 and fourteen families had arrived with "Col. Hayes" on the 7th and added that "unless those Colonists obtain their titles they will abandon the Country..."[11] It is quite evident that the immigrants were camped near the land office.[12]

In registering in Robertson's colony Childress stated that he had a "Child Charles aged 10 months."[13]

Among the first settlers of Robertson's colony was Goldsby Childers, his wife, and a large family of children. Many writers have confused the names of *Childress* and *Childers*. Morrell, for instance, stated that he preached his first sermon in Texas at the home of Mrs. Childress, while as a matter of fact it was at the home of Mrs. Goldsby Childers.[14]

Approximately 250 votes were cast in the Municipality of Milam February 1, 1836, to elect two delegates to the Constitutional Convention to be held at Washington on the Brazos beginning March 1. Following are the results at the various voting boxes:

At Tenoxtitlan, William H. Smith, John Teal and Capt. L. B. Franks were judges and Robert Barr, teller. George C. Childress received 55 votes; Capt. L. B. Franks, 48; Alexander Thomson, 48; Thomas Morrow, 45; Lieut. A. Benton, 30; Lieut. J. Boring, 24; Sterling C. Robertson, 14; J. G. W. Pierson, 7; A. Henson, 2; and J. Trude, 1.

N. F. Smith was the judge and D. Laughlin and M. Farley tellers at the town of Milam. Among those who voted there were E. S. C. Robertson, John R. Childress, and William H. Steele. Sterling C. Robertson received 46 votes; Childress, 45; A. G. Perry, 22; J. G. W. Pierson, 12; and Alexander Thomson, 1.

Elijah Powers was the election judge at New Nashville, assisted by L. D. Brown, substitute for M. Canles. Robertson received 37 votes; Chiidress, 34; Thomson, 4; and Perry, 1. All of the 38 voters expressed themselves as favoring independence.

At the home of Jesse Webb in the "Municipality of Robertson," Webb, John D. Smith, and J. R. Harding were judges. Childress led the ticket, receiving 15 votes. Robertson received 14 and Thomson, one.

Goldsby Childers was the judge of the election held at his house and Joel Moore the teller. Robertson and Childress each received all of the 21 votes.

At the home of W. H. Walker thirteen votes were cast. Robertson received 12; Childress, 10; and Thomson, 3 votes. Walker and John Bailey were the judges.

The judges at the election held at the home of J. W. Parker were Elisha Anglin, Silas H. Bates, and Richard Duty. Luther T. H. Plummer was the clerk. The vote: J. G. W. Pierson, 22; Robertson, 15; Thomson, 9; A. G. Perry, 1; and Childress, 1. The voters expressed themselves 20 to 1 against independence. This may account for the poor showing made by Childress at this box.

At the home of James Dunn, 35 votes were polled, distributed as follows: Robertson, 35; Childress, 28; and Thomson, 7. The election judges were Dunn and Daniel Dunham.

The total votes received by the candidates in the municipality were: Childress, 209; Robertson, 194; Thomson, 73; Franks, 48; Morrow, 45; Pierson, 41; A. Benton, 30; J. Boring, 24; A. G. Perry, 24; A. Henson, 2; and J. Trude, 1.[15]

Childress took his seat at the Convention March 1.[16] On the same day he moved that a committee of five be appointed to draft a Declaration of Independence. The Convention adopted the resolution and Childress was named chairman of the committee composed of Edward Conrad, Collin McKinney, Bailey Hardeman and James Gaines.[17]

On March 12:

> Mr. Childress introduced the following resolution: Re-
> solved that a single star of five points, either of gold or silver,
> be adopted as the peculiar emblem of this republic: & that
> every officer and soldier of the army and members of this
> convention, and all friends of Texas be requested to wear it
> on their hats or bosoms: which was adopted.[18]

On March 19 President Burnet appointed Childress as
agent of the Government at Washington, D. C. His duties
were to open negotiations with the United States cabinet
"inviting on the part of that Cabinet a recognition of the
Sovereignty and Independence of Texas, and the establishment of such relations between the two Governments as
may comport with the mutual interest, the common origin, and kindred ties of their constituents." Childress was
in Natchitoches, Louisiana, on March 8.[19] He was in Nashville, Tennessee, April 18,[20] and in Washington May 21. He
remained there as late as June 10.[21]

From New York City, July 9, Samuel Swartwout wrote a
letter to Stephen F. Austin in which, among other things
he said:

> ...let your Lands pay the expenses of the war, if you sell
> them for only 5 cents an acre. You must yet have large sums
> and that promptly and nothing else will bring them — Chil-
> dress left this city just a week ago, I did not see him, he left
> his card for me, but I did not see him to converse with him.[22]

Childress and the other agents of the Republic who had
been sent to the United States were recalled by President
Burnet, May 27, 1836.[23] Childress returned to his home in
Nashville, Tennessee, and there in 1837 he was married
to Rebecca Jennings, daughter of Rev. Obadiah Jennings,
D.D., pastor of the First Presbyterian Church.

The records in the County Clerk's office in Nacogdoches
disclose that on January 23, 1838, Childress applied for a

74

headright certificate to the Board of Land Commissioners of Nacogdoches County, composed of Dr. James H. Starr, president, and William Hart and Adolphus Sterne, members.

Childress stated that when he first came to Texas in January, 1836, he was single, but that in 1837 he had married.[24] In stating that he was single when he first came to Texas he evidently meant that he was a widower. The county court records of Davidson County, Tennessee, of which Nashville is the county seat, show that Childress was married to Margaret L. Vance in June, 1828, by Rev. William Hume. Mrs. Childress died July 27, 1835.[25]

At the town of Milam, Sabine County, January 29, 1838, Childress sold his rights to his headright certificate to Daniel L. Richardson for $1,000. In the deed of transfer he stated that his home was in Nacogdoches County.[26]

Moses Austin Bryan at Houston on January 10, 1839, wrote a letter to James F. Perry, Brazoria, in which he said:

> Childress from Tennessee got me to see Gen. Lamar and know if he would be willing to let him have access to Uncle's [Stephen F. Austin's] papers as he [Childress] is writing a history of Texas and says he knows many important matters of the history of Texas can only be had from Uncle's papers and he intends incorporating a biographical of all the principal characters of Texas and he told me Uncle's name and character was inseparable from the history of Texas, but the old Gen. says he wants to finish the work he has commenced and is unwilling to give up anything and told me to send Childress to you and you can give him what you think proper—I have not seen Childress since, but will see him tomorrow and will send him to see Gen. Lamar and may give him a letter to you and you can give him what you think proper...I think it would be well to let him have some information relative to Uncle's history as he told me he felt capable and willing to do him justice—Childress is the man who drew up the declaration of Independence at Washing-

ton and when it passed, stepped up to me and said "Did you remark a clause alluding to your Uncle?" I said I did. "Well," says he, "We thought it was due him"—it all amounts to nothing as no one or but a few know that the allusion as Uncle's name is not mentioned. Childress stands well I believe in the U. States.[27]

By using the pronoun "we" Childress was generous enough not to claim full credit for writing the Declaration. The clause to which he referred was:

It incarcerated in a dungeon for a long time, one of our citizens [Stephen P. Austin], for no other cause but a zealous endeavour to procure the acceptance of our Constitution and the establishment of a State government.

That Childress was practicing law in Houston in 1839 is shown by his professional card inserted in the *Weekly Picayune*, New Orleans, April 1, 1839: "George C. Childress, Attorney at Law, will attend the Supreme Court, and the District Courts of Harrisburg, and some of the adjacent counties. Office at the City of Houston..." He returned to Nashville, but on March 26, 1841, he wrote to Dr. Ashbel Smith from New Orleans: "Mrs. Childress and I are now here, on our way to Galveston." On June 9, 1841, from Galveston, he wrote to President Lamar and applied for a government appointment, preferably as secretary to the President.

Early in the morning of October 6, 1841, Childress, at the boarding house of a Mrs. Crittenden in Galveston, inflicted on himself several wounds in the abdomen with a bowie knife, from which he died at about nine o'clock. His friend Dr. Ashbel Smith was sent for and arrived at his room at six o'clock in the morning, remaining with him until he expired. Childress was rational to the end and conversed freely with Dr. Smith. He gave Dr. Smith three letters for him to mail. In one addressed to Dr. T. R. Jennings, Nashville, he wrote: "I cannot bear to live longer and I consider it an act of justice in dying to declare that my unhappiness has in no part arisen from the conduct of my wife, your sister. She has made the best of wives, and is the greatest and most perfect character I have ever known." To Franklin Morgan in Philadelphia, he wrote: "To you and your wife, Mary, I bequeath My little daughter, Ellen. Should she lose her mother, adopt and raise her as your own child." To his brother-in-law, Hon. John Catron of Nashville, Tennessee, later a justice of the United States Supreme Court, he wrote: "To you and your wife I bequeath the father-ship and protection of my dear daughter, Anne. Should she be so unfortunate as to lose her mother, please adopt her and raise her as your child."[28]

Childress County, Texas, when created August 21, 1876, was named "in honor of George C. Childress, the author of the Declaration of Texas Independence."[29]

The State of Texas erected a monument in memory of Childress in the Episcopal Cemetery at Galveston. It was unveiled February 10, 1934, by the Sidney Sherman Chapter of the Daughters of the Republic, State Senator Thomas J. Holbrook of Galveston being the orator of the occasion. A bronze statue of Childress, authorized by the Commission of Control for Texas Centennial Celebrations at a cost of $7,500, was unveiled at Washington, Texas, March 2, 1939. After the death of her husband Mrs. Childress made her home at that of her brother's, Dr. Thomas Read Jennings, who had adopted her daughters, Annie and Ellen Childress. Mrs. Childress died December 16, 1847, at Tuscaloosa, Alabama, and her remains are buried in the tomb of those of her uncle, Thomas Kennedy Jennings, in the Tuscaloosa Cemetery.[30]

Ellen Childress, daughter of George C. Childress, was married to Dr. Henderson Pearce Crute. The three children of this union who reached maturity were Katie Bell, Frank, and William Dowe Crute.

Annie Childress, daughter of George C. Childress, was married to William D. Dowe. Miss Harriet Hall Dowe, a daughter of this union, was in 1940 residing in Melrose, Massachusetts.[31]

WILLIAM CLARK, JR.
of
SABINE MUNICIPALITY

78

*W*illiam Clark, Jr., was born in North Carolina,[1] April 14, 1798.[2] He came to Texas from Georgia,[3] in 1835.[4] The Municipality of Sabine was organized December 15, 1835, from the Municipality of San Augustine and allowed two delegates to the Constitutional Convention.[5] On February 1, 1836, at the balloting places in the town of Milam, Seaborn J. Robinson was elected president; Hardy W. B. Price and Jacob Lewis, judges, and A. W. Canfield secretary. The return to the convention does not tabulate the votes but states only that Clark and James Gaines were elected.[6] Clark was seated in the Convention on March 1.[7]

After the Convention, Clark does not appear to have served in the Texas Army. He represented Sabine County in the House of Representatives of the Second Congress, September 25, 1837, to May 24, 1838.[8] As late as April 1, 1850, he was residing in Sabine County. Later he moved to Nacogdoches, where he

> ...engaged in the mercantile and land business, living at two or three different places in town, as land traders usually do, until he purchased the Planters Hotel from the estate of

John J. Simpson, across North Street from Church Plaza, on January 7, 1859. He continued to live there and operate the hotel until his death...[9]

He died January 3, 1871.[10] In 1936, the Commission of Control for Texas Centennial Celebrations erected a joint monument at the graves of Mr. and Mrs. Clark in Oak Grove Cemetery, Nacogdoches,[11] and a marker at the site of their last home. Clark was married to Martha B. Wall, who was born May 16, 1801, and who died February 4, 1863. According to the 1835 census of Sabine Municipality, the Clarks were Methodists.[12]

Children of Mr. and Mrs. Clark were Margaret W., who married William H. Harris; Sarah Jane, who married Dr. Lycurgus Edward Griffith; William, who married Amelia Taylor, daughter of Charles S. Taylor, a signer of the Texas Declaration of Independence; and Francis A. Clark, who died at the age of five.

Some of the surviving grandchildren of Mr. and Mrs. Clark in 1940 were Thomas B. Griffith, 3411 University Avenue, Dallas; Miss Julia Clark; Adolphus Clark; Mrs. Anna Schott; and Mrs. Mary Hardiman, all of Nacogdoches.

ROBERT M. COLEMAN
of
MINA MUNICIPALITY

Robert M. Coleman was born in Kentucky in about 1799 and came from that state[1] to Texas in 1832[2] and settled in what is now Bastrop County.

In the summer of 1835 Coleman commanded one of four volunteer companies organized to attack the Tehuacanas at the spring of that name now in Limestone County.[3] He commanded the "Mina (Bastrop) Volunteers" from September 28 to December 16, 1835. His company was stationed before Bexar at the storming of that place December 5 to 10, 1835, but it did not enter the town. According to Edward Burleson, commander-in-chief, "several parties were sent out mounted, under Capts. [James] Chessher, [Robert M.] Coleman and [John A.] Roberts, to scour the country, and endeavor to intercept Ugartechea, who was expected, and ultimately forced an entry, with reenforcements for General Cos."[4]

Approximately 88 votes were polled in the election held February 1, 1836, to select three delegates from the Municipality of Mina to the Constitutional Convention.

At the home of Mrs. Nancy Blakey, Precinct of Perry, the election judges were S. J. Whatley, James Rogers, J. B. Walters, W. Duty and David F. Owen. John Caldwell received 25 votes; Thomas J. Rabb, 24; Thomas J. Gazley, 21; John W. Bunton, 17; Robert M. Coleman, 16; Robert M. Williamson, 9; Edward Burleson, 7; and D. C. Barrett, 1.

James Robison was president, David Berry and John W. Scallorn, judges, and William Gorham and F. T. Cottle, secretaries at the other voting box in the municipality. There Rabb received 32 votes; Gazley, 26; Bunton, 22; Burleson, 20; Coleman, 19; Williamson, 16; Caldwell, 4; and Barrett, 4.

The total votes cast for the various candidates were: Rabb, 56; Gazley, 47; Bunton, 39; Coleman, 35; Caldwell, 29; Burleson, 27; Williamson, 25; and Barrett, 5.[5]

Rabb did not attend the Convention and since Coleman had received the fourth largest number of votes he was seated in his stead, March 1.[6]

Coleman, probably with the rank of major, was an aide-de-camp to General Houston from April 1, to July 15, 1836, acting in that capacity in the Battle of San Jacinto.[7] After receiving his discharge he raised a regiment of rangers of which he was colonel to at least November 30, 1836.

The *Telegraph and Texas Register*, Columbia, of July 23, 1836, carried the following notice about him:

Col. R. M. Coleman has left this place with his men, to go and protect the inhabitants of the Colorado from the incursions of marauding Indians, and to enable the farmers to attend to their crops and gather them. A fort will be erected in that district, probably at the three forks of Little River, or at the foot of the mountain on the Colorado.

For a cause unknown to the author, Coleman was arrested at Velasco in 1837 by order of General Houston. Colonel Gray recorded in his diary February 22, 1837:

[At Velasco] Met Colonel Rob. M. Coleman, who I had known at Washington, a member of Convention. He is now a prisoner, under military arrest, by order of General Houston. From his representation his treatment has been harsh and arbitrary. He says he is poor, without money, and offers to sell one or two leagues of land in Robinson's Colony; asked 1 per acre; afterwards said he would take 75 cents. I feel interested for him, and would like to serve him.[8]

On February 24 he wrote:

[At Quintana] I went over to Velasco again to see Coleman, who expressed a wish to see me before I left there. His object was to request me to say to the President, as from myself, not from him, that he, Coleman, was very anxious for a trial; that his situation was very uncomfortable, and he wished to have a decision of his case, etc. This I promised to do, if opportunity offered.[9]

In 1837 a pamphlet attributed to Coleman, but thought by some to have been dictated by him but written by Judge Algernon P. Thompson of Houston, was widely distributed. It was entitled *Houston Displayed, or Who Won the*

Battle of San Jacinto, By a Farmer in the Army. In the pamphlet, General Houston was severely criticized.

Coleman, while bathing in the Brazos River at Velasco, drowned about July 1, 1837.[10]

Coleman County, Texas, when created February 1, 1858, was named in honor of "Col. Robert M. Coleman, deceased."[11] In 1931 the State of Texas erected a monument in Freeport, Brazoria County, in honor of Colonel Coleman who was drowned nearby.

On February 18, 1839, Mrs. Coleman and her oldest son, Albert V., aged fourteen, were killed by Indians. The Indians had surrounded and fired upon their log cabin home near where the town of Webberville, Travis County, was later built. Mrs. Coleman and Albert defended themselves as best they could by firing between the cracks of the logs. Mrs. Coleman was first to fall, being shot with an arrow. James W., second oldest son, had escaped when the Indians were first seen. Thomas, the baby, aged five years, was carried away by the Indians, the other children, Sarah Elizabeth, Sarah Ann and Rebecca M., remained in the house and were not harmed.

James W. Coleman, son of Robert M. Coleman, died in about 1855 at the age of seventeen. He is buried in the Baptist cemetery at Spring Prairie, five miles from Dime Box in Lee County. His grave, though unmarked, is known.

Sarah Elizabeth Coleman, daughter of Robert M. Coleman, was married to William J. McClellan. Mrs. McClellan was born in Bastrop, Texas, and died in Tennessee in 1856. She is buried in the McClellan family cemetery four miles from Franklin, Tennessee. Surviving children of Mr. and Mrs. McClellan in October, 1941, were Albert Wilson and William Thomas McClellan.

Albert Wilson McClellan was born near Franklin, Tennessee, and came to Texas in 1858. He was married to Sarah Matthews. Mr. and Mrs. McClellan were residing at Dime

82

Box, Lee County, Texas, in 1941. Their children were Anna, Cora, Arthur and Alice McClellan.

William Thomas McClellan was born near Dime Box, Texas, in 1853. He was married to Lela Chambers. Mr. and Mrs. McClellan were residing in Ninekah, Oklahoma, in 1942. Their children were William, Robert and Sallie Mc-Clellan.

Rebecca M. Coleman was married to Robert J. Russell, and both are deceased. Mrs. Russell died in Dime Box, Lee County, in 1852. Their children were Marcy C., Jane, Izora and Alice Russell.[12]

JAMES COLLINSWORTH
of
BRAZORIA MUNICIPALITY

83

James Collinsworth was born in Tennessee in 1806.[1] He was educated in the common schools, studied law and began to practice in 1826.[2] From April 30, 1829, to sometime in 1834 he was United States District Attorney for the Western District of Tennessee.[3] He came to Texas in about February, 1835, and located in what is now Brazoria County.[4] There is but little doubt that the reason prompting Collinsworth to emigrate to Texas was to keep alive the flames of the revolution which had been started, and later to fight for her independence. He early became a member of the "war party."

A petition bearing 99 names and dated Brazoria, August 9, 1835, stated that it was the belief of the signers that a

convention of the people is best calculated to quiet the present excitement, and to promote the general interest of Texas.

We acknowledge the doctrine of the right of instruction and we therefore recommend to our fellow citizens the call of a convention.[5]

A meeting was held at Columbia on August 15, and the petition then bore 134 names. Some of those who signed it, however, were unable to attend the meeting. Among the signers of the petition who later signed the Texas Declaration of Independence were Collinsworth, John W. Moore, and Edwin Waller.[6] Appended to the Brazoria petition was an address signed by "Jastus" who gave reasons for the need of a convention:

UNION.

The writer of this has thus far taken no active part in the political excitements and discussions which of late has so much agitated the people of Texas. His habits of life have inclined him to quiet and retirement and nothing but the clearest conviction of duty could at this time force him before the public...

The people of Texas, sir, have but one common interest. Although some may be more deeply interested in its prosperity than others; it is preposterous to say, that there is a single man in the whole community, who would be willing to take any step that he believed would be injurious in its consequences: We all aim at the same great end, but there must necessarily be great difference of opinion, as to the most successful mode of effecting it.

The people at this time may be said to be divided into three parties. The first has been denominated the war party. These compose a large and very respectable portion of the community, and they urge with very great plausibility, that Texas is now by the repeated acts of the general Government entirely released from her alliance to the late republic of Mexico...

The second party (and that which the writer believes to be the largest) is composed of those men who are willing to pledge their lives and fortunes for the good of their country, but before any final or decisive step is taken these conceive

that the whole of Texas ought to be consulted; that the majority in all states or communities ought to control and that
where the opinion of the majority is clearly expressed it
should there be acquiesced in by the minority.

These sentiments do honor to the head as well as to the
heart. They urge that "the welfare and happiness of Texas
is their motto," and that they are willing to unite heart and
hand in promoting that object, so soon as the voice of the
people can be heard.

The next party may be denominated the Neutralist. Their
name gives a sufficient definition. They are as contemptible
in numbers as in character.

The last classification has been styled the submission
party. This embraces a large number of very good men, but,
who either alarmed or misguided, are willing to lie supinely
on their backs, declaring that there is no case of alarm, and
tamely submit to all the insults and indignities which military despotism may think proper to heap upon us.

The General Council of the Provisional Government of
Texas on November 28, 1835, elected Collinsworth, captain, Leander McNeil, first lieutenant, and Pleasant Bull,
second lieutenant of the Texas Regiment of Infantry.[7] This
company was probably never organized.

On December 13, 1835, Charles Wilson, First Judge at
Matagorda, notified Gov. Henry Smith that he had appointed Collinsworth prosecuting attorney. He had no
authority to make the appointment, and Collinsworth did
not serve.[8]

On February 1, 1836, Collinsworth, Asa Brigham, John
S. D. Byrom, and Edwin Waller were elected to represent
Brazoria Municipality in the Constitutional Convention.[9]
Collinsworth was seated March 1[10] and on the 4th he nom-
inated General Houston for commander-in-chief of the
Texas army.[11]

To President Lamar, Collinsworth made some notes on
the proceedings of the Constitutional Convention:

A convention of the people of Texas met at Washington the first day of March 1836. When I arrived it seemed to be understood that Richard Ellis from that part of Red River under the Convential Jurisdiction of the U. States was to be President.

He was accordingly nominated to that station without opposition.

And the very first acts done by him in the appointment of his committees he clearly exhibited the course he subsequently intended to pursue. He united himself with Robert Potter of famous memory and other avarious [sic] land speculators who in order to carry their own speculations where they had pretended to purchase & had actually procured conveyances to head many of [them] had never been bona fide settled: Attempted to pass the famous agrarian law declaring all grants of land for [more] than one league of land absolutely void. This measure was warmly opposed by myself in the Judiciary the Committee in a speech which I shall shortly lay before the world. The committee voted down the proposition by a small majority. But Mr. Childress who together with Ellis Hamilton Robertson & others were deeply interested in defeating these claims, modified the measure so as to make all grants for more than eleven leagues void and all eleven league claims not located in strict conformity with law void as to their location (See Constitution). During the short space of [ ] days the present Constitution was formed and the late government ad interim organized. You know all about that. Burnet & Carson were run for President, Carson then was elected Secretary of State. Rusk beat Potter for Secy of War, Potter then beat Fisher for Secy of the Navy. All the candidates nominated for atty genl offered to name their claims in my favor if I would accept which I declined upon the ground that a battle decisive of the existence of the Country was obliged soon to [be] fought as I then stated when the lives of my friends & the existence my Country was to be periled I chose to be with them. I shall never forget the alarm manifested by many honorable members of the Convention the night the news arrived of the fall of the Alamo. The venerable President of that body rose in his seat with much trepidation and pulling a small pistol from his pocket proposed adjourning to Bradshaws, as the enemy would [be] upon us before morning. This was objected to & overruled. But the news of the fall of the Alamo was unpleasing music to the ears of these aforesaid land speculators and they were willing to lead the retreat & abandon for a time their unhallowed speculations. And when now [sic] they when the souls of men were tried. The Commander in Chief was also appointed by the Convention and as Chairman of the Committee on military affairs I reported a resolution appointing Sam Houston &c.

This met with but little opposition except from Robert Potter who opposed it in a long & animated speech in which he urged many objections.

(I wish you could [read] Farris notes & journal as it would throw much light on this subject.)

My return to Brazoria and subsequently rejoining the army and all the subsequent operations are as well known to yourself as to me all of which you saw...My health from the time I came to the Country had precluded me from taking any part in the proceedings that led to, and what was done in the Consultation, hence you will be enabled to get better information from others.

And in the San Antonio expedition there were few things of much interest except the battle of Conception our demands surrender promises to that effect chasing the white crane and sundry little anecdotes of which I have occasionally spoken to.[12]

After the hasty adjournment of the Convention on the 17th Collinsworth repaired to the army. On April 8, 1836, at Washington, he wrote General Houston:

Sir:

In compliance with your order I have attempted to organize the force at this place subject to duty. When I arrived Maj. Williamson had but few men enrolled for duty. I have now almost an entire company of Volunteers who performed their duty with great alacrity and good order.

Things here now in great confusion, many families of all classes are camped in the bottoms on the east side of the Brazos and in a most deplorable condition. Men women and children subject to all the inconveniences of the dampness of a low bottom much overflowed & without medical attention. Under these circumstances I have appointed Dr. B. B. Goodrich Surgeon at this post until further ordered by yourself.

Pettis has left in search of some deserters before I arrived at this Post & has not returned. I have thus far continued Maj. Williamson with me because my want of information in regard to this part of the country rendered it necessary.

I crossed the river yesterday and finding the bottom a scene of drunkeness & debauchery, when ladies of proud claims to decency and respectability were insulted in my presence, in compliance with your order I destroyed without reserve all the spirits I could find to which altho' there was no actual resistance but many murmurs & threats. I was more than rewarded for these in hearing the prayers of a venerable matron sent up to heaven in my behalf for the act without being conscious that I was in hearing. I think there will be good order here among those we may be enable to embody. The militia law is defective in requiring the persons subject to duty to be notified, after notice is given it should be their duty to enroll themselves.

In conclusion I have to say we have no information of the enemy having been nearer than Bastrop on the West side of the Colorado. I hope I shall be discharged from this place as soon as possible as I have performed all the duty contemplated. The troops here conduct themselves with the most perfect good order.[13]

On April 8, Collinsworth was made a major and appointed aide-de-camp to General Houston.[14] At San Jacinto, according to General Houston, he "bore himself as a chief." General Rusk, in his official report of the battle, said of him, "While I do justice to all in expressing my high admiration of the bravery and gallant conduct of both officers and men, I hope I may be indulged in the expression of my highest approbation of the chivalrous conduct of Major Collinsworth in almost every part of the engagement."[15]

President Burnet at Harrisburg, April 12, 1836, wrote Collinsworth:

Dear Sir

It has become necessary to establish a court with maratime jurisdiction.

A Prize, [the brig *Pocket*] of considerable value, was brought into Galveston a few days ago, by Capt. J. Brown, and until a competent court is obtained to adjudicate the case, and it is obviously improper to detain her long before a trial is had.

The Government has passed a decree to establish the District Court, and the Supreme Court under the constitution. But we find a difficulty in selecting the several Judges. You are spoken of as the Chief Justice, and would be immediately tendered that appointment, could we, then get along well. But we want an able judge in the District Court, where the trial must commence and where it will probably terminate. Under this view of the subject; possibly the demanding of an appeal may render it necessary to fill the appointment. These are my views, and I believe the cabinet present [concur] with me.

Will you then, Sir, accept the office of District Judge, for the district of Brazoria, "*ad interim*". Your compliance will confer a favor on the Country...[16]

Collinsworth, however, declined the appointment, and it was given to Benjamin C. Franklin. On April 29, Collinsworth was appointed acting secretary of state[17] and served as such until May 23.[18]

Although Collinsworth had only been in Texas for fifteen months, in a letter to the President and Cabinet, dated

Velasco, May 13, 1836, in which he tendered his resignation as acting secretary of state, he indicated that one of the reasons that prompted his resignation was the government's recently conferring "the highest office in your gift, such as foreign minister, Brigadier General, foreign agencies and many other appointments upon persons who have never been in the country except temporarily upon speculations, injurious to its best interests, to the exclusion of many better qualified who had taken up their permanent residence among you & done the State some service."

In commenting on the appointments referred to, Binkley said: "The references here are probably to the appointment of Childress as commissioner to the United States, of Green as brigadier general, and of Triplett as financial agent."

There is no doubt that Collinsworth had rendered Texas a distinct service, but further in his letter he indicated that he himself had come to Texas only to help win the revolution and then to return to Tennessee. He wrote:

> I left the place of my nativity about fifteen months ago with the intention of returning in a short time to settle considerable business which I had on hand both of a publick & private nature. Sickness in the first place & the interest I felt in your struggles for Liberty afterwards, has detained me, up to this period. And without claiming to merit applause, I shall be more than satisfied for the little I have done either in the field or the cabinet should I escape just ground of censure. The result however has been to bring upon me considerable pecuniary loss at home and absolute indigence here, having expended what little of means I brought with me and accumulated some debts without having ever called or received one cent in any way whatever or one acre of land from the government, while many in your country arriving here long since I did & performing no publick services have received large grants of the most valuable lands in your country.[19]

At Velasco May 26, 1836, President Burnet and Secretary of State William H. Jack addressed a joint letter to Major Collinsworth and Peter W. Grayson:

> By these presents you are appointed Commissioners on the part of this Government to proceed to the City of Washington in the United States and obtaining access to the Executive and Cabinet of that Government present yourselves as duly empowered and instructed by the Executive and Cabinet of the Government ad interim of Texas, to solicit the friendly mediation of the former, to produce a cessation of the war, between Texas and Mexico, upon terms just and honorable to both parties to the end of procuring the recognition of the Independence of Texas by Mexico and you will also use your best exertions to procure the acknowledgment of that Independence by the Government of the United States.
>
> You are further instructed to say; that in the opinion of this Government, the annexation of Texas to the United States as a member of that confederacy, would be for many weighty reasons highly acceptable to the people of this Country. You will in the event of your being received with the frankness and consideration due to your Commission and with indications of a desire to hold communication with you on this subject, respectfully enquire the terms upon which in the opinion of the authorities you address, the proposed event might be attained and you will on your part state with candor the terms upon which as you think, it would be acceptable to the people of Texas.[20]

Thus on the 35th day after Texas had won her independence from Mexico, she knocked at the door of the United States for admittance.

On the following day, William H. Jack, Secretary of State, wrote to "S. F. Austin and Others" (Dr. Branch T. Archer and William H. Wharton):

> I am instructed by the President and Cabinet to inform you that inasmuch as important changes have recently occurred

it has been deemed necessary to despatch to Washington two commissioners for the purpose of representing this Government there. It was conceived most advisable to select gentlemen who are now in this country because they could be more fully informed on the views of this Govt. and the wishes and interests of the people. These gentlemen are Peter W. Grayson and James Collinsworth Esqrs. to whom you will be pleased to communicate any valuable information which you may possess, affording them at the same time every possible facility in consummating the objects of this mission.[21]

Grayson and Collinsworth arrived at Washington on July 8 after the adjournment of Congress. President Andrew Jackson was preparing to leave for Nashville, and the commissioners were unable to obtain an audience with him.

It was decided that Grayson should remain in Washington and that Collinsworth should go to Nashville with the hope of being able to talk to the President. At Washington they had presented their credentials to John Forsyth, Secretary of State, who formally objected to the credentials, from which the seal of Texas was omitted.

At Nashville, Tennessee, Major Collinsworth talked with President Jackson on several occasions and was told by him "that nothing could be done until the Congress of Texas met and organized a more formal and regular government, then in existence."[22] Collinsworth left for Texas October 22.

President Houston on October 26, 1836, appointed Major Collinsworth attorney general of the Republic.[23] He declined the office on November 24 on account of personal circumstances.[24] He was seated as senator from Brazoria District, November 30, 1836, having been elected to fill the vacancy created by the resignation of William H. Wharton, who was confirmed as minister to the United States.[25] On December 16 Collinsworth was elected at a joint session of

Congress chief justice of the newly created Supreme Court of Texas.[26]

William Fairfax Gray at Brazoria, on February 25, 1837, recorded in his remarkable diary:

> Saw Judge Collingsworth, who received me very cordially, and proffered his friendship and counsel. This kindness increases my already favorable opinion of the man. His court does not sit until November. Salary $5,000. I fear his habits will prevent his discharging the duties of his office with the credit and ability that his talents and honesty would lead the world to expect of him.[27]

Collinsworth, in 1838, while a candidate for the presidency against Gen. Mirabeau B. Lamar and Peter W. Grayson committed suicide by jumping off a boat into Galveston Bay. *The Telegraph and Texas Register*, of July 21, 1838, refers to his "melancholy death." The following day his body arrived in Houston by boat and was placed in the capitol building which stood on the present site of the Rice Hotel. On July 24 he was buried in the city cemetery, with the first Masonic funeral in Texas. The procession formed at 10 a.m. Tuesday at the lodge room and proceeded to the courthouse where Vice President Lamar and other officers, civil and military, of the republic, together with a large concourse of citizens, were gathered.

93

> The fraternity then moved with the procession to the Capitol (where the corpse was deposited) and listened to an eloquent eulogy pronounced by our worthy fellow-citizen, A. M. Tompkins, Esq., preceded by a few pertinent remarks from Brother Lawrence, officer of the day. The procession was again formed and proceeded to the graveyard of the City of Houston, where the remains of Brother Collingsworth were deposited with solemn and Masonic prayers, ceremonies and honors.[28]

Commenting on the suicides of Collinsworth and Grayson, Dr. Anson Jones on July 29, 1838, wrote:

I shall be surprised at no one's committing suicide after hearing of Col. Grayson's doing so. It is the first time in my life that anyone in the circle of my acquaintance has done such an act; and it has shocked me more than the death of a dozen others would have done in the usual course. I believe party abuse has been the cause, acting upon some predisposition to morbid melancholy. Col. Collinsworth's drowning himself was a thing of course. I had expected it, as I knew him to be deranged, and, when excited by liquor, almost mad. In all the annals of suicide, perhaps no parallel to these two cases can be found. Two years ago they were in this house, and on their way to Washington together, as Commissioners on the part of Texas to procure recognition, &c; and, at the time of their deaths, both candidates for the highest office in the republic. Both committed suicide about the same time, and at the distance of 2,000 miles from each other; both at the time holding high and responsible offices in the Republic of Texas.[29]

94

Here it is interesting to note that Dr. Jones himself committed suicide at Houston, January 9, 1858.

Yoakum commented on the death of Collinsworth:

Among the distinguished dead of Texas this year may be mentioned James Collingsworth and John A. Wharton. Collingsworth was the first chief-justice of the supreme court of the republic. He was a man of fine talents, great urbanity, and a devoted and valuable friend of Texas in her struggle. He had a pleasant wit, was a most admirable companion, and of scrupulous integrity. He had emigrated to Texas to rid himself of a false habit, which unfortunately pursued, and brought him to a premature grave.[30]

Collinsworth was one of the organizers of the Texas Railroad, Navigation, and Banking Company, December 10, 1836.[31] He was one of the founders of the town of Richmond, Texas, in 1837.[32] He was the first secretary of Holland Lodge No. 36 (now Holland Lodge No. 1, Houston), A. F. & A. M., Brazoria, in February, 1836.[33]

The State of Texas erected a monument at the grave of Major Collinsworth in the old City Cemetery, Houston. It was dedicated August 15, 1931, by Senator Clint Small, whose home at that time was in Collinsworth County.

The historian Henderson Yoakum erroneously spelled Collinsworth's name *Collingsworth*, as have many others.[34] The State Legislature at the creation of a new county, August 21, 1876, passed the following act: "The county of Collingsworth is named in honor of James Collingsworth, the first Chief Justice of the Republic of Texas."[35]

EDWARD[1] CONRAD
of
REFUGIO MUNICIPALITY

Edward Conrad, son of John[2] and Elizabeth or Liza (Kittera) Conrad, was born in Philadelphia about April, 1811.[3] He came to Texas, via Natchitoches, Louisiana, in December, 1835. In Nacogdoches on December 10, the United States Independent Volunteer Cavalry Company was organized with Benjamin L. Lawrence captain, John M. Harris first lieutenant, and Conrad second lieutenant. At San Antonio de Bexar on December 24, the company was consolidated with Capt. James Tarleton's company of Kentuckians, and David Thomas succeeded John M. Harris as first lieutenant.[4] Although the land offices were closed, Conrad, anticipating their re-opening, applied February 18, 1836, for land in Austin's Colony, stating in his petition that he was single, a printer by trade, and had emigrated from Pennsylvania in 1835.[5]

At the election held in Refugio Municipality, February 1, 1836, to select delegates to the Constitutional Convention, Sam Houston of Nacogdoches, commander-in-chief of the Texas Army, having recently inspected the troops in Refugio, and James Power were chosen to represent Refugio Municipality. Though the soldiers stationed at Refugio had no objections to Houston and Power, they nevertheless thought the army should be represented by two of its soldiers. Consequently, on about February 4, they elected David Thomas and Conrad, who carried with them to Washington a memorial stating the soldiers' reasons and requesting that Conrad and Thomas be seated.[6] En route to the convention Conrad recovered a horse that had been stolen from him.[7] Without objection, Conrad and Thomas as well as Houston and Power were accepted by the Convention as delegates from Refugio Municipality. Conrad was seated March 1.[8] He remained at the Convention until adjournment on March 17, when he rejoined the army. From his headquarters on Camp Mill Creek, on March 29, 1836, Houston, in a letter to William Christy of New Orleans, outlined Conrad's orders:

> I have ordered Captain David N. Burke and Edward Conrad to New Orleans, to procure men for the army of Texas. The present is probably the most important moment we have to experience. We now stand before the world as a nation, and stand almost alone. But for the assistance upon which we confidently rely from our brethren in the United States, we shall not be enabled to maintain the position we have assumed. With equal confidence I look to you for the immediate use of all the influence in your power to sustain our cause. I look to you the most efficient and zealous agent of our country. Do exert all the talent and means you can command, for now is the time of need. Captain Burke and

Mr. Conrad will bear this letter to you, with my orders; be good enough to render them all the assistance in your power.[9]

Burke was soon given other orders,[10] and Conrad proceeded to New Orleans alone. At New Orleans on April 30, in a letter sent by Edward O'Connor, Conrad reported to Houston:

I arrived in this city on the 28th ult after a protracted and uncomfortable voyage of 12 days from Galveston Bay. I was detained in Galveston Bay about a week by head winds and whilst there assisted in the fortifications in progress. Capt. Burk and myself arrived in Houston about the 1st inst. and could not receive even on our own private account one cent from the Govt. This was truly disheartening and Capt. Burk after remaining some days in Galveston Bay abandoned the object of our mission for you and accepted the post of Capt. of Marines from the Secty of the Navy. I delivered your letter to Mr. Christy, he thinks nothing [can] be done here in raising men & says he has already done all that he can do. I expect no assistance from any agent but have no doubt in another way of being able to effect something.

News rec'd here from every part of the U. S. is very cheering—the cruelty of the Mexicans & their disgraceful treachery has created a general burst of indignation from North to South—30 men leave here today by way of Galveston. Genl. Felix Huston leaves Natchez on the 5th of May with 5 to 700 men. He will be accompanied by Reson Bowie brother of Col. Bowie who fell in the Alamo. They will march through lower Louisiana directly to Harrisburg or wherever your Head Quarters may be established—50 men have left Phild and by the latest papers from that city I see a country & town meeting has been called for the relief of Texas. A meeting has been called also in Baltimore. Men are gathering in Tennessee & Kentucky & in short in every part of the U. S. the barbarity of the Mexicans has harrowed up the hearts of all American & a storm is gathering the thunders of which will rock the centre of Mexico. The whole American press is in our favour & in a number of papers which I have seen it has been strongly and boldly urged that the Mexican Minister be dismissed from Washington City as the agent of a people that are unworthy to be classed among civilized nations. A number of Jackson's strongest friends are said to urge this course upon the Executive. In case our arms are successful I hope the soldiers will not allow their passions to urge them to any act of barbarity to deprive us of the immense moral strength we now possess for the sympathy and respect to all civilized men. The barbarity of the Mexicans has injured them more than our arms could have done & retaliation on our part I fear would be equally fatal to Texas.

I am happy in apprising you that you possess many warm friends in the U. S. & that the prudent course you have pursued has inspired universal confidence as to the eventual result of the war. It is generally wished that a doubtful engagement will not be risqued by you as a very short time must give force enough to place the contest beyond hazard.

A vessel arrived in this City last evening 13 [original MSS torn] for Matamoros. She brings no news to cause us despair. The *Montezuma* driven around J [original MSS torn] Brown has since gone to pieces in the breakers. No force was fitting out against Galveston. Only 500 soldiers were in Matamoros & one vessel of war of 90 tons. The corvette so long expected has not yet arrived. Capt. Liveis [?] sent on board the Mexican ship before the engagement with the *Montezuma* & taken prisoner has since been shot in conformity with the savage use of the enemy.

As respects to the mission with which you have been pleased to honor me I can only say under the unfavourable circumstances which I am placed I will do all that can be done & repair as soon as possible to camp."

On May 14, Edward Hall at New Orleans wrote President Burnet that "Some Coffee and Sugar is about to be shipped by Mr. Conrad." Conrad and F. W. Thornton, on June 6, received a statement from Thomas Toby & Brother for $1722.22, payment due for 37 bags of coffee and 10 boxes of Havana sugar which had been delivered at Quintana.[12]

On March 29, the day after he arrived in New Orleans, Conrad appears to have enrolled as first lieutenant of Company D, an infantry company under Capt. Francis W. Thornton.[13] While serving in this capacity, Conrad died at Victoria, July 13 or 14, 1836. *Poulson's American Daily Advertiser*, published in Philadelphia, on October 14, announced:

> Died on the 14th of July at Vietoire, Texas, Mr. Edward Conrad, son of John Conrad, Esq., of this city, in the 26th year of his age.[14]

The Commission of Control for Texas Centennial Celebrations in 1936 provided for the erection of a monument in Evergreen Cemetery, Victoria, to Conrad's memory. It seems, however, that the monument was placed on a downtown street in Victoria by the Victoria County Board.

Conrad's heirs did not obtain the headright or bounty lands due him. It seems that Col. William Fairfax Gray made some attempt to get the land, for on February 23, 1837, at Velasco, he wrote in his diary:

> The *Wm Bryan* went to sea this evening. [Captain Benjamin L.] Thornton and Smith went with her. Wrote by Smith to Mrs. Gray. T. Green and Jno. Conrad, respecting his son's claims on Texas.[15]

OUR (unlikely) FATHERS

WILLIAM CARROL CRAWFORD
of
SHELBY MUNICIPALITY

*W*illiam Carrol Crawford,[1] the last surviving signer
of the Texas Declaration of Independence, was
related to Charles Carroll, the last surviving signer of the
United States Declaration of Independence. Nancy Carroll, a first cousin once removed of Charles Carroll, was
married to Archibald Crawford, son of Sir Robert Crawford.
William Carrol Crawford, the first son of this union was
born in Fayetteville, North Carolina, September 13, 1804.[2]
During his infancy his parents moved to Georgia where
they both died in about 1821. William Carrol, then seven
years of age, found a home with a family who reared him.
At the age of eighteen he became a tailor's apprentice, following that trade until 1830 when he became a Methodist
minister and was assigned to a circuit in Alabama. In 1834
he was married to Rhoda Jackson Watkins, daughter of
Lewis and Polly Watkins. Later in the year 1834, his health
having failed him, he decided to emigrate to Texas with
Watkins and his family. The caravan arrived in Texas in
January, 1835.[3] Watkins and his family and Rev. Mr. Crawford and his wife settled near Shelbyville in what is now
Shelby County. Watkins joined the Texas Army and served
at various times in the companies of James Chessher, John
M. Bradley and Richard Hooper.[4]

An election was held in the town of Nashville, February
1, 1836, to select two delegates to represent Shelby Municipality at the Constitutional Convention. Crawford and
Sydney O. Penington were elected. The judges were B. H.
Simpson and George V. Lusk, the clerks William Woods
and Joseph Percival. The number of votes cast were not
reported to the Convention.[5] Crawford was seated as a delegate March 1.[6]

In 1836 Crawford moved to Shelbyville, then being laid out. He was made postmaster there in 1843 and served until Texas entered the Union. He was county treasurer of Shelby County, January 30, 1844, when he addressed the following letter from Shelbyville to President Anson Jones:

I have been acting as county treasurer in this county for better than twelve months and with this mail my successors bond is sent. You will see that I have not resigned and lest there should be some representations made to you on a par with some made to the court when I was superceded I have thought that I would write you a few line showing how it happened that the court turned me out of office, which is as follows to wit—A certain member of the court who has a little weight with it, in my absence and entirely unknown to me, rose and informed the court that I did not consider myself the Treasurer of this county, he had heard me say so, and that it was necessary that they should elect another, (he has allways been inimical to my interest and this is the second time he has thus clandestinely thrown me a clear fall, his name is Alfred A. George) where upon the court proceeded to elect Dr. W. P. Landrum. There has been nor can there by any fault found to me as treasurer. I make these remarks not because I care so much about the office, but as I hold office of Post Master, I would Explain the matter lest some supposition might appear authorized from the proceedings of the court prejudicial to my Character.

With great respect and high consideration permit me to subscribe myself your humble servant.

Wm. C. Crawford[7]

In 1859 Mr. Crawford moved to Pittsburgh, Camp County. He was postmaster there from 1874 to 1881. His wife died January 18, 1881, and in that year he moved to Hill County where he remained for four years. In 1884 he moved to Alvarado, Johnson County, where he made his home with one of his daughters.

The *Northern Standard,* published at Clarksville, on February 6, 1885, carried a notice of the Reverend Mr. Crawford:

> Rev. H. M. Glass of Alvarado writes to the Texas Christian Advocate: Rev. William C. Crawford, aged 81 years, emigrated to Shelby County, Texas, on January 5, 1835; was a signer of the declaration of independence, March, 1836. He was among the first to erect a family altar in Texas. In Georgia he heard Bishop Pierce preach among his first sermons. He travelled two years in the Georgia conference, and two years in the Alabama conference. In 1834 he started for Texas, a confirmed dyspeptic, expecting to be buried by the way, but he is an efficient local elder in Alvarado at this writing...[8]

Following is a copy of a letter written by Crawford to Gov. James Stephen Hogg:

> At Home Near Alverado Tex
> Nov 1st 1892
>
> To His Excellency Governor J. S. Hog
>
> Dear Sir
> Infirmities prevent me the pleasure of seeing you today. Many of your staunch friends are in similar fix (two of my sons in Law); we supported you last election and will support you again. There are many strong men in Texas; I am proud of them. They are my sons; I am a father to all Texans, the only surviving Signer of Texas Independence. I saw you once when you were a bony young man. I hear that you have become corpulent. Be strong and guide Texas to Prosperity and God help you for she is a refractory fellow. Since the year A. D. 1835 I have tried with all my power to guide her in the ways of righteousness. God bless Texas and her sons.
> Very Respectfully, your fellow helper,
> W. C. Crawford.[9]

While visiting his son at his home near Dublin, Erath County, Crawford died September 3, 1895. He was buried in the Cow Creek Cemetery, about five miles north of Dublin. The State of Texas had his remains exhumed and, on Sunday, February 16, 1936, they were reinterred in the State Cemetery at Austin. Later a monument was erected at his grave. It was intended to also remove the remains of Mrs. Crawford, but her grave in Pittsburgh could not be located. She was born in Murfreesboro, Tennessee, January 11, 1816.

Children of Rev. William C. and Rhoda Jackson (Watkins) Crawford were Charles Wesley, who married Margaret Davenport; William Carroll, Jr., who married Mattie Ross; Julia, who married James Harkness; Emily, who married Samuel Clark; Texana, who married James Clark; Alice Casey, who married Dan Koonce; Sadie J., who married Peter Burke; Rhoda Elizabeth, who married Benjamin Blanton Moore; and Frances Crawford who married M. C. Fewell.

Mrs. Rhoda E. Crawford Moore, last surviving child of Crawford, was residing in 1939 at 919 North Buffalo Street, Cleburne.

Some of the surviving grandchildren, in 1939, of Rev. and Mrs. William C. Crawford were B. B. Moore and Mrs. T. E. Holt, Cleburne; Mr. J. F Moore, 1714 East 62d Street, Seattle, Washington; Fred C. Crawford, Saginaw, Michigan; Claude and E. C. Fewell, Dublin, Texas.

RICHARD ELLIS
of
PECAN POINT AND VICINITY

Richard Ellis was born February 14, 1781,[1] in Virginia. Receiving a common school education he studied law and was admitted to the bar. In 1817, he moved to Huntsville, Alabama. The next year he removed to Tuscumbia, then in Franklin County. He was one of the two delegates elected from Franklin County to the Alabama Constitutional Convention of 1819, and at the organization of the circuit courts, was elected over John McKinley and Beverly Hughes to a judgeship.[2] This automatically made him a member of the Supreme Court of Alabama, which he served creditably for six years.

104

As early as the year 1825, Ellis had considered moving to Austin's Colony. On August 23, 1825, Richard R. Royall from Tuscumbia, Alabama, wrote to Austin:

> ...many gentlemen possessing Large Estates and of high character speak with much interest of Texas, and several have determined to visit your Colony before spring. I think probably the Hon. R. Ellis, and my Father-in-Law will be of the latter number...[3]

On February 21, 1826, Royall again wrote:

> Judge Ellis and some other gentlemen will be to see it [your country] this Spring.[4]

Ellis visited Texas in 1826, not as a colonist, but in an effort to collect a debt. Austin sent James Cummins, James Kerr, and Ellis to Nacogdoches to try to induce Haden Edwards to abandon his revolt against the Mexican government.[5] In the meantime, Ellis's wife in Franklin County, Alabama, became alarmed and, on September 3, 1827, wrote Austin:

Richard Ellis

Dear Sir

I am the wife of Judge Ellis from Alabama. He went to Texas to Collect a debt due from Col. Pettus which debt he was security for and Pettus ran away from here and left him to pay, and I wish you to state to Judge Ellis if he don't come home directly he will have his property sold. For Pettus the ballance due is usery, that part I suppose Pettus will not pay. Col. Pettus has treated Judge Ellis very ill and bad about it. I have not herd from my husband since the 30 of May. For god sake let me know what has become of him since that time and whare he is; if he is thare let him see this letter. For god sake write me and let me know, and if he is dead take care of his property untill I can send for it. This from a poore woman that [is] in deepist destress. Pray write immediately and direct your letter to Tuscumby, Franklin County Alabama and I will take it as a great favor.[6]

Safely back in Tuscumbia, Ellis, on January 3, 1828, wrote Austin:

...in the short time since my arrival at home I have ascertained beyond question that 40 or 50 families would emigrate with me next fall to your country if they could introduce their slaves, many of them are large holders of that description of property; and I consider it a duty I owe myself as well as you, to assure you that I shall move to your country next fall if I can with safety bring mine; for I find I have not one slave that he is willing to be sold from me.

I feel a deep interest in the prosperity of your country and hope you will do me the favour (for I shall prize it highly) to write to me by the first safe hand after the receipt of this letter; let me know if we will be allowed to bring in slaves under any circumstances, if not what are the future prospects—what has been done with my petition, can locate the Heseander [hacienda] on the west back of the Colorado river.

If I can bring in fifty families, I believe I can get $50 a league from them, and I should give you one half of it if you will reserve good land for them as I have always thought that compensation not enough for the founder of a colony in addition to his premium lands—but this will depend on the Slave Question. Can fifty good Leagues be got between the Colorado and auroyo lavaca—that is now vacant?[7]

On June 16, 1830, Austin, in reply to a letter written January 30 by Ellis, wrote discouraging news:

The law [of April 6, 1830] requires that passports should be brought by the emigrants from a Mexican consul, and this must be done—the government has ordered most positively that the 13th article of the State constitution shall be rigidly inforced, and I am of the opinion that Texas will never become a Slave state or country. I will be candid with you on this point, and say that I hope it never may.[8]

It was not until four years later, on February 22, 1834,[9] that Ellis moved to what in later years proved to be Texas, settling in "Pecan Point," in what is now Bowie County.

The name Pecan Point originally applied to a small settlement that was made on the north side of Red River, east of the present Red River County, but was eventually applied to a vast area on Red River.[10] In 1835 it embraced all of the present Fannin, Lamar, Red River, Bowie, and possibly other counties. Both Arkansas and Mexico claimed the area, and after March 2, 1836, Texas added its claim.

The first Territorial Legislature in Arkansas (known as the General Assembly) was elected November 20, 1819. The first governor of the territory, General James Miller, of New Hampshire called it in session on February 7, 1820. The same legislature held its second session in October of that year. The first Miller County was created April 1, 1820.[11]

Shawneetown, now in Oklahoma, was the first county seat of Miller County. A treaty with the Choctaws, which gave them lands in the Indian Territory, took from Arkansas the jurisdiction that territory had exercised over the north side of Red River.[12] On October 22, 1832, Jonesboro,

RICHARD ELLIS

the site of which is now in Red River County, Texas, was made the county seat of Miller County.[13]

So far as Mexico was concerned the Pecan Point settlers chose to consider themselves citizens of Arkansas and of the United States.

When in October, 1835, the Arkansas Territorial Legislature provided for a constitutional convention to meet at Little Rock, January 4, 1836, Miller and Sevier Counties were each authorized to send a delegate and to jointly elect a third delegate.[14] Richard Ellis was chosen the joint delegate. When the Convention met on January 4, Ellis "was too much indisposed to attend," and it was "feared he would not attend."[15] Ellis resigned his position, and on January 21, George Halbrook, his successor, took his seat.[16]

The residents in the Pecan Point area, separated as they were by almost unknown and untraveled country from the settlements in Texas proper, had shown little interest in the inevitable Texas revolution. Likewise until November, 1835, Texas paid little attention to them. No delegates to the First and Second Conventions of Texas, held in San Felipe in 1832 and 1833, were solicited from Pecan Point. It was the Consultation of 1835 that, on November 11, resolved:

> That as the settlements on Red River is remote from other settlements in Texas, that they be formed into a separate municipality, and that they be invited to send delegates to this convention, which is to meet on the first day of March next, and that they elect immediately, and send a member of the council of Texas.[17]

On December 10, 1835, the General Council of the Provisional Government of Texas voted to permit the "citizens of Pecan Point" to send two delegates to the Constitutional Convention. When the news of this reached Pecan Point some of the residents there decided to send James

107

Clark to San Felipe to discuss the matter more fully with the Council, and to suggest that three municipalities be created in the Pecan Point area, with two delegates from each municipality. This is indicated in a letter written at Nacogdoches, December 23, 1835, by John Forbes and addressed "To his Excellency James W. Robinson, Lieut. Gov. & President of Council":

> Permit me to introduce to your acquaintance Mr. James Clark of Pecan Point, Red River and who has been appointed by a Committee of the Citizens of that portion of our territory, to represent their interests at St Felipe. You will find him a very intelligent Gentleman, very conversant with the interests of Red River and Texas generally and truly desirous of promoting the welfare of the Colonist and Country...
>
> On account of the increased population of Red River as you will be fully informed by Mr. Clark it would be very desirable to have more than One Municipality in that Section. I am of Opinion *three* Municipalities or Jurisdictions would be formed there and which would entitle them, to a representation of Six members in the General Convention. I should be gratifyed to receive from the Council to organize two additional Municipalities on Red River that the Settlers there be fully represented in that Body.[18]

There is no record to show that the Council amended the act of December 10, but the citizens of Pecan Point, without organizing so much as one municipality, thought they were entitled to at least five and possibly six delegates.

Despite there being no Municipality of Red River or Republic of Texas, and that the General Council stipulated February 1 as the date of the election for delegates to the Convention,[19] Pecan Point sent the following statement:

> Municipality of Red River Jan. 27th, 1836
>
> We the undersigned Judges appointed in the Resolutions passed at Collin McKinneys to compare the polls of the different elections after examining the same do certify

that Collin McKinney, Robert Hamilton, Samuel P. Carson, Richard Ellis and James H. Robinson are duly elected to the General Convention to be held at Washington in the Republic of Texas on the first day of March next for the purpose of framing a Constitution.

> Ashley McKinney
> Joseph Savage
> George Collom.[20]

The Pecan Point delegation was indeed unique. Though Robinson did not attend, with A. H. Latimer, it was larger than that of any municipality. All five of the delegates claimed to be residents of Arkansas, and none of them had received any land from the Spanish or Mexican governments. It is doubtful that Carson was, at any time prior to March 2, 1836, even technically, a citizen of Texas. He was either a citizen of North Carolina or of Arkansas. It is not known that he was in Texas on March 2, when by an act of the Convention on March 10, mere physical presence in Texas made one a citizen, for he did not reach the Washington until March 10. Carson's home was definitely in La Fayette County, Arkansas, in a section not involved in the boundary dispute. It is also possible that Robert Hamilton's home was in this same area.

Ellis, it will be recalled, had attended a constitutional convention in Alabama and had been elected a delegate to one in Arkansas. On March 1, 1836, he was seated at the Texas Convention as a delegate from "the municipality of Pecan Point and vicinity,"[21] and on Stephen H. Everitt's motion he was unanimously elected president of the convention.[22]

Ellis was a senator in the First,[23] Second,[24] Third,[25] and Fourth[26] Congresses of the Republic, October 3, 1836, to February 5, 1840, representing the district composed of Red River County in the First and Second Congresses and Red River and Fannin Counties in the Third and Fourth.

He died December 20, 1846, and was buried in the Ellis family cemetery three miles from the present New Boston. His remains, and those of his wife, were exhumed, and on October 6, 1929, reinterred in the State Cemetery at Austin, with a joint monument.

When Ellis County was created October 20, 1849, the Legislature did not state for whom it was named,[27] but Thrall in 1879 stated it was named for Richard Ellis.[28] In 1936 the Commission of Control for Texas Centennial Celebrations erected a bronze statue of Judge Ellis at Waxahachie, the county seat of Ellis County. In 1940, one of the rooms of Ellis's home was owned by his great grandchildren, Robert Ellis Williams and Mrs. C. V. Bunn.

Mrs. Ellis, nee Mary W. Danridge, was born in 1787 and died October 30, 1837.

Two of the children of Judge and Mrs. Ellis were Nathanial Danridge Ellis and a daughter who married James M. Smith. William Fairfax Gray, on January 31, 1837, met in Mobile, Alabama, R. Ellis, Jr., presumably the son of Richard Ellis.[29]

Surviving great grandchildren of Judge and Mrs. Ellis in 1942 were Richard Ellis Williams and J. John Ellis, New Boston; Robert Williams, Foreman, Arkansas; James Hubbard Ellis, Oklahoma City, Oklahoma; and Mrs. C. V. Bunn, North Carolina.

STEPHEN HENDRICKSON EVERITT[1]
of
JASPER MUNICIPALITY

*D*r. Stephen Hendrickson Everitt was born in New York in about 1806 and came to Texas from his native state.[2] The May 1, 1835, census of Bevil (Jasper) Municipality lists him as a merchant, 29 years of age, whose wife, Alta, was 21.[3]

Everitt came to Texas in 1834. On February 28, 1835, he received title to one league of land in Zavala's Colony, situated in what is now Jasper County.[4] He was a delegate from Bevil (Jasper) Municipality to the Consultation held at San Felipe de Austin in 1835.

On November 13, 1835, the Consultation decreed:

> That all land commissioners, empresarios, surveyors, or persons in anywise concerned in the location of lands, be ordered forthwith to cease their operation during the agitated and unsettled state of the country, and continue to desist from further locations until the land office can be properly systemized by the proper authority, which may hereafter be established; that fit and suitable persons be appointed to take charge of all the archives belonging to the different land offices, and deposit the same in safe places, secure from the ravages of fire, or the devastation of enemies; and that the persons so appointed by fully authorized to carry the same into effect...[5]

Everitt, John Leplesser, and A. E. C. Johnson were appointed commissioners to close the land offices in the Department of Nacogdoches. Of the empresarios throughout Texas, Stephen F. Austin, George W. Smyth, and perhaps others, complied with the law and closed their offices. Sterling C. Robertson was at this time in Tennessee recruiting settlers for his colony. His commissioner, William H. Steele, at first refused to recognize the authority of the government, and his arrest was ordered by the General Council on December 2.[6] Steele appeared before the Council on December 17 and after agreeing to close the office was discharged.[7] Robertson on December 18 in a letter to the government told of the efforts he had made to bring colonists to Texas and requested the Council to "take their [Robertson's Colony's] case in consideration, and so afford him and his colonists such protection & relief, as ever directs a just and prudent Govt. in the exercise of legal & equitable trust reposed in them by the people."[8] In the Department of Nacogdoches, Everitt on March 17, 1836, reported to President Burnet:

> I have to inform you that the Honl. George W. Smyth promptly closed his office, and the documents &c connected with his office are at your disposal, in his hands, —Mr. C. S. Taylor refused to close his office and has, as I have been credibly informed, issued many titles since the order was issued to him. Mr. George A. Nixon has closed his office and has left the country. I respectfully suggest to your Excellency the propriety of having the papers and documents attached to Mr. Nixon's office, forthwith secured, as they are truly important to the settlers of our country. Mr. R[adford] Berry refused to obey the order issued to him saying that he was a Constitutional officer and that he would not obey anything but a Constitutional officer...[9]

On November 25, 1835, Postmaster General John Rice Jones awarded Dr. Everitt a contract to carry the mail from Jefferson, Liberty Municipality, to San Augustine.[10]

The number of votes cast in the election held in Jasper Municipality February 1, 1836, to elect two delegates to the Constitutional Convention is not known. The election judges, Joseph Mott, Barney C. Lowe, Hannibal Good, and John Miller, simply notified the convention that George W. Smyth and Stephen H. Everitt had been elected to represent the municipality.[11] Everitt was seated March 1.[12] Everitt

112

was elected to the Senate of the First,[13] Second,[14] Third,[15] Fourth[16] and Fifth Congresses[17] of the Republic from the district composed of Jasper and Jefferson Counties, serving from October 3, 1836, to December 9, 1840, when he resigned.[18] He joined Holland Lodge No. 1, A. F. and A. M., of Houston, June 3, 1838.[19]

Everitt was not a practicing physician in Texas, but he was generally referred to as "Doctor" Everitt.[20] Many of his letters to his close friend, Mirabeau Buonaparte Lamar, are owned by the Texas State Library.[21]

Dr. Everitt, in New York City, on August 31, 1843, deeded half of his extensive properties in Texas to James Cam Everitt of New York City.[22] On November 19, Everitt wrote Anson Jones, then Secretary of State of Texas:

> I wrote you from New York while in that city. After spending some forty days at that place, I started on my return to Texas, taking Philadelphia, Baltimore, Washington City, and other places, in my way.[23]

113

Everitt died in New York City on July 12, 1844.[24] Z. William Eddy was the administrator of his estate, September 10, 1844. In November, 1856, the estate was divided among Louisa R. Broad, William Hendrickson Everitt, Sarah Ann Everitt and James C. Everitt.[25]

Dr. Everitt was married to Alta Zera Williams, daughter of William and Sidney Williams. William Williams was a son of Stephen Williams, Sr., a Revolutionary soldier who died in Jasper County, Texas. Dr. and Mrs. Everitt had four children: Louisa, who married a man named Broad; William Hendrickson; Sarah Ann; and James C. Everitt. Dr. Everitt's widow married Col. Randolph C. Doom and died in 1883. Mrs. Thomas W. Causey, a child of this union, was residing in Kirbyville, Texas, in 1937.

JOHN FISHER
of
GONZALES MUNICIPALITY

*J*ohn Fisher was born in Richmond, Virginia, January 18, 1800, son of James and Margaret (Nimmo) Fisher.[1] Two of John's brothers played prominent parts in Texas history. William S. Fisher commanded a company at the Battle of San Jacinto and was the commander of the Mier Expedition. Henry Fisher, in 1835, was purser on the *Liberty* in the Texas Navy.[2]

John Fisher, on February 16, 1836, applied for land in Austin's Colonies, but the closing of the land office prevented his receiving it. In his application he stated: "From Virginia arrived in April, 1832; applied Feby. 16, 1836; family with us; wants land, resident of Gonzales."[3]

At Gonzales on November 3, 1835, Fisher wrote to Stephen F. Austin:

> As secretary of the Committee of safety for this municipality I have to address you upon a matter revolting to the feelings of every American not destitute of every moral principle. Yesterday the troops from Ayish Bayou [San Augustine] arrived in this place. In consequence of the Boat being turned over to be put in a situation for service, the Troops were compelled to remain until this morning. Last night a scene such as in all probability never was exhibited in any civilized country presented itself to us—Upon the Army's leaving this place not more than 12 men and 3 or 4 guns were left; most of the men were invalids, the balance of the population composed of women (whose Husbands are in the Army) and children. Those men (the Ayish Bayou) entered private houses, compelled women to leave their house with their children and seek protection from their neighbours, broke open doors, robbed of money, clothing

114

and everything they could lay their hands on and dragged
Dr. Smithers from his bed and would have murdered him,
but for the interference of some of the company who pos-
sessed some little more of the milk of human kindness than
the balance. I am directed by the committee to ask for a detachment of 20 men from the Main Army to protect this
place and to assist in sustaining the forces as they come on
Capt. Johnson, English, and Sublet can in all probability
give information as to the ringleaders in this Matter.

N. B. The families of this place unless protected, are
determined to risk the Indians, rather than such men as represented above, some of whom seem determined to remove
at once, rather than risk the passing of the reinforcement
coming on.

(Addressed:) Genl Stephen F. Austin Commander in Chief
of the Texas forces Mission St. Juan."[4]

Approximately 65 votes were cast in the election held in
Gonzales Municipality, February 1, 1836, to elect two delegates to the Constitutional Convention. Elections were
held in the town of Gonzales and in the Precinct of Upper Lavaca. At Gonzales the election judge was William
W. Arrington; A. N. Brill was first teller and L. W. Aster
second teller; and George W. Davis was secretary. Mathew
Caldwell received 44 votes; John Fisher, 43; Byrd Lockhart, 16; and Joseph D. Clements, 13. Andrew Kent and
Isaac Millsapps were the election judges at the box on the
Lavaca and Henry C. G. Summers, the clerk. Pleasant Bull
received 7 votes; Clements, 7; and Lockhart, 5. The total
votes received by the candidates were Caldwell, 44; Fisher, 43; Lockhart, 21; Clements, 20; and Bull, 7.[5] Fisher was
seated at the convention March 1.[6] When that body hastily
adjourned on the 17th, Fisher joined the Runaway Scrape.
On April 20 Colonel Gray met him on the Neches River,
headed for the United States.[7] On November 17, 1837, at
Houston Fisher wrote to President Houston:

To His Excy, Sam Houston

Sir

Understanding that there is now before the House a bill authorising you to appoint a Notary Public each for Galveston & Velasco, my object in this communication is to ask the appointment to Velasco should the Bill pass, as I intend making that place my residence—as to my qualifications I have only to say I have been for sixteen years extensively engaged in foreign & domestic business in shipping and the duties of a Notary were nearly daily required—I would not make the application but have been nearly 5 months sick unable to do anything, exhausted my means and am compelled to resort to something by which I can earn an honest livelyhood for myself and a small family—Should you think proper to honor me with the appointment please communicate to me at Velasco & oblige.

Respectfully,
Yr frd & well wisher
Jno Fisher[8]

116

Fisher assigned to Peter W. Grayson his rights to the headright certificate for the one league and one labor of land he was entitled to receive from the Republic of Texas.[9] That he early returned to his home in Virginia is stated in a letter he wrote to Governor Houston, dated at Richmond, Virginia, February 6, 1860.

As an old friend & acquaintance I take the liberty of asking your aid if not inconsistent with your position in a matter of interest to me.

I petitioned the Legislature of Texas to grant me a league of land which you will find by the enclosed letter has been rejected by the Senate, which I consider a very hard case under the circumstances, in as much as I was entitled to it under the Colonization laws & guaranteed to me by the action of the Convention that made the declaration of Independence, both you & myself being members of it. Not only this but I complied with all the requesitions; my land was

surveyed, but in consequence of frauds having been prac-
tised upon the land office could not obtain my patent, the
land office being afterwards burnt destroyed the evidence
of my claim. There have been laws passed since with regard
to the course to be pursued all of which I am ignorant of. I
left Texas for Virginia intending to return with my family,
upon my arrival here found two old ladies 60 & 70 years of
age relatives & members of my family perfectly blind, which
rendered it impossible for me to return. What I have to ask
of you as I before remarked if not inconsistent with your position is to get the Senate to reconsider their vote & render
me as I consider an act of Justice & I know in your kindness
of heart you will do so. I am now getting advanced in life &
in limited circumstances & this little boon would help me
very much.[10]

In the 1860 Richmond City Directory Fisher is listed as
"tobacco stemmery, corner 7th and Arch, [home] Cary between 1st and 2d." In the classified list of industries the
name of John Fisher, with the same address, appears under
the heading: "Tobacconists."[11] He died in Charlotte, North
Carolina, August 13, 1865, and was buried in Hollywood
Cemetery, Richmond.[12]

Fisher was married to Margaret Connor McKim who was
born in Richmond, Virginia, September 16, 1810, and died
there March 22, 1879.[13]

The Fishers had two children, John Robert Fisher and
a child who died in infancy. John Robert Fisher was married to Florence Mallory. Their children were Russell W.,
who died in childhood; Estelle M., who was never married;
James McKim, who married Sophie G. Bibb, and had no
children; John W., who married Anna R. Spratt; Robert M.,
who died in childhood; and William N. Fisher, who was
never married. All of the children of John Robert Fisher are
deceased. Mrs. J. M. Fisher, widow of James McKim Fisher,
resides at 1400 Fairmont Street, N. W., Washington, D. C.

John W. and Anna R. (Spratt) Fisher had several children, two of whom lived to maturity. One died unmarried and the other married to Dr. Neilson Strawbridge, had one child.

Mr. and Mrs. Fisher and some of their children are buried in marked graves on Lot B in Hollywood Cemetery, just west of Richmond, Virginia. Their burial plot is marked "Perpetual care."

There are eight graves on the Fisher lot, those of Elizabeth McKim, wife of Robert McKim, born March 15, 1783, died December 19, 1855; John Fisher; Margaret C. Fisher; James R. Fisher, born September 16, 1829, died December 29, 1893; Florence McKim Fisher, wife of James R. Fisher, born September 4, 1839, died October 25, 1901; Dr. William M. Fisher, died June 27, 1902; James McKim Fisher, son of James R. and Florence McKim Fisher and husband of Sophie Gilmer Bibb Fisher, born July 20, 1864, died December 9, 1929; and Estelle M. Fisher, who died in Washington, D. C., and was buried in Richmond, December 29, 1938.[14]

SAMUEL RHOADS FISHER
of
MATAGORDA MUNICIPALITY

Samuel Rhoads Fisher was born in Pennsylvania, December 31, 1794. He came to Texas in 1830 from his native state and settled at Matagorda where he remained the rest of his life.[1]

From Northumberland, Northumberland County, Pennsylvania, August 14, 1830, Fisher wrote Stephen F. Austin:

...am making every arrangement to start from Philadelphia: by sea in the course of next month, say the latter part
of it, so that with reasonable luck I shall put into Matagorda
by the last of October—Major [Ira] Ingram has promised to
have a place of shelter for my family, and I trust he will not
disappoint me...Your observations with respect to Zavala's
grant are noted and assented to...like yourself I detest Slavery, but conceive the general views I have there taken are
correct, and am firmly persuaded that the free admission
of Slaves into the State of Texas, authorised by act of our
legislature, would tend more to the rapid introduction of
respectable emigrants than any other course which could be
pursued...Colonel, I will give you a gratuitous opinion, The
most valuable emigrant you have ever had is James Bowie, I
consider him of the first order of men...[2]

Fisher, in addition to being a planter, also owned and
operated one or more schooners. In a letter to Austin,
dated January 10, 1831, he stated that he went to Harrisburg to load the schooner *Champion* with lumber for
Tampico.[3]

In a letter to Gov. Henry Smith and the General Council,
dated at Matagorda, December 11, 1835, James W. Fannin,
Jr., in substance charged that Fisher and Capt. Norman
Hurd had appropriated to their own use merchandise on
the schooner *Hannah Elizabeth* which had been run ashore
near Matagorda by the Mexican armed vessel *Bravo*.[4] In
a printed handbill dated January 12, 1836, Fisher branded
the charges as false and implied an invitation for Fannin to
challenge him to a duel.

The General Council of the Provisional Government on
December 16 referred the matter to the committee on the
State and Judiciary, composed of Thomas Barnett, James
Collinsworth, and Robert H. Williams. Barnett went to
Matagorda to investigate the charges, but due to the fact
that the other two members did not join him he returned
without making any recommendations.[5]

Approximately 175 votes were polled in the election held in Matagorda Municipality, February 1, 1836, to select two delegates to the Constitutional Convention. Following are the votes received by the candidates at the various boxes:

At "Head of Bay Prairie" Isham Thompson was election judge and B. J. White and John Huff, tellers. Ira Ingram received 18 votes; Daniel Elam, 17; Bailey Hardeman, 4; S. Rhoads Fisher, 4; and Thomas Cayce, 2. None of the voters expressed themselves in favor of independence.

Francis Keller was judge at his home in Trespalacios District. R. R. Royall led the field with 11 votes; Bailey Hardeman received 10; and Fisher, 1. All voters favored the Constitution of 1824 rather than independence. Five soldiers, former members of Captain William G. Cooke's Company of New Orleans Greys, Seth Carey, Michael Cronican, Sidney S. Callender, Adam Mosier and Lewis F. Amelung voted at this box.

A. B. Fleury was judge and John Redman secretary at Matagorda. There Fisher received 49 votes; Royall, 43; Elam, 29; Ingram, 16; Hardeman, 14; Cayce, 4; and Benjamin F. Sanders, 1.

At the Peach Creek District box Isham B. Phillips was judge and Jefferson George secretary. The vote: Hardeman, 18; Fisher, 12; and Elam, 2.

Thomas M. Blake and Lewis De Moss were election judges at the box in Elisha Hall's District, where Hardeman received 18 votes; Fisher, 11; and Ingram, 5. Four votes were cast for independence.

At his home in the Caney Lower Settlement, Thomas McCoy was judge, G. W. Whiteside and William Page, tellers, and William Baxter, secretary. Hardeman led with 17 votes; Ingram, 11; Royall, 10; and Elam, 4. No one voted for Mr. Fisher.

Allen Larrison was the judge and Benjamin Harrison and J. J. Avery the election clerks at the box in Larsche's District. Elam received 14 votes; Ingram, 8; Hardeman, 4; and Fisher, 1.

An election was held among the volunteers in the army at Goliad (Goliad Municipality) January 5, 1836, to select delegates from Matagorda Municipality to the convention. B. L. Reding was elected judge and Joseph Cadle secretary. At this election Royall received 16 votes; Ingram, 16; Hardeman, 4; and Elam, 1.

It appears, also, that three volunteers had voted January 12 and had shortly afterward returned to the United States.

The total votes sent to the convention for the various candidates were Royall, 83; Fisher, 79; Hardeman, 75; Ingram, 74; Elam, 67; Cayce, 6; and Sanders, 1.

Fisher, at Matagorda, February 22, 1836, wrote to the Convention:

> Herewith you have certified copies of all the electoral returns from which you will perceive that [Richard R.] Royall has 83 votes and, I, 79—but by examination you will perceive that there appears from Squire [James] Norton's certificate, 5 votes altered on the [Thomas] McCoy return and that there is a difference of 1 vote in the tallied count, and the written figures of Larche's return—these you can look into—and many other irregularities I am willing to pass by—but I shall oppose 'in toto' the returns of the Goliad election, as by the statement of Dugald McFarlane who drew up the discharge of the volunteers, they were all at liberty to return to their homes on the 12th Jany; and were not, either in service nor in the field—this will take from Royall 16—see Cady's certificate against the 5 volunteer votes on the Trespalacios, taken after night (Washington Greys) (New Orleans Greys) on their return to the U. States, when the law says *Citizen* volunteers, I shall object to—this will make to be deducted from Royall 21—and Dan Rawls will say upon oath, that he voted for me, tho' it is put down differently—that will be 22 to be deducted from 93, which leaves Royall 71 votes— (many of which are doubtful) but giving me a majority of 8

votes—Mr. McFarlane told me he would go before the convention and make his statement under oath—*memo*—did you know 'till now that any others than Royall & Ingram were voted for at Goliad?

The votes at Buckners I shall object, to, as no election was ordered to be held there—(See R. Hood's Certificate) in evidence of which you have herewith the original orders for an election as taken from the court House after the election—The above are in Squire Norton's handwriting as you will perceive—Mem: Major [Ira B.] Lewis has certificates that the Lt. [James] Rawls voted for me.[6]

On March 4, 1836, Mr. Everitt, chairman of the committee on privileges and elections, made the following report:

Your committee on privileges and elections ask leave respectfully to report, that after a patient examination of various documents laid before your committee, in regard to an election held in the municipality of Matagorda, (said election being contested by Messrs. [Richard] Royall and Fisher) have come to the conclusion that Mr. S. Rhodes Fisher is legally elected and entitled to a seat in this house. In drawing this conclusion, your committee would respectfully state to the house, that among the returns of elections, is one from Goliad, held among the volunteers on the fifth of January; at that election Mr. Royall received sixteen votes. The person who discharged that post, appeared before your committee, and testified that he discharged said volunteers on the evening of the 11th and morning of the 12th January, and it appears further in evidence, that a part at least of said volunteers voted again, and your committee are unanimously of opinion, that said votes were not legal votes, and that they ought not to be counted, and in making up their report, they have left them entirely out.

It appears further in evidence that three men on their way from the army to the United States, did vote at a house where they stopped for the night, and as is certified, their votes were taken between the hours of 8 and 9 o'clock at night, your committee are unanimously of opinion that the above three votes should not be counted, as they were clearly illegal, and have accordingly thrown them out, as said persons who voted, did immediately thereafter leave the country, and also that the votes were taken after the time of the election.

Your committee are therefore of opinion, that Mr. S. Rhodes Fisher, named, ought to be enrolled among the members of this house.

The minutes of March 6 show that Fisher appeared and, agreeable to the report of the committee on privileges and elections, took his seat as a delegate of the Convention.[7]

On March 7, "Messrs. S. Rhodes Fisher, John W. Moore, John W. Bowers [sic], and Samuel A. Maverick, being absent at the adoption of the Declaration of Independence, asked and obtained leave to sign the same."[8]

On October 26, 1836, President Houston nominated Fisher to be Secretary of the Navy.[9] On October 28 the Senate unanimously confirmed his nomination.[10]

In October, 1837, President Houston suspended him from office. The Senate, on October 11, resented the suspension.

Mr. [William H.] Wharton offered a substitute for the Resolution introduced on Saturday, directing the President to reinstate the Hon. S. R. Fisher which was received, read and adopted. Mr. [Robert] Wilson entering his protest against the same.

Resolved that a committee of two be appointed to wait on his Excellency [the President] and inform him that his message of the 6th Instant in regard to the reinstation of the Secretary of the Navy is deemed by the Senate disrespectful, dictatorial and evincive of a disposition on the part of the Executive to annihilate those co-ordinate powers conferred upon the senate by the constitution in all cases of the appointment or removal of Cabinet Officers. The welfare of the country and the respect due to the chief Magistrate greatly dispose the senate to act in concert and harmony with him, but the oath which [they have] taken to support the constitution imperatively bind them to prevent their legitimate powers from being infringed by another department of the Government. They deem the message of his Excellency referred to as an attempt at such infringement and therefore reject and return it with an earnest reiteration of their resolution requesting the reinstation of the Secr[etar]y of the Navy or a presentation of the charges which induced his suspension from office.

The senate do not deny in toto the power of the Executive to suspend a Cabinet Office, but they conceive that such suspension ought only to be made under very extraordinary circumstances and then that justice to the Individual and respect for the co-ordinate powers of the senate would justify and indeed require an immediate convocation of that body that the suspension might be concurred in or rejected. Mr. President of the Senate [Mirabeau B. Lamar] and Mr. [Isaac W.] Burton were appointed a committee to wait on his Excellency with the same."[11]

124

On October 18, 1837, the Senate directed

...that the Hon. S. Rhoads Fisher be instructed to immediately resume the active exercise of his duties as Secretary of the Navy.[12]

Fisher replied to the Senate on October 20:

Having on the 18th inst been furnished with a copy of a Resolution of your Hon Body of that date, in relation to my resuming the duties of my office, I have to state that I yesterday addressed the acting Secretary of the Navy, Wm. M. Shepherd, a note of which you herewith have a copy; and on the evening of the same day received his reply which is also enclosed. Having now Gentlemen laid before you the facts, and copies of the correspondence in relation to your Resolution, I await the further orders of your Honorable Body.[13]

In a letter to Fisher, Shepherd said:

In reply to which I beg leave respectfully to remark, that having obtained the appointment which I hold from the Executive, I cannot yield the papers of the Department, without instructions from the same source.[14]

On October 26 President Houston in a letter to the Senate stated that he was preparing charges and specifications against Fisher and would send them to the Senate.[15] The charges were presented on November 7 but were not recorded in the Senate Journal. What are purported to be the charges are printed in *The Papers of Mirabeau Buonaparte Lamar*, I, 584-585. Among them were the following:

> Proposition to Thos. Toby to engage in a speculation in Tobacco, to be *smuggled* into the enemy's country & traded with the enemy, on their joint acct. and for their private advantage—Vessels of Texas Navy to be disposed of by the Sec. as to give protection to the illicit traffic—Horses and mules, got in exchange for the Tobacco, to be sold to the Texas Government.—See letter Fisher to Toby Jan. 9th, 1837 (B, No. 1)...
>
> "Taking a cruise with the Navy," against the enemy, without the approbation of the President, and contrary to his known wishes and express denial. Done surreptitiously, under pretence of recruiting his health and spirits. (See his publications in the *Telegraph* of Sept. 9th and 16th.)— (Application for and grant of leave of absence, A. 2 and 3.)—Took a position on board, which, while it exempted him from the legal responsibilities of the command, gave him in fact the superintendence and effectual control of the squadron and its movement...
>
> Discreditable character of the Cruise—Plundering—burning and destroying the property of defenceless and unoffending Mexicans not warranted by laws of Wars and Nations—(see Wheaton fol. 249). Disobedience of orders—leaving the Texan Coast unguarded—700 miles from it—parting Company three times—ordered to cruise a month or 6 weeks, staid nearly 3 months.

125

Attack on Sisal contrary to orders—impolitic, endangered loss of vessels...On November 28, the Senate Resolved, that the Senate on the grounds of harmony and expediency advise and consent to the removal of the Hon S. Rhoads Fisher from the office of Sec of the Navy, but in doing so they must do the Secretary the justice to say that President has not adduced sufficient evidence that proves him guilty of dishonorable conduct.[16]

Fisher was shot and killed on March 14, 1839. Albert G. Newton who was charged with the murder was acquitted March 2, 1840.[17]

Fisher was married to Ann Pleasants, who was born January 26, 1796, and died October 21, 1862.[18] Mr. and Mrs. Fisher are buried in marked graves in the cemetery at Matagorda.

When Fisher County was created August 21, 1876, it was named "in honor of S. Rhoads Fisher, a distinguished officer of the Republic."[19]

Near the graves of Mr. and Mrs. Fisher are those of Rebecca Fisher, who was born July 6, 1830, and died September 26, 1862; and John Calhoun Perry, husband of Rebecca Fisher, born October 26, 1818, and died October 12, 1861. Mrs. Perry was probably a daughter of S. Rhoads Fisher.

Samuel W. Fisher, son of Samuel Rhoads Fisher, was born May 29, 1819. On August 16, 1848, he was married to Eliza Ophelia Smith, who was born January 17, 1823, and died April 30, 1877. Mr. Fisher died September 15, 1874. The two are buried in marked graves in the cemetery in Matagorda.

Dr. W. C. Fisher, son of Samuel W. Fisher, was born in Matagorda County, January 18, 1860. He was married to Alice Porter. Children of this union were W. C. Fisher, Jr., Galveston; Sidney L. Fisher, who died in France during the first World War; Capt. Royden Kener Fisher, U. S. A.; a daughter who married W. C. Cromby, El Paso; and a daughter who married C. C. Forskey, Houston.

Rhoads Fisher, a son of Samuel Rhoads Fisher, was born March 18, 1832, and died in 1911. He was married to Sophia Rollins Harris, who was born in 1840 and died February 5, 1889. The two are buried in marked graves in Oakwood Cemetery, Austin. Some of the children of this union were Annie F., who married Thomas L. Ormond; a daughter, who married Dayton Moses of Ft. Worth; a daughter, who married Andrew Moses of Washington, D. C.; and Lewis Fisher, who married May Masterson, and who in February, 1942, was residing at 232 Marshall Street, Houston.

Ann Pleasants Fisher, daughter of S. Rhoads Fisher, on October 1, 1845, was married to James Wilmer Dallam, for whom Dallam County, Texas, was named. Annie Wilmer Dallam, a daughter of this union, was married to Judge Branch T. Masterson.

Children of Judge Branch T. and Annie Wilmer (Dallam) Masterson were May; Thomas W., who married Beatrice Thomson; Rebecca; and Wilmer Dallam Masterson, who married Marilla Anthony. May Masterson, daughter of Judge Branch T. and Wilmer (Dallam) Masterson, as has been stated, was married to Judge Lewis Fisher.

127

JAMES GAINES
of
SABINE MUNICIPALITY

*J*ames Gaines, son of Richard and Jemina (Pendleton) Gaines, and first cousin of Gen. Edmund Pendleton Gaines,[1] was born in Culpeper County, Virginia, in about 1776.[2]

OUR (unlikely) FATHERS

In 1803 James Gaines aided Edmund P. Gaines, then a lieutenant in the United States Army, in making a survey of the waterway extending from Nashville down the Cumberland River to the Ohio and from there to New Orleans. In 1805 he went with the troops to Fort Jessup near Natchitoches, Louisiana.

Although James Gaines in several instances stated that he came to Texas in 1812 to make it his home, when, on March 31, 1818, he sold a tract of land in Texas to Stephen Barker he gave as his home Natchitoches Parish, Louisiana.[3]

A boundary dispute between the United States and Spain arose. In 1806, with a detachment of United States troops under Gen. James Wilkinson facing a Spanish army under Simon de Herrera, Governor of Nuevo Leon, across the Sabine River, a battle seemed inevitable. On November 5, 1806, Herrera, however, entered into an agreement with General Wilkinson, that, until the question of boundary between the two governments was settled, all the territory between the Sabine and the Arroyo Hondo, in Louisiana, should be a *neutral ground*, not to be occupied by either party. Thus the conflict was avoided.[4] Gaines's home was just across the Sabine from the neutral ground.

In 1812 Augustus W. Magee, who had been a lieutenant in the United States Army, and Jose Bernardo Gutierrez concentrated their forces in the neutral ground, while preparing for what is recorded as the Guiterrez-Magee Expedition. They planned to wrest Texas from Spain and to build up a republican state. Gaines joined the expedition, recruited and commanded a company of Mexicans. He participated in the battle of Rasolis near San Antonio in 1813, but with other Anglo-Americans he resigned in disgust and went home when the Mexicans executed prominent Spanish prisoners captured in the battle.

Yoakum intimated that Captain Gaines participated in Dr. James Long's expedition,[5] but a letter Gaines and Ramon Quirk, at Sabinas, on September 20, 1820, wrote the governor of Texas indicates the contrary.

> After having paid my respects to Your Lordship and wished you a long and prosperous life, I would inform you of the situation of affairs, so far as the interest of the vassals of His Majesty is interested.
>
> I have visited the territory between this place and the Opelusas and Rapids & have an opportunity of seeing the small band who call themselves Long's Army; I have also ascertained the whole truth concerning Galveston Island; and I can assure Your Excellency that Long has now with him nearly 800 men, and is daily making recruits. La Fitte, the notorious pirate, has returned, it is said, under the colors of South America, and was bearer of commissions for Long and the officers of his party. Recruiting is carried on at the Rapids, and the men are to join Long overland, either at Galveston, or at Atascosito.
>
> I cannot state positively which point they intend to attack; the ones say La Bahia, the others Soto La Marina. What is certain is that they intend to attack travellers on the road from La Bahia to San Antonio, and to rob them. A general of experience and renown is to take the command of Long's forces, and the expedition shall set out during the next month. Quirk will leave, in November to obtain further information, and if before that epoch any new occurrence should take place, one of us would at once go to inform Your Lordship.
>
> P. S. I have to inform Your Lordship that Colonel Perez allowed me to remain in my settlement at the Lower crossing of the Sabine.[6]

The District of Sabine was probably first organized in 1823 or early 1824, for in a petition signed by the settlers of the area on February 15, 1824, there is reference to the fact that James Dill, Alcalde of Nacogdoches, had ordered election of Alcaldes in various districts. Although there are no records of this election, it is probable that James Gaines was the first alcalde, since correspondence is found from him in that capacity as early as May 15, 1824.[7]

In 1826 Haden Edwards started the Fredonian War in East Texas with Martin Parmer, who later with Gaines signed the Texas Declaration of Independence, as one of his ranking officers. Gaines joined the opposition. He had married a sister of Samuel Norris, who had identified himself with the Mexican population in Nacogdoches, and it was Norris who on January 4, 1827, temporarily captured Nacogdoches from the Fredonians. Edwards accused Gaines of being largely responsible for the trouble that caused the "war."

On December 15, 1835, the General Council of the Provisional Government of Texas elected Gaines first judge of the Municipality of Sabine.[8]

On January 23, 1836, Gen. Edmund P. Gaines received orders from the Secretary of War of the United States to take command of the troops on the Mexican boundary and to prevent either of the contending parties from crossing the frontier in arms.[9]

James Gaines and William Clark, Jr., were elected from Sabine Municipality to the Constitutional Convention. Votes were received at the town of Milam. The return to the convention does not capitulate the votes but states that Gaines and Clark were elected.[10] Gaines was seated in the Convention March 1,[11] and on that date was appointed a member of the committee to draft a declaration of independence.[12]

For a time in 1836 a post office named Sabine was established at Gaines Ferry with James Gaines as the postmaster.[13]

On May 19, 1837, President Houston nominated Gaines to be Collector of Customs for Gaines Ferry, to extend as far as the 32° of North Latitude, but on the same day his nomination was unanimously rejected by the Senate.[14] He was a member of the Senate from the district composed of Shelby, Sabine and Harrison Counties of the Fourth,[15] Fifth[16] and Sixth Congresses,[17] November 11, 1839, to February 5, 1842. He resigned after the close of the regular session of the Sixth Congress.[18] In 1843 he moved to Nacogdoches County. In 1849 he joined the gold rush for California and died in the long-since abandoned mining town of Quartsburg, California, in November, 1856. The San Francisco *Daily Alta California* of November 25, 1856, carried an obituary:

> Very rarely are California Journals called upon to record the demise of one, in this State, who has lived the "Three score and ten years" allotted to mortals. A large proportion of the population of the cities and larger towns is composed, perhaps, of men in middle life; but even in the greatest assemblages, the venerable heirs that betoken age are seldom seen. The sparsely settled portions of the interior, however, contain but here and there one whose locks are silvered o'er, and those communities may be said to be entirely peopled by the young men. We were, therefore, somewhat surprised on seeing chronicled in a late number of the *Mariposa Democrat* the death of a citizen of that county who has attained the good old age of eighty. The deceased Colonel Gaines of Quartsburg, was remarkable for the interest he manifested in the political affairs of the county.

131

A town was surveyed by William McFarland near the ferry and named Pendleton, probably in honor of Edmund Pendleton Gaines, cousin of James Gaines, and several years before the Texas State Highway Department completed, in 1937, a modern bridge at the site of the old ferry, the ferry had been called Pendleton Perry.

When Gaines County, Texas, was organized August 21, 1876, it was named "in honor of James Gaines, an old Texan and valuable citizen."[19]

James Gaines was married to Susanna Norris, a daughter of Ramond Norris. Norris settled in what is now Nacogdoches County in about 1805 on four leagues of land. He left Texas at the beginning of the revolution of 1813 and settled in Louisiana, but returned in 1821 to his Texas land, where he remained until his death in 1828. Norris's wife died in Nacogdoches County in about 1851.

Children of Ramond Norris were Samuel, Nathaniel, Julia Ann, Thomas, Susannah and John Norris, all of whom died before February 13, 1858, except John.

Susannah Norris, daughter of Ramond Norris, was married to James Gaines, subject of this sketch. Of this union there were five children—Edmund Pendleton, John Baptist, James S., Sarah Ann and William Gaines.[20]

In the Nacogdoches Archives of 1835 the names and the ages of the Gaines family, except the grown son, Edmund P. Gaines, are given. Mr. Gaines gave his age as 53 and that of his wife Susannah as 36. Their children were John, 17; James, 8; Sarah Ann, 4; and William Gaines, five months of age.

The following information pertaining to his life is the testimony of James Gaines given during the trial of Case No. 221—Russell heirs vs. James Mason in the District Court of Shelby County, filed April 1, 1851. The case was originally filed and tried in Sabine County but was taken to Shelby County on a change of venue:

> JAMES GAINES being sworn as a witness by deposition stated that he was sixty-eight years of age. That he moved to Texas in the year 1812 and has lived in principally ever since. That he purchased the Ferry known as the Gaines Ferry on the Sabine in the year 1819 and owned the same until the 20th of November 1844; that he commenced living at said Ferry in 1819, and lived there principally until 1843 when he removed to Nacogdoches County. There has always been a Boat or Flat at Gaines Ferry since 1814, but at Crows and other ferries on the Sabine there have been frequently no boats. Among the Mexicans my ferry was al-

132

ways known as the "Paso del Chalan." The Baregas crossing was always known as the place where the road leading from Nacogdoches to Natchitoches crossed the Baregas at where Milam now stands. The Road by Gaines Ferry was known among the Mexicans as the Camino Carreterro. The place where the upper or Crows Ferry Road crossed the Baregas waters which were very small there was called Cedars Crossing. In 1819 and indeed ever since I lived at the Ferry called Gaines Ferry; this Ferry was the main traveled road from Nacogdoches to Natchitoches. Crows Ferry was frequently abandoned. The hauling for the troops was always to the best of my recollection done on the Gaines Ferry Road. The Crow Ferry Road crossed the Patroon some six miles this side of the Sabine River, but the Gaines Ferry Road does not cross the said Patroon. The Patroon is an uncommonly large Bayou and in very high waters it was impossible to cross it, there being no Bridge across it in those days.

Dr. Edmund Pendleton Gaines, a son of James Gaines, was married to Mahalia Mackey. The 1835 census of Sabine Municipality shows that in that year Gaines was twenty years of age and his wife, Mahalia, was seventeen. Dr. Gaines in 1900, then 84 years of age, died at Luling, Texas, while visiting his granddaughter, Lily Chandoin. His remains were placed beside those of his wife in the Mackey cemetery at Prairie Lea, Caldwell County.[21]

133

Dr. and Mrs. Gaines had two children, Charles Pendleton and Amanda Gaines.

Charles Pendleton Gaines, on May 4, 1859, was married to Cass Kyle, daughter of Claiborne and Lucy (Bugg) Kyle. Children of this union were Emma Marion and Charles Kyle Gaines.

THOMAS JEFFERSON GAZLEY
of
MINA MUNICIPALITY

*D*r. Thomas Jefferson Gazley was born January 8, 1801,[1] in Dutchess County, New York, where he received an academic education. At Baltimore he was graduated as a physician.[2] In 1828 he moved to Louisiana. Shortly afterward he returned to Baltimore to wed his fiancee, Eliza Boyce. From Louisiana the two came to Texas in 1829 and settled in what is now Bastrop County.[3]

On April 29, 1829, Dr. Gazley applied for a license to practice medicine in the town of San Felipe de Austin.

> The Ayuntamiento of Austin met in special session, the president and two *regidores* present and the *sindico procurador* absent. Citizen Thomas J. Gazley presented two certificates from Scientific bodies (corporaciones scientificos) in the States of the North, accrediting his knowledge and skill in the practice of medicine. The ayuntamiento agreed to grant him a provisional license to practice his profession as a physician, pending the resolution of the supreme government, and for that purpose ordered that the said documents be sent to the government for its discussion.[4]

On February 1, 1830:

> Thomas J. Gazley was appointed clerk of the ayuntamiento to discharge such duties as may be required to him by that body until a secretary acquainted with the Castilian language can be procured and to us his name as secretary Pro Tem, during that time.[5]

He held the office of acting secretary until May 3, 1830.[6] The First Convention of Texas at San Felipe de Austin, October 5, 1832, appointed Dr. Gazley, Richard Andrews, and

Bartlett Sims members of a sub-committee of Safety and Vigilance for the District of Bastrop.[7] Dr. Gazley was a delegate to the Second Convention of Texas held in San Felipe in April, 1833.[8]

Dr. Gazley was surgeon of Capt. Michael E. Goheen's Company from September 28 to November 9, 1835.[9]

From Gonzales on October 6, 1835, Dr. Gazley, Peter W. Grayson, Patrick C. Jack, James W. Fannin, Jr., J. W. E. Wallace, John J. Linn, S. E. Millard and Dr. Amos Pollard jointly wrote Stephen F. Austin:

> You will receive important dispatches by the bearer that Col. Ugartachea and probably Genl. Cos—are now on their march here, with all their forces to take the Gun if it is not delivered—You will see by Ugartachea's letter to you, he proposed a sort of compromise. That will give us an opportunity to entertain him a little while, upon the suggestion that you are sent for, until we can get in more men. We, who subscribe this, request you earnestly to come on immediately, bringing all the aid you possibly can—we want powder and lead. Do all you can to send on instantly as much as possible.[10]

On the following day Dr. Gazley and the following other physicians, William P. Smith, T. Kenney, Joseph E. Field and Amos Pollard, offered their services to Colonel John H. Moore:

> You are hereby requested to accept the medical services of the undersigned, who without any distinction of grade, have with a special eye to the good of their country, constituted themselves a board for the volunteer army of Texas —with sentiments of high consideration we subscribe ourselves. Yours sincerely,[11]

Dr. Gazley, John W. Bunton, and Robert M. Coleman were elected to represent Mina (Bastrop) Municipality in the Constitutional Convention.

One of the two voting boxes in the municipality was at the home of Mrs. Nancy Blakey, mother of Lemuel S. Blakey who was later killed at the Battle of San Jacinto. There S. J. Whatley, James Rogers, J. B. Walters, William Duty, and David P. Owens were the election judges. John Caldwell received 25 votes; Thomas J. Rabb, 24; Thomas J. Gazley, 21; John W. Bunton, 17; Robert M. Coleman, 16; Robert M. Williamson, 9; Edward Burleson, 7; and D. C. Barrett, 1.

At the other box, not identified in the election returns sent to the convention, James Robison was president, David Berry, John W. Scallorn, F. T. Cottle, William Gorham were the secretaries. Rabb received 32 votes; Gazley, 26; Bunton, 22; Burleson, 20; Coleman, 19; Williamson, 16; Caldwell, 4; and Barrett, 4.

The total vote received by the various candidates: Rabb, 56; Gazley, 47; Bunton, 39; Coleman, 35; Caldwell, 29; Burleson, 27; Williamson, 25; and Barrett, 5.[12] Rabb, Gazley and Bunton were elected. Rabb, however, did not attend the convention and Coleman having received the fourth highest number of votes, was seated in his stead. Gazley was seated March 1.[13]

During the afternoon session of March 16 of the convention: "Mr. Gazley asked to be discharged from further attendance as a delegate of the Convention, which was done."[14] There is no evidence in the General Land Office that he joined the army.[15]

After the revolution Dr. Gazley moved to Houston where he resided for several years. On September 4, 1837, he was elected from Harrisburg County to a seat in the House of Representatives of the Second Congress of the Republic, September 25, 1837, to May 24, 1838.[16] In 1837 he was a law partner of John Birdsall.

Dr. Gazley moved from Houston to Bastrop County and settled near the site of the present town of Smithville.[17]

There he died October 31, 1853. His remains were exhumed in 1937 and on February 27 of that year re-interred in the State Cemetery at Austin by the Commission of Control for Texas Centennial Celebrations and a monument erected at his new grave. It was planned also to remove the remains of Mrs. Gazley but unfortunately her grave could not be found. At the death of Dr. Gazley she made her home at Waco with her son, Alfred Francis Gazley. There she died in 1884.

Dr. Gazley was a member of Holland Lodge No. 36, A. F. & A. M., Houston, in 1837. He was listed as: "Age 40, Lawyer."[18] He was senior warden of the lodge in 1837 and 1838,[19] and was a charter member of the Grand Lodge of Texas, organized at Houston, December 20, 1837.[20]

Children of Dr. and Mrs. Gazley were Thomas Jefferson, Jr.; William H., who married Margaret Ann Shepherd; Dr. Edwin T., who married Anna C. Hadsel; and Alfred Francis Gazley.

Some of the surviving grandchildren of Dr. and Mrs. Thomas J. Gazley are Henry L. Gazley, 525 East Park Avenue, San Antonio; Mrs. Lila William, Skidmore; Erwin T. Gazley, 301 West 8th Street, Austin; Chas. C. Gazley, Los Angeles; Mrs. Gustie Dordap, Houston; and Albert N. Gazley, Houston.

137

BENJAMIN BRIGGS GOODRICH
of
WASHINGTON MUNICIPALITY

*D*r. Benjamin Briggs Goodrich was born in Brunswick County, Virginia, February 24, 1799, son of John Goodrich.

As a small child Benjamin Briggs Goodrich was taken with his parents from Virginia to Tennessee, where he grew into manhood and was given an academic education. He later graduated from a medical college in Baltimore[1] and began the practice of medicine there. Returning to Tennessee he went, thence, to Mississippi and practiced medicine for a time near Vicksburg; going, thence, to Tuscaloosa, Alabama; thence to Tallahasse, Florida; thence back to Alabama, where he served one term in the legislature of that state.[2]

Dr. Goodrich and his younger brother, John Calvin Goodrich, arrived in Texas, April 30, 1834.[3] Dr. Goodrich purchased a lot in the town of Washington, December 16, 1835,[4] and was living in the town at the time the Convention was held there in March, 1836. He later settled near the site of the present town of Anderson, Grimes County.

Dr. Goodrich, Jesse Grimes, Dr. George W. Barnett, and James G. Swisher represented the Municipality of Washington at the Constitutional Convention. The election returns of the municipality are not among the Convention Papers in the Texas State Library. Goodrich was seated as a delegate March 1.[5]

While attending the convention, Dr. Goodrich obtained from each delegate present his age, place of birth and the name of the state in which he was living when he emigrated to Texas. Samuel P. Carson did not arrive at the convention until March 11 and unfortunately Dr. Goodrich failed to interview him. The information collected by Dr. Goodrich was published by Henderson Yoakum in 1855 in his *History of Texas*[6] and the omission by Dr. Goodrich of Carson's name has misled many people into believing that only 58 men signed the Texas Declaration of Independence.

Colonel Gray arrived at "the new town of Washington" February 13, 1836, and recorded in his diary:

> Was introduced to Dr. Goodrich, a physician of the place, and a member-elect of the new Convention, a strenuous Independence man.[7]

While Dr. Goodrich was attending the convention be learned that his 27-year-old brother, John Calvin Goodrich, had fallen at the Alamo on March 6. On March 15 he wrote his brother, Edmund Goodrich, in Nashville, Tennessee:

> Texas is in mourning, and it becomes my painful duty to inform my relations in Tennessee of the massacre of my poor brother John. He was murdered in the Texas fortress of San Antonio de Bexar (known as the Alamo) on the night of the 6th of this month, together with one hundred and eighty of our brave countrymen, gallantly defending that place against an invading army of Mexicans, eight thousand strong; not one escaped to tell the dreadful tale. The Alamo had been surrounded for many days by a besieging army of the Mexicans, variously at from 3 to 8 thousand men, commanded by Genl. Lopez de Santa Anna in person; the fortress, as before stated, was besieged, and it fell and every man was put to the sword. They effected their purpose by a general charge aided by scaling ladders. Upward of five hundred of the enemy were killed and as many more mortally or dangerously wounded. Col. Travis, the commander of the fortress, sooner than fall into the hands of the enemy, stabbed himself to the heart and instantly died.
>
> Seven of our brave men, being all that were left alive, called for quarter and to see Santa Anna, but were instantly shot by the order of the fiendish tyrant. Col. Bowie was murdered sick in bed. Among the number of our acquaintances,

murdered in the Alamo, were Col. David Crockett, Micajah Autry, formerly of Haysborough, John Hays, son of Andrew Hays of Nashville, and my unfortunate brother, John C. Goodrich; but they died like men, and posterity will do them justice. Santa Anna is now in Texas with an invading army of eight or ten thousand men strong—determined to carry on a war of extermination. We will meet him and teach the unprincipled scoundrel that freemen can never be conquered by the hireling soldiery of a military despot.

The struggle is great and our difficulties many—but the army of the patriot is doubly nerved, when his fireside and his liberties are invaded—we rush to the combat, and our motto is *Revenge, Liberty or Death*. Approach our poor old mother cautiously with this awful news, for I fear her much worn out constitution will not survive the shock. Publish this information if you think proper. We ask for help and in the name of everything that is sacred to Liberty and Independence.

140

So soon as the Convention adjourns, I shall proceed forthwith to the army.—The blood of a Goodrich has already crimsoned the soil of Texas and another victim shall be added to the list or I see Texas free and Independent.—Give my love to my dear mother, sisters and brothers and friends generally—

BENJ. BRIGGS GOODRICH

P. S. News has just reached that the enemy are on their march to this place and we know not at what moment we shall be compelled to move our women and children beyond their reach. Their mode of warfare is strictly savage; they fight under a *Red Banner*, and we ask nor expect to quarter in the future,—I will advise you from time to time (if alive) and would highly appreciate hearing from you.—Direct your letters to Cantonment Jessup, pay postage and I will be sure to get them.[8]

In a letter dated at Washington, Texas, in April, 1836, James Collinsworth wrote to General Houston, relative to Dr. Goodrich:

Things here now in great confusion, many families of all classes are camped in the bottoms on the east side of the Brassos and in a most deplorable condition. Men women and children subject to all the inconveniences of the dampness of a low bottom much overflowed & without medical attention. Under these circumstances I have appointed Dr. B. B. Goodrich Surgeon at this post until further ordered by yourself.[9]

Dr. Goodrich died November 16, 1860. His wife, Serena (Corothers) Goodrich was born May 11, 1807, in Barren County, Kentucky, and died April 27, 1884. The State of Texas in 1932 erected a joint monument at their graves in Odd Fellows Cemetery in Anderson, Grimes County. From the old headstone that stood at their graves the dates of their births and deaths were obtained.

The names of the children of Dr. and Mrs. Goodrich were furnished the author in 1940 by Mrs. W. C. Gibson, Navasota, Texas. They were: John, who married Mary Eliza Rogers; Virginia, who married John B. Harris and, after his death, A. W. Scables; Serena, who married Lemuel P. Rogers and, after his death, John Carroll; Benjamin, who married Mary Terrell; Eugenia, who married B. W. Pearce; Elizabeth, who married James L. Scott; Mary, who married James H. Muldrew; Briggs, who first married Rhoda Meador and after her death was twice married; and Dr. William Goodrich, who was married but had no children.

In 1942 some of the surviving grandchildren of Dr. and Mrs. Benjamin B. Goodrich were: Mrs. J. D. Covlet, 1508 Hemphill Street, Ft. Worth; Beaumont Carroll, Houston; Mrs. Latham Boone, Navasota; Mrs. H. H. Scott, 909 Truxillo Street, Houston; and Mrs. Lillie Wilkerson and Mrs. W. C. Gibson, Navasota, Texas.

JESSE GRIMES
of
WASHINGTON MUNICIPALITY

*J*esse Grimes was born in what is now Duplin County, North Carolina, February 6, 1788,[1] son of Sampson and Bethsheba (Winder) Grimes. He left home in 1817 and went to Washington County, Alabama. He came to Texas in 1827[2] and located temporarily on the San Jacinto River in what is now Harris County, about ten miles above its junction with Buffalo Bayou. In the fall of 1827 he settled on the league of land to which he received title from the Mexican government in 1831, The settlement in which he located early became known as Grimes Prairie and is in the present Grimes County.

On March 21, 1829, the Ayuntamiento of San Felipe de Austin elected Grimes first lieutenant of the First Company, Battalion of Austin.[3] He was elected *sindico procurator*, precinct of Viesca, Jurisdiction of Austin, Department of Bexar, on December 12, 1830,[4] and on December 11, 1831, one of *regidors* of the Ayuntamiento.[5]

The First Convention of Texas at San Felipe in October, 1832, created a central Committee of Safety and Vigilance with sub-committees for the various districts. Grimes was not a member of the Convention, but on October 5 he was put on the sub-committee as one of the representatives from the District of Viesca,[6] On the following day he was appointed treasurer of the district.[7]

On November 5, 1835, Grimes was seated by the Consultation at San Felipe as a delegate from Washington Municipality.[8] By that body he was elected, on November 14, a member of the General Council of the Provisional Government of Texas.[9]

James Hass, elected judge of the municipality, reported to the Convention at Washington on March 1 that in the election held February 1, 1836, Grimes, Dr. George W. Barnett, Dr. Benjamin B. Goodrich, and James G. Swisher had been elected to represent Washington Municipality. The number of votes polled was not stated.[10] These gentlemen were all seated March 1.[11]

While Grimes was attending the convention, his eighteen-year-old son, Alfred Calvin Grimes, fell at the Alamo on March 6, 1836.

On April 17, 1836, Judge Grimes wrote President Burnet:

> A great many widows and women whose husbands are in the Army have been compelled to leave their homes and seek safety by retiring East of the Trinity many of whom must certainly suffer if no provision is made for them. On reflecting upon the situation of these unfortunate families the following suggested itself to me: That if such families as are not in a situation to support themselves were requested to situate themselves in some two, three or more places and agents appointed to procure them provisions on the public credit wherever to be found. It would not only have the good effect to save them from starvation but it would admit many men to go to the army who would otherwise be compelled to remain with their families to procure for them a subsistence and it would induce some to join the Army so that their families might be taken care of.
>
> There are not more than three or four families remaining within twenty miles of me and I shall sound a retreat tomorrow morning.[12]

On June 3, 1836, Grimes enrolled a company of volunteers "for a tour of three months service in the Texas Army, East Side of the Brazos River, Washington County."[13]

When Lamar was collecting material for a history of Texas he intended to write, he obtained from Judge Grimes, some time in the year 1838, an account of the Convention:

143

Whilst the convention was in session at Washington, its business was subject to constant interruptions from alarms about the approach of the enemy. On the 16th March, intelligence (but false) was received, that Guiano [Antonio Gaona], who was supposed to be on his way to Nacogdoches, above Tenoxtitlan was marching down upon Washington; and would be very soon in the town. This threw the members of the convention into great consternation. They knew not what to do. Captain Teel [Henry Teal] had just passed through the city on his way to Gonzales with a company of regulars, who however had no arms. It was known that there was some muskets and ammunition at San philippe [San Felipe de Austin]. John Alcorn and Simon Miller volunteered their services to bear an order to Teel to repair forthwith to San philippe, arm his men and return to Washington. The only authority in the country then was the convention. The president of the body [Richard Ellis] granted the necessary order; and the two gentlemen above named proceeded on after Teel. They had gone but a few miles, before they returned in full speed, under whip and spur and all breathless, with the alarming tiding that Gouiana was upon the city—The convention was then in session, then late at night; and being seized with dreadful apprehensions, immediately adopted the Constitution, then lying on the Table, and passing a Resolution authorizing the Secretary [Herbert Simms Kimble) to sign the names of the members of that body to the Instrument, adjourned in great confusion. The alarm proved to be false—Alcorn and Miller had overheard two Mexicans who were out in the prairie, guarding a cavayard of horses, in conversation, as they were lying on the grass and mistook them for spies of Gouiana. The convention met the next day, and after appointing the officers of the Govt. ad interim then dissolved—consult the journals to see the precise date when the officers of the Govt. ad interim were appointed; uncertain whether it was on the 16 or 17.[14]

Grimes was a member of the Senate of the First Congress of the Republic, October 3, 1836, to September 25,

1837, from the District composed of Washington County.[15] He was a member of the House of Representatives in the Sixth[16] and Seventh[17] Congresses from Montgomery County, November 1, 1841, to December 8, 1843. Robert M. Williamson's seat in the Senate was declared vacant January 4, 1844, and Judge Grimes succeeded him January 22, representing the district composed of Washington, Montgomery and Brazos Counties in the Eighth Congress.[18] He was reelected to the Ninth and final congress which ended June 28, 1845.[19] He represented the Ninth District, composed of Montgomery County, in the Senate of the First[20] and Second[21] Legislatures, February 14, 1846, to November 5, 1849, and he was in the Senate of the Third Legislature from the Thirteenth District, composed of Montgomery, Walker and Grimes Counties, November 5, 1849, to November 3, 1851,[22] and was likewise a Senator in the Fourth Legislature, November 3, 1851 to November 7, 1853.[23] He was not a member of the Fifth Legislature but was a member of the Senate of the Sixth,[24] Seventh[25] and Eighth Legislatures,[26] November 5, 1855, to November 4, 1861.

In the Act of the Legislature of April 6, 1846, which created Grimes County, Texas, it is not stated for whom it was named.[27] Homer S. Thrall, in 1879, said it was named for Jesse Grimes.[28]

Judge Grimes was first married to Martha Smith, who was born in Alabama, August 4, 1789, and died in that state in 1824. Children of this union were Robert Henry, who married Elizabeth Highsmith; Harrie Elizabeth; Albert Calvin, born December 20, 1817; Rufus; Lucinda, who died in childhood; Jacob; Mary Jane, who died in childhood; William Ward, who died in childhood; and Martha Ann, twin of William Ward Grimes.

In 1826 Judge Grimes was married to a young widow, Mrs. Rosanna Ward Britton, who had married at the age of sixteen and whose husband had drowned shortly after their

145

marriage. She was a daughter of Francis and Mary Ward. Their children were Gordon, who died in early childhood; Harvey; Leonard, who died in childhood; Helen, who married Robert Love; Emily, who was twice married, first to John Bowen, and after his death to George Gannaway; and Nancy Grimes, who married Charles H. Ehlinger.

Judge Grimes died March 15, 1866. Mrs. Grimes was born October 31, 1803, and died December 6, 1871.[29] Both were buried in the John McGintry cemetery about ten miles east of Navasota. The cemetery was eventually abandoned. The State of Texas had the remains of Judge and Mrs. Grimes exhumed and on October 17, 1929, reinterred in the State Cemetery at Austin.

In 1940 some of the surviving grandchildren of Judge and Mrs. Jesse Grimes were Mrs. Ben Harris, Ft. Worth; Mrs, George Breitenstein, Boulder, Colorado; Mrs. W. C. Preston, Ft. Worth; George Grimes, Brownwood; and Mrs. J. W. Kenedy, Lampasas, Texas.

ROBERT HAMILTON
of
PECAN POINT AND VICINITY

Robert Hamilton was born in Scotland, in about 1783.[1] His parents, William and Euphemia (Alston) Hamilton, had ten children: Isabella, John, George, James, William, Robert, Alexander, Patrick, Jean and Euphemia Hamilton.

All of the seven Hamilton brothers, except George, emigrated to America from Scotland. Five came in about

1807 and settled in Granville County, North Carolina.[2] John did not arrive until about 1826. In 1812 the brothers associated themselves jointly in commercial business, apparently combining branches of business which each had been prosecuting individually before that time. Each branch was under a different firm name, viz: James Hamilton & Co., Robert Hamilton & Co., Alexander Hamilton & Co., and Patrick Hamilton & Co. The capital stock of the concern was £25,000 of Virginia currency, of which each was to hold £5,000. Each contributed the investments of his own business at valuations, including estates, houses, mercantile stocks, and accounts receivable outstanding each at a special valuation, and each one continued his own business as "managing partner," but for the benefit of the concern. This excluded William, who was not a managing partner.

After some years Robert dissolved his connection with his brothers and removed to an area on Red River claimed both by Arkansas and Texas. According to his sworn statement made March 15, 1838, before the Red River County Board of Land Commissioners, he arrived in this area on December 15, 1834, a single man.[3]

In 1838, however, Red River County was still claimed by the United States as a part of Miller County, Arkansas.

Much of the Hamilton family genealogy used in this sketch was compiled by the late Patrick Hamilton Baskerville, grandson of James Hamilton, brother of Robert. Regarding Robert he wrote:

> Robert Hamilton, the fifth son, never married. We do not know the date of his birth or emigration. His property, which was contributed to the concern, consisted of two plantations, one on Flat Creek, and the other on Tabs Creek, with mills and other industries established thereon, and with all the stock and other appurtenances valued at eight thousand four hundred and fifty-five pounds fourteen shillings and

eleven pence half penny Virginia currency. And the character of the improvements seem to indicate that he must have lived there in order to manage them. After some years, we do not know how many, he dissolved the connection with his brothers, and removed to Texas, where dealing largely in Red River lands he acquired a large estate, which at his death was inherited chiefly as stated, by the two children of his brother James.[4]

Hamilton, Richard Ellis and Collin McKinney on March 1, 1836, were seated at the Constitutional Convention as delegates "From the Municipality of Pecan Point and vicinity."[5] At the afternoon session of March 2, "Mr. A. H. Latimer, from the Municipality of Pecan Point and vicinity, appeared, produced his credentials, and took his seat."[6] And at the afternoon session of March 10, "Mr. Samuel P. Carson, from Red River, appeared, produced his credentials and took his seat..."[7] Strange to say, there was no municipality of Pecan Point or Red River at that or any other time. Carson's home was definitely in Arkansas[8] and the others resided in territory claimed by the United States as a part of Arkansas and by Mexico as a part of Texas.[9]

148

On March 19, 1836, Hamilton and George C. Childress were commissioned by President David G. Burnet and his cabinet to go to Washington on a very important mission:

> Childress, acting with Robert Hamilton, is to open negotiations with the Cabinet at Washington, D. C. inviting on the part of that Cabinet a recognition of the Sovereignty and Independence of Texas, and the establishment of such relations between the two Governments, as may comport with the mutual interest the common origin, and kindred ties of their constituents.[10]

Hamilton and Childress were at Natchitoches, Louisiana, on March 28.[11] On April 18, Childress wrote from Nashville, Tennessee, to President Burnet and among other things he said:

I reached this place a day or two since on my way to Washington City. Mr. Hamilton and I parted company at Natchitoches, he having gone by his plantation on Red River. We are to rendezvous at Washington on the first day of May...[12]

On June 1, 1836, Secretary of State Samuel P. Carson wrote to Gen. R. G. Dunlap a letter in which he said:

I will direct Robert Hamilton Esq. the authorized agent of the government of Texas, to negotiate a loan to refund the amount with not exceeding *ten per centum per annum* interest thereon, if he should obtain a loan in the Northern cities, where he at this time is...[13]

On July 3, 1836, Carson from Washington, wrote to President Burnet that "Mr. Hamilton is in Philadelphia, feeling the pulse of the capitalists, and will proceed to New York..."[14]

Due to frauds perpetrated by persons professing to represent Texas, President Burnet, on June 10, issued a proclamation that after that date only Toby & Brother and B. F. Triplett of New Orleans would be recognized as agents. The proclamation was published in New Orleans and New York papers and was read by Carson and Hamilton while they were in New York. How it affected them is told in a lengthy letter written November 28, 1836, by Carson from Pulaski County, Arkansas, to President Sam Houston:

...Meeting with Messres Hamilton and Childress on my arrival at Washington City we adopted such plans and measures for the furtherance of the objects which we were charged, as seemed most expedient at the moment—Under the authority granted to the Executive Govt. to obtain a loan of money to supply the wants of the Army etc. Robert Hamilton Esqr. was thought by the cabinet to be the most suitable person to effect that object in part. He was therefore commissioned by the President on the 2d day of April last. His commission was confided to me for delivery to Mr. Hamilton, which I bore and delivered to him at Washington City...

Upon this Mr. Hamilton and myself proceeded to New York sounded the money market and were arranging our plans of operation, when to our surprise and astonishment there appeared in the Gazettes of New York the following proclamation extracted from the New Orleans Papers...

To judge our feelings and decide upon our deep mortification could only be done by persons placed in similar situations. But great as our chagrin we deemed it better for the cause of Texas to bear it in silence—had we taken any other course we should have been compelled to give *flat contradiction* to the President and publish in the public prints the authority under which we acted and had presumed to borrow money upon—but we preferred submitting to the injury, rather than bring the authorities of the Republic, into disrepute in the only country from which we could expect aid, and in which our dissentions at home, had been sufficiently magnified and done sufficient injury. I also thought and hoped that the omission of the name of Mr. Hamilton, as one of the Govt. Agents to obtain money, in the Proclamation of the President was a mere inadvertence or 'Casus ommissis' which would be rectified immediately but in this I have been disappointed and Mr. Hamilton and myself remain to this day under the odious light of having attempted to obtain money without authority from the Govt. which we profess to be serving. And this the more extraordinary as the commission of Mr. Hamilton is not only signed by Pres. Burnet in his official capacity but every word of the Commission is also in his own handwriting...

From New York Mr. Hamilton and myself returned to Washington City when we met with Cols. Collinsworth and Grayson who seemed to be charged with all the duties necessary to be discharged for the benefit of the Republic.[15]

On December 20, 1836, President Houston nominated Robert Hamilton as the chief justice of Red River County, and the Senate confirmed the nomination on the same day.[16]

Hamilton was probably the wealthiest man to sign the Texas Declaration of Independence. In a report to the Senate in October, 1836, David G. Burnet said of him:

> The appointment of Messrs Childress and Hamilton was predicated on the high character and enthusiastic patriotism of the one and the financial experience, the unblemished integrity and the personal wealth and extensive pecuniary connections of the other.[17]

Becoming seriously ill at Saratoga Springs, New York, a noted health resort, and believing his death was near, Hamilton, a guest at the Pavillion Hotel, signed his will on August 16, 1843. It was witnessed by Dr. Thomas D. Mutter of Philadelphia, Lewis Webb of Richmond, Virginia, and Roscoe Cole of Pittsburgh, Virginia, all guests of the hotel.

IN THE NAME OF GOD AMEN:

I, Robert Hamilton of Red River, being of sound mind and memory, do make, constitute and ordain this my last Will and Testament in manner and form following (in premises) my will is that all my just debts be paid by my executors out of the first funds coming into their hands from my estate. It is my will that my plantations and negroes, and all and everything necessary to carrying on my planting business, as I leave it at my decease, should be kept together without being sold, for ten years from the first of January after my decease, and the net proceeds of said plantations arising from the sale of crops, shall be paid over after my debts are paid, to my legatees, viz: One third of my Brother John's Widow and children, one third to my Nephew William Frederick Hamilton, and one third to my Brother Patrick Hamilton.

Item,—I will and devise, give and bequeath unto my Brother John's widow and children the net one third of my estate, real, personal and perishable to them their heirs and assigns forever. Until the debts of the estate are paid, my executors will annually pay to said widow and children Eight Hundred Dollars, which amount or amounts, will with interest thereon be deducted from their proportion of my estate, devised to them herein; and should all of the children die without issue, their part of my estate will go to the other legatees, in the same proportion as the balance of my estate as herein willed.

Item,—I will and devise, give and bequeath unto my nephew William Frederick Hamilton, son of my brother James Hamilton, one third of all my estate, real, personal and perishable, to him, his heirs and assigns forever, he paying to his Nephew James Hamilton McIntosh, son of my niece Euphemia Alston McIntosh daughter of my brother James on his becoming twenty one years of age Ten Thousand Dollars on said James Hamilton McIntosh relinquishing on his Grand Fathers, my Brother James Estate as well as any claim he may have through his Mother Euphemia A. McIntosh, to any part of the Nine Oak Tract of land Granville County, North Carolina, but should he recover from his Grand Fathers, My Brother James Estate, as much as Fifteen Thousand Dollars, then my Nephew William F. Hamilton will only pay him Five Thousand Dollars, on his relinquishing the interest above stated.

Item,—I will and devise, give and bequeath unto my Brother Patrick Hamilton, one third of my estate, real, personal and perishable, to him, his heirs and assigns forever.

And lastly I nominate and appoint my Nephew William Frederick Hamilton, and James Hamilton, son of Patrick my Brother, Executors of this my Last Will and Testament, who are also my trustees in having the plantations carried on as my Will directs, the acting trustee or trustees to have five per centum on the net amount of the crop, and the acting executor or executors, shall have also upon the amount of the estate, independent of the crops on Final settlement Five Per Cent. My Executors not to be required to give security.

IN WITNESS WHEREOF, I hereunto affix my hand and seal this Sixteenth day of August, Anno Domino, One Thousand Eight Hundred and Forty Three.[18]

Hamilton died on the day he signed his will, but evidently the news of his death did not reach his heirs until late in the year 1845. The Probate Records of Red River County, Texas, show:

> December 30th, A. D., 1845. The Court met according to law. Same officers present as yesterday.
> William F. Hamilton this day presented a certain copy of the last will and testament of Robert Hamilton, Dec'd for Probate, the original being on file in Hempstead County, State of Arkansas.—
> Again :
> Petition of William F. Hamilton, represent and show that heretofore to wit: the ...... day of 1843 one Robert Hamilton departed this life, that on the same day he made and executed his last will and testament...[19]

Accompanying the will were depositions of Roscoe Cole, Dr. Thomas D. Mutter, and Lewis Webb. Cole testified:

> Roscoe Cole, late of Pittsburgh, Virginia, now of the City of New York, Gentlemen, aged sixty-three or thereabouts, a witness produced, who having been first duly sworn according to law deposeth and says I am one of the subscribing witnesses, I saw the testator Robert Hamilton sign and seal the said will, and I heard at the time acknowledge and declare it to be his last WILL AND TESTAMENT, in addition to which I asked him the question if he executed it as his Will and he declared that he did, this was at the Pavilion Hotel at Saratoga Springs in the State of New York in the Month of August 1843 at or about the time of the date of said Will. Dr. Mutter of Philadelphia and Lewis Webb of Richmond, Virginia was also present, and saw and heard the same as I did. Mr. Hamilton requested us all to subscribe our names as witnesses to the execution of the Will, which we did in his presence and in the presence of each other and to the best of my knowledge and belief he was at the time of executing said Will of sound and disposing mind and memory

and understanding. We was all on a visit to the Springs at that time for health or pleasure. We all boarded together at the Pavilion Hotel except Dr. Mutter, who frequently visited that establishment.

Samuel P. Carson in completing his will, which he signed January 1, 1838, wrote:

> In conclusion I nominate and appoint my friend Robert Hamilton, Esqr, Col. Thomas W. Williamson & Jesse H. Hall Executors of this my last will and Testament.

Carson died November 2, 1838, and Robert Hamilton, one of the administrators of his estate, having died in 1843, William F. Hamilton of New Orleans was granted letters of administration *De Bonis Non* of Carson's estate, February 5, 1846, by the Probate Court of Lafayette County, Arkansas.[20]

Believing that Hamilton died in Red River County, the Commission of Control for Texas Centennial Celebrations erected a monument in his memory in the old Rowland Cemetery, twenty-two miles northeast of Clarksville, on a site selected by Mr. Pat B. Clark of Clarksville.

The fact that Hamilton died at Saratoga Springs, New York, did not become known to the author until after the monument in Red River County had been erected. Attempts to locate his grave have been futile.[21]

Patrick Hamilton, brother of Robert Hamilton, was born in Burnside, Scotland, May 31, and died at his residence, "Burnside," Granville County, North Carolina, June 28, 1850. He was married December 14, 1812, to Mary Eaton Baskerville, who was born in Virginia, March 12, 1796, and died in North Carolina, January 5, 1837. Their children were William Baskerville, Mary Euphemia, Charles Eaton, Robert Alston, James, Isabella Alston, and Alexander Hamilton.

Isabella Alston Hamilton, daughter of Patrick Hamilton, was married to Henry Embra Coleman Baskerville of

154

Mecklenburg County, Virginia. Their children were Patrick Hamilton, Isabella Alston, Mary Eaton and Henry Embra Coleman Baskerville.

Patrick Hamilton Baskerville, son of Henry Embra Coleman Baskerville and grandson of Patrick Hamilton, was married to Elise Meade Skelton. Their children were John Skelton Baskerville, deceased, and Hamilton Meade Baskerville and who resides (in 1943) at 217 Nottingham Road, Richmond, Virginia.

155

BAILEY HARDEMAN
of
MATAGORDA MUNICIPALITY

*B*ailey Hardeman was born February 26, 1795,[1] in Davidson County, Tennessee, about three miles from Nashville. He was a son of Thomas and Mary (Perkins) Hardeman, whose children were Nicholas Perkins, Nancy, John, Constant, Eleazar, Julia Ann, Peter, Dorothy, Thomas Jones, Blackstone, Elizabeth, Bailey, Franklin and Pitt Hardeman.

Thomas Hardeman, the father, was born in Virginia in 1750. He was married first to Mary Perkins, daughter of Nicholas Perkins of Tuckahoe Creek, Henrico County, Virginia, and after her death in 1798 he was married to a widow, Mrs. Susan (Perkins) Marr, his former wife's sister. Thomas was a soldier in the Revolutionary War, being a member of Capt. William Bean's company of "Watauga Riflemen."[2] In 1782 he moved from Pittsylvania County, Virginia, to the Watauga settlement in East Tennessee.[3] Later he moved to Middle Tennessee and settled near Nashville in Davidson County. In 1796 he was elected a delegate from Davidson County to the first constitutional convention in Tennessee, which met at Knoxville.[4] Later he was elected to the State Senate. In 1803 he moved to Williamson County, Tennessee, and in 1816 to Howard County, Missouri. He returned to Williamson County in 1830 and is thought to have died there in 1833 or 1834.[5]

The brothers, Bailey and Thomas Jones Hardeman were lawyers, and both were veterans of the War of 1812. In the early 1820's Thomas Jones settled in Hardin County, Tennessee. In 1823 he helped to organize Hardeman County, created from Hardin County and named in his honor.[6] He was the first county clerk of the county. Bailey was an early resident of Hardeman County but most of his life in Tennessee was spent in Williamson County.[7]

Bailey Hardeman, during the War of 1812, in Capt. Ota Cantrell's company, Second Regiment of Mounted Gunmen (cannons), West Tennessee Volunteers, served as a private from September 24 to October 28, 1813, and as a first lieutenant from October 28 to December 10.[8] Accompanied by his brother, Thomas Jones Hardeman, he left Tennessee and arrived in Texas in the fall of 1835.[9]

The General Council of the Provisional Government on November 28, 1835, elected Hardeman, Jefferson George, and Hamilton L. Cook commissioners to organize the militia for Matagorda Municipality.[10]

Hardeman and Samuel Rhoads Fisher on February 1, 1836, were elected delegates to represent Matagorda Municipality in the Constitutional Convention.[11] Hardeman on March 1 was seated in the convention[12] and on the fol-

156

lowing day he, Edward Conrad, George C. Childress, James
Gaines, and Collin McKinney were named a committee to
draft a declaration of independence.[13] At the formation of
the ad interim government of the newly formed republic,
March 17, Hardeman was elected Secretary of the Treasury,[14]
a position he held until the permanent government was
formed. Secretary of State Samuel P. Carson being absent,
Hardeman became Acting Secretary of State. On April 1,
1836, he twice signed a document, once as Secretary of the
Treasury and again as Secretary of State.[15] With President
Burnet, Secretary of State James Collinsworth and Peter
W. Grayson, Attorney General, Hardeman signed an open
and a secret agreement with Santa Anna at Velasco, May
14, 1836.[16] On May 27 Lorenzo de Zavala and Hardeman
were appointed commissioners to accompany Santa Anna
to Vera Cruz to negotiate a treaty.[17] They planned to sail on
the *Invincible* on June 1, but for some reason the boat was
delayed. On June 3, at the insistence of indignant soldiers,
most of whom had but recently arrived from the United
States, Santa Anna was removed from the vessel and kept
a prisoner for several months.

157

Hardeman died of congestive fever at his home on Caney
Creek in Matagorda County, September 24, 1836. The *Telegraph and Texas Register* of September 27 announced his
death but did not give the date. His widow later filed a
claim for his salary as secretary of the treasury from March
17 to September 24.[18]

On February 28, 1837, Mrs. Rebecca Hardeman petitioned Silas Dinsmore, Chief Justice of Matagorda County:

> The Resident Rebecca Hardeman of the County of
> Matagorda in the best form she may comes and represents
> that on or about the twenty fourth day of September last
> her husband Bailey Hardeman late a resident of this county
> died at his residence leaving considerable property and ef-
> fect as such real, personal and mixed and died without a

will or Testament, and that your petitioner has children, the lawful issue of said husband deceased.[10]

Hardeman's remains were ordered exhumed by the Commission of Control for Texas Centennial Celebrations and, on August 29, 1936, reinterred in the State Cemetery at Austin with a monument placed at his new grave.[20] Likewise were the remains of his brother, Thomas Jones Hardeman[21] removed from a family cemetery in Bastrop County and reinterred June 18, 1937, in the State Cemetery.

When Hardeman County, Texas, was created February 21, 1858, it was named "in honor of the deceased brothers Bailey and Thomas J. Hardeman."[22]

Bailey Hardeman was married to Rebecca A. F. Wilson in Williamson, Tennessee, June 19, 1820.[23]

Mrs. Rebecca A. F. Hardeman, widow of Bailey Hardeman, on February 1, 1848, was married to William P. Hardeman, nephew of Bailey Hardeman.[24] Mrs. Hardeman died October 15, 1853.

158

AUGUSTINE BLACKBURN HARDIN
of
LIBERTY MUNICIPALITY

Augustine Blackburn Hardin was born in Franklin County, Georgia, July 18, 1797,[1] son of Swan and Jerusha (Blackburn) Hardin, who moved from Maury County, Tennessee in 1807. In April, 1824, Augustine B. Hardin was appointed constable of Maury County, Tennessee.[2]

Members of the Hardin family came to Texas and settled on the Trinity River in what is now Liberty County. The brothers Benjamin Watson, Augustine B., William, Franklin, and Milton A. Hardin became prominent in the affairs of Texas and, in consequence, when Hardin County was created January 22, 1858, it was named "in honor of the Hardins of Liberty."[3]

Augustine B. Hardin arrived in Texas in 1825.[4] On January 16, 1827, he enlisted in Capt. Hugh B. Johnston's volunteer company.[5] Although he was not a member of the First and Second Conventions of Texas,[6] the First Convention at San Felipe de Austin, on October 5, 1832, appointed Hardin a member of the sub-committee of Safety and Vigilance for the District of Liberty.[7]

A meeting was held in the town of Liberty, August 30, 1835, at which Hardin was elected chairman and Daniel P. Coit, secretary. Edward Tanner, P. J. Menard, and H. W. Farley were appointed members of a committee to arrange for an election to be held to select delegates to the Consultation to be held at San Felipe. Those chosen at the election to represent Liberty Municipality were Hardin, George M. Patrick, William P. Harris, Henry Millard, and James B. Woods.[8]

Approximately 90 votes were cast in the election held in the Municipality of Liberty February 1, 1836, to select three delegates to the Constitutional Convention.

At Liberty, William Hardin was elected president, Hugh B. Johnston, and B. M. Sinks, tellers, and George W. Miles, secretary. A. B. Hardin led the field with 56 votes; M. B. Menard received 42; James B. Wood, 40; E. T. Branch, 19; Rogers, 11; and Cole, 4.

H. W. Farley and Peter J. Menard were the judges at the election held at Peter J. Menard's home. There, M. B. Menard received 14 votes; Hardin, 14; Woods, 12; and Reason Green, 1.

At the home of William Duncan, Precinct of Old River, Charles C. P. Welch and Edward McFerrow were the judges. Samuel Rogers led the field with 10 votes; Bryan received 6; Woods, 5; Menard, 3; and Cole, 1.

Joseph E. Pulsifer, Hezekiah Williams, and James Drake were the judges, and Thomas E. Shell and Hutson B. Little-field were the secretaries at the home of John C. Read. At this box Joseph Bryan received 54 votes; James Cole, 53; and Samuel Rogers, 52.

G. S. Thomas was the judge and Franklin Hardin and William A. Smith the clerks at Anahuac. There Menard led with 17 votes; Hardin received 16; Woods, 16; and Branch, 2.

Following are the total number of votes shown by the election returns as having been cast in the municipality for each candidate: A. B. Hardin, 89; M. B. Menard, 76; James B. Woods, 73; Joseph Bryan, 73; Samuel Rogers, 73; James Cole, 73; Edward T. Branch, 21; and Reason Green, 1. Hardin and Menard were declared elected. Since the next three highest candidates had received the same number of votes a run-off election was held on February 20, at which time Mr. Woods received all of the votes, 81, and was declared elected.[9] Hardin was seated at the Convention March 3.[10]

In returning to their homes after the hasty adjournment of the convention, Col. William Fairfax Gray, Hardin and M. B. Menard spent the night of March 17 at the log house of James Whitesides, which stood on the site of the present town of Independence.

Colonel Gray, returning to his home in the United States on April 20, saw Hardin who was also headed for the United States. Colonel Gray wrote in his diary:

> Left Williams' at 7 o'clock; $1. As we approached the Neches, we found there was great uncertainty about crossing the river. The boats were said to have been taken from all the ferries and carried down to the lower bluff. Thither we bent our way, passing great numbers of fugitives, men, women, and children, black and white, with all the accustomed marks of dismay. Arrived about noon at the lower bluff.

160

The report of the Mexicans being on Cow Creek is not credited here. It is believed to have been circulated by Rains, McLaughlin, etc. There are many families here waiting to be ferried across the bay, a distance of seven or eight miles, and put on the United States shore. There are at least 1,000 fugitives here, among them Menifee, A. B. Hardin, Smith [Smyth] John Fisher, all members of the convention.[11]

Hardin died in Liberty County, July 22, 1871.[12] In 1936 the Commission of Control for Texas Centennial Celebrations erected monuments at the unmarked graves of Hardin and his brother William in the Hardin family cemetery near Liberty.

The late Gus Hardin of Liberty told the author that A. B. Hardin, the signer of the Texas Declaration of Independence, and his first wife had a son, A. B. Hardin, Jr. He stated that a separation took place between the Hardins and that when Hardin came to Texas, his wife and child did not accompany him. Later Mrs. Hardin and the son, A. B. Hardin, Jr., came to Texas. They did not become reconciled, but Hardin agreed to raise his son. Some of the relatives of A. B. Hardin, the signer, contend that Hardin married but one time and that he had no son by the name of Augustine Blackburn, Jr.

It is certain, one "A. B. Hardin, Jr., emigrated to the Republic of Texas prior to the 5th day of December, 1839, and was at that time a single man over seventeen years of age."[13] On December 5, 1839, A. B. Hardin, Jr., was issued Conditional Headright Certificate 119 for 320 acres of land by the Liberty County Board of Land Commissioners.[14] On March 30, 1859, the certificate, by a decision rendered by the District Court of the Fifteenth Judicial District, held in Liberty County, was declared unconditional. A. B. Hardin, Jr., was at that time living in Leon County.[15]

Frank A. Hardin of Oakwood, Texas, a grandson of Augustine Blackburn Hardin, Jr., wrote to the author that he had heard that the first wife of A. B. Hardin, Sr., was married in Texas to a Mr. Van McAnalty. According to Frank A. Hardin, his grandfather, Augustine B. Hardin, Jr., was twice married. His first wife was Mary Garner. Two children of this union were A. B. Hardin and Swan Hardin. Swan Hardin was married to Sallie Titley. Frank A. Hardin is a child of this union. His surviving children are George Cecil Hardin, Oakwood; Mrs. O. L. Gragg, Palestine; and R. W. Hardin, Ft. Worth.

Genealogical information regarding the children of Augustine B. Hardin, the signer of the Texas Declaration of Independence, and his wife, Mariah Hardin, is found in the records of a lawsuit tried in the 75th District Court of Liberty County, Cause No. 7653. On March 22, 1893, W. F. Hardin and J. D. Lum deposed:

> ...that they were well acquainted with the said A. B. Hardin in the County of Liberty during his lifetime. That the said A. B. Hardin died in Liberty County, in 1871; that we were not acquainted with Mariah Hardin but from common report the said Mariah Hardin died about the year 1841. That said A. B. Hardin and Mariah Hardin had born to them as the issue of their marriage the following children: (1) S. A. Hardin, (2) Swan Hardin, (3) Sarah H. Hardin, who married Abner McMurtry, (4) Jerusha Hardin who married Stephen Green, (5) Cornelia Hardin who married Jeremiah Van Deventer who departed this life in 1866 then the said Cornelia married C. C. Neil.

(1) Sanders A. Hardin was married to Hannah Jane Rogers, daughter of James Rogers. Mrs. Hardin was born January 11, 1835, and died March 31, 1892. She is buried in a marked grave in the cemetery at Liberty. Her husband was buried beside her at his death, but the date of his birth and death are no longer legible on the modest marker that stands at his grave.

A. B. Hardin

Some of the children of Sanders A. Hardin were R. Blackburn Hardin; Minnie Hardin, who married William Nolan; Lillie Hardin, who married J. B. Jones; and Gus Hardin.

(2) Swan Hardin died at some time after October 24, 1901. A son of his, William F. Hardin, died April 5, 1908. A daughter, Helen B., was married to George W. Eaton. Mrs. Eaton died in Ft. Worth, March 5, 1914.

(3) Sarah H. Hardin was married to Abner McMurtry. Their children were Liscum, Abner Jr., Augustine, Cornelia and Sallie McMurtry.

(4) Jerusha Hardin was married to Stephen Green. Their children were W. B. Green, Jeff and Reasie Green.

(5) Cornelia Hardin was married to Jeremiah Van Deventer. Their children, all deceased, were Quitman, Sanders and Joseph Van Deventer. Jeremiah Van Deventer died in 1866, and later his widow was married to Charles D. McNeil. Children of this union, now all deceased, were Kolita McNeil, who married Frank J. Polka, and Dee McNeil. Mrs. Cornelia McNeil died in 1883.

163

A. B. Hardin, the signer of the Declaration of Independence, served in the volunteer company of his brother, Capt. Franklin Hardin, from July 7 to October 7, 1836.[16] It appears that he was married three times. His widow, Mrs. Martha Jane Hardin was alive as late as February 20, 1886. Someone in filling in the blanks in a printed application form for a Veterans Donation of 1280 acres of land, dated December 9, 1885, stated that Martha Jane Harden [sic] was the widow of A. B. Hardin, who had served in the company of F. Hardin from July 7 to October 7, 1836. Mrs. Hardin evidently could not write, since she signed the application with a mark. Her petition was granted and on February 20, 1886, Veterans Donation Certificate 1223 for 1280 acres of land was issued to Martha Jane Hardin, who was at that time residing in Anderson County. On December 9, 1885, Mrs. Hardin had given a power of attorney to

J. H. Stewart and A. E. Habicht to obtain the certificate and sell it for her. The certificate was sold for six hundred dollars on February 20, 1886, to Hyman and Blum of New York.[17]

A. B. Hardin

SAMUEL HOUSTON
of
REPRESENTING REFUGIO MUNICIPALITY

Samuel Houston, fifth son of Samuel and Elizabeth (Paxton) Houston, was born March 2, 1793, at Rockbridge, near Lexington, Rockbridge County, Virginia. In the spring of 1807 his widowed mother moved to Blount County, Tennessee, and settled on a tract of land that had belonged to her husband. Young Sam, not studious and dissatisfied with school, left home and joined a band of Cherokees, camped not far away. For three years, he spent most of his time with the Indians, returning home only when in need of clothing. He read much during his idle time, and in 1812 left the Indian camp to conduct a private school a few miles from the town of Marysville.

On March 24, 1813,[1] during the War of 1812, Houston, at Marysville, enlisted as a private in the 39th Infantry of the United States Army. Shortly afterwards he was made a sergeant. He became an ensign on July 29, 1813, and a third lieutenant on December 31, 1813. On March 28, 1814, he was wounded at the Battle of Tohopeka. His gallantry at this battle won the admiration of Maj. Gen. Andrew Jackson. He was promoted to second lieutenant on May 20, 1814, and was transferred to the Seventh Infantry May

164

17, 1815. He was assigned to the adjutant-general's office at Nashville January 1, 1817, and became a first lieutenant May 1, 1817. In November he was sent as a sub-agent to the Cherokees.[2] He resigned his commission March 1, 1818.

In June, 1819, Houston began to read law in the office of James Trimble at Nashville. Six months later, having been admitted to the bar, he opened a law office at Lebanon, Tennessee.[3] While thus engaged he was appointed adjutant-general of the Tennessee Militia, with the rank of colonel. In the same year he was elected prosecuting attorney for the Davidson District and moved to Nashville.[4] He served in this capacity for about a year and then resigned. In 1821 the field officers of the State Militia elected him major general. In 1822 and again in 1825 he was elected to the United States House of Representatives, and served from March 4, 1823, to March 3, 1827.[5] He was elected governor of Tennessee in 1827 and was inaugurated on October 1.[6]

On January 22, 1829, Houston was married to Eliza H. Allen, daughter of Col. and Mrs. John Allen of Gallatin, Tennessee.[7] The marriage proved unfortunate, and, on April 16, 1829, Houston resigned the governorship and on the 23rd he left by steamer for Little Rock, Arkansas. Continuing his journey, he reached Cantonment Gibson where the tribe of Cherokees he had formerly lived with were encamped. Ooloo-te-ka, or John Jolly, as he was known to the whites, principal chief of the tribe, welcomed his return, and on October 21, 1829, Houston became an official member of the tribe.[8]

On January 13, 1830, Houston, dressed as an Indian, reached Washington, D. C. The purpose of his visit was to obtain a contract with the United States government to supply rations to Indians. He was unsuccessful, however, and soon returned to his home. In December, 1831, he was again in Washington with a delegation of Indians. On March 31, 1832, William Stanbery, a member of Congress from Ohio, from the floor of the House accused President Jackson of attempting fraudulently to award the ration contract to Houston. Shortly afterward Houston met Stanbery on a street and struck him with his walking cane. For this, after a trial in Congress in which he was found guilty, Houston was reprimanded by Speaker Andrew Stevenson, May 14. Houston and John H. Watson were then investigated by a committee of the House on the ration charge and acquitted.

The following was extracted from a letter written at New Orleans, June 2, 1832, by John A. Wharton to Sam Houston, Washington, D. C.:

> I gave Dr. Branch T. Archer of Virginia a letter of introduction to you; Dr. Archer has been in Texas for upwards of twelve months, is intimately acquainted with matters and things there, and is in the confidence of all of their leading men. He is of the opinion that there will be some fighting there next fall, and that a fine country will be gained without much bloodshed, he is very desirous that you should go there, and believes that you can be of more service than any other man; he left for Virginia today, and should you fall in with him, I expect that he will put you in the notion of going. Texas does undoubtedly present a fine field for fame, enterprise, and usefulness, and whenever they are ready for action, I will be with them. I expect to visit my Brother [William H. Wharton] in August, and as matters are getting worse there every day I should like to be provided with a passport, if you will procure one for me. I will be very thankful, and should it ever lay in my power to confer a favour on you, I will not forget your kindness.[9]

166

Leaving the Cherokee tribe, Houston crossed Red River at Fort Towson into Texas, December 2, 1832.[10] He was on an official trip for President Andrew Jackson to report on the condition of Indians at San Antonio. He passed through Nacogdoches both on his way to and from San Antonio, and while in Texas he determined to return and make it his future home. According to the Spanish Archives, on January 9, 1833, Houston received title to one league of land in Austin's Third Colony, stating in his petition, "my status is that of a married man." On January 13, 1833, at Natchitoches, Louisiana, Houston wrote to President Jackson:

Having been so far as Bexar, in the province of Texas, where I had an interview with the Comanche Indians, I am in possession of some information which will doubtless be interesting to you, and may be calculated to forward your views, if you should entertain any, touching the acquisition of Texas by the Government of the United States. That such a measure is desired by nineteen-twentieths of the population of the province, I can not doubt. They are now without laws to govern or protect them. Mexico is involved in civil war. The Federal Constitution has never been in operation. The Government is essentially despotic, and must be so for years to come. The rules have not honesty, and the people have not intelligence. The people of Texas are determined to form a State Government, and separate from Coahuila, and unless Mexico is soon restored to order, and the Constitution revived and re-enacted, the Province of Texas will remain separate from the Confederacy of Mexico.

She has already beaten and repelled all the troops of Mexico from her soil, nor will she permit them to return; she can defend herself against the whole power of Mexico, for really Mexico is powerless and penniless to all intents and purposes. Her want of money taken in connection with the course Texas *must and will adopt*, will render a transfer of Texas to some power inevitable, and if the United States does not press for it, England will, most assuredly, obtain it by some means. Now is a very important crisis for Texas. As relates to her future prosperity and safety, as well as the relations which it is to bear to the United States, it is now in the most favorable attitude, perhaps, that it can be, obtain it on fair terms. England is pressing her suit for it, but its citizens will resist, if any transfer should be made of them to any power but the United States.

167

I have travelled nearly five hundred miles across Texas, and am now enabled to judge pretty correctly of the soil and resources of the country, and I have no hesitancy in pronouncing it the finest country, for its extent, upon the globe; for the greater portion of it is richer and more healthy than West Tennessee. There can be no doubt that the country east of the river Grand, of the North, would sustain a population of ten millions of souls.

My opinion is that Texas, by her members in Convention, will by 1st of April, declare all that country as Texas proper, and form a State Constitution. I expect to be present at the Convention, and will appraise you of the course adopted, as soon as its members have taken a final action. It is probable that I may make Texas my abiding-place. In adopting this course *I will never forget* the country of my birth. I will notify from this point the Commissioners of the Indians at Fort Gibson of my success, which will reach you through the War Department.

I have, with much pride and expressible satisfaction, seen your message and proclamation,—touching the nullifiers of the South, and their "peaceable remedies." God grant that you may save the Union! It does seem to me that it is reserved for you, and you alone, to render to millions so great a blessing. I hear all voices commend your course, even in Texas; where is felt the liveliest interest for the preservation of the Republic. Permit me to tender you my sincere thanks, felicitations, and most earnest solicitude for your health and happiness, and your future glory, connected with the prosperity of the Union.[12]

Returning to Nacogdoches from San Antonio he found that he had been elected a delegate from the Nacogdoches Municipality to the Second Convention of Texas, which opened at San Felipe de Austin, April 1, 1833.[13] Reporting to Jackson in Washington, early in 1833, he then returned to Texas.

At a mass meeting held in Nacogdoches, September 14, 1835, called to discuss the advisability of holding a convention or consultation, John K. Allen's motion to elect Houston chairman carried. When the Consultation was called, Houston was elected a delegate.[14] On November 12, 1835, the General Council of the Provisional Government of Texas on motion of Merriwether W. Smith elected Houston major general of the Texas Army.[15]

General Houston left Washington-on-the-Brazos on January 8, 1836, and arrived at Goliad on the 14th. Here and at Refugio, on the 20th, he conferred with the officers relative to the proposed expedition to Matamoros. He was back in Washington on January 30.[16]

On February 1, 1836, when delegates were elected to the Constitutional Convention, Houston's popularity was at low ebb. In his home municipality, Nacogdoches, he was unmercifully defeated, receiving but 55 votes out of about 610. In the town of Nacogdoches, he received but three votes.[16] At Refugio, someone, probably James Power, influenced the voters to elect Houston a delegate from the thinly populated municipality. Were it not for this, Houston's subsequent career might have been materially different from the brilliant one now recorded.

When Houston and Power went to the Convention, they carried with them the certificate of their election:

> At an election held in the Town of Refugio and Municipality of the same name for the purpose of Electing two Delegates to represent this municipality in a convention to be held in Washington on the first day of March next in accordance with a Decree of the General Council passed Dec. 1835 General Samuel Houston Rec'd 44 votes, James Power Rec'd 42 votes and Martin Lawlor Rec'd 26 votes.
>
> We therefore declare General Saml. Houston and James Power to be duly Elected Delegates to the aforenamed convention.
>
> Refugio, Feb 1, 1836
> Hugh McDonald Fraser   Ira Westover, Presiding Judge
> L. Ayers, Secretary[18]

One hundred and seventy-seven soldiers stationed at Refugio, who were not permitted by the citizens to vote in the election, held an election of their own and chose two of their members, David Thomas and Edward Conrad, to represent the army. Thus General Houston was rejected both by his neighbors in Nacogdoches and his soldiers at Refugio.[19]

On February 23, 1836, General Houston and John Forbes signed a treaty with the Cherokees and associated tribes at Bowl's village. The treaty, however, was rejected by the Senate of the Congress of the Republic of Texas, December 16, 1837.[20]

Houston arrived at Washington February 29. From the opening of the Convention until he left to rejoin the army, he was one of the dominating figures. Near the close of the afternoon session of March 4, James Collinsworth's motion that Houston be made commander-in-chief of the Texas Army carried. Robert Potter was the only member who spoke in opposition.[21] On March 6 Colonel Gray wrote in his diary:

> A great many persons are starting and preparing to start to the seat of war. In the afternoon Houston, left accompanied by his staff, Capt. [William G.] Cooke, Capt. [James] Tarleton, etc.[22]

Houston served as major general from November 11, 1835, to October 22, 1836. During this time he received a salary of two hundred dollars a month.[23] He commanded the army at San Jacinto and was badly wounded in the left ankle during the engagement of April 21. On May 11 aboard the schooner *Flora*, Houston left Galveston for New Orleans to have his wounds treated. Arriving at New Orleans on the 22nd, he stayed at William Christy's. This wound never completely healed. On June 4, 1860, Drs. M. A. Taylor and E. D. Renfro of Austin examined the wound. "It is our opinion," they reported, "after careful examination, that said wound is a bodily injury for life, and beyond the power of medical aid to produce a permanent cure which disqualified him from bodily labor."[24] In June, 1836, with William G. Cooke, Houston left New Orleans, passing through Natchitoches,[25] on his way to San Augustine, where he visited Col. Philip Sublet.

On September 5, 1836, Houston was elected president of the Republic of Texas. He was inaugurated at Columbia, October 3. In accordance with the provisions of the Constitution, which forbade a president to succeed himself, he served but one term. Houston, then, in order to help shape the destinies of the new republic, was elected from San Augustine County to the House of Representatives of the Fourth[26] and Fifth[27] Congresses, November 11, 1839, to February 5, 1841.

In a lengthy speech delivered December 22, 1839, in the House of Representatives of the Fourth Congress, General Houston was caustic in his criticism of the Constitutional Convention. Among other things he said:

171

> Under this situation of affairs, the convention assembled; and it was not strange that apprehension and caution should have been the order of the day. It is recollected by more than one member upon this floor, that when the convention was called to order, that the presiding officer, on putting his hand into his pocket for a paper, drew forth a horseman's pistol, and laid it upon the speaker's table. He mentioned this anecdote to show the feeling which prevailed among the members. But they had assembled for the purpose of forming and organizing a government.—The people expected it of them, and they were compelled to stay until they had accomplished it. They could not go home and say to the people, we cannot adopt a form of government—the country already filled with anarchy, would have been ruined by such a course. But for all the necessity for grave deliberation, they remained in session but seventeen

days; they assembled on the 1st, and on the 17th of March they left Washington: how did they leave? It had been frequently described, and he would not repeat it here. But one thing he would say, that the constitution submitted to the people was not the one adopted by the convention. The constitution was not engrossed previous to the adjournment, but all the papers were thrown into a box and carried by the clerks to Groce's Retreat where they attempted to make out a correct copy of the Constitution. When a question arose as to what composed a part of the Constitution, the Clerks took a vote among themselves, and a majority either adopted or rejected it. In this way articles which had been rejected by the Convention had been adopted by the Clerks, and incorporated into the body of the Constitution. He did not mention this as a censure upon the Clerks, he believed they had done the best they could under the circumstances, for the country. But to explain things which would be inexplicable, if found in a constitution adopted in an ordinary way by a grave deliberate assembly. This constitution was submitted to the people, and the necessity of having some form of government, induced them to ratify it, and it became the organic law of the land. But many of the members of the Convention whose name was attached to that instrument had never seen it. When he saw what purported to be the Constitution, six months after the Convention, he was very much astonished to find his name attached to it. He had never placed it there himself, and it was a base forgery. He would have solemnly protest in the face of Heaven, that the first time he had ever seen it, his name was attached to it. He did not know whether it had been placed there by some kind friend, to make the whole number complete, or by some one who wished to mortify him, by appending his name to so imperfect an instrument.[28]

On September 6, 1841, Houston was again elected president of the Republic. He was succeeded December 9, 1844, by Anson Jones.

Houston was elected a delegate from Montgomery County to the Annexation Convention held at Austin, from July 4 to August 27, 1845. He did not attend, however, for at the time it met, he was in the United States hastening to the death-bed of his friend, Gen. Andrew Jackson.

On February 21, 1846, the Legislature elected Houston and Thomas Jefferson Rusk to the United States Senate. Rusk drew the longer term. Houston served in the Twenty-Ninth, Thirtieth, and Thirty-First Congresses, serving from February 21, 1846, to March 3, 1859.[29]

Running for governor on a platform that closely resembled Know-Nothingism, Houston was defeated by Hardin R. Runnels, August 1, 1857. On August 1, 1859, however, he defeated Runnels. He was inaugurated December 21, 1859. As governor, no less than as senator, Houston voiced his opposition to secession. On September 22, 1860, addressing a mass meeting at Austin, he denounced disunionists as reckless and mischievous agitators.[30] By refusing to subscribe to the Confederacy, he removed himself from office on March 16, 1861.

173

Houston retired to Huntsville and died July 26, 1863. Some years later the State of Texas erected a $10,000 monument at his grave in Oakwood Cemetery, Huntsville.

When, in 1836, J. K. and A. C. Allen were attempting to induce Congress to move the capital of the Republic to their new town on the Buffalo Bayou, they named the town Houston. The act of Congress of June 12, 1837, by which Houston County was created, does not state for whom it was named.[31] Thrall, in 1879, said it was named for Gen. Sam Houston.[32]

When Houston, in conformity to the Mexican colonization laws, became a member of the Roman Catholic Church, at Nacogdoches, he took, in accordance to Roman Catholic custom, a saint's name, Pablo or Paul, and thus became Paul Sam Houston.[33] On January 19, 1854, he joined the Baptist Church at Independence and was baptized by Dr. Rufus C. Burleson.[34]

Houston had several homes, from time to time, in Texas. In an affidavit made June 14, 1849, regarding his places of residence he said "that at first he became domiciled in Nacogdoches in Feby. 1833 and that he continued to claim his domiciliation and residence in Nacogdoches and no other place up to the year 1839."[35] In 1839 he moved to San Augustine. After the adjournment of Congress he removed to Grand Cane, then in Liberty County but now in Chambers County.[36] There he lived until as late as March 3, 1845.[37] Shortly after his election to the United States Senate he moved to a place fourteen miles south of Huntsville, at a place he named "Raven Hill." When seated in the Twenty-Ninth Congress, on March 30, 1846, he gave Raven Hill as his home. On March 4, 1847, when seated in the Thirtieth Congress, he again gave Raven Hill as his place of residence. In 1853 he removed to Independence in Washington County.[38] While serving in the Thirty-First Congress, 1853 to 1859, his home was in Huntsville, Walker County. In 1860 Houston built a summer home on Galveston Bay in what is now Chambers County. There he lived for a time in 1861 and 1862. When he moved to Austin in 1859, he sold his home in Huntsville. It was to a rented house in the northeast part of Huntsville that Houston retired and died.

Houston received his share of land grants from Texas. On June 30, 1838, he received Bounty Certificate 3894 for 1,280 acres of land for having served in the army from November 11, 1835, to October 20, 1836,[39] and on July 2, 640 acres for having participated in the Battle of San Jacinto.[40] Pursuant to an act of the Legislature, approved June 5, 1860, he was issued Headright Certificate 29/300 for one league of land for having been permanently wounded at San Jacinto.[41] In addition Houston made extensive land purchases.

174

General Houston was made a member of Cumberland Lodge No. 8, Ancient Free and Accepted Masons, of Nashville, Tennessee, on July 22, 1817.[42] On November 13, 1837, he became a member of Holland Lodge No. 36 (now No. 1), Houston.[43]

On May 9, 1840, at the home of her parents, Temple and Nancy Lea, in Mobile, Alabama, Houston was married to Margaret Moffette Lea, who was born in Perry County, Alabama, April 11, 1819. Of Mrs. Houston, Dr. William Carey Crane wrote:

> She was a thorough student of the Bible, and was devoutedly attached to the principles of practical Christianity. The writer first met her in Marion, Alabama in 1839, at a time when she was regarded as the most attractive and fascinating young lady in that part of Alabama. She became a member of Siloam Baptist Church, Marion, and was baptized by Rev. Peter Crawford, then pastor of that church.
>
> On a visit to Mobile she first met Gen. Houston. He was at that time given to occasional excesses in drinking, by which he had acquired the name among the Indians of "Big Drunk." His romantic history, his brilliant career as the savior of Texas, his commanding figure, winning manners, and vivacious conversation, won the heart of the young Alabamian.
>
> She was asked by the writer why she ran the risk of unhappiness and misfortune by consenting to link her destinies with, those of Gen. Houston, at a time when he gave way to such excesses? She replied, that "not only had he won her heart, but she had conceived the idea that she could be the means of reforming him, and she meant to devote herself to the work."
>
> According to her wishes, and to the astonishment of her friends, she was married to Gen. Sam Houston at Marion, Alabama, May 9th, 1840.
>
> It was not long before her influence induced him to give up strong drink, to which he never returned.[44]

Shortly after the death of her husband, Mrs. Houston took her children to Independence, where Baylor University was then located. She died there on December 3, 1867. She probably would have preferred to have been buried beside her husband in Huntsville, but having died of yellow fever her remains could not be transported. A simple marker stands at her grave in Independence, just across the road from the old Baptist Church. In 1936 the Commission of Control for Texas Centennial Celebrations appropriated $1,000 to be used in burying Mrs. Houston's remains besides those of her husband. This met with the entire approval of Gen. Andrew Jackson Houston, her only surviving child, and with most of her grandchildren. Since, however, it was opposed by other grandchildren, the appropriation was cancelled.

By his first wife, Eliza H. Allen, Houston had no children. Margaret Lea bore him eight children, all of whom are now deceased: Sam Houston, Jr., who married Lucy Anderson; Nancy Elizabeth, who married J. C. S. Morrow; Margaret Lea, who married Weston L. Williams; Mary Willie, who married J. S. Morrow, first cousin of J. C. S. Morrow; Antoinette Power, who married Major W. S. L. Bringhurst; Andrew Jackson, who married Carrie Glen, and after her death, Elizabeth Hart Good; William Rogers, who never married; and Temple Lea Houston, who married Laura Cross.

Surviving grandchildren of General Houston in 1942 were: Mrs. Jennie Bell Decker, 3208-1/2 Smith; Mrs. Madge W. Hearne, 2112 Dryden; Mrs. Robert A. John, 2120 LaBranch; Franklin W. Williams, 1117 Milford; and James Royston Williams, all of Houston; Miss Ariadne Houston and Miss Marguerite Houston, both of LaPorte; Temple Houston Morrow, of 1003 South Rosemont, Dallas; Mrs. David A. Paulus, of Moresville; Mrs. Maude Louise Heitchew and Mrs. R. E. McDonald, of Abilene; Sam Houston

III, of Claremore, Oklahoma; Richard Coldon Houston, of Woodward, Oklahoma; Mrs. William C. Henderson, of Tulsa, Oklahoma; Mrs. Gail H. Loe, 149 Princeton Drive, Toledo, Ohio; Mrs. C. R. Whittemore, of Pittsburgh, Pennsylvania; and Mrs. Margaret Bell Houston, 404 Riverside Drive, New York.

WILLIAM DEMETRIS LACEY[1]
of
COLORADO MUNICIPALITY

William Demetris Lacey was born in Virginia in 1808[2] but was raised in Paducah, Kentucky. He came to Texas in 1831[3] from Tennessee and established a tan yard and saddle shop in what is now Colorado County, near the site of the present Columbus.[4]

Lacey was one of the delegates from the District of Alfred to the First Convention of Texas, which convened at San Felipe de Austin, October 1, 1832.[5] On January 9, 1836, William Menefee was elected first judge and Lacey second judge of the Municipality of Colorado by the General Council of the Provisional Government of Texas.[6]

Approximately 112 votes were cast in the election held at two voting places in the Municipality of Colorado, February 1, 1836, to elect two delegates to the Constitutional

Convention. At one box the election commissioners were Robert Brotherton, William D. Lacey and Eli Mercer. M. D. Ramsey, the Alcalde, seems to have been in charge. William D. Lacey received 105 votes; William Menefee, 60; and James Wright, 50.

One vote was cast for Francis Keller at the home of Pumphrey Burnett. Menefee and Lacey each received 5 votes there.

Total votes received by the candidates were Lacey, 110; Menefee, 65; Wright, 50; and Francis Keller 1.[7] Lacey was seated at the Convention on March 1.[8]

Leaving the Convention, Lacey escorted his family and other refugees to Galveston Island. On April 18 he joined the army and was stationed at Galveston under Col. James Morgan until May 12. On July 8 he joined Capt. George Sutherland's company and served in it until September 17.[9]

Upon retiring from the army, Lacey settled on Tres Palacios River in Matagorda County. In May, 1848, with his family he moved to Paducah, Kentucky, where he died on October 14, 1848. Mrs. Lacey returned to Texas with her children and made Matagorda County her home until her death.

In September, 1929, the author visited at Palacios, Texas, Mrs. S. J. Pybus, one of Lacey's daughters. She was so young when her father died that she remembered very little about him. She had the date of his death, but she did not know where he was buried.

Lacey's wife was thrice married. Born Sarah Ann Bright, daughter of David Bright, a member of one of Austin's "Old Three Hundred," she was first married to a Mr. Hunter. Lavina Hunter was a daughter of this union. After the death of her husband, Mrs. Hunter was married to John McCrosky, also one of Austin's first colonists. By this marriage there was born one child, John McCrosky, Jr. After the death of her husband, Mrs. McCrosky in 1832 was married to Lacey. Mrs. Lacey was alive as late as June 18, 1872.[10]

Children of Mr. and Mrs. Lacey were Nannie, Sally Jane, Fanny and Richard Lacey.

Nannie Lacey was married to Jonathan Edward Pierce, who came to Texas from Rhode Island in the early part of 1850. Surviving children of this union in 1942 were: Abel Pierce of Blessing, Texas, and Grace Pierce Heffelfinger of Minneapolis, Minnesota.

Fanny Lacey was married to Abel Head Pierce, generally called "Shanghai Pierce," brother of Jonathan Edward Pierce, who married Nannie Lacey. To this union was born only one child who lived, Mamie, who married Henry Malcom Withers of Kansas City. The surviving children of this union in 1941 were Lacy Armour and Mary Runnels of Chicago, and Pierce Withers who was residing at his grandfather's old ranch headquarters home at Pierce, Texas.

179

ALBERT HAMILTON LATIMER
of
PECAN POINT AND VICINITY

Albert Hamilton Latimer, son of James and Jane (Hamilton) Latimer, was born in 1800[1] in Huntingdon, Carroll County, Tennessee, and was reared and educated there. He was admitted to the bar in 1831.

Members of the Latimer family with some of their relatives and friends in Tennessee decided to emigrate to Texas. Those who were to make the trip assembled at the plantation home of James Latimer. Included in the group were eleven of the fifteen children of James Latimer, their wives, husbands and children. They had all gathered around the house, each family with all their possessions loaded on ox-wagons. There were about fifty slaves, most of whom belonged to James Latimer. The calvacades started in April, 1833. They crossed the Mississippi at Chicksaw Bluff, where the City of Memphis, now stands. The Arkansas was crossed at Little Rock. They crossed Red River at Mill Creek Ferry.[2]

The Latimers arrived in what later proved to be Texas, December 3, 1833,[3] and settled in an area known as "Pecan Point," claimed until 1841 by the United States as a part of Arkansas and by the Republic of Mexico as a part of the State of Coahuila and Texas. After March 2, 1836, it was claimed by the Republic of Texas. There is ample evidence that most of the settlers of the area, who had arrived prior to the year 1835, considered themselves citizens of Miller County, Arkansas. In about 1834 James Latimer, for instance, was elected to the legislature of Arkansas Territory.[4]

180

The General Council of the Provisional Government, on December 12, 1835, adopted a resolution calling for an election to be held throughout Texas on February 1, 1836, to select delegates to a convention to be held in Washington beginning March 1. After designating the number of delegates from each of the established municipalities, the resolution ended by stating that the "citizens of Pecan Point" would be permitted to send two delegates.[5] The printed proceedings of the Council do not show that the law was revised to allow additional representatives from Pecan Point, but, according to Latimer, the number was first increased to five and later to six.

Although the elections were ordered to be held on February 1 the election judges of "Red River Municipality" met at the home of Collin McKinney January 27, and certified that McKinney, Robert Hamilton, Samuel P. Carson, Richard Ellis and James H. Johnson had been elected "to the General Convention to be held at Washington in the Republic of Texas on the first day of March next for the purpose of forming a Constitution."[6]

Latimer went to Washington, appeared before the committee on elections, and asked to be seated as a delegate from Pecan Point, claiming the area was large enough to justify six delegates. He did not state that he had been elected as a delegate. Upon the recommendation of the Election Committee, Stephen H. Everitt, Robert M. Coleman and Charles B. Stewart, Latimer was seated.[7] It so happened that Johnson did not attend the Convention, Had he done so Pecan Point would have been represented by six delegates instead of two, as originally contemplated.

At the afternoon session of March 2, "Mr. A. H. Latimer, from the Municipality of Pecan Point and vicinity, appeared, produced his credentials, and took his seat"[8] On March 10, "Mr. Samuel P. Carson, from Red River appeared, produced his credentials and took his seat, and asked and obtained leave to sign the declaration of Independence."[9]

There was at no time a municipality of Pecan Point or Red River. The boundaries of Red River County were fixed by the Congress of the Republic December 18, 1837,[10] but the United States claimed the territory as a part of Miller County, Arkansas, until 1841, when an international survey put it definitely in Texas.

Albert H. Latimer, Jr., wrote a lengthy sketch of his father.[11] In describing his exit at the hasty adjournment of the Convention he said:

> Albert H. Latimer rushed out and mounted his mule that had been tied to a nearby tree, and started in a hurry on his four hundred mile trip through a trackless wilderness to his home near Red River. In telling of this instance afterwards he said: "I never knew that a mule could run as fast as the one I

was riding." On this long ride the only provisions he carried was a bag of parched corn, depending on his rifle for meat.

On the sixth day from Washington, he was riding through a dense growth of pine and came out suddenly into a small glade in plain view of an Indian village. He attempted to withdraw, but the dogs had scented him and sent up a howl. Several young bucks came running toward him with their bows and arrows ready. Latimer held up his hands, giving the peace sign, but the young men came on ready to shoot, Latimer was getting ready to sell his life dearly when the chief came out of his tent and called to the young Bucks who stopped instantly.

It appears that Latimer had befriended the chief several years previously, and this act probably saved Latimer's life on this occasion.

Latimer, according to his son, shortly after reaching his home, joined a squad of men who were engaged in rounding up wild cattle for the Texas Army. Latimer served in Capt. William Becknell's company from July 14 to October 14, 1836.[12]

In 1834 the Latimers moved to a place about three miles northeast of the site of the present town of Clarksville. There they and others founded the town of La Grange, which was incorporated November 18, 1837.[13] It was provided in an Act of Congress, approved December 18, 1837, by which the boundaries of Red River County were defined, that the first court of the county should be held in La Grange on the second Monday of January, 1838.[14] Clarksville and Jonesboro were incorporated December 29, 1837, under the laws of Texas,[15] but Jonesboro at that time was considered by the United States as the county seat of Miller County, Arkansas. Clarksville later succeeded La Grange as the county seat of Red River County.[16]

Latimer was member of the House of Representatives from Red River County in the Fifth[17] and Sixth[18] Congresses

182

of the Republic, November 2, 1840, to November 14, 1842. He was a delegate to the Constitutional Convention held at Austin from July 4 to August 27, 1845,[19] Albert H. Latimer was a member of the Senate of the Third Legislature, November 5, 1849, to November 3, 1851, having been elected from the Second District, composed of Red River and Lamar Counties.[20]

At the outbreak of the War Between the States, Latimer wholeheartedly espoused the cause of the Union. Some of his sons, however, entered the Confederate Army.

In 1867 Maj. Gen. P. H. Sheridan, the commanding general, removed the justices of the Supreme Court upon the ground as alleged in his order, "of their known hostility to the Government of the United States."[21] Latimer was appointed an associate justice to succeed Judge Asa H. Willie, removed, a former officer in the Confederate Army.

At the election held November 30, 1869, E. J. Davis was elected governor of Texas. Judge Latimer was a candidate for lieutenant governor on the Republican party ticket but was defeated.[22] He died of a cancer at Clarksville in 1877. Although a Presbyterian he is buried in a marked grave in the Baptist Cemetery at Clarksville. He was a charter member of the Shiloh Cumberland Presbyterian Church, organized in what is now Red River County in June, 1833, by Rev. Milton Estill.[23] He became a member of De Kalb Lodge No. 9, A. F. and A. M., October 10, 1839, and was a member of the Texas Veterans Association.

Latimer was married three times. His first wife, whom he married in 1827 in Tennessee, was Elritta Smith. Of this union there were four children. His second wife, whom he also married in Tennessee, was Elizabeth Richey, to whom there were born eight children. Daniel R., the eldest, was born in Red River County, Texas, November 10, 1837. During the War Between the States he served in the Confederate Army. On June 5, 1858, Daniel was married to

Mary E. McCasley, daughter of George W. and Olivia (Perry) McCasley, of Tennessee, who came to Texas in 1836. Of this union there was one child, George A. Latimer.[24]

In Texas Albert H. Latimer was married to Mary Gattis of Mississippi, by whom he had seven children.

Four of the children of Judge A. H. Latimer were: Morgan Gattis, Henry Russell, Albert Hamilton and Ella Latimer. The last was married to a Mr. Parks and in 1940 resided in Clarksville, Texas.

Some of the surviving grandchildren of Albert H. Latimer in 1940 were: Mrs. Summerville Brooks, Chickasha, Oklahoma; Albert Latimer, Oklahoma City; Albert Gattis Latimer, Corpus Christi; Mrs. Bernard Sunkle, Longview; Mrs. Owenby Norwood, Clarksville; Mrs. Louise Machael, Marble Falls; and Mrs. James Thompson, Hot Springs, Arkansas.

184

EDWIN OSWALD LeGRAND
of
SAN AUGUSTINE MUNICIPALITY

*E*dwin Oswald LeGrand, son of Abner LeGrand,[1] was born in North Carolina in about 1803.[2] He removed from Alabama to Texas in 1834,[3] and settled near the present town of San Augustine.

As a member of Capt. George English's company, LeGrand participated in the storming of Bexar, December 5 to 10, 1835.[4]

The Municipality of San Augustine was first allowed four delegates to the Convention to be held at Washington beginning March 1, but the number was reduced to three at the creation of the Municipality of Sabine, December 15, 1835.[5] At the election held in San Augustine on February 1, 1836, approximately 170 persons voted. Joseph Burleson and Robert C. McDaniel were election judges, and E. B. Lockridge and Sanford Holman secretaries. The votes were distributed as follows: LeGrand, 162; Martin Parmer, 145; Stephen W. Blount, 118; Dr. Caleb S. Brown, 115; Dr. Joseph Rowe, 79; A. E. C. Johnson, 70; Jacob Garrett, 66; David A. Cunningham, 62; Robert Kuykendall, 40; Thomas S. McFarland, 23; and William N. Sigler, 2. LeGrand, Parmer and Blount were declared elected.[6]

At the adjournment of the Convention on the 17th, LeGrand promptly re-entered the service, joining the main army at its camp on the Brazos. He participated in the Battle of San Jacinto on April 21 as a member of the Eighth Company, Second Regiment, Texas Volunteers, of which William Kimbro was captain and Sidney Sherman, colonel.[7]

During congressional recess, President Houston appointed LeGrand chief justice, an official corresponding to the present county judge, of San Augustine County, to serve out the unexpired term of Robert H. Foote. On April 25, 1838, Houston submitted the nomination to the Senate for confirmation, and the Senate promptly complied.[8] At the election held on February 4, 1839, John C. Brooke was elected chief justice, though it is not known that LeGrand stood for re-election.[9]

On November 18, 1839, LeGrand was elected inspector general of the Third Brigade.

James Branch LeGrand, Judge LeGrand's brother, and W. C. Norwood, E. O. LeGrand's brother-in-law, came to Texas in about 1846 and settled about ten miles south of San

Augustine. With them LeGrand, who never married, made his home until his death. J. A. Norwood, son of W. C., was living in the old home in 1929 when the author visited it. Norwood pointed out Judge LeGrand's unmarked grave in near by Graham Cemetery, but he had no record of the date of his death. He thought, however, that it occurred in 1870. In 1936, when the Commission of Control for Texas Centennial Celebrations erected a monument at LeGrand's grave, the author was responsible for the inscription stating that LeGrand died in 1870. Since then the definite date of his death has been ascertained. The *Red Land Express*, San Augustine, Friday, October 18, 1861, said:

> Judge E. O. Le Grand, for a long time a citizen of this county, died on the 10th inst., of dropsy.

186

SAMUEL AUGUSTUS MAVERICK
of
BEXAR MUNICIPALITY

Samuel Augustus Maverick was born July 23, 1803,[1] in Pendleton, South Carolina, son of Samuel and Elizabeth (Anderson) Maverick. He entered Yale College in 1822 and received a bachelor of arts degree in 1825.[2] In Winchester, Virginia, he studied law in the office of Henry St. George Tucker. Returning to South Carolina he was admitted to the bar. His friends expected him to enter politics, but, unable to accept the doctrine of nullification that John C. Calhoun was agitating, he could see no political future in South Carolina. His father likewise disagreed with Calhoun and so intemperately was he criticized for opposing nullification that his son, Samuel A., dueled one critic and wounded him, but nursed him to recovery.[3] Leaving his native state Maverick resided for a short time in Alabama. He arrived in Texas in 1835 from Alabama,[4] and promptly joined the volunteer army then being raised by the colonists. He, John W. Smith and A. C. Holmes were arrested by the Mexicans shortly after the capture of Goliad, October 2, 1835, and kept under surveillance at San Antonio. On the morning of December 3 they made their escape and reached the Texas camp. When San Antonio was attacked on December 5, Maverick rendered valuable service as a guide until the surrender of the town on the 10th.[5] After this encounter he remained in San Antonio as a member of the Alamo garrison.

Bexar Municipality had not been represented at the Conventions of Texas held in 1832 and 1833 at San Felipe de Austin, and no delegates were present at the Consultation at San Felipe in 1835 when the Provisional Government of Texas was formed. This was because of the heavy Mexican population. Some of them having demonstrated, however, that their sympathies were with Texas, the General Council of the Provisional Government passed an act which was approved December 10, 1835, whereby Bexar Municipality was allowed four delegates to the Constitutional Convention.[6] The returns of the election held in the municipality on February 1, 1836, are not in the archives of Texas State Library, but William Fairfax Gray, who attended the convention as a spectator and kept a diary of what he saw and heard, recorded that the four delegates elected from Bexar were Francisco Ruiz, J. Antonio Navarro, Miguel Arciniega and Juan N. Seguin.[7] Of these only Ruiz and Navarro attended the convention.

The Anglo-American soldiers stationed at the Alamo— and most of whom lost their lives there on March 6—were not permitted to vote by the Mexican election judges because they were not residents of Bexar. Accordingly, an election was ordered by Lieut. Col. J. C. Neill to be held in the Alamo on February 1 at which time two soldiers, Jesse B. Badgett and Samuel A. Maverick, were elected to represent the soldiers stationed at the Alamo. Badgett carried with him to the Convention a petition signed by the officers of the Alamo requesting that he and Maverick be seated along with the Mexican delegates. They were seated without debate.

Maverick did not reach Washington until March 5, after the day's session had adjourned to meet Monday, the 7th. On Sunday morning, however, President Ellis convened the Convention and informed the delegates that he had received by express a letter from Col. W. B. Travis, commandant of the Alamo, "which required immediate action of the convention." The letter was dated March 3 and was the last one sent from the Alamo. John W. Smith was the bearer,[8] and it appears that he was accompanied by Maverick, who left the Alamo on March 2.[9] Following the reading of the despatch it is recorded that: "Mr. Samuel A. Maverick, from the municipality of Bejar, appeared, produced his credentials and took his seat as a member of the convention."[10] He signed the Declaration of Independence March 7.[11]

At the adjournment of the Convention Maverick apparently did not tarry long in Texas. The records of the General Land Office do not indicate that he rejoined the army. On Thursday, August 4, 1836, at the home of the bride's widowed mother, three miles north of Tuscaloosa, Alabama, he was married to Mary Ann Adams. In January, 1838, with his wife and baby, he returned to Texas and settled at San Antonio. He served as mayor of the city from January 8, 1839, to January 8, 1840.

In addition to the practice of law, Maverick invested heavily in land certificates. These certificates entitled the holder to locate the stipulated number of acres on any of the unappropriated public domain. By this time, however, most of the land in the more thickly populated sections of Texas had been taken, and all that remained was the western lands infested with Indians. So expensive was the surveying of single tracts of land in this area that many holders sold their certificates to investors who bought with a view of holding them until conditions were more settled, but others, among them Maverick, sent out parties to run the lines. On October 20, 1838, while one of Maverick's parties, consisting of five men, were surveying on Leon Creek about four miles from San Antonio they were attacked by Indians and all of the men killed except one. Moses Lapham, one of the surveyors, who had participated in the Battle of San Jacinto, was among those slain.[12]

Later in February, 1842, word reached San Antonio that a Mexican army was en route to capture the town. Maverick and others decided to remove their families to places of safety. "Hasty preparations were made," said Mrs. Maverick, "and on March 1st, 1842, our little band started on the trip which we have always spoken of since as the Runaway of '42."[13]

The Mavericks settled temporarily near the home of J. W. Dancy across the Colorado from La Grange. On August 22, 1842, Maverick left for San Antonio to attend the fall session of the district court. On the opening day, September 5, he represented Dr. Shields Booker in a suit against the city of San Antonio.[14]

On September 9, San Antonio was full of rumor that a Mexican army was approaching. Though the rumor was generally discredited, on the next day a public meeting made provisions to defend the town. Early on Sunday morning, September 11, Gen. Adrian Woll with 1,200 men entered the town. Maverick, George Van Ness, C. W. Peterson and William E. Jones, as commissioners for the citizens, offered to surrender. Fifty-five, mostly those in attendance at court, were made prisoners and carried to Mexico.[15] On March 30, 1843, the United States Minister to Mexico, Gen. Waddy Thompson, effected the release of Maverick, Jones and Judge Anderson Hutchinson. Maverick joined his family on the Colorado on May 4, 1843.[16]

Maverick was elected to represent Bexar County in the House of Representatives of the Seventh Congress, which convened November 14, 1842, at Washington-on-the-Brazos, but since he and William E. Jones, member-elect of Gonzales County, were in prison in Mexico, their seats, on December 2, 1842, were declared vacant, by a vote of 25 to 7.[17] Though he had not actually resided in San Antonio since March 1, 1842, he was elected from Bexar County to the Eighth Congress, and served from December 4, 1843, to February 5, 1844.[18] From December 8, 1844, to October 15, 1847, he lived on a farm and ranch on Decrows Point in Matagorda County. In October, 1847, he removed his home to San Antonio.[19] He represented the forty-fourth legislative district, composed of Bexar and Medina Counties, in the Extra Session of the Fourth Legislature.[20] In the Fifth Legislature he was a member of the House of Representatives from Bexar County,[21] and in the Sixth[22] and Seventh[23] he was a senator from the thirty-first district, composed of Bexar, Gillespie and Medina and Uvalde Counties. In the Eighth Legislature he represented Bexar County in the House of Representatives,[24] and in the Ninth Legislature he represented the seventy-second district, composed of Bexar, Medina, Uvalde, Kinney, Maverick and Dawson Counties.[25] He served in the Legislature continuously from January 10, 1853, to November 2, 1863.

The Secession Convention which met at Austin, January 28, 1861, appointed a "Committee of Safety," which on February 2 appointed Maverick, Thomas J. Devine, Philip N. Luckett and James H. Rogers commissioners to demand from General D. E. Twiggs, commander of the United States military forces in Texas, such munitions of war as were in arsenals in Texas. "Having matured their plans for the seizure of the property in the hands of the Federal officers in the State, proceeded to perform that duty."[26]

During the 1850's Maverick was treasurer of the San Antonio & Mexican Gulf Railroad Company, which was building a line from Victoria to San Antonio.[27]

Maverick died in San Antonio September 2, 1870,[28] and was buried in City Cemetery No. 1. When Maverick County was created February 2, 1856, the act of the legislature did not state for whom it was named,[29] but Thrall, in 1879, said it was named for S. A. Maverick.[30]

The word maverick as applied to unbranded cattle owes its origin to Samuel A. Maverick. *The Century Dictionary*, copyright 1890, gave the following definition:

> So called from one Samuel Maverick, a Texan cattle-raiser, who, according to one account, relying upon the natural conformation of his cattle-range to prevent escape, neglected to brand his cattle, which having on one occasion stampeded and scattered over the surrounding country, became confused with other unbranded cattle in that region, all such being presumed to be Maverick's, whence the term maverick for all such unbranded animals in that cattle region.[31]

Mrs. Maverick who was born March 16, 1818, in Tuscaloosa County, Alabama, daughter of William and Agatha Strother (Lewis) Adams, died February 24, 1898. She is buried beside her husband.

Children of Mr. and Mrs. Maverick were: Samuel, Lewis Antonio, Agatha, Augustus, George Madison, William Harvey, John Hays, Mary Brown and Albert Maverick. Of these, Agatha, Augusta and John Hays died while young.

Samuel Maverick was born in Pendleton, South Carolina, May 14, 1837. He was married to Sarah (Sallie) Frost.

Their children were Samuel Augustus, who married Frances Cure; John Frost, who married Ann Luth; Mary Agatha, who married O. Sammons; Sallie, who married A. A. Gray; Elizabeth G., who died young; Emily Virginia, who married Edmund Thorton, and Georgia Maverick, who married Eugene Alden Harris.

Lewis Antonio Maverick was born in San Antonio May 23, 1839. He was married to his cousin, Ada Bradley. There were no children. After Maverick's death his widow married Jacob Frederick Waelder.

George Madison Maverick was born September 7, 1845. He was married to Mary Elizabeth Vance. Their children were: Mary Rowena, who married Robert B. Green; Lola, who married William Bross Lloyd; George, who married Laura Brocker, and after her death, Mrs. Glenn Worthington; Lucy Madison; Augusta Lewis, who married Nicholas Kelley; and Lewis Adams Maverick, who first married Jennie Byrd Rosseau, and later Pirie Davidson.

William Harvey Maverick was born December 24, 1847. He was married to Emilie Virginia Chilton. Their children were: William Chilton, who married Grace Fox; Lewis, who married Ada Robards; Laura Wise, who married Amos Groves; Robert Van Wych, who married Laura Grice, and after her death, Mrs. Stella Cutrer; and Augustus Maverick.

Mary Brown Maverick was born June 17, 1851. She was married to Edwin H. Terrell. Their children were Maverick; George Holland; Edwin H., who died young; Martha, who married Richard Miller; Lewis; Mary, who married a Mr. Giesting; and Dorothy Terrell.

Albert Maverick was born May 7, 1854. He was married to Jane Lewis Maury. Their children were Jessie, who married James S. McNeel; Agatha, who married N. J. Welsh; Ellen, who married Louis A. Wright; Albert, who married Lilian Williams; Reuben; Phillip, who married Jean Evans; Virginia, who married Murray S. Crosette; James Slayden,

who married Hazel Davis; Mary, who married Robert Mc-
Garraugh; George Madison, who married Ruth Newell;
and Fontaine Maury Maverick, who married Terrel Dobbs.

COLLIN McKINNEY
of
PECAN POINT AND VICINITY

Collin McKinney was born April 17, 1766,[1] son of Daniel and Massie (Blatchley) McKinney, who came to the United States from Scotland in 1750, settled in New Jersey, and later moved to Virginia. In 1780 they moved to Lincoln County, Kentucky. In December, 1824, Collin and his brother Daniel, with their families, settled in Arkansas, six miles east of the site of the present city of Texarkana. In 1831 Collin McKinney and family moved to Hickman's Prairie on Red River, thought then to be in Miller County, Arkansas, but found, in 1841, to be in the present Bowie County, Texas.[2] As late as July 20, 1835, McKinney considered himself a citizen of Arkansas.[3]

At McKinney's home on January 27, 1836, the judges of election for "Red River Municipality" certified that McKinney, Richard Ellis, Samuel P. Carson, Robert Hamilton and James H. Robinson had been "duly elected to the General Convention to be held at Washington in the Republic of Texas on the first day of March next for the purpose of framing a Constitution."[4] There was, of course, no Republic

193

of Texas at that time, and there was no Red River Municipality in Texas. Robinson did not attend the Convention. Albert H. Latimer, who had not been "duly elected," appeared at Washington and was seated as a delegate from Pecan Point. McKinney, Hamilton and Ellis were seated March 1 as delegates from "the Municipality of Pecan Point and vicinity."[5]

Although McKinney was a member of the House of Representatives from Red River County in the First[6] and Second[7] and Fourth[8] Congresses of the Republic, the question of whether he lived in Texas or Arkansas had not been settled to the satisfaction of either Texas or the United States when his term of office expired. In 1838 the Texas Congress created Colon (not Collin) County from Red River County. On May 21, 1838, President Houston vetoed the bill.[9] In 1844 McKinney moved to the present county of Collin.[10]

194

McKinney died September 8, 1861, and is buried in a marked grave in the cemetery at Van Alstyne, Collin County, Texas.

The Act of the Legislature, approved April 3, 1846, creating Collin County, failed to state for whom the county was named.[11] The county seat was first named Buckner, but on March 16, 1848, the name was changed to McKinney.[12] The act, however, failed to state for whom the town was renamed. Thrall,[13] in 1879, and Brown,[14] in 1893, stated that the county and town were named in honor of Collin McKinney.

The Commission of Control for Texas Centennial Celebrations in 1936 appropriated $1,000 to be used in having the McKinney residence moved to Finch Park in McKinney and there repaired.

McKinney, on February 13, 1792, was married to Amy Moore. Of this union four children were born, two of whom, Ashley and Polly, grew to maturity.[15] Ashley was married to his cousin Sallie McKinney and Polly was married to her cousin, James McKinney.

Mrs. Collin McKinney died May 8, 1804, and, on April 14, 1805, McKinney was married to Betsy E. Coleman, who was born May 2, 1786, and died August 2, 1862. She is buried beside her husband in the cemetery in Van Alstyne, Collin County, Texas.

Children of Collin and Betsy E. (Coleman) McKinney were: William C. who married Margaret Dolley; Amy, who married Joseph James; Peggy (twin of Amy), who married Jarrett James, brother of Joseph James; Anna C, who married James Sloan; Eliza, who married Jefferson Milam, bother of Benjamin Rush Milam; and Younger Scott McKinney, who married Sarah Janes.

All of the grandchildren of Collin McKinney are deceased. Some of the many surviving great-grandchildren in 1942 were: Jack McKinney, James W. McKinney, Si McKinney, Lee McKinney, Sewell McKinney, Mrs. Mattie Emerson, Mrs. Jennie Benton, Mrs. John Neill, Mrs. Maggie Kelly, Mrs. J. L. Kelly, Mr. R. S. Fulton, James Kelly, Jefferson Milam and Collin Milam, all of Van Alstyne; Mrs. Chis W. Thomasson, 4502 Rawlins Street, Dallas; Miss Laura Milam and Mrs. L. M. Anderson, 713 Medina Street, Houston; Mrs. W. C. Bryant, Anna, Texas, and Mrs. Birdie Trube, 406 East 23d Street, Austin, Texas.

195

MICHEL BRANAMOUR MENARD[1]
of
LIBERTY MUNICIPALITY

*M*chel Branamour Menard was born December 5, 1805,[2] in the village of La Prairie, near Montreal, P. Q., Canada. His parents were French. At the age of fourteen he left home to seek adventure. He roamed the Northwest overland and up and down the rivers, living with the trappers and trading with the Indians. During these early years, he joined the service of the Northwest Fur Company with headquarters at Detroit. In about 1823 he went to Kaskaskia, Illinois, to make his home with his uncle, Pierre Menard, an Indian agent. There he learned to speak English. He entered the employ of his uncle as an Indian trader and moved with Indians to territory west of the Mississippi, establishing himself in the Arkansas area. Here he traded with the Shawnees on White River, making friends with the tribe and eventually becoming a chief. After 1825 the Indians migrated into the Louisiana region, and Menard moved to Shreveport in 1826. He arrived in Texas November 28, 1829, and traded for some time among the Mexicans and Indians at Nacogdoches.[3] He returned to Illinois and did not come back until 1832.[4]

On February 1, 1836, Menard, Augustine B. Hardin and James B. Woods were elected as delegates from Liberty Municipality to the Constitutional Convention.[5] Menard was seated March 2.[6]

It is probable that after the adjournment of the Convention, Menard temporarily left Texas. On March 18, William Fairfax Gray saw him in company with Charles S. Taylor headed for Nacogdoches.[7] There is no record in the General Land Office of his having joined the army.

M. B. MENARD

On November 30, 1836, President Houston appointed Menard and A. J. Yates commissioners to negotiate a loan on the bonds of the Government of Texas of $5,000,000.[8]

On December 9, 1836, Menard purchased for $50,000 from the First Congress of the Republic one league and one labor of land on Galveston Island.[9] He later laid out the town of Galveston. Associating with himself a number of others, he formed the Galveston City Company, with which he was identified until his death. He was a member from Galveston County of the House of Representatives in the Fifth Congress of the Republic, November 2, 1840, to February 5, 1841.[10]

Menard, although a Roman Catholic, was a member of Harmony Lodge No. 6, Ancient Free and Accepted Masons, Galveston.[11] He died September 2, 1856, and is buried in a marked grave in the old Catholic cemetery in Galveston.

When Menard County was created January 22, 1858, it was named "in honor of Col. Michael [sic] B. Menard, deceased."[12]

Menard was married four times. He was first married to Marie Diana La Clere, who was born at Ste. Genevieve, Missouri, June 9, 1813, a daughter of Francois Le Clere, a native of Kaskaskia, Illinois. Mrs. Menard died in Ste. Genevieve, May 14, 1833. On November 13, 1837, Menard was married to a second cousin, Catherine Maxwell, of Kaskaskia, Illinois. She was born in 1815, a daughter of Hugh H. and Marie Odille (Menard) Maxwell and a sister of Peter Menard Maxwell. The second Mrs. Menard died in Kaskaskia July 12, 1838, and her daughter died June 23, 1839. Menard was next married to Mary Jane Riddle of St. Louis. Mrs. Menard died of yellow fever in Galveston in 1847.

On September 5, 1850, Menard was married to Mrs. Rebecca Mary Bass, whose children, Helen and Clara Bass, he adopted. There was one child born of this union, Doswell Menard, who died in early manhood.

After the death of her husband, Mrs. Menard was married to John S. Thrasher. The *Weekly Telegraph*, Houston, on July 16, 1869, announced that Mrs. John S. Thrasher, formerly Mrs. M. B. Menard of Galveston, died in New York some few days previously.

Susan Le Clere, twin sister of the first wife of M. B. Menard, came to Texas in 1837 with her brother, Isidore S. Le Clere, and settled at Galveston, as did Medard Menard, a cousin of Michel B., on November 1, 1838. Medard Menard married Susan Le Clere.

WILLIAM MENEFEE
of
COLORADO MUNICIPALITY

William Menefee was born May 11, 1796,[1] in Knox County, Tennessee, son of John and Frances (Rhodes) Menefee. He studied law and was admitted to the bar.

The Menefees moved to Morgan County, Alabama, in 1824 and settled near Decatur. In 1830 the families of William and John Menefee came to Texas with families of the Heards, Sutherlands and others from the vicinity of Tuscumbia and Decatur.[2] Determined to settle in Austin's colonies they decided, in 1829, to send George Sutherland, Jesse White, brother-in-law of Sutherland, and Anthony Winston to Texas to arrange for land. These three and Stephen F. Austin at San Felipe de Austin, February 19, 1830, entered into a contract for land for the families of William Menefee, Thomas Menefee, William J. E. Heard, Joseph

Rector, William Pride, Jesse White, Benjamin J. White, Samuel Rogers and Robert J. Crozier. Upon their return to Alabama, George Sutherland and Jesse White immediately began their preparations to remove to Texas. It was decided that George Sutherland would lead a part of the prospective colony overland, while Jesse White would follow up by the water route. In writing of the overland trip John S. Menefee said:

> Those who came by land were Thomas and William Menefee and families, George Sutherland and family, William J. E. Heard and family and mother, and Thomas J. Reed and wife.
>
> We started out October 30, and came through the Choctaw nation by Natchez to the Mississippi at the mouth of the Red River, where we found the boat out of repair and the ferryman not well, consequently we had to repair the boat and set ourselves over except the ferryman steered the boat and collected for ferriage. We crossed the Sabine at Gaines Ferry and came by Nacogdoches and crossed the Trinity at Robbins Ferry, and the Brazos at San Felipe. Between Nacogdoches and the Trinity there were but few houses and none on the road that I recollect from Trinity to the Brazos. Leaving San Felipe, we crossed the Colorado at Beason's Ferry—a little below where Columbus is, and followed the old Attascosita Road, crossing the Navidad at Hardy's, thence to Major James Kerr's on the Lavaca, from which we followed wagon tracks made by F. G. Keller moving to Keller's Creek; and arrived at our destination on the N. Navidad, seven miles above where Texana is, on the 9th of December, 1830.[3]

Menefee was sent as a delegate from the District of Lavaca to the First Convention of Texas which convened at San Felipe de Austin October 1, 1832.[4] He was likewise a delegate to the Second Convention of Texas at San Felipe in 1833.[5] Elected from Austin Municipality, he was seated as a delegate to the Consultation at San Felipe on the day it

199

opened, October 16, 1835.[6] On December 8 he was seated as a member of the General Council of the Provisional Government of Texas.[7]

Colorado Municipality was created January 8, 1836, from the Municipality of Austin.[8] On the following day Menefee was elected first judge and William D. Lacey, second judge of the Municipality.[9] On February 1 these two were elected delegates to the Constitutional Convention.[10] Menefee was seated March 1.[11]

Following the adjournment of the Convention, Menefee joined the Runaway Scrape. Gray saw him on April 20 near the Louisiana border.[12]

Menefee was the first chief justice of Colorado County, having been appointed to that position by President Houston, December 20, 1836.[13] President Lamar nominated Menefee secretary of treasury of the Republic December 23, 1840.[14] The Senate took no action by January 21, 1841, and the nomination was withdrawn.[15]

By an Act of Congress, approved January 14, 1839, by President Lamar, three commissioners were elected by the House of Representatives and two by the Senate of Congress, whose duty was to select a site for the location of the seat of government. The site selected was required to be at some point between the Trinity and Colorado Rivers and above the San Antonio Road. When selected the site was to be named Austin. In compliance the House elected Menefee, Isaac Campbell and Louis P. Cooke. In the Senate Albert C. Horton and Isaac W. Burton were elected. On April 13, 1839, the commissioners met at Houston to vote on the site. Horton, Menefee and Cooke voted for some site on the Colorado. Burton and Campbell favored a site on the Brazos. Next a vote was taken as to whether the capitol should be placed at Bastrop or Waterloo. Waterloo was chosen by unanimous vote.[16] Later the name of the town was changed to Austin.

Menefee represented Colorado District in the House of Representatives of the Second,[17] Third,[18] Fourth[19] and Fifth[20] Congresses of the Republic, September 25, 1837, to November 1, 1841, and in the Ninth Congress,[21] December 2, 1844 to February 3, 1845.

Menefee was a candidate for the vice-presidency of the Republic but was defeated by Gen. Edward Burleson in the election held September 6, 1841. In 1842 he participated in the Vasquez campaign. He was elected chief justice of Colorado County July 13, 1846.

Judge Menefee moved to Fayette County in 1846 and represented that county in the House of Representatives in the Fifth Legislature, November 7, 1853, to November 5, 1857.[22] He died October 29, 1875, and was buried in the Pine Springs Cemetery six miles from Flatonia in Fayette County. The State of Texas removed his remains and those of his wife to the State Cemetery at Austin.

Judge Menefee married Agnes Sutherland, daughter of Mr. and Mrs. George Sutherland. Mrs. Menefee was born in Virginia August 22, 1794, and died February 28, 1859.

Children of Judge and Mrs. Menefee were: Sarah S. Menefee, born September 14, 1818, married Eli Mercer; Thomas Shelton Menefee, born September 27, 1820, married Mary Elizabeth Penn (widow of his brother, Quinn), and died February 2, 1912; John L. Menefee, born July 27, 1822; Talitha Ann Menefee, born June 5, 1824, married to Rev. John W. Devilbiss, and died August 15, 1846; William Menefee, born May 5, 1826, married to Susan B. Smith; George Menefee, born May 6, 1828, and died August 25, 1829; Quinn Morton, born August 11, 1830, married Mary Elizabeth Penn October 10, 1855, and died September 5, 1867; Elizabeth Frances Menefee, born in Egypt, Texas, September 14, 1833, and died in Fayette County, April 11, 1853.

Following are the names of some of the surviving grandchildren of Judge and Mrs. William Menefee in 1942:

Mrs. George Butler, Edna; Thomas B. Menefee, 1530
Fifth Street, Port Arthur; Henry A. Menefee, 2331 Angelina
Street, Beaumont; Miss Hattie Menefee, Edna; Mrs. Sue
McAnelly, 404 Iberia Street, Franklin, Louisiana; Robert S.
Menefee, 802 Euclid Street, San Antonio; George Q. Mene-
fee, 205 East Seventh Street, Austin; Mrs. Nannie Menefee
Basford, 101 Archway, Austin; Mrs. Lazelle Menefee Wil-
cox, 205 Archway, Austin; Mrs. Agnes Luty, 1426 Bennett
Avenue, Dallas.

JOHN W. MOORE
of
HARRISBURG MUNICIPALITY

John W. Moore was born in Pennsylvania in about
1797, and came to Texas from Tennessee.[1] He arrived
in 1830[2] and settled in Harrisburg Municipality.

The Ayuntamiento of San Felipe de Austin announced
December 18, 1831, that in the elections held on December
11 and 13, Moore had been elected *comisario* (commissary
of police) of the Precinct of San Jacinto (Harrisburg), Jurisdiction of Austin, Department of Bexar.[3]

Moore was a close friend of William B. Travis and was
with him June 30, 1835, when a company of volunteers under Travis forced the capitulation of Capt. Antonio Tenorio,
commanding about forty men at the fort at Anahuac. On
August 31, 1835, Travis wrote a letter to Moore which was
published in the *Morning Star*, Houston, March 14, 1840,
and from which the following was extracted:

> Principle was gradually working out this glorious end and
> preparing the way for the march of freedom, when the or-
> der came for my being arrested and given up to the military

to be shot for engaging in the expedition to Anahuac, etc. That was too much for the people to bear; it was too great a sacrifice for them to make and they unanimously exclaimed against this order and its supporters. The devil has shown his cloven foot and his lies will be believed no longer.

Commenting on the letter, Daniel H. Fitch, editor of the paper said:

> The following letter from the pen of the immortal Travis will be read with peculiar interest. Every line that has been penned by that noblest of Texian patriots will ever command the admiration and respect of Texians. Who can read their lines and not feel his bosom glow with the fire of liberty that animated their illustrious author. This letter was addressed to Major J. W. Moore and the original is now in his possession; it will some day become a valuable autograph. Colonel Moore was the first who raised the starred banner among the brave Harrisburgers, to whom Travis alluded, and has on many occasions by his bravery and devotion to the cause of freedom, proved himself worthy of this noble correspondent.

203

Moore was seated November 1, 1835, as a delegate from Harrisburg Municipality to the Consultation held at San Felipe.[4] On November 18 the General Council of the Provisional Government elected him contractor for the army.[5]

The General Council, on January 2, 1836, adopted the following resolution:

> Resolved, that John W. Moore be allowed an additional sum of three dollars per diem, for his services as contractor for supplies to the volunteer army, and that he be put upon the same footing, as to any bounty that may be allowed to volunteers that were at the taking of Bexar.[6]

On the day following on motion of R. R. Royall:

John W. Moore was discharged from any further duties as contractor for the volunteer army, and the thanks of the House were voted to Mr. Moore, for the prompt and efficient manner in which he has discharged the duties of contractor.[7]

Approximately 132 votes were cast in the election held in the Municipality of Harrisburg, February 1, 1836, to elect two delegates to the Constitutional Convention. Votes were polled at John Owen's, the town of Harrisburg, New Kentucky, Lynchburg and Stafford's Prairie Home. Moses Shipman was president of the election, H. H. League, judge, David Hanson, secretary, and James East and Leo Roark tellers at the home of John Owen. Lorenzo de Zavala and Andrew Briscoe each received 7 votes. Apparently there were only two voters other than the election officials.

At Harrisburg, William P. Harris and William H. Steele were the tellers and J. F. Ailers the secretary. Briscoe received 19 votes; Zavala, 17; John W. Moore, 13; and Daniel Perry, 2.

Abram Roberts was president of the election at his home at New Kentucky; William Bushby and J. H. Callihan, the tellers, and James Cooper secretary. Here Zavala and Moore each received 9 votes.

In the returns, the names of the officials who conducted the election at Lynchburg are not shown. Zavala led the field with 65 votes; Briscoe received 29; James Morgan, 23; Moore, 13; and Daniel Perry, 2. One of the voters registered as "Peter the Great."

M. M. Battle was president, De Witt C. Harris secretary, and Joel Wheaton and Daniel Perry, tellers at the election held at Stafford's Prairie House. There Briscoe led with 25 votes; Zavala was next with 17; and J. W. Moore received 8.

Total votes of the candidates in the municipality were: Zavala, 115; Briscoe, 80; Moore, 43; and Perry, 4. Zavala and Briscoe were declared elected.[8] Briscoe, however, was in the United States at the time of the election and not having returned by February 25, H. H. League, judge of elections, wrote Moore:

> Department of Brazos
> Municipality of Harrisburg

To Citizen John W. Moore. You are hereby notified that Andrew Briscoe was Elected a member of the Convention of Texas to meet at the Town of Washington on the First day of March ensuing—and in as much as the Said Briscoe is absent from the government, and knows not of his Election—and in as much as the people of this municipality feels a Vital interest in the political affares of Texas at this time; and wish to be fully represented in the Convention.

Therefore; in as much as the laws governing Elections provide that if any member Elect shall fail, or refuse to take his seat in conformity with the law; after presenting himself and taking the oath prescribed. That the Candidate having the next highest number of Votes, on the return list of the candidates shall serve in his place—

Therefore; this is to inform you that owing to the total failure of Andrew Briscoe; and your Standing next highest on the list of Candidates—you are hereby required (as the law directs) to proceed to the Town of Washington on the First day of March Ensuing, then and there to take your Seat in manner and form as prescribed by law Given under my hand at office that 25th February 1836—

H. H. League, Judge[9]

Moore was seated in the Convention and signed the Declaration of Independence, on March 7.[10] Captain Briscoe presented himself on March 11 and, on motion of Martin Parmer, was "invited to take a seat in this convention."[11] Thus, Harrisburg Municipality was represented by three delegates instead of by two.

From an order issued March 17, 1836, by General Rusk it appears that Moore as contractor for the army held the rank of captain and that after the Convention adjourned he was, for a time at least, engaged in organizing troops.[12]

Moore was seated October 3, 1836, as a member from Harrisburg County of the House of Representatives in the First Congress of the Republic.[13] His election was contested however, and on October 11 the House voted to seat Jesse

H. Cartwright in his stead.[14] Andrew Briscoe, chief justice of Harrisburg County, ordered an election of county officers and officers of militia districts to be held January 25, 1837. At this time Moore was elected captain of the Second Militia District and sheriff of Harrisburg County.[15] He was installed as sheriff February 27. He was re-elected February 4, 1838,[16] and continued to office until at least November 30, 1840. On January 6, 1840, he was elected an alderman of the city of Houston and took the oath of office two days later.[17]

Moore was a charter member of the first Independent Order of Odd Fellows Lodge of Texas, organized at Houston, July 25, 1838.

Moore's wife having died after April 28, 1831, the date on which Captain Moore had received a league of land in Austin's Second Colony, Captain Moore on February 21, 1839, was married to Eliza Belknap in Houston.[18]

Captain Moore died in Houston in 1846 and was buried in the City Cemetery. In 1936, the Commission of Control for Texas Centennial Celebrations erected a monument in the cemetery in his honor.

On March 30, 1846, Mrs. Moore petitioned to have Captain Moore's will, signed on June 6, 1845, probated.[19] In the will Captain Moore left one dollar each to his brothers, James, Joseph, William, Hugh W. and Samuel Moore, and to his sisters, Jane Birsben and Lucy Miller. The balance of his property he left to his widow, Mrs. Eliza Moore.

From a petition in the Memorials and Petition files in the Archives of the Texas State Library, Austin,[20] it appears that when in 1836 Harrisburg was burned by the Mexican army, Moore's residence was the only house left standing. Following is a copy of the petition:

To the Honourable, the Senate & House of Representatives of the Republic of Texas, in Congress assembled.

Your Petitioner Citizens of the County of Harrisburg, one

of the Counties of this Republic most respectfully beg leave to represent to your Honourable bodies, that on or about the fourteenth day of April last [1836] they were compelled to leave their homes and property, to protect their families &c., there being no military troops or force stationed at this place, and having been informed that the hostile Mexicans under the commandancy of Gen. Santanna had then crossed the Brazos River at or near the fort settlement and were then on their march to this place, where they arrived on or about the sixteenth of said month (April), they having plundered the aforesaid town of Harrisburg, of what valuable property had been left by the Citizens and then set fire to all the buildings in said town except one, the dwelling house of John W. Moore—Your petitioners therefore pray your Honourable bodies to pass a law to indemnify them in all their losses, spoliations &c. and also to appoint a court of commissioners to hear the claimants and their testimony to be authorised to call for and obtain bills of said spoliation by fire or otherwise, as any other papers that may be calculated to show the amount of damages sustained by any person or persons and report the same to your Honourable bodies for their confirmation or rejection—and as in duty bound your petitioners will ever pray—

Harrisburgh, Octr 31st, 1836

Wm P. Harris	A. Larsson [Allen Larrison]
John W. Moore	Edward Wray
Wm E. Harris	A. Briscoe & Co.
Heinrich Thurwachter [Henry Tierwester]	
De W. Clinton Harris	McCaskill & Dobie

By D. W. C. Harris, agent

Laid on the table, Dec. 6, 1836.

May 17, 1837, taken up and Indefinitely postponed

JUNIUS WILLIAM MOTTLEY
of
GOLIAD MUNICIPALITY

*J*unius William Mottley, usually referred to as "Dr. Mottley," was born in Virginia about 1812,[1] and came to Texas from Kentucky.[2]

On April 7, 1931, Mrs. Charles F. Norton, librarian of Transylvania College, formerly Transylvania University, Lexington, Kentucky, wrote the author:

> In regard to Dr. William Mottley of whom you write, I find that *Junius William Mottley* matriculated as a first year student in the medical college of Transylvania University in the fall of 1833. His residence is given as Greensburg, Kentucky, and his preceptor—the physician with whom he "read medicine" at home—is Charles Hay, M.D., T. U. 1829. Charles Hay was the father of the statesman and writer, John Hay.
>
> Mottley matriculated again in the fall of 1834 giving the same place of residence and the same preceptor but his name does not appear in the list of graduates. Nor is his thesis filed with those of other graduates, nor is his name given in the faculty minutes recording the examination of graduates. Two years is the usual length of the course so Dr. Mottley must have left for Texas before March 18, 1835, the date of the conferring of degrees. There were two hundred and fifty nine matriculates in the medical department that year and eighty three graduates. Dr. William Welsh of Baltimore said recently, "Transylvania was the best of schools." No entry concerning the age or the parents of students is made. Your spelling of the name is verified by our records.

Residing in Bowling Green, Warren County, Kentucky, in 1912 was Col. Erasmus L. Mottley, related, no doubt, to the subject of this sketch. Of Erasmus L. Mottley, E. Polk Johnson wrote:

208

J. W. Mottley

He was born in Greensburg, Green County, Kentucky, n the 3d of September, 1838, and is a son of James D. and Eliza L. (Hobson) Mottley, the former of whom was born at Amelia Court House, Virginia, and the latter of whom was a native of Green County, Kentucky. The Mottley family traces its ancestry back to English origin, the original progenitor in America being one Mottley, who emigrated from Kent County, England, to America in the year 1600. Mottley of Revolutionary fame was connected with the Ninth Virginia Cavalry. James D. Mottley, father of Erasmus L. Mottley, was an extensive slave holder and a prominent merchant in the Blue Grass State. He was the owner of about one hundred slaves prior to the inception of the Civil War. William Hobson, maternal grandfather of Colonel Mottley, was a captain in the War of 1812.[3]

Dr. Junius William Mottley came to Texas in 1835 to fight for the independence of Texas from Mexico. He was appointed surgeon for the Post of Goliad January 24, 1836, by General Houston. He furnished the Post of Goliad with surgical instruments worth at least $125.[4]

Approximately 45 votes were cast at one voting box in Goliad Municipality February 1, 1836, to select two delegates to the Constitutional Convention. Dr. J. William Mottley and Incarnacion Vasquez were elected. Of the total number of votes, Dr. Mottley received 45; Vasquez, 43; Victor Loupez, 32; Joseph Watson, 30; and Capt. John Chenoweth, 1. The election judges were Joseph Watson, Roberto Galan and Samuel Williams. Jose Miguel Aldrete was secretary.

Vasquez did not attend the convention. Dr. Mottley left Goliad early for Washington, carrying with him the election returns and this statement:

Municipality of Goliad, Town of Goliad
February 4, 1836, His Excellency, the Governor of Texas

By virtue of the order of Your Excellency of the 18th, the

election took place of two delegates to go to that place for the forming of a new convention on the first of next March: By the computation inclosed herewith, Your Excellency will be advised of the individuals who have been named Delegates to represent the rights of this municipality, and I am now making possible their immediate departure, soliciting their support in order that they may not fail in such an important object. At the same time, I take pleasure in assuring Your Excellency of my greatest respects.

God and Liberty,
Jose Miguel Aldrete, Secretary[5]

William Fairfax Gray left San Felipe February 19, expecting to return to the headquarters of Robertson's Colony near the falls of the Brazos. Reaching Colonel Edwards's he was advised not to attempt to make the trip alone on account of possible attack by Indians. He remained at Edwards's until the 21st when he set out for Washington. On the 19th he recorded in his diary:

> After breakfast rode as far as Col. Edwards', where I found Mr. Childers [probably George C. Childress]. Waited until after dinner, expecting [Thomas J.] Chambers and [Ira P.] Lewis. They did not come. After night Chambers arrived, in company with a Dr. Motley, a delegate to the convention from Goliad.—They also persuaded me not to attempt to go to the Falls alone.—[6]

On February 21, he wrote:

> Left Col. Edwards at half past 8 o'clock with company with Dr. Motley, a member of the Convention from Goliad, who is going to Washington.[7]

Dr. Mottley was seated at the convention March 1.[8] He did not resign from the army, and when the Convention was dissolved he hastened to rejoin the military forces. He was aide-de-camp to Secretary of War Thomas J. Rusk at San Jacinto, and was mortally wounded in the engagement. He died on the night of April 21 and was buried on the battlefield as were seven of the others who were killed or mortally wounded. Olwyn J. Trask, mortally wounded, was placed on board a boat and taken to Galveston Island for medical treatment and where he died.

On January 1, 1838, William G. Cooke was appointed administrator of the estate of Dr. Mottley by the Probate Court of Harris County. His heirs evidently could not be located, for on December 4, 1849, Dr. Mottley's donation certificate was sold at auction on the courthouse steps in Houston to the highest bidder by the sheriff, David Russell, to satisfy an "execution issued from the office of the clerk of the county court of Harris County on the eighth day of November, 1849, commanding the sheriff of said county to levy the sum of $90.75 on the goods, chattels, lands and tenements of William Mottley, deceased."[9] The certificate was purchased for fifteen dollars by W. R. Baker.[10]

When Motley (sic) County, Texas, was created August 21, 1876, it was named "in honor of Dr. William Motley (sic), who was mortally wounded at San Jacinto."[11]

William Mottley

JOSE ANTONIO BALDOMERO NAVARRO
of
BEXAR MUNICIPALITY

Jose Antonio Baldomero Navarro was born in San Antonio, a son of Angel Navarro and Maria Josefa Ruiz y Peña. His mother was a daughter of Manuel Ruiz de Posia and Manuel de la Pena, and was a sister of Francisco Ruiz,[1] a signer of the Texas Declaration of Independence.

OUR (unlikely) FATHERS

Angel Navarro was born in Ajaccio, Corsica. He left his native island in 1772, when about thirteen or fourteen years of age; visited in Genoa, Barcelona and Cadiz; and after service in the Spanish army, emigrated to Mexico. He was a resident of Real de Bayecillos for eight years, and came to San Antonio in the capacity of a merchant, in about 1777. He was alcalde in 1790.[2]

Mirabeau B. Lamar gathered from pioneer citizens of Texas material for use in a history of Texas he contemplated writing. Navarro furnished him with an autobiographical sketch:

> I was born in the City of San Antonio de Bexar, on the 27th February 1795, my father was Angel Navarro a native of the Island of Corsica; my father arrived [in the Kingdom] of New Spain [in] the service of the King [ ] been an Officer, and having resigned his [commission] he settled in Bexar and married [Mary Joseph] Ruiz, afterwards my mother, which lady [descended] from a Spanish family of the City of Saltillo.—I cannot say that my father descended from any of the first European families but I can assure that his virtues and honest life sufficiently indicate that he appertained to those of some distinction in Corsica. My father acquired by means of Commerce in Bexar a sufficient fortune to maintain us with decency and to obtain for his children a rank and education, which in those days of obscurity and obstacles to [the] American Civilization, which the Government of Spain never lost sight of, may have been called superior.
>
> Of the marriage of my father resulted six children, who survived him—My father left Bexar and this world on the last day of October, 1808.
>
> In consequence of the death of my father, we were left orphans and at the side of our widowed mother we six stood. The oldest was my Brother Jose Angel, followed by Maria Josefa, Jose Antonio [the writer of this], Maria Antonia, Jose Luciana and the last and the youngest of all Jose Eugenio.—[3]

212

During the ill-fated revolution of 1813, Navarro was intimately connected with the Bexar revolutionists who joined with Augustus W. Magee, a graduate of West Point, and Bernardo Gutierrez, a former adherent of Miguel Hidalgo, in their attempt against the Spanish authority. Navarro's uncle, Francisco Ruiz, was lieutenant colonel, first under Gutierrez and later under his successor, Jose Alvarez Toledo. When Toledo was routed on the Medina River August 18, 1813, by the Spanish general, Joaquin Arrendondo, Veramendi, Ruiz, Navarro and many others fled to Louisiana. In 1815, the King of Spain pardoned the insurgents, and the next year Navarro returned to Bexar. In 1821 Navarro joined Augustin Iturbide in his struggle for the independence of Mexico. It was his brother, Jose Angeles, who proclaimed in Bexar the plan of Iturbide and to whom Antonio Maria Martinez, Spanish governor of Texas, surrendered.

Navarro was elected in 1821 to represent Bexar in the House of Representatives of the Legislature of Coahuila and Texas.[4] In 1831 he was appointed land commissioner for De Witt's Colony.[5] On October 6, 1831, he received title to four leagues of land from Commissioner J. M. Salinas, surveyed in what is now Atascosa County.[6] On July 2, 1832, he was issued title to seven leagues by Commissioner M. Arciniega, surveyed two-thirds in the present county of Travis and one-third in what is now Bastrop County.[7]

In 1833, Navarro was elected suppletory representative in the Legislature.[8] In 1834-35 he was land commissioner for Bexar District.[9] On March 2, 1835, the Legislature elected him one of two senators to represent the State of Coahuila and Texas in the Congress of the Republic of Mexico.[10] In April, 1835, he wrote Congress that due to illness he could not attend that body.[11]

An act of the General Council of the Provisional Government of Texas, approved December 10, 1835, allowed Bexar

213

Municipality four delegates to the Constitutional Convention.[12] The incomplete election returns in the Archives of the Texas State Library do not reveal all of those elected from Bexar, but William Fairfax Gray, who as a spectator at the Convention recorded in his diary what he saw and heard, wrote that Bexar Municipality, on February 1, 1836, elected Francisco Ruiz, J. Antonio Navarro, Miguel Arciniega and Juan N. Seguin.[13] Of these only Navarro and his uncle, Ruiz, attended.

The Anglo-American soldiers stationed at the Alamo, most of whom lost their lives there on March 6, were not permitted to vote by the Mexican election judges of Bexar because they were not citizens of Bexar. Accordingly an election was ordered by Lieut. Col. J. C. Neill to be held in the Alamo on February 1 at which time two men, Jesse B. Badgett and Samuel A. Maverick, were elected to represent the soldiers stationed there. Badgett carried to the convention a petition signed by the officers stationed at the Alamo requesting that he and Maverick be seated along with the Mexican delegates.[14] They were accepted without debate. Navarro took his seat March 1.[15]

At Washington, Navarro, Ruiz, Zavala, Badgett and William Fairfax Gray occupied a room in a building owned by Samuel Heath, a carpenter.[16]

The printed proceedings of the Convention do not show that Navarro took an active part in the deliberations of that body. After adjournment he did not join the army. He was in New Orleans May 12, 1836.[17]

Navarro was a member of the House of Representatives from the Bexar District to the Third Congress of the Republic of Texas, November 5, 1838, to January 24, 1839.[18] He represented Bexar County in the Fourth Congress, which met at Austin beginning November 11, 1839, but was unable to make the trip to the capital, due to sudden illness, and resigned.[19]

JOSE A. B. NAVARRO

In 1841 Navarro was appointed by President Lamar one of the commissioners of the ill-fated Santa Fe Expedition. He was captured October 5, 1841, marched overland with his companions to the City of Mexico and there imprisoned. Navarro was incarcerated in one of the dungeons of the Acordada, brought to trial by order of Santa Anna and sentenced to death. The sentence was later modified to life imprisonment and he was transferred to a dungeon of San Juan de Ulloa at Vera Cruz.[20] His brother, Luciana Navarro, went to Mexico during the year 1842 to try to obtain his release and was himself thrown into prison.

Navarro, with the assistance of some Anglo-Americans, made his escape January 2, 1845, arrived at New Orleans by boat on the 18th and at Galveston February 3rd, where he was warmly welcomed by friends and admirers.[21]

In 1845, Navarro was a delegate to the convention which framed the constitution of the State of Texas.[22] He moved back to San Antonio and was elected Senator from the Eighteenth District to the First[23] and Second Legislatures,[24] serving from February 16, 1846, to November 5, 1849.

The act of the Legislature of April 25, 1846, creating Navarro County failed to state for whom it was named.[25] Thrall, in 1879, said it was named for Jose Antonio Navarro.[26] Fulmore wrote: "His father was a native of Corsica and in compliment to Navarro the county seat was named Corsicana."[27]

Although Navarro was a Roman Catholic he was a member of the Masonic fraternity, being a member of Virtue Lodge No. 10, Saltillo, Mexico. He visited the Grand Lodge of Texas, November 10, 1838.[28]

Navarro was married to Margarita de la Garza, who was born in Mier, Mexico, October 17, 1801, and died July 6, 1861. Navarro died Saturday morning, January 13, 1871, and his remains were interred beside those of his wife in San Fernando Cemetery No. 1, San Antonio. The Commission of Control for Texas Centennial Celebrations had a joint monument erected at their graves in 1936. The Commission also had a statue of Navarro, costing $14,000, placed at Corsicana, Navarro County.

Children of the Navarros were: (1) Jose Antonio George, (2) Celso Cornelio, (3) Angel, (4) Sixto Eusebio and (5) Josefa Navarro.

(1) Jose Antonio George Navarro was married to Juana Chaves.

(2) Celso Cornelio Navarro was married to Agapita Garcia.

(3) Angel Navarro was married to Concepcion Ramon Callaghan, widow of Bryan Callaghan. Two of the children of this union, Eugenio and Angelita Navarro de Mores were alive in 1936.

(4) Sixto Eusebio Navarro was born in San Antonio March 5, 1833. He was married to Genoveva Cortinas of Nacogdoches. Their home was in Atascosa County.

(5) Josefa Navarro was married to Daniel Tobin. Mrs. Margarita Navarro Barrera, blind, a great-granddaughter of Antonio Navarro in October, 1941, was living at 2716 East Fifth Street, Austin, with her daughter, Mrs. Josephine Barrera Kelly. Living with Mrs. Kelly, also, were her children, Gilbert Kelly and Rosa Mary Kelly.

216

MARTIN PARMER
of
SAN AUGUSTINE MUNICIPALITY

*M*artin Parmer was born in Virginia, June 4, 1778.[1] At the age of twenty he moved to Dickson County, Tennessee, where for some time he was superintendent of the works of Montgomery Bell.[2] According to a letter from Capt. William Becknell to Gen. Sam Houston, dated May 28, 1838, Parmer served in the War of 1812,[3] but the United States War Department has no record of such service.[4]

In about 1816, Parmer moved to Missouri, for in the next year he hunted and trapped in what is now Carroll County.[5] He represented Howard County in the first General Assembly of Missouri, which sat at St. Louis from September 18 to December 12, 1820, and at St. Charles from June 4 to June 29, 1821.[6] He was living on Fishing River in Clay County[7] when he was elected to the Senate of the third General Assembly, which met at St. Charles from November 15, 1824, to February 21, 1825.[8] At the end of this session Parmer, with another member, James Kerr, came to Texas.[9] When the special session of the General Assembly met on January 19, 1826, a committee was appointed to inquire into the absence of a number of the senators, among them Martin Parmer.[10] The committee later reported that Parmer had "removed...out of the State."[11]

On October 2, 1826, the Mexican government cancelled (unjustly so, many think) the empresario contract it had awarded to Haden Edwards April 18, 1825, by which he was authorized to settle 800 families in and around Nacogdoches. Lawlessness prevailed in that area and a small revolution was in the making. It was then that four men who were in later years to sign the Declaration of Independence appeared upon the scene to play important roles in the drama then unfolding: Martin Parmer, John S. Roberts, James Gaines and Francisco Ruiz.

Conditions at that time were described in detail by Henry S. Foote, as related to him by Benjamin W. Edwards, brother of Haden Edwards. The Anglo-Americans had held an election January 1, 1826, at which time Chichester Chaplin, son-in-law of Martin Parmer,[12] received the largest number of votes for Alcalde but Samuel Norris had declared himself reelected and continued to rule with a high hand.

> Nacogdoches now became a scene of wild uproar and confusion; acts of lawless and cruel violence marked the history of every day, and indeed of every hour; hands of *Regulators* as they were called, pervaded the whole country, under the ostensible sanction of the Alcalde, and ready to execute any mandate to which he might give utterance.[13]

218

Yoakum adds:

> The Mexican population, in anticipation, immediately set up claim to all the valuable places occupied by the Americans! The servile alcalde, Norris, granted all the orders they asked; and Gaines, his brother-in-law, was ready with a company of *Regulators* to enforce them. By these means, the Americans were dispossessed, driven from their homes, fined and imprisoned. Matters had become intolerable.[14]

Finally the opposition organized and on November 23, 1826, brought Samuel Norris and Jose Antonio Sepulveda to trial before a court composed of Colonel Parmer, president, Capt. B. J. Thompson, Maj. John S. Roberts, J. W. Mayo and William Jones.[15]

On November 25, 1826, a proclamation was issued offering a reward of $100 for the body, dead or alive, of James Gaines charged with high crimes and misdemeanors.[16]

On the 25th both Norris and Sepulveda were found guilty and removed from office.[17] On January 1, 1827, Stephen F. Austin issued a circular from which the following was extracted:

> A small party of infatuated madmen at Nacogdoches have declared Independence and invited the Indians from Sabine to Rio Grande to join them and wage a war of murder, plunder and desolation on the innocent inhabitants of the frontier—The leader of this party is Martin Parmer, and Jim Collier, Bill English, the Yoakums, and the men of that character are his associates.[18]

This was the beginning of the Fredonian War, which ended March 31, 1827, when the Fredonians crossed the Sabine in exile. Francisco Ruiz, then an officer in the Mexican Army, had been sent to Nacogdoches to help quell the revolution.

Parmer returned to Texas in 1831 but was quickly expelled by the Mexican authorities.[19] He returned again in 1835, and in that year was elected a delegate to the Consultation.[20] He bore the sobriquet "Ringtailed Panther."[21]

On motion of Parmer the district of Tenehaw on November 11, 1835, was made a municipality of that name by the Consultation, with Nashville as the seat of government,[22] On November 12, Parmer was elected a member of the General Council from Tenehaw Municipality.[23] His resignation from that body was accepted December 15.[24] He, Stephen W. Blount and E. O. Le Grand on February 1, 1836, were elected from San Augustine Municipality as delegates to the Constitutional Convention.[25] Parmer was seated March 1.[26]

On March 16 Parmer, Thomas J. Gazley and Edwin Waller, members of the Convention, and Isham Parmer, door-keeper, left for their homes.[27] Regarding their departure Colonel Gray wrote in his diary:

219

Some members are going home. Col. Parmer, Mr. Waller and Mr. Gazley have obtained leave of absence. Col. Parmer was authorized by resolution to press wagons, horses, etc., and to take possession of the public arms at Nacogdoches, etc.[28]

It appears that one of the first horses impressed for the army by Parmer was one belonging to Mrs. James W. Robinson, wife of the former Lieutenant Governor of the Provisional Government. Governor Robinson before joining the army had provided a horse for Mrs. Robinson's use in the Runaway Scrape. At the home of James Whitesides in the present county of Washington Colonel Palmer "pressed" the horse for the army much to the chagrin of Mrs. Robinson. Referring to the incident Colonel Gray said:

> [Mrs. Robinson] made loud complaint against Col. Palmer, who had pressed into the public service her horse, which her husband, who was gone to the army, had left for her to retreat upon. She was now afoot, and in her indignation she said she would be durned if she did not take the first horse she could find.

On August 16, 1839, Parmer was appointed chief justice of Jasper County by President Lamar,[29] being succeeded January 30, 1840, by M. B. Lewis.[30]

Col. Martin Parmer died March 2, 1850,[31] while preparing to move to Walker County and was buried on the A. C. Parmer survey about twelve miles southeast of Jasper, Jasper County. The Commission of Control for Texas Centennial Celebrations had his remains exhumed, and, on June 6, 1936, re-interred in the State Cemetery at Austin and had a monument erected at his new grave.

When Parmer County, Texas, was created August 21, 1876, it was named "in honor of Martin Parmer, an eccentric Texan of the olden time, and one of the signers of the Declaration of Texas Independence."[32]

Parmer was married four or five times, depending upon the legality of his marriage with Candace Midkiff, Peter Ellis Bean's Texas wife, who admitted that she was not legally married to Bean. The noted Peter Ellis Bean, an Anglo-American who bore the title of colonel in the Mexican Army and who divided his time between his Anglo-American wife in East Texas and his Mexican wife in Mexico had been on an extended visit to the latter when the Fredonian War started. He was ordered to Texas by the Mexican government to help pacify the Indians with whom he had great influence. Upon his arrival he found two very good reasons for opposing Martin Parmer, one because he was a Fredonian and the other because just prior to his arrival Parmer had married Bean's Texas wife.

In a letter written at Iola, Grimes County, Texas, August 30, 1902, by William P. Zuber to A. W. Morris, Willis, Texas, Zuber, who married a granddaughter of Colonel Parmer, tells in detail of the romantic marriage of Colonel Parmer and Candace Midkiff-Bean.

221

It appears that word had reached Texas that Colonel Bean was dead. Shortly after receiving this news, and shortly after the death of Colonel Parmer's wife, according to Zuber, Colonel Parmer and Mrs. Bean were married "by bond, I think, no priest being convenient." "My opinion," he wrote, "is that he [Parmer] proposed to give up his place to his children, and live on Bean's place, which was then believed to be Mrs. Bean's property and would have been such if Bean had been really dead."

"I now approach the heart of the event," continued Mr. Zuber:

> Colonel Parmer went to Mrs. Bean's residence, married her and stayed there with her during that day and the night following, also during the second day and night. But on the third day a reliable man came from the west and called to inform him that Bean was not dead. That notable man was

alive, in good health and on his way to his Texas home. He had halted at San Felipe where business had detained him during a few days, and the informant had seen him there and talked with him.

This intelligence abruptly ended a newly begun wedded life, about forty-eight hours after its commencement. Colonel Parmer, probably unwilling for Bean to find him there, departed for his own residence and never returned. One or more days later Bean arrived at home; with what emotions he and his wife met, probably no one but themselves ever knew. The recent unfortunate event did not separate them, but he continued to live with her as formerly, acknowledging her as his wife, but not amicably as I shall show.

It seems surprising that Bean did not kill Parmer; probably he may have considered Parmer's unfortunate belief that he was dead. Nevertheless, he was always thereafter Parmer's bitter enemy. I do not know that he and Parmer ever met after that unfortunate affair. It may be that both avoided meetings, as one would have been bitterly unpleasant to both.

222

Mention of the marriage of Colonel Parmer and Mrs. Bean is made in a letter dated "Trinity December the 31st 1826," written by Colonel Bean to Stephen F. Austin. He intimates that when he returned home Colonel Parmer fled across the Sabine. He wrote:

> With this I send you a proven certificate Declerid Before esqr. Grisham. It is in english; you will Do me the favour to translate this [into Spanish] and send it on. This is a favour that I Ever shall esteem. This woman was married to Parmer but when she hear of my [coming] on she left him and has given him a bill of sail of all my stock of catel and hogs.
>
> Mr. Hais [Hays] that was the magistrit that staited she swore she was married to [me] and took the Bill of Sail for my Property. Run off when he heard of my Coming and Past [the] Sabine. I am sir with Dew Respect your Sincer friend."[33]

Colonel Bean referred to the following certificate:

Deposition of Candes Metcalf
State of Cowehey and Texus
District of the Natches
December 28th, 1826

This day appeared Candes Metcalf and after Being duly sworn deposeth and answereth to the within named questions as follows.

Question the first: Did you ever Swear before Demetrie Hays, Alcalda for the District of Natches in the above named State that you was lawfully married to Peter Ellis Bean. To question the first She anawereth no that she never Did.

Question the 2d: Did not the above Demetrie Hays state to you that if you had not answered his questions that Samuel Norris the Chief Commandent at Nacogdoches would send Malitia and have you taken? Answereth to the third question that She did state before the said Hays on examination that She was lawfully married to Peter Ellis Bean.

Question the fourth: Why did you answer in the way you did to the third question? She answereth to the fourth question the cause why she answered the third question as she did was to save the property of Peter Ellis Bean in her hands as she supposed he never would return.

Question the fifth: Was you ever Lawfully married to Peter Ellis Bean? To this question She answereth she never was.

Sworn to Before me this day and Date above written.

[signed, her mark]
Candes Metcalf

223

Parmer was first married to Sarah Hardick. Next he married a widow, Mrs. Lornt. His third wife was another widow, Mrs. Margaret Neal. His fourth wife, Zina Kelly, survived him and lived for a number of years in Waller.

Only the names of the children of the first marriage of Parmer are known to the author. They were Charlotte, who married William Idles; William, who married a cousin, Lucinda Caldwell in Arkansas; Martha, who married William

Driskill in Arkansas; Emily, who was married to Chichester Chaplin in Texas; Isham, who was never married; Thomas, who married Rachel Teal; Nancy, who married Daniel Moore; and Mary Palmer, who married Henry Black. All of the children of Martin Parmer spelled their name "Palmer."

The census of 1835 of San Augustine shows Parmer living with his second wife, who before marriage was Mrs. Sevina Lornt, a widow. Some of the children listed were doubtless those of his wife by a former marriage. The census also shows that Parmer did not give his correct age to the census taker. He is shown as aged 50; his wife, Sevina, 43. The children were Bailey, nineteen; Antone, eighteen; Indiana D., nine; Matilda and Ruth, twins, seven; John, five; and Martin, two years of age.[34]

William P. Zuber, who as a boy served in the Texas Army in 1836, was married to a granddaughter of Martin Parmer. Zuber's wife was a daughter of William and Charlotte (Parmer) Liles.

In 1941 some of the surviving grandchildren of Martin Parmer were Mrs. Low Parker, Trinity, Texas, a daughter of William Parmer, son of Martin Parmer by his first marriage; and Mrs. T. M. Brewer, 103 Dresden Street, Houston, a daughter of Martin and Zina Kelly Parmer.

Other descendants were Mrs. G. J. Creighton, Conroe; Mrs. Phil H. Sticker, 1403 Holman, Houston; and Mrs. J. E. McQuillen, 3401 Avenue K, Galveston.

SYDNEY O. PENINGTON[1]
of
SHELBY MUNICIPALITY

Sydney O. Penington came to Texas from Arkansas Territory[2] in 1834.[3] He was born in Christian County, Kentucky, February 27, 1809, proof of which will be given later in this sketch. He settled in a part of San Augustine Municipality now in Shelby County, where he engaged in surveying. On October 17, 1835, he enrolled in Capt. John M. Bradley's Company of Volunteers. He was elected second lieutenant November 22. He participated in the storming and capture of Bexar, December 5 to 10, 1835,[4] and was honorably discharged December 17.[5]

Shelby Municipality was created from San Augustine Municipality December 15, 1835, was allowed two delegates to the Constitutional Convention.[6] On February 1, 1836, the voters in the municipality elected Penington and Rev. William C. Crawford to represent them at the Convention. The number of votes cast were not reported to the Convention.[7] Penington was seated March 1.[8]

On March 23, 1836, Sydney O. and Joseph Penington enlisted in Capt. James Chesser's Company of Jasper Volunteers.[9] Joseph was first corporal of the company July 26, 1836.[10] Sydney O. was transferred to Capt. John M. Bradley's Company of "San Augustine Volunteers," April 30.[11] The author has no evidence that Sydney O. and Joseph Penington were related.

Penington was a member of the House of Representatives from Shelby County in the First Congress of the Republic, October 3, 1836, to June 14, 1837.[12] In a letter dated Shelby County, August 1, 1837, he said: "My health is still very bad."[13] He died October 28, 1837. The Commission of Control for Texas Centennial Celebrations had a monument erected at his grave in the cemetery in Shelbyville in 1936.[14] Pertinent information relative to Sydney O. Penington was unearthed in the lawsuit styled "James C. Atkinson vs W. J. Lister et al." which was tried in Shelby County in 1896.[15] Atkinson, a grandson of Penington's mother, was suing to recover some of the headright land which had originally been granted to the heirs of Penington and surveyed in Shelby County, Texas, not far from Logansport, Louisiana. The files in the case contain depositions of several old men then residing in Christian County, Kentucky, who had known Penington since he was a boy, as well as Atkinson's deposition. A torn and badly worn letter purportedly written by Penington from San Augustine, Texas, May 24, 1835, to his half brother, Samuel C. Atkinson, was also offered as evidence. Penington's signature, however, had been torn off.

226

Penington's name is usually misspelled Pennington, even by those who were acquainted with him, but his signature on the Declaration of Independence and on a letter he wrote May 15, 1836, is definitely *Penington*.

All of the witnesses agreed that Sydney O. Penington and his sister, Jane A. Penington, were illegitimate children of Nancy Rigsdale. All of them claimed that they did not know who the father was.[16] Nancy Rigsdale later married Amos Atkinson and bore him several children. The attorneys tried to prove that Sydney and Jane Penington were also children of Amos Atkinson and Nancy Rigsdale, born out of wedlock, and given the name of Penington, but they failed to do so, the witnesses contending that they did not know who the father was. None gave Sydney O. Penington's full name. The "Oswald" seems to have been supplied by Sam Houston Dixon.

The following testimony offered by Atkinson was not disputed: Nancy Rigsdale had two children out of wedlock,

Sydney O. and Jane A. Penington. Sydney O. Penington was born February 27, 1809, in Christian County, Kentucky, and died in Shelby County, Texas, October 28, 1837. He was never married. Jane A. Penington was born May 2, 1814, and died in Kentucky, March 16, 1888. She was married to James Manahan.

Nancy Rigsdale was married to Amos Atkinson in about 1815 and died in Christian County, Kentucky, July 15, 1851. Children of this union were: Samuel C., Sarah E., Francis M., Pembroke S. and Elisha F. Atkinson.

Samuel C. Atkinson was born August 10, 1817, and died February 14, 1889. He was married to Theodocia Bailey.

Sarah E. Atkinson was born April 3, 1822, and died November 16, 1887. She was married to Nathaniel Tandy.

Francis M. Atkinson was born September 14, 1827, and died in 1870. He was married to Elizabeth Power.

Pembroke S. Atkinson was born September 11, 1829, and died September 27, 1867. He was married to Mary J. Clark. A son of this union, James G. Atkinson, was residing in Christian County, Kentucky, in 1896.

227

Elisha F. Atkinson was born May 27, 1831, and died April 13, 1862, at Chattanooga, Tennessee, while serving in the Confederate Army. He had never married.

Following is the text of Sydney O. Penington's will:

> In the name of God, Amen: I, S. O. Penington being in my proper mind make this my last will and Testament.
>
> I wish William S. Watson to Administer on my estate and expose to sale enough to pay my just debts as soon as practicable. The residue, if any, I will bequeath to Nancy Atkinson, my mother, in Christian County, Ky.
>
> Sydney O. Penington.
>
> P. S. I further will and ordain that Five Hundred Dollars of my estate shall be given to Sydney O. Hennies.
>
> Mr. Watson: I want you to lay out my own order of Survey on the place where George Gooden lived. O'Bannion's

is Hennie's—my other lands and land matters you can see what should be done with them. Some is in the hands of Mr. Dunn and some in Mr. White's hands.

Sydney O. Penington.[17]

Following is a copy of a letter written by Mr. Penington:

San Augustine, Texas
May 24th, 1835
Mr. Samuel Atkinson

Dear Brother, I have just returned from the Trinity River after a trip of 4 months. I have had good health and tolerable good luck. We have a new commissioner [original is torn] to the titles [original is torn] survey some sand & am going in a few days to the Trinity again. In fact I am doing as well as I wish. I have a plenty to do and that at the highest sort of wages. I have to hire a hand to run the lines and it requires a man of smartness and they very soon find that they had as well run lines for themselves and soon quit or ask $2 per day. If you will come and stay with me 6 months I will give you $180 in Cash or a Compass and instruments to survey with and a commission. Come this fall as soon as the sickly season is over or write that you wont come and I will then be satisfied and not hope to see a brother that I greatly love. Stand behind the [illegible in original] point and be called something of importance. Kill my hopes or verify them, I humbly beg. Just Write that you will come and you can have the money remited to you to bear your expenses.

Just please to write and direct it to San Augustine Texas. Bolins has been here and stay[ed] an hour or two and left. I did not see them. [The rest of the letter is missing.]

Clearly and distinctly the following letter was signed by Sydney O. Penington:

Fort Bend, May 15th, 1836
To the Honl. The President of the Republic of Texas

Dear Sir, During the existence of the Provincial Govrmt of Texas E. Raines was appointed primary Judge, and James

228

English asassistant Judge for the Municipality of Shelby. Since the decesion & decree of the convention ordering that all Judicial proceedings only in criminal cases should cease, they have Continued to Issue warrants & Try cases, Issue Executions, & sell property &c.

Judge English has, in one case, sat as Judge and gave a decision when he was the security to one of the Partys. Their dicisions and official acts has caused much Dissatisfaction in the county, and it's humbly hoped that you will Require and account of them how they have discharged their duties, as soon as they return to Texas, for they have both left and will no doubt remain as long as there is any danger in the Country. The sheriff who was elected by the people for that county has also left the Republic. Let me beg of you to order them at any rate to cease all civil operations at law, for official Robery is too bad.

Sir with Esteem I have the Honor to subscribe myself your Most obt & Humble servt.

Sydney O. Penington[18]

ROBERT POTTER
of
NACOGDOCHES MUNICIPALITY

Robert Potter was born in Granville County, near Williamsboro, North Carolina, in June, 1799.[1] In a speech in the North Carolina House of Commons in March, 1827, he said: "While a boy, of the age of fifteen years, I left the humble home of my youth, and went forth to do whatever my humble arm could in behalf of my country...During six years, in the very Spring time of life, from the age of fifteen to twenty one, I bore the arms of my country in the Navy of the United States."[2]

On March 2, 1815, he was appointed midshipman. At Oxford, North Carolina, 26 days later he accepted. On June 24, he was ordered to report for duty to Charlestown (now a part of Boston), Massachusetts. He served on the schooner *Java* from August 10 to September 23, and on the brig *Prometheus*, engaged in revenue duty, from October 30 to sometime in 1816. For the two years from 1816 to 1818 he was on the steamer *Independence* at Charlestown. Later he served aboard the *Congress*, the frigate *Constellation*, the *John Adams*, and the frigate *United States*. From the last, at Norfolk, Virginia, on March 20, 1821, he tendered his resignation, which was accepted a few days later.[3]

> Feeling an obligation towards dependent members of his family and seeing no prospect of being able to help them by continuing in that service, he resigned...the Navy, and settled in Halifax, studying law in the office of Thomas Surges, an eminent lawyer of that day.[4]

Potter began the practice of law at Halifax and, in 1826, was elected from Halifax County to the North Carolina House of Commons, defeating Jesse A. Bynum. In July, 1827, he returned to his native county of Granville, where, according to Robert Watson Winston,

> —he immediately announced himself for the House of Commons on this platform: "Destruction of the State Bank, reduction of all salaries, and cutting down the fees and charges of attorneys, commissioners ,and others. No judge to have a salary above a thousand dollars, no lawyer to have a fee above ten dollars." On these issues, Potter went to the people and was elected to the House of Commons by a great majority—a triumph, indeed, for the restless iconoclast, his canvass having been so brilliant it thrilled the state and swept him into the halls of Congress. In August, he had been elected to the legislature; in November, three months

later, he was sent to Congress—the main issue being the destruction of the banks.

August 28, 1831 fell on Sunday. Potter was at home [in Oxford] that day with his wife, a good woman, and North Carolina and Virginia stock, a Miss Pelham. Mrs. Potter had two cousins who often visited the home, Reverend Louis Taylor, a minister of the Methodist Church, about fifty-five years old, and Louis Wiley, a youth of seventeen. Potter had conceived a dark malignant hatred for these two men and had charged his wife with criminal intimacy with both. That day, Sunday, August 28, Taylor came out to Potter's on a visit, not knowing Potter's feelings towards him. Potter laid the charge of adultery on Taylor and after a few angry words, pounced on him like a wild beast, beating him senseless. He then whipped out his keen sharp blade and (Maimed) the man, "Potterized" him.—Potter then set forth in search of Wiley, who lived three or four miles nearer Oxford then Reverend Mr. Taylor's home. Finding Wiley at home, Potter sprang upon him like a tiger, treating him as he had Taylor.

Next day, Monday, August 29, Potter was arrested and put in jail without being permitted to give bond, because it was claimed that his victims were in danger of dying and under these circumstances, bail was not allowable. On the following first Monday in September, he was tried in Oxford before Robert Strange, an eminent judge, and a jury. No lawyer would or did not appear for him and he therefore represented himself and, it must be said, had a fool for a client. His plea was the unwritten law—but he seems to have been without any evidence except his own on this point.— Potter was convicted of the charge of maim and sentenced to jail for two years and to pay a fine of a thousand dollars.— He was not [this time] imprisoned in the Oxford jail, where ordinarily he would have been, but in the Hillsboro [Orange County] jail, some distance away.

The next legislature met in November and the people of the state were so outraged by Potter's act that a bill was passed making his crime an offense punishable with death, "without benefit of clergy."[5]

231

It might be mentioned here that the law was revised in 1868 and the penalty was reduced to imprisonment, for not less than five years, nor more than 60 years.[6]

Upon being released from jail at the expiration of his term Potter hastened to Granville and announced his candidacy for the House of Commons and in the ensuing election, he was elected.

> Reaching the capital and taking his seat in the legislature in 1834, Potter found the House in the control of his enemies and solidly massed against him. They would not fight him a duel and they were no match for him in debate. They, therefore, concluded to get rid of him in some other way. This, Potter claimed, they did. In January, 1835, the moving orator, the magnetic daredevil was expelled and for what? He had been playing a game of cards unfairly, contrary to the rules! The vote to expel stood 62 to 52 and in the minority were some of the ablest men in the House. Undoubtedly Potter's real offense was not gambling, but the maiming of Taylor and Wiley.[7]

Bishop Cheshire's version of the card game differs somewhat from the ones usually given:

> On Christmas night about nine or ten o'clock he and a man named Cotten (I think it was R. C. Cotten; and I have heard of him as "Carney Cotten," a member of the House from Chatham County), sat down to a game of cards, a gambling game called "Thirteen the Odd." Stakes were high, and after a few hours Cotten had won all Potter's money. Potter said he would get more, and went off and returned with a new supply. After some hours Cotten had again stripped him. A new supply was again obtained. The hour was now very late—or rather, very early. The struggle was protracted until eight or nine o'clock the following morning, when Potter had been completely exhausted of funds. The money lay piled high on the table between them. Swearing a great oath that no rascal should cheat him, Potter suddenly seized the

232

money and crammed it into his pockets. Cotten sprang upon him, the table was overturned, and there was a desperate struggle. Finally Potter drew a pistol and held Cotten off with it; and thus got off with his booty.

The matter was brought to the attention of the House, and a committee of investigation was appointed, of which Edward B. Dudley, afterwards Governor, was the leading member. This committee reported the facts as above stated, and brought in a resolution that Potter be expelled. This was opposed by some on the ground that, if the House should undertake to investigate the private character of its members it would be hard to say just where such an investigation would stop. Finally, however, a vote was taken, the roll was called, and sixty-two members voted for expulsion, and forty-two against; so the resolution was adopted by a majority of twenty, January 2, 1835.[8]

Potter arrived in Texas on July 1, 1835.[9] On October 9 he enlisted in Capt. Thomas J. Rusk's company of Nacogdoches Independent Volunteers.[10] On November 21, evidently with the intention of joining the navy, he retired from the army. On November 30 during a session of the General Council of the Provisional Government of Texas at San Felipe, the President of that body tendered the services of Potter in the navy of Texas.[11] On motion of D. C. Barrett his services were accepted. On December 1 Potter wrote to

233

> The Govr. & council of Texas:
> The undersigned being desirous of serving the country in the present emergency, and believing from his experience in Naval service, he could render more effectual service at sea than elsewhere, has already apprised the government of Texas through a member of their honorable body of his readiness to serve them whenever they can procure an armed ship—in the mean time he solicits of the Govt. & council a commission with letter of marque to cruise on the coast of the enemy.[12]

On the same day on motion of Daniel Parker the application of Potter for a commission with letters of marque and
reprisal was granted.[13]

At the election held in Nacogdoches Municipality on
February 1, 1836, Potter, Thomas J. Rusk, Charles S. Taylor
and John S. Roberts were chosen to represent the municipality at the Constitutional Convention.[14]

Capt. Sidney Sherman's Company of Volunteers, recruited in Kentucky and Ohio, had recently arrived in
Nacogdoches to fight for the independence of Texas. They
presented themselves at the polls but at first were denied
the privilege of voting. Later, however, their votes were accepted. William Fairfax Gray tells of the part Potter played
in the election:

> Several of the candidates addressed the people, and
> among them the famous Robert Potter, of North Carolina,
> who had been here some months. On the volunteers offer-
> ing to vote they were refused by the judges, which caused an
> angry excitement. The company was drawn up with loaded
> rifles and the First Lieutenant, Woods, swore that the men
> should vote, or he would riddle the door of the Stone House,
> where the election was held, with rifle balls.

Potter appealed "to the passions of the men" and exhorted "them to perseverance in their determination to vote."[15]

There is little doubt that Potter owed his election to the
newly arrived soldiers. He was seated at the Convention
March 1.[16]

The Convention, on Saturday, March 5, adjourned until
Monday morning. On Sunday, the sixth, "The President
called the convention together, and informed them that he
had received by express a letter from Col. W. Barret Travis,
Commandant of the Alamo, at Bejar de San Antonio, which
required the immediate action of the convention." In the
letter, dated March 3, Travis said among other things, "I
hope your honorable body will hasten on reinforcements,

ammunition, and provisions to our aid as soon as possible." On motion of Potter, it was

> *Resolved,* That the safety of the country is threatened in a manner which makes it the duty of all her citizens to hasten to the field.
>
> *Resolved,* That the members of the convention, while they keep steadily in view the organization of the government, will, in the present emergency, adjourn to meet in the camp of our countrymen, there or elsewhere to complete the business of the convention.
>
> *Resolved,* That a committee of five members be appointed, clothed with all the powers residing in the Convention, to raise and organize the militia and volunteers, provide supplies and ammunition for the troops, and to draft an appeal to the people of Texas and to the United States, explaining our situation and the motives of our adjournment.
>
> Mr. Potter advocated the adoption of the resolution: Messrs. Collinsworth, Childress, and Rusk, in opposition thereto, and the question being taken thereon, it was decided in the negative.[17]

235

Viewing Potter's brilliance and his experience in the United States Navy, the Convention, on March 17, elected him *ad interim* secretary of the navy of the Republic of Texas. On April 20, President Burnet appointed him commander of the Port of Galveston.[18]

While stationed on Galveston Island with the President and some other members of his cabinet Potter became acquainted with Mrs. Soloman C. Page, nee Harriet A. Moore, daughter of Francis Moore and sister of John D. Moore.

Francis Moore, whose home was in Brazoria County, was at this time a refugee on Galveston Island while John D. Moore and Soloman C. Page were members of Capt. Peyton R. Splane's company in the Army of Texas.[19]

According to Mrs. Page (who in later years became Mrs. Harriet A. Ames) she and her two small children, a boy and a girl, were among the refugees who accepted Potter's invitation to occupy quarters on board a vessel of the Texas Navy.[20]

When Page went to Galveston for his wife she refused to go with him, claiming that he had mistreated her in many ways and had even deserted her.

> We all stayed on the ship [wrote Mrs. Ames], until after the battle of San Jacinto had been fought, and then I wanted to go to my grandmother's in Kentucky. I had parted forever from my husband, for he came on board the ship and begged me to return to him, but no inducement could turn me from my purpose, to go away from him and Texas forever. He had left his innocent, helpless little babies and young wife [in Brazoria County] to perish with starvation. No, never, never, would I trust myself nor them to his mercy again.
>
> ...When Col. Potter found how anxious I was to go to my Grandmother, he told me that he had promised Mr. Moore to take his daughter [Martha] to Kentucky where she was to live with her Grandmother, and go to school, and that he would take charge of both of us that far.[21]

In May, 1836, Potter, Mrs. Page and son, the daughter having died at Galveston, and Martha Moore, who appears not to have been related to Mrs. Page, sailed for New Orleans. After remaining there for a short time they boarded a steamer that landed them in Shreveport, Louisiana, on Red River, greatly to the surprise of herself and Martha Moore. Using one ruse after another, Potter, Mrs. Ames said, finally coaxed the two women to accompanying him to a house Potter owned, or had rented, on the Sabine River in Texas. En route on more than one occasion he had asked Mrs. Page to marry him but she had always declined on account of never having been legally divorced from her husband.

> One day [wrote Mrs. Ames], he came up to the house and said that he had some important questions to ask me

if I would answer them and when I assented he inquired whether my marriage with Page had been solemnized by a priest. I explained how the ceremony had been performed. We were not married by a priest. "Very well," he answered, "your marriage with Page was not legal, because in Texas a marriage not solemnized by a priest is not valid. Therefore you are just as free, according to the laws of Texas, as if you had never married." I listened to all he said and promised to think the matter over. He loved me very devotedly, and the more I thought about it the better it seemed out of my difficulties.

So one evening, according to the custom of the country, the little assembly gathered to see us wedded; the ceremony was a very simple one in those days in that country, but it was just as binding as judge and clergy were present. The only guests at our piney woods wedding, were Joe Miller, George Torents, Paddy Roling and Martha Moore.[22]

Potter and Mrs. Page resided for a year on the Sabine, in what is now Harrison County, then a part of Shelby County, building in the meanwhile a home at a site since known as "Potter's Point," on Caddo Lake in what is now Marion County. At that time the lake was known as Ferry, or Soda Lake, and it was in Red River County. Unable to persuade his wife to return to him, Page obtained a divorce from her May 11, 1840, in the Harris County District Court at Houston,[23] and later left Texas.

Potter did not participate in the Battle of San Jacinto, but after Santa Anna had been captured, he was in favor of hanging him. His conduct as a cabinet officer was severely criticized, but this did not prevent his election as senator to the Fifth[24] and Sixth[25] Congresses, November 2, 1840, to the time of his death, March 2, 1842, from the district composed of Red River and Fannin Counties. In 1841 he was a member of the law firm of Potter and Van Zandt, composed of Robert Potter of Paschal County and Isaac Van Zandt of Panola County.

OUR (unlikely) FATHERS

Capt. William Pinkney Rose, who, it has been claimed, commanded a company in the Battle of New Orleans, January 8, 1815, moved to Texas in the winter of 1839 and located about eight miles east of Marshall, Harrison County. Shortly afterwards he organized a band of citizens for the avowed purpose of ridding the country of lawless characters. Some of these men committed so many crimes against the law they purported to uphold that they soon became regarded as outlaws themselves. In consequence of the various ineffectual attempts to arrest Rose, who by his extraordinary adroitness in escaping, and the absolute sway which he held over a large following, he came to be known as the "Lion of the Lakes." He later moved to a place about seven miles east of where the present city of Jefferson now stands, in what was known as Caddo Bend.

An alienation arose between Rose and Potter which was intensified when Rose espoused the candidacy of John B. Denton, who was defeated for a seat in the Senate by Potter in the election held September 5, 1841.

President M. B. Lamar on November 15, 1841, offered a reward of $500 for the capture of Rose who was charged with assisting in the murder of John B. Campbell, sheriff of Panola County on January 31, 1841, and of murdering D. Minor and D. Morris, citizens of that county, on about September first. Potter was accused of prevailing upon Lamar to offer the reward. After the adjournment of Congress Potter set out to supervise the killing or capture of Rose. As a consequence he himself was killed on the morning of March 2, 1842. There are many versions of how he was killed. The account contained in the memoirs of Mrs. Ames, an eyewitness to the assassination, written at her home in New Orleans when she was 83 years of age, is used in this sketch:

> It was early in March when my husband [Robert Potter] brought the President's proclamation down to the Point,

and gathered a company of seventeen men to assist in capturing this outlaw. In those days Texas was ruled by two parties, the moderators and regulators; the former believed in administering justice in a legal way and the latter dealing it out in arbitrary and usually quite sudden fashion. Col. Potter belonged to the moderator's party and Old Rose was to be imprisoned and tried by law in the county courthouse.

Old Rose was busily engaged in supervising the work of his negroes who were clearing off a new piece of ground and burning the brush-wood upon it, piling the brush in heaps and then setting fire to it, when he saw a number of men riding towards his house. He realized that he was outnumbered and knew well what their visit portended, so down he fell upon the ground and ordered the negroes to pile brush-wood over him at once. He knew that Col. Potter had offered to plead against him when he was captured, and that at his request President Houston would take effective steps towards his arrest. The men were all armed when they rode up to Rose's house and presented their warrant, for they intended to overpower their prisoner and take him without bloodshed if possible. He was not there however, nor could they find him anywhere upon the place. It did not once occur to them to look under the brushwood piles for him. Preston Rose was a nice young man who had just been married a short while before this event; he was not at all like his father, and so, when they failed to find the old man, he begged my husband to go peaceably away, that he would make his father give himself up and be tried. Col. Potter believed him, the more readily perhaps, because he was tired out from his long trip to Austin. Preston assured my husband that if his father refused to go peacefully or if there was any danger to him or the men with him on account of this visit that he would notify us so that we might be prepared.

Satisfied that Old Rose would give himself up without further trouble, the men dispersed and my husband came home.

When I learned of the result of their mission I was distressed. "When Old Rose hears that you have been hunting

239

for him he will come here tonight and try to kill you," I said. I begged him to gather all the men he could and have them in the house with firearms ready for an attack, but he only laughed at my fears. He admitted that Rose might feel revengeful, but that it would be impossible for him to get men enough that night to make an attack. He was so tired that he would not listen to any thought of danger, and so went to rest. No sooner did Old Rose see from his safe retreat, his enemies ride away than he was up in a moment and dispatched runners in haste to his acquaintances asking them to come that night, and surround Col. Potter's house to kill him.

A request from Rose was a command which not one of the men dared to disobey. That all but the man Schott [John W. Scott] which were friends of the Colonel's indebted to him for innumerable kindnesses, did not count in the least with them in the face of old Rose's command.

When darkness had settled down over the forest and the angel of Peace had brought sleep to weary eyes, evil spirits were going to and fro plotting murder. Old Rose felt sure that if he could compass Col. Potter's death no one else would dare to molest him.

I felt very anxious as night advanced, and presently the barking of the dogs warned me that some stranger was around our home.

I woke my husband up and called his attention to this fact, but he would not believe that the house was being surrounded and said that he was so very tired to let him alone. I was too uneasy to sleep any myself and listened intently to the sounds outside; the barking and growling of dogs, the whirr of the crickets in the woods, and I could almost imagine the footfalls of human beings. So the night wore on until I felt that I could bear the suspense no longer. We always had our meal ground for breakfast in a steel mill, and it was almost time for the performance of that first morning duty.

I arose and woke the boy whose business it was to grind the meal, and told him it was time to get the meal ready for breakfast. The boy was obliged to cross the yard in order to reach the corn-crib and get a supply of corn for the mill. In a few moments he went out; he did not return, and as time went on the gray morning began to break into the dusk of night and shadows became less deep and dark, I roused my brother and told him about the boy's absence. He went out to look for him, and he, too, remained. We had an old man living with us who always fed the hogs and when he started to go out to his work I said to him it is very strange that George does not commence to grind the meal for breakfast. I wish you would see what is the matter. I waited awhile, and unable to stand the anxiety any longer I decided to go myself.

I stepped out into the early morning and started toward the kitchen. Just as the man Hezekiah [George] went over the stile some little distance from the left hand side of the house, I was halfway to the kitchen. A posse shot him down and tried to take me prisoner. I was very active and I darted away from them and ran into the house. Several shots were fired and their round awoke my husband. "What does that mean?" he asked me, as I came into the house. "It means that the house is surrounded, and that we will have fight or die," I replied. "Where are all the men?" he inquired, at once on the alert, and then I said what I always regretted saying, for I think it was a terrible blow to him, that probably discouraged him from making any defense. "I suppose the men are all killed; they have just killed one," I answered. Then he wanted to escape from the house, but I begged him not to go, and his little daughter whom he loved tenderly, cried and screamed for her Papa not to leave her. I think he was unnerved by the loss of the men and thought that his only safety lay in getting away from the house. "I want to tell you something," he said at three different times, but I was so anxious trying to persuade him to remain with me and defend himself that I did not ask him what it was, nor did I understand the meaning of his words until afterwards.

He looked through a small crack in the wall at the back of the house and seeing the number of the attacking party he said that the only thing for him to do was to get down to

241

the lake where he would be safe as he was a fine swimmer. We had a cannon and plenty of firearms all loaded, and I reminded him that I could load guns as fast as he could.

"We can defend ourselves," I said. "I will stand by you as long as we both live. If you will just kill old Rose and Schott, [John W. Scott] the difficulty will be at an end." But in the haste and excitement of the moment he paid no attention to the argument.

Some weight seemed to be on his mind, something that he wanted to tell me.

As he left the house he said, "They cannot hurt you anyhow." I learned afterwards that his words bore another meaning. He ran from the house and jumped the fence. Six shots were fired at him. Just by the fence stood Sandy Miller and Stephen Peters.

"Why, these are my friends," he called out to me.

"No, they are not friends," I answered back, and as he jumped over the rails both men fired at him; the group who had been stationed behind the house yelled like Indians as they fired after Col. Potter's retreating form, and pointed the way he had gone. He ran down the hill and along the beach under the cliff unhurt by the bullets which whistled after him. We had cut steps down the steep bank to the spring and, at the foot of these grew three magnificent cypress trees.

Leaning his gun against one of these trees my husband sprang into the lake, and dived out of sight of his pursuers. Schott [Scott] ran down the bank behind him, while Old Rose levelled his gun at me and ordered me to go into the house.

What careless spirit could have entered my husband's mind and caused him to leave his gun on the shore is more than I could ever comprehend. Schott [Scott] seized it, and as Col. Potter's head rose out in the Lake he fired.

Old Rose still with his gun drawn on me tried to force me to go in, but I told him that I would not move a step nor did I.

Presently Schott [Scott] came up the bank and said to Rose, with some indignation, "What are you abusing Mrs.

242

Potter for? She has never done you any harm; come on let's go, we have done what we came to do."

I thought they were just talking to annoy me, now that my husband had escaped them. But before he would go Old Rose determined to wound me in some way. Turning, he said with a cruel sneer, "Now what do you think of your pretty Bobby?" Our small cannon loaded with buckshot stood beside me, but I had been unable to find the matches to fire it with.

When Old Rose spoke to me I exclaimed, "If only I had a match to touch off this cannon I would shoot your tongue down your throat."

What the wretch would have done I do not know but Schott said I was too brave a woman to kill, and took him away.

The other men released the boy and my brother whom they had taken prisoners, and I went with George to see if Hezekiah was quite dead. We found him living and dressed his wounds; from which he finally recovered. When Hezekiah had been cared for we began to look for Col. Potter. He was not on the islands nor on the shore; we searched all that day for him until I despaired of ever finding him alive and thought that, after all, Schott had killed him when he fired into the lake with his gun.

How horrible that broad sheet of water seemed to me, who had once thought it so beautiful; what dreadful secret did it hold from me? That night as if the elements were in sympathy with my tortured mind, there was a terrible thunderstorm. In the morning we decided to take the cannon down to the lake and fire it across the water, so that if Col. Potter had indeed been drowned we might recover his body.

We had rowed about the lake all day before, searching it well with a large spy-glass and nothing else was left for us to do.

We got the cannon down to the place from which he had jumped into the lake, for his tracks were plainly visible, but there was no need to fire it, for there in the early morning light lay my husband asleep upon the water.

243

That was a terrible time for me; we carried him up to the house and found that he had been shot in the back of his head.

In his trousers pocket was the match I had needed so sorely to fire the cannon upon his murderers. There were only two among all the men whom he had befriended who dared to come and help me to bury him.

There was a beautiful knoll on the hill in front of the house where a clump of tall trees grew. My husband had often said that when he died he would like to be buried there.

So we bore his body to the grave beneath the clump of trees that he had loved, and laid it there to rest...[26]

Potter's having been a signer of the Texas Declaration of Independence, secretary of the navy, and member of congress, it was appropriate that his remains should have been exhumed and, on October 9, 1928, reinterred in the State Cemetery, with a monument erected at the grave. When Potter County, Texas, was created August 21, 1876, it was named "in honor of Robert Potter, a distinguished Texan in the days of the Republic."[27]

244

On March 25, Mrs. Page, signing her name Harriet A. Potter, appeared before John T. Mills of the Seventh District of the Republic and preferred charges against William P. Rose, Preston Rose, John W. Scott, Stephen Peters, Samuel Perkins, Sandy Miller, James Williams, William Smith, Isaac Jones, and Calvin Puller for having murdered Robert Potter, March 2, 1842.[28] On March 26 Judge Mills ordered Edward West, Sheriff of Red River County, to arrest the persons named above.

The Roses and John Scott were arrested March 29 and Isaac Jones was arrested March 31, "by taking their bodies and bringing them to Clarksville." West was assisted by a company of 30 or 40 men raised by Col. R. H. Hamilton. On April 6 the grand jury of Red River County, of which James Latimer was foreman, returned a true bill.

William P. Rose, Preston Rose, John W. Scott, Samuel Petters, Samuel Perkins, William Smith and Calvin Puller, not having the fear of God Before their eyes, But being moved and seduced by the instigation of the Devil, on the second day of March in the year of our Lord one thousand eight hundred and forty two, with force and arms at and in the County of Red River and Republic of Texas, feloniously wilfully and maliciously and of their malice aforethought, in and upon one Robert Potter, in the peace of God and our said Republic, then and there Being did make an assault, and that said William P. Rose [and the others named] a certain Gun at the value of Twenty Dollars, then and there charged and loaded with Gun Powder and divers laden shot, which said Gun the said William P. Rose, [and the others named] in their hands then and there had and held to, against and upon the body of the said Robert Potter, then and there feloniously, wilfully and maliciously, and of their malice aforethought did shoot and discharge, and that the said William P. Rose [and the others named] with the laden Shot, aforesaid, Shot, discharged and sent forth as aforesaid, the aforesaid Robert Potter in and upon the back part of the head of him the said Robert Potter—one wound of the depth of five inches and the Breadth of two inches, of which, said wound, the said Robert Potter then and there instantly died.

245

On April 13, William P. Rose, John W. Scott, Preston Rose, and Isaac Jones prayed that the case be continued. They claimed that, since the accusation had been preferred against them, they had been held in strict confinement and for that reason had been unable to have present at court their defence witnesses, S. B. Alford, R. R. Perry, James Swanson, Joseph Perry, Logan B. Anderson, William H. Adams, Wiley Coon, William McMillan, Mrs. McMillan, William F. Johnson, Nathaniel King, Robert Smith, Mathias Ward, and Memucan Hunt. The case was continued until the next term of court.

On April 15, Ebenezer Allen, W. N. Porter, B. H. Martin, Edward H. Tarrant, W. Young, and A. H. Latimer, attorneys for the defendants, applied for bail for their clients. This was opposed by District Attorney Jesse Benton assisted by R. D. Ellis and William R. Scurry. Bail was denied on the 16th. There being no jail nearer than the one at Nacogdoches, distance 125 miles, Sheriff West with an order from Judge Mills, dated April 18, took the prisoners to Nacogdoches, at which place they arrived April 27. Sheriff David Rusk of Nacogdoches County refused to receive them on the plea that the Nacogdoches jail was not secure. West then left the prisoners in charge of guards and proceeded to Shelbyville, where Judge William B. Ochiltree, of the Fifth Judicial District, was holding court, who ordered Sheriff Rusk, to confine the prisoners in the Nacogdoches jail. Rusk, on May 2, made affidavit that the jail was "unsafe and insufficient to detain prisoners with security and safety, and could easily be broken open either by prisoners from within or persons without."

246

In the meantime the defendants' attorneys had been joined by Thomas J. Rusk and J. Pinckney Henderson who sued out a writ of *habeas corpus* in Judge Ochiltree's Court. On May 4, the prisoners were granted bail, William P. Rose's being fixed at $25,000, Scott's at $10,000 and Preston Rose's at $5,000. The case was transferred to Nacogdoches County to be tried May 6, 1843, but was dismissed before reaching trial.

Potter's will made at Austin, February 11, 1842, less than a month before he was killed, witnessed by Morgan C. Hamilton, T. Henderson, and N. B. Tancy, left his homestead on Ferry Lake to Sophia Ann Mayfield, wife of Col. James S. Mayfield. To Mrs. Mary W. Chalmers, wife of Dr. John G. Chalmers, he willed sections seventeen, eighteen, and nineteen on Ferry Lake, east of his homestead. Regarding Mrs. Page, Potter wrote in his will:

I give and bequeath to Mrs. Harriet A. Page all that part of my headlight, being part of my estate aforesaid lying north of section twelve before mentioned and west of section six as mentioned, except one thousand acres to be set apart by Mrs. Page and reserved for her brother John D. Moore. I also give and bequeath to her, two mares to be chosen by herself, my stock of cattle, and three negroes, to wit, George, Hannah and Matilda, and also my household and kitchen furniture, and farming utensils.

To Col. James B. Mayfield he gave his horse, Shakespeare. To his friend John W. Crunk he left a negro girl, Mary, and to Dr. Chalmers, "All my estate, real and personal that may remain after and satisfying the several bequests and objects herein before expressed."

247

JAMES POWER
of
REFUGIO MUNICIPALITY

*J*ames Power was born in County Wexford, Ireland in 1788.[1] In 1809 he emigrated to the United States and settled in New Orleans, where he lived until about 1822, when he went to Mexico. Visiting Texas in 1823, he began planning a colony there.[2] In this venture he interested Dr. James Hewetson, a fellow Irishman. On February 6, 1829, Congress, in accordance with article 31 of the colonization law of March 24, 1825, which made easy the naturalization of aliens who had married Mexican citizens,[3] declared

Power, who had married a Mexican, a citizen.[4] On June 11, 1828, the Legislature granted Power and Hewetson a contract to settle 200 families, half Irish and half Mexican, between the Guadalupe River and Lavaca Creek. This area was found insufficient, and, in March, 1829, the Legislature extended the colony to the Nueces. The colony was subject to continual difficulties: disputes with other empresarios, death of colonists, and shipwreck. Despite the extension of the contract—lengthening the time and permitting citizens of England, Germany, and the United States—the contract was never fulfilled.[5]

Power received large tracts of land in what is now Refugio County. On September 10, 1834, he was granted title to one league, on November 28, 1834, eleven leagues, and on October 20, 1834, with his son, one and a half leagues.[6]

On October 8, 1835, Power, Hugh McDonald Fraser, and John Malone were elected to represent Refugio Municipality in the Consultation set to meet at San Felipe de Austin, October 15,[7] but not one of the three attended; all probably were in the army. Power served under Capt. Ira Westover at the capture of the Mexican Fort Lipantitlan on the Nueces, November 4. He arrived at San Felipe, November 22, eight days after the Consultation had adjourned. He was seated as a member of the General Council of the Provisional Government.[8] On December 7 he wrote to John Malone to come to San Felipe and to take his place. By January 15, 1836, Malone had not arrived, and the Council directed that Hugh McFrazier (Hugh McDonald Fraser) attend.[9]

In December, 1835, Gen. Jose Antonio Mexia, with a fragment of the ill-fated Tampico expedition, arrived in Texas, and offered his services in the Texas Army. Governor Smith vetoed the Council's resolution inviting Mexia to join the army, but the Council disregarded the veto. Power offered to call on General Mexia and to inform him of the Council's action. To the Council, on December 17, Power reported:

I have called on General Mexia at Columbia. He has declined to go to Bejar to join our people. His object is to go Copano to join with the two hundred Mexicans who are at Palo Blanco; and from thence to take Matamoras if possible. Mr. [Jorge] Fisher, who is acting Secretary to the General, stated to me that the General could not place his military character at stake by accepting a command under the Provisional Government of Texas as Mr. Viesca is not Governor. I further understand that General Mexia will be here in a short time, with a view of seeing the Governor and Council, in hopes that they will place armed vessels to blockade the ports to Matamoros, where they can discharge their cargo, as there seems to be no doubt of the latter port falling into the hands of the liberal party. Mr. Fisher further stated that he was bearer of dispatches to General Mexia, that in February next there is a general plan of revolutionizing all over Mexico. Under these circumstances I thought it most prudent to return and inform the council, and subject myself to their further orders of this subject.[10]

249

At the election held in Refugio Municipality on February 1, 1836, Power and Sam Houston were elected delegates to the Constitutional Convention.[11] Soldiers garrisoned at the mission presented themselves at the ballot box, but the election officials refused them, asserting they were not citizens. The soldiers then returned to the mission, elected two of their members, David Thomas and Edward Conrad, to represent the army and signed a petition explaining their conduct.[12] Power, Houston, Thomas and Conrad were all seated at the Convention, March 1.[13]

After the adjournment of the Convention, Power did not rejoin the army. He was in New Orleans when the Battle of San Jacinto was fought.

Following the Revolution, Power laid out Aransas City on Live Oak Point and served as mayor in 1839. On January 9, 1838, he represented Texas in a treaty with the Lipan Indians at Live Oak Point. Later in the year he was captured by

Mexican raiders and imprisoned for a short while in Matamoros. Again in September, 1841, he was taken prisoner
to Matamoros but after a few weeks released.[14]

Power represented Refugio County in the House of Representatives for part of the Second Congress,[15] and in the
Constitutional Convention which met in Austin in 1845.[16]
He died August 15, 1852,[17] at his home on Live Oak Point
and was buried on his land. His remains were later removed to Mount Calvary Cemetery in Refugio, where a
monument marks his new grave.

Colonel Power was twice married. The two wives were
sisters, daughters of Capt. Felipe Roque Portilla, a former
officer of the Mexican Army and a colonist of Power and
Hewetson. Power first married Dolores Portilla, in Mon-
terrey. Their children were (1) James and (2) Dolores Power.
Mrs. Power died in 1836 and later Colonel Power married,
in San Patricio, Tomasita P. Portilla, who survived him and
who died in Refugio in 1893. Children of this union were:
(3) Tomasita C., (4) Eliza J., (5) Agnes E., (6) Mary F., and
(7) Phillip Power.

(1) James Power, Jr., son of the empresario, married Frances Bower, daughter of John White Bower, signer of the
Texas Declaration of Independence. This occurred June
21, 1866, at Copano House, a hotel the elder Power was
building at the time of his death. Children of James and
Frances Bower were: Mary Frances, who married Lewis
Henry Woodworth; Agnes, who married John F. Shelly;
and James F. Power, who, in January, 1940, was residing in
Refugio, Texas.

(2) Dolores Power was born in 1835. She married John
Welder, who with his parents and brother came to Texas
in 1835 as members of the Beale and Grant Colony. James
F. Welder, a son of this union was married to Katie Owens,
daughter of Richard and Elizabeth (McAnulty) Owens.
Surviving children of this union in 1942, were James P.

250

Welder, Victoria; Mrs. James B. Woods, Victoria; Mrs. W. J. Crabb; and Mrs. W. A. Smith, Houston.

(3) Tomasita Claire Power was born at Live Oak Point, September 9, 1839, and died at Refugio, May 8, 1932. She was married to Walter Lambert. Their children were James W., Philip, Allie C. and Lalla R. Lambert.

(4) Eliza J. Power was married to William Wilson.

(5) Agnes E. Power was married to John Franklin.

(6) Mary F. Power was never married.

(7) Philip Power was born at Live Oak Point, December 27, 1845, and died at Refugio in 1934.

JOHN S. ROBERTS
of
NACOGDOCHES MUNICIPALITY

John S. Roberts was born in Virginia, July 13, 1796.[1] In 1826, while he was deputy sheriff of Natchitoches Parish, Louisiana, just across the Sabine River from what is now Sabine County, Texas, the Fredonian War broke out, and he entered Texas and served as major in Haden Edwards's army. In 1827, after the suppression of the rebellion, he moved to Nacogdoches and there spent the remainder of his life.[2] On August 2, 1832, Roberts participated in the Battle of Nacogdoches when the Texans expelled from Nacogdoches the Mexican troops under Col. Jose de las Pedras.

Major Roberts, on October 4, 1835, the date of organization, was made first lieutenant of the Nacogdoches

Independent Volunteers of which Thomas J. Rusk was captain. The company joined the army before Bexar, November 25. When the Consultation designated Rusk recruiting officer at Nacogdoches, Roberts took command of the company and was with it when Cos and his army were driven from San Antonio on December 10, 1835. His company did not enter the town, for, according to Edward Burleson, commander-in-chief, "several parties were sent out mounted, under Capts. [James] Chessher, [Robert M.] Coleman and [John S.] Roberts, to scour the country, and endeavor to intercept Ugartechea, who was expected, and ultimately forced an entry, with reinforcements for General Cos. At three o'clock on the morning of the 5th instant Col. Neill, with a piece of artillery, protected by Capt. [John S.] Roberts and his company, was sent across the river to attack, at five o'clock, the Alamo, on the north side, to draw the attention of the enemy from the advance of the division which had to attack the suburbs of the town, under Colonels [Benjamin R.] Milam and [Francis W.] Johnson. This service was effected to my entire satisfaction; and the party returned to camp at nine o'clock a.m."[3]

Roberts received 640 acres of land from the Republic of Texas for having participated in the storming and capture of Bexar, December 5 to 10, 1835.[4] On the very day that he entered Bexar, December 5, 1835, he was issued title to 44,280 acres of land by the corrupt legislature of Coahuila and Texas for having served in the Mexican army against Indians, for a period of one year[5]—a service he had not performed. He, however, was not the only prominent Texan who had received such gigantic grants from the legislature.

A central executive committee called the "permanent council" was organized at San Felipe October 11 [1835], and on Sunday, the 18th, General Sam Houston, a member of it, proposed a resolution recommending that the consultation, when it met, should investigate and declare null all extensive grants of land made by the legislature under suspicious circumstances since 1833. The resolution was adopted, and a thousand copies in handbill form distributed through the country. It was probably needed to convince many of the citizens that the war just beginning was not a speculators "war," but it naturally drew a protest from the interested persons.[6]

The grants made to Major Roberts and to many others were cancelled by the Republic of Texas. Roberts, Thomas J. Rusk, Robert Potter and Charles S. Taylor were elected delegates to the Constitutional Convention. Roberts was seated March 2.[7] Two of the other delegates were Martin Parmer from San Augustine and James Gaines from Sabine Municipality. Parmer and Roberts in 1826 had aided Haden Edwards in his "Fredonian War," while Gaines was with the opposing faction. Roberts sat as a member of a court martial, of which Parmer was president, at Nacogdoches November 25, 1826, which offered a reward of $100 for the capture of Gaines, dead or alive.[8]

253

In 1838, during the Cordova rebellion, Gen. Rusk appointed Major Roberts quartermaster of the army. President Houston confirmed the appointment December 11, 1838.[9]

On December 26, 1826, Major Roberts was married to Mrs. Harriet Collier, widow of Robert Collier, a wealthy planter who lived near the present town of Milam in Sabine County and who had been assassinated. Collier had been married twice. By his first marriage he had two daughters who were grown at the time of his death. By his second wife, Harriet, Collier had four children, Susan, Rebecca, Nathaniel and John F. Collier. Maj. John S. and Harriet Roberts had at least four children: Susan A. H., Josephine Maria, Lycurgus S. and J. S. Roberts.

Rebecca Collier, daughter of Robert and Harriet Collier and step-daughter of John S. Roberts, was married to

Zachariah P. Fenley, and they settled on Fenley Lake near Angelina River in what is now Angelina County. Shortly after the breaking out of the Cordova rebellion, August 8, 1838, one of Fenley's slaves was induced to join the conspiracy. Fenley, who went in pursuit of the slave, was himself captured and murdered. On December 1, 1839, Mrs. Fenley sued Vincent Cordova for theft of her slave, William, alleging damages to the amount of $1,500 and recovered judgment against him. To satisfy the judgment, Cordova's half interest in the "stone house" was sold at auction to Rebecca Fenley, who transferred the title to her mother, Mrs. Harriet Roberts. Thus the title to the Old Stone Fort passed into the Roberts family, where it remained until purchased by Perkins Brothers in 1901.[10]

After the Texas Revolution, Major Roberts, John Durst and George Allen formed a partnership in the mercantile business in a building across the street from the Old Stone Fort. Later Frederick T. Phillips bought an interest in the firm which operated under the name of Roberts, Allen and Company. In March, 1838, Allen sold his interest in the business to Durst and moved to Houston, a town founded in 1836 by his brothers, Augustus C. and John K. Allen.

Eventually Major Roberts opened in the Old Stone Fort a saloon which he operated for many years until his death. He died August 9, 1871. His wife was born in Alabama, April 7, 1796, and died April 5, 1874. The Commission of Control for Texas Centennial Celebrations had a joint monument erected at their graves in Oak Grove Cemetery in Nacogdoches.

Major Roberts was a charter member of Milam Lodge No. 40, Ancient Free and Accepted Masons, Nacogdoches.[11]

When Roberts County, Texas, was created August 21, 1876, it was named "in honor of John S. Roberts, one of the signers of the Declaration of Texas Independence, and other distinguished Texans of that name."[12]

254

John F. Collier, stepson of Maj. John S. Roberts, was adopted by Major Roberts January 10, 1839, and his name changed by law to John Finley Roberts.[13] A grandson of his, John F. Roberts, in 1940 resided in Nacogdoches.

STERLING CLACK ROBERTSON
of
MILAM MUNICIPALITY

Sterling Clack Robertson, son of Elijah Robertson, was born October 2, 1785,[1] in Nashville, then in North Carolina but now the capital of Tennessee. He rose to the rank of major in the War of 1812[2] and with that rank served on the staff of Gen. William Carroll at the Battle of New Orleans, January 8, 1815.[3]

Early in the year 1822 a group of citizens of Davidson County, Tennessee, formed a "Texas Association" for the purpose of applying for a grant of land in Texas similar to that made to Austin. Robert Leftwich, the agent of the association, was sent to Mexico, where, with the assistance of Stephen F. Austin, he received a contract from the Legislature of Coahuila and Texas on April 15, 1825, to settle 800 families within six years on a large tract lying above the old San Antonio-Nacogdoches road. Leftwich had the contract made in his name, much to the dissatisfaction of his associates. Finally on October 15, 1827, a new contract was made with the company itself, but no settlers were introduced. On October 1, 1830, Sterling C. Robertson, one of the original stockholders, became the agent of the "Nash-

255

ville Company," a sub-company which had been formed.[4] He had visited Texas in 1825 or 1826 and had been, from the first, the most active member of the colonization project.

On April 6, 1830, six months before Robertson was made the agent for the Nashville Company, the Mexican government passed a law which virtually prohibited further immigration from the United States to Texas.

> In November, 1830, just a few months before the expiration of the contract, Sterling C. Robertson and Alexander Thomson with eight or nine families attempted to reach the territory of the Nashville Company. Since they did not possess the passports required of all Americans by the Law of April 6, 1830, Colonel Piedras, the military commander at Nacogdoches, refused to allow them to proceed to the colony. But Colonel Piedras did grant permission to Robertson and Thomson to go to Austin's colony to attend to some business. The permission was granted on the condition that they leave the families at Nacogdoches to await their return, that they return in twenty days, and then leave the Republic. After a few days Robertson and Thomson returned one dark night, stole the families away and rushed on to Austin's colony. When the Mexican authorities were aware of what had happened, they issued orders to all military and civil authorities in Texas to expel them from the nation.[5]

Upon the receipt of the ordinance of April 6, the Legislature of Coahuila and Texas cancelled the contract of the Nashville Company

> ...and the region embraced in his contract was given over to Austin and Williams February 25, 1831. It took over three years for Robertson to have this order annulled and the Nashville Company restored which was done April 29, 1834. Desiring that settlers already in his colony should not be left to themselves and to carry out his contract at all hazards, he continued to introduce settlers but on the 18th of May, 1835, it was restored to Austin and Williams and matters were in

256

this situation when the Texas Revolution broke out in October, 1835.[6]

On November 14, 1835, the Consultation ordered all of the land offices in Texas closed.[7] Robert Peebles and Clement C. Dyer were appointed commissioners to close the office of Robertson's Colony. These men at Viesca, the headquarters of the colony, the site of which is on the Brazos near the city of Marlin, Falls County, on November 27 demanded from William H. Steele all the books, documents and papers kept there pertaining to the colony.[8] Steele, in a written communication addressed to Peebles and Dyer, declined to deliver the documents, stating that he did not recognize in the Consultation or any person acting for it the authority and right to demand the Archives of the colony.[9] On December 2, the General Council of the Provisional Government ordered J. L. Hood to arrest Steele and to bring him before the council.[10] The minutes of the General Council of December 17 show that

> Mr. Steel came before the Council and stated that the warrant to arrest him had not been served upon him, but hearing that one had been issued, he appeared for the purpose of explaining the circumstances of his refusal.
>
> He stated that the citizens of Viesca did not consider that their delegates were clothed with conventional powers, but that they generally approved of the doings of the Convention, so far as they were informed of them; that he lived at a great distance from the seat of Government from which communications were very uncertain. That as he had been informed of the provisions of the organic law, no such powers were given as claimed by the commissioners, one of whom was a commissioner for issuing titles under Austin and Williams, who claimed to be empresarios of that colony. That the refusal was made through misunderstanding, and in the moment of excitement, and not from any disrespect to the Government or its authorities. With this explanation he submitted himself to the Council.

On motion of Mr. Royall...

> *Resolved*, that this council is satisfied with the explanation made by Mr. Steel, that his refusal to deliver up the archives of the land office under his charge, was made under a misunderstanding, and not from any disrespect to the Government of its authorities.[11]

During this controversy, Robertson was in Tennessee, where he had been since July, trying to induce citizens there to emigrate to Texas and to settle in his colony. On his return he arrived at Viesca, December 6, with fifteen families, some families having preceded him and others on their way.

On December 18 he petitioned the Provisional Government to permit him to issue land titles to those with whom he had contracted. In his petition he stated that when he left Texas in July "all was then favorable & pacific in the country, except some local discontents, which he had no expectation would either involve the country in war, or operate a change of Govt."[12]

Sarahville de Viesca, near the falls of the Brazos, the headquarters of Robertson's Colony was named for Robertson's mother, Sarah, and Jose Maria Viesca, Governor of Coahuila and Texas. Later Robertson laid out the town of Nashville, farther down the Brazos, the site of which is in the present Milam County, and which he named for his birthplace, Nashville, Tennessee.

On January 17, 1836, Robertson recruited a company of volunteers of which he was elected captain. The names of the 64 men who formed the company are listed on page 119 of the army rolls in the General Land Office, Austin, under the caption: "Muster Roll of Capt. Robertson's Co. Rangers mustered into service on the 17th January, 1836, afterwards commanded by Capt. Calvin Boales." This company disbanded, however, before the spring campaign.

STERLING C. ROBERTSON

On February 1, 1836, Robertson and his nephew, George C. Childress, who had been in Texas for about a month, were elected to represent Milam Municipality at the Constitutional Convention. On that date Robertson happened to be near the present town of Wheelock, Robertson County, and voted at the home of James Dunn.[13] He was seated in the Convention, March 1.

Robertson joined the army on April 20, 1836, and on the following day he was opposite Harrisburg at the camp of the Texans who had been detailed to guard baggage.[14] Following the Battle of San Jacinto Robertson went in pursuit of the Mexicans who had escaped from the battlefield. In May, 1836, he was in San Augustine on recruiting service.[15]

(From the *Nashville Banner*)

Extract of a letter, from Colonel Sterling C. Robertson of Texas, to his friend at Nashville, dated May 26, 1836, at San Augustine, Texas.

...I am sent here, by the commanding general, to try and raise some recruits for the army which is now on its march to San Antonio; at which place there are some fears, that the Mexican army, may make another stand; though they have been ordered by Santa Anna, to march out of the country, to Monte del Rey in the State of Nova Leon. The panic prevalent among the citizens of Texas, was not to be compared with that of the Mexican army, when they heard of the defeat and capture of Santa Anna, Cos, Almonte, &c. I went in pursuit of those who escaped from the field of battle, and those that were in the rear of the reinforcement, commanded by Cos; and left as a guard for his bagage.—They appeared to have been frightened nearly to death. Every hundred yards on the road, for twenty miles they had thrown away some of their plunder, and a whole mule load could have been collected, frequently in the distance of a mile; and often the mule with his pack on his back, being run down, was left on the roadside. They left the main road, and went through the prairie; and traveled all night, to enable them to reach the Brazos;

where the division of Sezema lay, or was crossing the river, at a place called Fort Bend; about forty miles below San Felipe.

I there joined a detachment of mounted men and went on a reconnoitering trip, in pursuit of Sezema, and Filasola, on their retreat out of the country. From every appearance presented, by scattered baggage, muskets thrown away, and mules left bogged in the mud, the panic appeared even greater, than among the fugitives from the field of battle. They left fifty mules and fourteen baggage wagons, in the mud in the distance of ten miles, buried one piece of cannon and threw at least one thousand of arms in the river San Bernard.

When the advance of the detachment came up with them, they said they were getting out of the country as fast they could; and would obey the orders of Santa Anna, and go on to Monte Del Ray, by the way of San Antonio—we could have taken at least 1,000 men of them, with all their mules, and baggage and cannon, if we had been allowed to do so, but as a treaty was on hand we were ordered not to molest them. If I had had the command, I would have endeavoured to have misconstrued my orders, and at least taken their cannon and arms from them. They had ten pieces of cannon —six pounders; and an immense quality of plunder, which they had taken from the houses of the citizens of Texas, after they had left them.

Our men were all anxious for the contest; flushed with victory, and full of resentment against the Mexicans. On the other hand, the officers and soldiers, were nearly frightened to death; and would have surrendered, in one moment, and I think without the firing of a gun. I have no doubt General Rusk regrets that it was not done, as nothing has been done with regard to the treaty; and he is now on his march after them to San Antonio; at which place I expect we shall have them to fight, unless we can show a respectable army. If we do, I think they will acknowledge our independence. Two expresses, in the last two days, have gone on from General Gaines, to the headquarters of the Texian and Mexican armies. Some think he offers mediation of the United States

260

between the parties, and others, that the United States have bought the country.

Yours respectfully,
STERLING C. ROBERTSON

The records in Spanish Archives in the General Land Office show that between January 5 and July 2, 1835, Major Robertson received title from the Mexican government to a total of 34 leagues and one labor of land.

Major Robertson was a member of the Senate of the First and Second Congresses of the Republic, representing the district of Milam County. He died in Robertson County, March 4, 1842, and was buried across the Brazos River in the cemetery at Nashville, Milam County. His remains were removed by the State of Texas and, on December 28, 1935, reinterred in the State Cemetery at Austin, where a monument was erected at his new grave.

The act of the Legislature creating Robertson County, Texas, December 14, 1837, failed to state for whom it was named.[16] Thrall, in 1879, said it was named for Sterling C. Robertson.[17]

Elijah Sterling Clack Robertson was a son of Sterling C. Robertson and Fanny King. James Maclin Robertson was a son of Sterling C. Robertson and Rachael Smith.[18] The author has been unable to find any information regarding any of these except Elijah Sterling Clack Robertson. He was born in Giles County, Tennessee, August 23, 1820. He was married July 29, 1846, in Robertson County by H. Reed, Probate Judge, to Eliza Hamer Robertson, who was born December 15, 1824, in Davidson County, Tennessee, and died March 25, 1852, at Austin, Texas.

By the union the following children were born: Sterling, born August 7, 1847, in Robertson County and died August 26, 1847; Sterling Clack, born April 20, 1849, in Austin and died January 2, 1915, in San Antonio and was buried in Salado; and Eliza Medora Susan Robertson, born in Austin, Texas, December 29, 1851, and died August 10, 1858, at Salado.

Gen. E. S. C. Robertson was married November 8, 1852, at Austin by Rev. B. J. Smith to Mary Elizabeth Dickey, who was born September 22, 1834, at Paris, Henry County, Tennessee, and died December 11, 1882. General Robertson died October 8, 1879. The two are buried in marked graves in the Robertson family cemetery in Salado, Texas.

Children of E. S. C. and Mary E. (Dickey) Robertson were Randolph, who married Mrs. Mary Huckabee Cochrane; Lauella, who married Zachary Taylor Fulmore; Huling Parker, who married Mary Gatlin Cooke; Marion, who married Lola Mary Taylor; Maclin, who married Alice Johnson Woods; Mary Sterling, who married Richard Henry Harrison; Eliza Sophia, who married Cone Johnson; Imogene, who married James Archibald Gamel; Lela S., who married Eugene Floyd Ikard; and Celeta Teresa Robertson, who married James W. Durst. Of these, three were survivors in August, 1942, Mrs. Gamel, Mrs. Durst and Mrs. Lela S. Robertson, formerly Mrs. Ikard.

Some of the surviving grandchildren of E. S. C. Robertson in August, 1942, were Iran Randolph Robertson, 1742 West Grammercy Place, San Antonio; Maclin Robertson, Salado; Elijah Sterling C. Robertson, Salado; Gordon Robertson, 4149 Prescott Street, Dallas; Mrs. Thomas Shelton Sutherland, Austin; Mrs. Dallas Duncan McLean, Washington, D. C.; Mrs. Birdie Alice Howell, 1600 Congress Avenue, Austin; Mrs. James M. West, 2106 Crawford Street, Houston; Mrs. William C. Harlee, 1753 Lamont Avenue, Washington, D. C.; Sterling R. Fulmore, Austin; Sterling C. Robertson, El Paso; Miss Lorena Robertson, Charles Robertson, San Antonio; Mrs. Grady H. Harrison, Houston; Z. T. Fulmore, Los Angeles; Mrs. Parnorrow Turner, Miami, Florida; Marion Robertson, Oil City, Pennsylvania; Mrs. J. H. Knost, Jr., El Paso; Mrs. Thomas Stiles, El Paso; Mrs. J.

B. McNamara, New York City; J. A. Gamel, Mexico City; James M. Harrison, Los Angeles; R. H. Harrison, Los Angeles; Gilbert P. Robertson, Brandenburg, Kentucky; Sophie Durst, Los Angeles; and Mary Celeta Durst, Los Angeles.

JOSE FRANCISCO RUIZ
of
BEXAR MUNICIPALITY

Jose Francisco Ruiz was born in San Antonio, January 29, 1783, son of Juan Manuel Ruiz and Manuela de la Peña.[1]

During the revolution of 1813 Ruiz joined the insurgent army at San Antonio, serving first under Gutierrez and later under Jose Alvarez Toledo. He participated in the Battle of Medina, August 18, 1813. At the collapse of the revolutionary army, Ruiz, Juan Martin de Veramendi and other prominent leaders fled from San Antonio to escape death at the hands of Arredondo.[2] Ruiz remained in the United States until 1822, when he returned to Texas. He later became an officer in the Army of the Republic of Mexico, and he remained a loyal Mexican subject until sometime in the year 1834.

The activities of Ruiz as an officer in the Mexican Army are traced through the Bexar Archives.[3] On March 3, 1826, he wrote a letter from San Carlos, across the Rio Grande, to the governor of Texas, informing him that he was on his way to Tampico to obtain funds for the Bexar troops. Three days later he wrote from Tampico that he was having

263

trouble getting the money. On April 18 he wrote that he had obtained the money and was preparing to set out for Bexar. The following day he wrote that he was setting out that day with 46,000 pesos for the Bexar troops.

On June 22, 1826, Ruiz wrote a letter to the President of Mexico requesting the command of a post. By April 3, 1827, he was commandant of the detachment station of Nacogdoches.

Ruiz in 1827 was sent to Nacogdoches to help quell the Fredonian War.[4] In this connection it is interesting to note that four participants in this disturbance were later to sign the Texas Declaration of Independence. John S. Roberts and Martin Parmer were "Fredonians," while Ruiz and James Gaines were on the opposing side.

On April 6, 1830, the Mexican Congress passed a drastic decree aimed at Texas. Among other things it virtually forbade the introduction into Texas of anymore citizens from the United States. It provided for the condemnation of land on which fortifications, public works or arsenals should be built to accommodate the convict soldiers who were to be sent to Texas to enforce the decree. It further provided that:

> When the time of their imprisonment is terminated, if they should desire to remain as colonists, they shall be given lands and agricultural implements, and their provision shall be continued through the first year of their colonization.[5]

On April 24, 1830, Manuel de Mier y Teran issued the order for the construction of a fort which he named Tenoxtitlan, the site of which is in Burleson County on the Brazos. Ruiz, chosen to command the fort, set out from San Antonio, June 25, and reached the Brazos on July 13, where shortly afterward he selected the site of the fort.[6] Toward the end of August, 1832, he left the fort and returned to San Antonio.[7] He was well liked by the settlers around Tenoxtitlan.

In 1834 Ruiz received title to eleven leagues (48,708 acres) of land from the Mexican government. Title to nine leagues was issued March 16, 1834, by Commissioner Luke Lesassier, of which four leagues were surveyed in Robertson County, two in Brazos, two in Milam, and one in Burleson.[8] On March 16, 1834, he received from Commissioner Juan N. Seguin title to nine leagues surveyed in what is now Karnes County.[9] While none of the land was in any of his colonies, Stephen F. Austin, at Columbia, December 5, 1836, addressed a letter to the President of the Senate of Texas in which he stated that the large grants made to Ruiz were due to the preference that native Mexicans had under the Mexican Colonization Law.[10]

In the election held February 1, 1836, Ruiz, his nephew, Jose Antonio Navarro, Miguel Arciniega and Juan N. Seguin were chosen by the resident voters of Bexar Municipality as delegates to the Constitutional Convention.[11] The Anglo-American soldiers stationed at the Alamo did not protest the election of the Mexican delegates, but, in a petition addressed to the Convention, they urged that two of their members, Samuel A. Maverick and Jesse B. Badgett, be accepted also as delegates from Bexar Municipality. "A large portion of this army," they said, "whilst they possess the declared right of voting for members of this Convention, do not yet possess any local habitation whatsoever."[12]

265

Ruiz, Navarro, Badgett and Maverick were all seated without debate. Seguin and Arciniega did not attend the Convention.

Ruiz, unable to speak English, did not take an active part in the Convention. His name is mentioned but once in the published proceedings of that body, that when he was seated.[13]

As Ruiz, Jesse Grimes and Dr. Benjamin B. Goodrich sat together in the convention hall they did not know that a son of Ruiz had been directed by Santa Anna to help burn the bodies of those who had died martyrs at the Alamo. Among the bodies burned were those of Alfred Calvin Grimes, son of Jesse Grimes, and John Calvin Goodrich, younger brother of Dr. Goodrich. According to Chabot: "As alcalde of San Antonio at the time of the Fall of the Alamo, Colonel [Francisco] Ruiz, [Jr.] thought he should remain neutral, and took orders from Santa Anna."[14]

There is no evidence in the General Land Office that the elder Ruiz joined the army after the adjournment of the Convention. Chabot quotes a descendant of Ruiz who said: "When the Mexicans entered Texas, Francisco Ruiz is said to have sought refuge among the wild Indians."[15] This, however, does not seem probable.

Ruiz represented the District of Bexar in the Senate of the First Congress of the Republic, October 3, 1836, to September 25, 1837. He died at his home in San Antonio, January 19, 1840, and was buried in San Fernando Church. The Burial Records of San Fernando Church, 1817-1860, show:

> January 1840. In this city of San Fernando de Bexar on the 20th January, I, the priest, Don Refugio de la Garza, curate proper of this city, buried in this parish, at a depth of ten feet the body of Lieutenant Colonel Don Francisco Ruiz, widower. He made his last will and did not bequeath anything to Works of Mercy. He received the Holy Sacraments and died of hydropsy at sixty-one years of age.[16]

Dixon's sketch of Ruiz is amusing. To begin with he states that Ruiz was born August 31, 1772. Then, regarding his death he said:

> When the question arose of entering Texas into the United States as a State, Mr. Ruiz openly opposed it. He claimed that the matter should be left entirely to those who had made the sacrifice necessary to wrest Texas from Mexico and not to those who had but recently come to the State and did not appreciate the struggles through which the early pio-

neers had passed. When the Republic became a State of the Union, Mr. Ruiz left the country. He said he could not live in Mexico because he would not tolerate their government, so he sought a home among the Indians on the frontier—As old age crept upon him he returned to his home in San Antonio where he soon thereafter died.[17]

Col. Francisco Ruiz was married March 18, 1804, to Josefa Hernandez, daughter of Placido Hernandez and Rosalia Montes.[18] Of this union there were two children, Maria Antonia Ruiz and Francisco Antonio Ruiz.

Maria Antonia Ruiz was born in 1809 and was married to Bias Herrera. Their children were Jacoba, who married Miguel de la Garza; Francisco, who married Luisa Ramirez; Benito, who married Narcisa Calderon; Antonia, who married Josiah Cobs; Blas, who married Sabina Salinas; Juan Jose; Manuel, who married Refugia Tijerina; Jose Maria, who married Josefa Perez; and Josefa Herrera, who married Fernando Sandoval.[19]

267

Francisco Antonio Ruiz was married to Concepcion Soto. Their children were Francisco Antonio; Alejandro Modesto; Eugenio, who married Carlota Garcia; and Francisco Ruiz, III, who married Rosa Campbell. Francisco Ruiz, Jr., died October 18, 1876, at his residence on the south side of Military Plaza. He was buried in the Ruiz family cemetery on the Medina.

Francisco and Rosa (Campbell) Ruiz had seven children, all of whom were deceased in October, 1941, except Miss Anita A. Ruiz, 1310 Myrtle Avenue, El Paso, Texas.[20]

Some of the surviving descendants of Colonel Ruiz who were residing in San Antonio in 1940 were: R. G. Herrera, Thomas Herrera, Mrs. Maria H. Patino, Mrs. Frank Leyton, Benito Herrera, III; and Mrs. Sara H. Ruiz, Route 1, Von Ormy.

THOMAS JEFFERSON RUSK
of
Nacogdoches Municipality

Thomas Jefferson Rusk was born December 5, 1803,[1] in Pendleton District, South Carolina. His father had emigrated from Ireland and was a stone mason, and lived upon land belonging to John C. Calhoun. Thomas, at an early day, displayed such strength and capacity of mind as to attract the attention of Calhoun, who at once took a decided interest in the boy. Through his influence Thomas was placed in the office of William Grisham, for many years clerk of Pendleton District, where Thomas studied law and was soon admitted to the bar. He subsequently removed to Clarksville, Habersham County, Georgia, where he married.

In 1832 Rusk, enjoying a lucrative practice, invested heavily in the stock of a company of miners and land speculators, whose corrupt managers absconded with the company's property in 1835. Rusk followed them to Texas with the hope of recovering some of the funds. He overtook them only to find that they had squandered and gambled away the whole of their ill-gotten gains.[2]

Thomas J. Rusk was one of the seven children of John and Mary (Sterritt) Rusk. The other children were David, Esther Sterritt, Mary, Nancy, Jane and Rachel Rusk. Thomas J. arrived in Texas in February, 1835,[3] and settled at Nacogdoches.

At the outbreak of the Revolution in 1835 Rusk organized a company in the volunteer army in Nacogdoches of which he was elected captain. His company of cavalry joined the forces before San Antonio in October, 1835. General Cos, strongly fortified in Bexar, would not attack the Texans, and the Texans found that an assault on the town would involve too great a sacrifice of men; hence a regular siege was ordered by Gen. Stephen F. Austin. Efforts made to draw the enemy into the open were futile. Yoakum tells of the part Rusk played in trying to induce the Mexicans to leave their fortification:

> Various attempts were made to entice the enemy beyond his walls. On one occasion a detachment of one hundred and ninety Texans marched up within the range of the Mexican six-pounders; on another, Colonel Thomas J. Rusk, at the head of forty cavalry, took a position within three hundred yards of their walls and remained there twenty minutes; still they could not be drawn from their work.[4]

Finally on December 5 about 300 Texans, under the command of Benjamin R. Milam, began an assault on Bexar. Rusk, in the meanwhile, had withdrawn from the siege. On the 6th General Burleson and Milam sent a despatch to the government at San Felipe requesting "an immediate supply of ammunition, as much powder and lead as can possibly be sent instantly...I hope that good mules or horses will be procured to send on these articles with the greatest possible speed...Reinforcements of men, are perhaps, indispensable to our salvation."[5]

On December 10, the General Council of the Provisional Government passed resolutions calling for additional volunteers for the army. James W. Fannin and Thomas J. Rusk were constituted agents, or contractors, for supplying ammunition, provisions and other necessities for carrying out the resolutions. They were vested with full power of the provisional government.[6] Rusk was directed to proceed east of the Trinity to forward troops to the theatre of war. To do this he surrendered his command to his first lieutenant.

At Nacogdoches on January 4, 1836, Rusk appealed to, and later received from, Charles S. Taylor $1,000 for the army, a portion of the fees Taylor, as special land commissioner for the State of Coahuila and Texas, had collected from those to whom land had been granted.[7]

From December 14, 1835, to February 26, 1836, Rusk served as Inspector General of the Army.

William Fairfax Gray was in Nacogdoches, February 1, 1836, the day of the election for delegates to the Constitutional Convention. In his remarkable and most valuable diary he told of the excitement that prevailed there.

Monday, February 1, 1836.

This is the day designated by the Provisional Council for a general election of members of the new Convention. There are a large number of candidates. This place is much divided on the questions of adhering to the Mexican Constitution of 1824, or declaring for absolute and immediate independence. Much excitement prevailed. The constitutional party have enlisted on their side all the Mexicans, or native Texans, who are a swarthy, dirty looking people, much resembling our mulattos, some of them nearly black, but having straight hair.

The company of Newport, Ky., Volunteers, has been detained here to vote; they are on the independence side. Several of the candidates addressed the people, and among them the famous Robert Potter, of North Carolina, who has been here some months. On the volunteers offering to vote they were refused to the judges, which caused an angry excitement. The company was drawn up with loaded rifles, and the First Lieutenant, Woods, swore that the men should vote, or he would riddle the door of the Stone House, where the election was held, with rifle balls. The Captain, who had only arrived the night before, had not yet resumed the command of the company, and determined not to interfere, but to let the company and the judges fight it out.

The citizens were then called on to decide by a count of heads whether the volunteers should vote or not, and on being polled the Constitutionalists outvoted the Independents some thirty votes. On this the Mexicans set up a shout of triumph, which enraged the volunteers, and it was feared they would fire on the citizens. Judge Hotchkiss and myself interfered to restrain them.

I addressed them publicly, and attempted to convince them that by the law of the country and the ordinance under which the Convention was held, they had not the right to vote—or that it was at least a questionable right; that it was unbecoming in them, coming into the country as soldiers, to be stickling at the threshold for the political rights; that it was derogatory to their character to be mingling in the political and personal squabbles of the country, contrary to all the principles of republicanism and destructive of the freedom of elections for soldiers with arms in their hands to interfere in elections; exhorted them to abstain from violence, reserve their weapons for the enemies of the country, etc. I think the address was effective, although *Mr. Potter* attempted to neutralize it by a short reply, *ad captandum*, appealing to the passions of the men, and exhorting them to perseverance in their determination to vote, etc. They were also addressed by Col. Rusk, one of the candidates, who stated that the judges were reconsidering the subject, and would announce their determination after dinner. Mr. J. K. Allen also said a few words, exculpating Lt. Woods from some charges that had been raised against him.

After dinner it was announced that the volunteers might vote if they chose. They had in the meantime consulted, and unanimously resolved that they would not vote, at which I was much gratified. I was more gratified at hearing it said by a citizen that I had been the means of preventing bloodshed. But the volunteers, with the waywardness of children, reconsidered their determination, and subsequently all voted. They were all day under arms, and frequently marched to and fro, with drum and fife, before the door of the Hustings—a shameful spectacle, which I never before witnessed. But, notwithstanding all, the Constitutionalists carried the day by a considerable majority. The polls, however, are to be opened again tomorrow.[8]

Tuesday, February 2, 1836.

The polls have been open all day, and 401 votes have been taken in the two days. Inasmuch as the volunteers, and all other *Free white males* have been permitted to vote, and I was desirous of becoming *a citizen* as soon as possible, I went forward and tendered my vote, which was cheerfully received, and I am now considered as identified with interests of the country, and entitled to all the rights of citizenship! This day has gone off quietly. The angry feelings excited yesterday are hushed, if not extinguished. The foremost candidates are Th. J. Rusk, 247; C. P. Taylor, 221; Jno. S. Roberts, 203; Jno. K. Allen, 200. These four are supposed to be elected, but there are other election precincts in the municipality, the returns from which may vary the result. The next highest were Robert Potter, 157; Haden Edwards, 133.

The weather for the two last days has been very fine, cool but clear, dry and elastic, like fine autumn weather in Virginia. I wear no overcoat.[9]

272

In a letter to Gov. Henry Smith and the General Council, written at Nacogdoches, Wyatt Hanks predicted that Rusk, Taylor, Roberts and John K. Allen would be elected.

Mr. W. F. Gray one of the Stockholders in the loan of $200,000 is now in this place—he is a Virginian & a Gent... There is a company of Volunteers (some 40) in full uniform from Cincinnati who leaves this place for the seat of war this morning—There was considerable excitement as regards the election on yesterday as to the right of the co. of volunteers exercising the right of suffrage but after warm harangues &c. they were permitted to vote & everything has settled down quietly—Col T. J. Rusk will get a much larger vote for the Convention than anyone else—I think Rusk, Taylor, Roberts & Allen will be elected from this municipality.[10]

When the returns from the outlying boxes were received, however, it was found that Robert Potter had defeated Allen by three votes. Potter, without doubt, had been elected by the recently arrived soldiers recruited in Ohio and Kentucky by Capt. Sidney Sherman.

Of the approximate 610 votes cast in the municipality Thomas J. Rusk received 392; John S. Roberts, 263; Charles S. Taylor, 258; Robert Potter, 235; John K. Allen, 232; Haden Edwards, 144; Daniel Parker, 128; David A. Hoffman, 119; Richard Sparks, 112; James Bradshaw, 104; Arthur Hendrie, 96; M. G. Whitaker, 88; Jesse Walling, 80; Frost Thorn, 74; T. J. Golightly, 56; Sam Houston, 55; and James W. Robinson, 3.

Following are the returns from the several voting boxes:

Precinct of Nacogdoches: Thomas J. Rusk, 247; Charles S. Taylor, 221; John S. Roberts, 203; John K. Allen, 200; Robert Potter, 151; Haden Edwards, 133; Jesse Walling, 80; M. G. Whitaker, 78; Richard Sparks, 72; T. J. Golightly, 55; D. A. Hoffman, 45; Frost Thorn, 28; Arthur Hendrie, 22; Daniel Parker, 5; J. W. Robinson, 3; Sam Houston, 3; James Bradshaw, 1.

Precinct of Masters: Rusk, 33; Houston, 28; Parker, 23; Sparks, 21; Thorn, 16; Bradshaw, 11; Roberts, 8; Whitaker, 7; and Hendrie, 6.

Precinct of Naches: Rusk, 49; James Bradshaw, 48; D. A. Hoffman, 37; Parker, 35; Robert Potter, 13; Sparks, 9; Arthur Hendrie, 7; Haden Edwards, 3; Whitaker, 2; Roberts, 1; Charles S. Taylor, 1; T. J. Golightly, 1; Frost Thorn, 1; and Houston, 1.

Precinct of Williams Settlement: Bradshaw, 24; Hoffman, 24; Parker, 23; Roberts, 16; Potter, 5; Hendrie, 3.

Precinct of Mustang Prairie: Potter, 18; Hendrie, 17; Parker, 17; Rusk, 4; and Houston, 2.

Precinct of Randolph at Robbins: Hendrie, 24; Houston, 21; Potter, 20; Sparks, 5; Hoffman, 3; Rusk, 2; and Parker, 2.

Precinct of Houston: Parker, 17; Rusk, 16; Hendrie, 15; Potter, 4; Sparks, 3; Thorn, 2; Whitaker, 1.

Precinct of Costley's Settlement: Roberts, 34; Allen, 31;

Taylor, 29; Bradshaw, 20; Hoffman, 10; Potter, 5; Thorn, 3; Sparks, 2; Hendrie, 2.

Precinct of Sabine: Thorn, 24; Rusk, 23; Potter, 19; Edwards, 8; Taylor, 7; Parker, 4; Roberts, 1: and Allen, 1.[11]

Rusk was seated at the Convention on March 2,[12] and on March 17 he was elected secretary of war.[13] On April 1, he left Harrisburg to join the army,[14] and after joining his duties as secretary of war ended. He participated in the Battle of San Jacinto.[15] From May 4 to October 31, 1836, he was brigadier-general in command of the Texas Army.

In selecting his cabinet, President Houston named Rusk as secretary of war, the position he had formerly held under President Burnet. His private affairs requiring his entire attention, he resigned after a few weeks. His constituents, however, insisted that he represent them in Congress. Against his wishes he did so, serving in the House of Representatives in the Second Congress from September 25, 1837, to May 24, 1838.[16] In 1838 he refused the earnest solicitation of his friends to seek the presidency of the Republic. General Lamar, who was elected, did not announce as a candidate until General Rusk had stated that he would not run.

In the late summer of 1838 a revolution of Mexicans and Indians, under the leadership of Vicente Cordova, in East Texas was threatened. Rusk prevented the uprising by a demonstration of force in marching 600 horsemen through their country.[17] In November, 1838, Rusk captured a portion of the Caddo tribe, disarmed and delivered them to their agent in Shreveport.[18] On December 12, 1838, at a joint meeting of Congress, Rusk was elected chief justice of the Supreme Court of Texas.[19] This office he resigned June 30, 1840. On July 16, 1839, in command of a regiment, he participated in the decisive battle with the Cherokees in which the famous Chief Bowls was killed and his band driven from Texas.[20]

By joint ballot of Congress January 16, 1843, Rusk was elected major general of the militia.[21] At the expiration of his term he refused to stand for reelection, desiring to devote his entire time to his law practice. On February 25, 1841, he and James Pinckney Henderson formed a partnership with offices at Nacogdoches and San Augustine. Rusk was chosen president of the convention which met at Austin July 4, 1845, to frame the constitution for the State of Texas.[22] By the joint session of the First Legislature, February 21, 1846, Rusk and Gen. Sam Houston were elected to the Senate of the Congress of the United States.[23] Rusk was seated March 26, 1846.[24] He was reelected in 1851 and 1857. He was elected president pro tempore of the Senate March 14, 1857, in a special session of the Senate.[25]

Rusk was a member of Milam Lodge No. 40, A. F. and A. M., Nacogdoches, in 1837[26] and was a charter member of the Grand Lodge of Texas, organized at Houston, December 20, 1837.[27]

275

In the Act of the Legislature of January 16, 1843, creating Rusk County, it is not stated for whom the county was named.[28] Thrall, in 1879, said it was named for Thomas J. Rusk.[29]

Rusk ended his own life at his home in Nacogdoches, July 29, 1857. The State of Texas erected a granite monument at his grave in Oak Grove Cemetery, Nacogdoches. The Commission of Control for Texas Centennial Celebrations erected a joint monument at the graves of John and (Mary Sterritt) Rusk, parents of Thomas J. Rusk, in the cemetery in Pendleton, South Carolina. The Commission erected a bronze statue of Rusk at Henderson, Rusk County, at a cost of $14,000, and placed a marker at the Rusk home in Nacogdoches.

Rusk was married January 4, 1827, to Mary F. Cleveland, daughter of Gen. John Cleveland, a prominent merchant of Clarksville, Georgia.[30] Mrs. Rusk was born August 14,

1809, and died of tuberculosis April 23, 1856. General Rusk was buried beside his wife.

Children of General and Mrs. Thomas J. Rusk were: (1) Benjamin Livingston, (2) John Cleveland, (3) Thomas Jefferson, Jr., (4) Cicero, (5) Alonzo, (6) Thomas David, and (7) Helena Argin Rusk.

(1) Benjamin Livingston Rusk was born in Georgia, February 24, 1838. On April 17, 1853, he was married to Rachael A. Crain, daughter of Giles Burditt and Rachel A. (Fulgham) Crain. Their children were: (a) Alice Helena, born February 19, 1855, (b) Cicero Benjamin, born July 4, 1856, (c) Mary Euphemia, born March 29, 1858, and (d) Giles Thomas Jefferson Rusk, born January 28, 1860, and died May 25, 1861.

(2) After the death of his first wife, John Cleveland Rusk, on December 11, 1862, was married to Cornelia E. Lawson, who was born July 19, 1845. Their children were: (a) John David, who was born January 15, 1864, and died June 6, 1865; (b) Margaret Helena, born December 22, 1865; (c) David Cleveland, born November 19, 1867, and died April 27, 1878; (d) Saritha, born July 15, 1870; and (e) William Benjamin Rusk, born July 15, 1872, and died October 6, 1872. John C. Rusk died in Van Zandt County.

(3) Thomas Jefferson Rusk, Jr., was born in Georgia, January 12, 1832, and died October 14, 1834.

(4) Cicero Rusk was born in Georgia October 5, 1834. He was killed while serving in the Confederate Army in the War Between the States.

(5) Alonzo Rusk was born August 12, 1837, and died August 17, 1838.

(6) Thomas David Rusk was born April 3, 1841. He died in Harrison County.

(7) Helena Argin Rusk was born November 27, 1845, and died at the age of about eighteen.

In 1940 there were two surviving grandchildren of General Rusk, A. K. Rusk of Canton and Mrs. T. P. David, 802 Johnson Street, Terrell, Texas.

Some of the surviving great grandchildren, in 1940, were: A. W. Rusk, J. C. Rusk, and Dr. Thomas Rusk Keahey, Canton; A. J. Kellam and L. Tunnell; Ben Wheeler; H. E., H. C, C. F. and M. L. Tunnell, Grand Saline; and Mrs. Margaret Rusk Darden, Sulphur Springs.

WILLIAM BENNETT SCATES
of
Jefferson Municipality

A lengthy account of the disturbance at Anahuac in 1832 was written October 1, 1871, by William Bennett Scates at his home at Osage, Colorado County, Texas. He began his narrative:

I see in the *Colorado Citizen* you desire to extend the list of surviving veterans of the Texas revolution, with a sketch of their lives and services in that revolution.

I take this opportunity of forwarding you my own, which I could have done sooner had I known that you desire it.

My name is William B. Scates. I was born in Hallifax County, Va., June 27, 1802.[1] My father emigrated from there to Christian county, Ky., where I remained with my father, who was a farmer, until 1820, when I went to New Orleans. I there followed clerking for some years, after which I went to work at the house carpentering business, which I followed until 1831, and in February of that year I concluded to visit Texas, as I had become tired of the bustle of the city, and on the 2d of March, 1831, I landed at Anahuac, situated near the head of Galveston bay and opposite the mouth of the Trinity.[2]

William B. Scates was a son of Joseph and Elizabeth Scates. Joseph was born February 3, 1775, and Mrs. Scates was born June 4, 1774. They were married September 28, 1801. Their children were William Bennett, born June 27, 1802; Harriet Fields, March 16, 1804; Joseph W., December 20, 1805; Walter B., January 18, 1808; Elizabeth Eggleston, February 3, 1810; Isaac Coleman, July 16, 1812; and John Scates, born August 20, 1814.[3]

Scates, in 1835, joined the army, in the company commanded by Capt. Samuel C. Blair. On February 1, 1836, he and Claiborne West were elected to represent Jefferson Municipality in the Constitutional Convention.[4] Scates was seated March 1.[5] On March 3 he was appointed a member of a committee to devise a flag for the Republic of Texas. It appears that the design recommended by the committee was officially adopted but never used.[6]

Leaving the Convention, Scates made his way to the Texas Army and joined Capt. Benjamin F. Bryant's company of Sabine Volunteers.[7] As a member of that organization he participated in the Battle of San Jacinto.[8] Captain Bryant's company having enlisted only for a period of 30 days, at the disbandment of the company, Scates joined Capt. Haden Arnold's Nacogdoches Company.[9]

On October 9, 1863, Scates "private, age 62" enlisted in Company F, Capt. J. M. Kirby commanding, 4th Battalion, Texas Cavalry, Colonel C. W. Tate, commanding, 22nd Brigade, General William G. Webb commanding, Texas State Troops. He furnished his horse, valued at $350; horse equipment, $30; arms, $140. The company was stationed at Fayetteville, Texas, November 9, 1863; at Spanish Camp, Wharton, February 9, 1864. The company was detailed as couriers, beef drivers, stevedores and other laborers from December 2, 1863, to February 9, 1864. W. B. Scates was a substitute for H. D. Rhodes. One muster roll dated November 19, 1863, and one muster and pay roll dated October 9, 1863, to February 1, 1864, are in the Archives of the Texas State Library,

Retiring from the Texas Army in 1836, Scates settled in Washington County where, on November 17, 1836, he was married to Theodocia Clardy Smith, daughter of Dr. William P. Smith.[10] By this marriage two children were born, Sarah Elizabeth, February 8, 1838, and James Robert Scates, July 8, 1840.

After the death of his wife (date not recorded), Scates on March 25, 1850, was married to Sarah McMillan, who was born July 28, 1819, and who died April 28, 1881. Scates died February 22, 1882. The two were buried in a cemetery near Osage, Colorado County, near the old road that runs from Columbus to La Grange. The State of Texas had their remains exhumed and, on September 15, 1929, reinterred in the State Cemetery at Austin, and a monument was erected at their graves.

Children of Mr. and Mrs. Scates were Ellen Virginia, who was married to J. C. Lowery; Mollie, who was married to S. S. Teat; Harriet Fields, who was married to Edward Simpson; Arrie Bell, who was married to George W. Goode and who died in Electra, Texas, July 7, 1939; and Alice Bennett Scates who was married to James Frank Richardson and who, in 1943, was living at Route 3, Box 262-A, Cleburne, Texas.

Some of the surviving grandchildren of William B. Scates in 1943 were Mrs. W. R. Martin, Electra; Mrs. B. B. Thigpen, Artesia, New Mexico; Obediah D. Goode, Austin, Texas; Mrs. Oscar Surratt, Dalhart; George W. Goode, 1821 Alamitos Street, Long Beach, California; James B. Goode, Electra; Mrs. C. V. Sanford, 2854 Serrano Road, San Ber-

279

nardino, California; Robert L. Goode, Wichita Falls, Texas; Edwin Roy Goode, Byers, Texas; Mrs. C. W. W. McConkey, Route 3, Box 26-A, Cleburne, Texas; Lee Douglas Richardson, 1480 California Street, Puente, California; William Grady Richardson, 803 Prairie Avenue, Cleburne, Texas; Dannie Teat, Odessa, Texas; and Lemuel Teat, Abilene, Texas.

GEORGE WASHINGTON SMYTH
of
JASPER MUNICIPALITY

280

George Washington Smyth was born in North Carolina May 16, 1803,[1] a son of a German millwright. When he was three years of age his parents moved to Fayetteville, Tennessee, and when fourteen, to Alabama. For about four months in 1820 or 1821 and for eight months in 1824, Smyth went to school in Maury County, Tennessee.

On January 20, 1830, George W. Smyth, greatly in opposition to the wishes of his parents, set out for Texas. He crossed the Sabine February 11,[2] and arrived at Nacogdoches on the 14th.

Smyth did not contemplate remaining in East Texas, for his destination was Austin's Colony on the Brazos. At the solicitation of some of the citizens, however, he agreed to remain a short time to teach school. After a month he received, through the influence of Thomas J. Chambers, appointment as surveyor for what was then called "Bevil's Settlement." About April 1 he arrived at the residence of

John Bevil, where the town of Jasper now stands, to begin work. Shortly afterwards he moved to the home of Joseph Grigsby, his future father-in-law.[3]

Following the passage of the famous law of April 6, 1830, surveying in East Texas ceased, and Smyth decided to visit Louisiana and then to continue around the coast to Austin's Colony. This he did, arriving at San Felipe de Austin near the first of December. Shortly after his arrival, J. Francisco Madero, commissioner to issue land titles, passed through the town on his way to the Atascosito crossing of the Trinity, near the site of the present town of Liberty. Smyth decided to follow him and to obtain a position of surveyor under him. In this he was successful but only for a short period. Madero was dismissed as commissioner, and all surveying was suspended. Smyth then returned to Bevil's settlement where he stayed for the remainder of the year 1831.[4]

At the outbreak of the trouble at Anahuac in June, 1832, Smyth and seven others of the Bevil settlement set out for the scene of action to assist, if necessary, the colonists. The matter, however, was settled with out bloodshed, and Smyth and the volunteers returned to their homes.[5]

In the summer of 1834, George Antonio Nixon, commissioner for the colonies of Zavala, Vehlein and Burnet, appointed Smyth surveyor. In the spring of 1835 he was appointed a land commissioner, with headquarters at Nacogdoches.[6] Wrote Smyth in his autobiography:

> I continued in the discharge of that office until the 19th of December, 1835, when the office was closed by Dr. S. H. Everett, one of the commissioners appointed by the consultation for that purpose. By a resolution of the provisional government of the 8th of December, 1835, it is provided "that a majority of the said commissioners shall have full power to act", (p. 76), but I obeyed the notice from a single member of the commission instead of a majority, as re-

quired by law, and closed the books, never to re-open in that capacity.[7]

On November 26, 1835, Smyth was appointed First Judge of the Municipality of Bevil (Jasper) by the General Council of the Provisional Government of Texas.[8]

On February 1, 1836, Smyth and Stephen H. Everitt were elected to represent Jasper Municipality at the Constitutional Convention.[9] Both were seated March 1.[10]

After the adjournment of the Constitutional Convention, Smyth with his family joined the Runaway Scrape.[11] On July 24, 1839, President Lamar appointed Smyth surveyor to run the boundary line between Texas and the United States.[12] On May 1, 1840, Lamar appointed Smyth commissioner to fix the boundary line,[13] replacing David Sample. The work was completed in June, 1841.

Smyth was elected a member of the House of Representatives from Jasper County to the Ninth Congress, and served from December 2, 1844, to June 28, 1845.[14]

Smyth was a delegate to the State Constitutional Convention held at Austin from July 4 to August 27, 1845.[15] He served as Commissioner of the General Land Office from March 20, 1848, to March 1, 1857.[16] At a convention held at Tyler in 1852, Smyth, "a dark horse" candidate, was nominated for a seat in the House of Representatives[17] in the United State Congress, and in the ensuing election he was elected and served from March 4, 1853, to March 3, 1855.[18] He did not seek reelection.

Smyth was opposed to secession, but, at the outbreak of the War Between the States, his son, George W., Jr., joined the Confederate Army with his father's consent.

Smyth was a delegate to the Constitutional Convention which met in Austin February 2, 1866. A few days later, on February 21, Smyth died. He was buried in the State Cemetery.

George W. Smyth

Smyth was married April 1, 1834, to Frances M. Grigsby, who was born in Green River, Kentucky, September 13, 1809, and who died in Jasper County, Texas, March 15, 1888. She was a daughter of Joseph Grigsby, who moved from Green River, Kentucky, to what is now Jefferson County, Texas. Grigsby's headright was located at what was for a long time known as "Grigsby's Bluff," now called Port Neches. Grigsby served as a representative in the Second, Third, Fourth and Fifth Congresses of the Republic.

Children of the Smyths were: Sarah, who married J. T. Armstrong; Susan, who married Samuel S. Adams; Matilda, who married Rev. R. T. Armstrong, a Methodist minister; George W., Jr.; Francis; Emily, who married W. Hansford Smith; and J. G. Smyth.

J. G. Smyth, son of George W. Smyth, was married to Ella Green. Of this union there were two children, Ella M. and Ethel G. Smyth. Mrs. Smyth died in 1883 and in 1884 Smyth was married to Epsie B. Miller. Their children were Lewis, Jennie, Joseph G., William H., Andrew, George W. and Murra G. Smyth.

In 1936 the Commission of Control for Texas Centennial Celebrations erected a marker at the site of the home built by Smyth ten miles southwest of Jasper in 1836.

283

ELIJAH STAPP
of
JACKSON MUNICIPALITY

Elijah Stapp was born in Virginia in about 1783 and came to Texas from Missouri.[1] On March 9, 1826, Green DeWitt, in New London, Ralls County, Missouri, wrote to Stephen F. Austin:

> Permit me to Introduce to your attention Col. Elijah Stapp and Mr. William Duncan; who came to Texas for the purpose of selecting lands for a number of families; who intend to migrate from this County to that Country, they are particularly bound for the Guadalupe on San Marco, as their intention is Mills, Cotton Ginns etc—[2]

It was not until 1830, however, that Stapp with his wife and six children came to Texas to make their home.[3] On July 16, 1831, he received title to one league of land in De Witt's Colony, located in what is now Victoria County.[4]

The following officers were elected December 6, 1835, for the newly created Municipality of Jackson by the General Council of the Provisional Government: Patrick Usher, first judge; Elijah Stapp, second judge; John Alley, William Millican and George Sutherland, commissioners for organizing the militia.[5] When the municipality was created December 2 from Matagorda Municipality it was provided that "the Capitol shall be the Town of Texana, lately called Santa Anna."[6]

Approximately 85 votes were cast in the election held in Jackson Municipality to elect two delegates to the Constitutional Convention. At the box at the home of James Kerr, on the Lavaca, where Elijah Stapp and John Alley were the judges and Samuel A. White, the secretary, the vote was: Kerr, 29; Stapp, 27; George Sutherland, 2; and Francis Menefee White, 2.

284

John S. Menefee and Francis M. White were the judges at Texana. There Sutherland received 38 votes; Stapp, 26; White, 24; and Kerr, 20.

Of the total number of votes cast, Stapp received 53; Kerr, 49; Sutherland, 40; and White, 40.[7]

Kerr and Stapp were declared elected. Stapp was seated at the Convention March 1.[8] Kerr did not attend.

There is no evidence in the General Land Office that Stapp joined the army after the adjournment of the Convention. The fact that he was on the Trinity River in April is an indication, at least, that he was in the Runaway Scrape. He wrote a letter April 9, 1836, at "Trinity" to President Burnet on behalf of J. J. Linn.[9] He was probably with William Menefee who also on April 9 wrote to Burnet in defense of Linn.[10] That he had not returned to his home before June 1, 1836, is stated in a letter he wrote to Gen. Thomas J. Rusk in June, 1836:

> June 1836, East of Colorado River
>
> Genl Rusk:
> When I was at the Convention with you, my family was driven from their home on the Lavaca, by the Enemy and they, the enemy, have destroyed, & driven off all that I had to support my family; I am over here destitute of money or provisions for my family which compels me to ask your assistance by granting me an order to draw from any public stores a sufficienty to support on; My family that I ask for is five children, Wife and Myself—two of my sons has been in the army almost ever since it first commenced last fall— There is now two; in a few days I send you another which is all that I have able to do Military duty—
> I am doing all I can to get men to rally to the Standard and fight the Battles of Texas;—any duty that my bodily strength would enable me to perform either in public or private that would advance the cause of Texas I feel anxious & ever ready to perform; as soon as I get shelter & something to Support my family, I intend to pay you a visit if health permits—Your

course of procedure is approved by the people so far as I can learn; they are of opinion when you whip the enemy that you pursue them closely across Rio grande, not permitting them to take any arms of Munitions of war with them.

Respectfully yours &c.
Elijah Stapp[11]

Stapp was postmaster at La Baca, Jackson County in 1840. He died in March, 1843.[12] He was buried in what later became known as the old Russell Ward Cemetery five miles northeast of Edna, Jackson County. In 1936 the Commission of Control for Texas Centennial Celebrations had a monument erected in the cemetery in his honor.

Stapp was married to Nancy Shannon. Their children were Preston; Darwin Massey; William Preston; Oliver; Hugh Shannon; Achilles; Walter; Le Grand; Rebecca; and Mary Stapp, who was married to William King.

Darwin Massey Stapp, son of Elijah Stapp, was born in 1815. He was thrice married. On November 8, 1837, he was married to Mrs. Maria O. Heard, who was twice a widow. His second wife was Miss Cecelia Thompson and his third, Mrs. Lulu Cunningham Robinson, a widow. There were no children by the first marriage. Children of his second marriage were Elijah, Revel and Edward Stapp. Darwin and Lula Stapp were children of his third marriage. Darwin Massey Stapp died February 28, 1875.

Hugh Shannon Stapp, son of Elijah Stapp, was born in Frankford, Kentucky, in 1820. On November 9, 1850, he was married to Elizabeth M. Rice, daughter of Dr. Charles Wesley and Margaret Rice. Their children were Cecelia; Callista, who was married to Isaac Newton Mitchell; Charles; Darwin; Walter; Elsie and Dalton Stapp.

William Preston Stapp, son of Elijah Stapp, was a member of the Mier Expedition in 1842.

Some of the surviving descendants of Mr. and Mrs. Elijah Stapp in 1939 were Mrs. Callista Mitchell, La Ward, Texas;

286

Mrs. Eunice Stokes, 745 Porter Street, San Antonio; C. S. Mitchell, Lolita, Texas; Hugh O. Mitchell, U. S. Coast & Geodetic Engineer, Washington, D. C.; Mrs. Ross R. Bailey, Houston; Mrs. Lena H. Stafford, Miami, Florida; J. J. Halfin, Beaumont; Preston E. Halfin, Victoria; and G. S. Halfin, Port Arthur.

DR. CHARLES BELLINGER STEWART
of
AUSTIN MUNICIPALITY

287

Charles Bellinger Stewart was born in Charleston, South Carolina, February 18, 1806, son of Charles and Adrianna (Bull) Stewart.[1] In 1827 he resided in Columbus, Georgia, and owned an interest in a drugstore. For a few months in 1828 he conducted a business in Cuba.[2] Later he was a commission merchant in New Orleans. He came to Texas in 1830[3] and ran a drugstore in the town of Brazoria. In June, 1832, he entered Francis W. Johnson's command, raised to attack the Mexican fort at Anahuac.[4] Although he was not a member of it, the first Convention of Texas at San Felipe, on October 5, 1832, appointed him, John Austin, Charles D. Sayre, George B. McKinstry, and Warren D. C. Hall members of a subcommittee of Safety and Vigilance for the District of Victoria (Brazoria). Their duties were to keep up a regular and stated correspondence "on all subjects relating to the tranquility of the interior."[5] On November 21, 1834, Judge Thomas J. Chambers appointed

Ira R. Lewis prosecuting attorney and Stewart secretary of the judicial district of Brazos.[6]

Stewart moved to San Felipe prior to July 17, 1835. On that date he was secretary of the delegation from the jurisdiction of Austin, composed of Wyly Martin, president, Alexander Somervell, John R. Jones, and Jesse Bartlett, which met at San Felipe with delegates from the jurisdictions of Columbia and Mina, "to take into consideration the state of the country and the alleged outrages against Mexico, 'namely William B. Travis' capture of twenty Mexican soldiers under Captain Tenorio at Anahuac.'"[7] The Committee of Safety and Correspondence for the Jurisdiction of Columbia of which Dr. Branch T. Archer was chairman, and William T. Austin secretary, at Velasco on August 19, 1835, wrote to Stewart that they, reposing the fullest confidence in his zeal, energy, fidelity, and ability, had appointed him as

288

> ...confidential Agent to act within the Jurisdiction of San Felipe for the purpose of obtaining a Consultation of all Texas through her representatives, conformably to the plan contained in the address of the committee which is herewith forwarded to you.
>
> We confidentially hope that you will leave no honorable means untried to produce this desired object, that you will be diligent in communication, to the Committee and to the people of all valuable information which you may acquire, and in the end that your efforts may be crowned with success.—[8]

On October 11, 1835, Stewart was elected secretary of the Permanent Council, a body organized to conduct matters of state until the meeting of the Consultation.[9] Upon the recommendation of Governor Smith who had been elected November 12, the General Council, on November 18, appointed Stewart secretary to the executive and enrollment clerk.[10] A misunderstanding arose between Smith and the

General Council, and on January 11, 1836, the Council ordered Smith "to forthwith cease the function of his office," and declared Robinson governor. Stewart, not recognizing Robinson as such, on January 16, asked permission to resign.[11] Instead of accepting his resignation, the Council suspended him and assessed a fine of $2,500 against him for contempt. It provided, however, that the fine would be remitted if Stewart would deliver to the Council before nine o'clock January 18, all of the official papers of his office. This Stewart did on January 17.[12]

On February 1, 1836, Stewart, Thomas Barnett, and Randal Jones were elected to represent Austin Municipality at the Constitutional Convention.[13] Stewart and Barnett were seated March 1.[14] Jones did not attend. In Washington, Stewart had business additional to the Convention. On March 8, James Hall, Primary Judge of Washington Municipality, authorized "W. W. Sheppard of Lake Creek to celebrate a contract of Marriage between Chas. B. Stewart and Julia Sheppard and to give to it the said contract the necessary formality before attesting witnesses."[15] The ceremony was performed March 11.

Stewart, on March 16, the day before the Convention adjourned, wrote Ira R. Lewis in Natchez:

> An opportunity offering, I write you, not with many pleasant feelings. The Alamo has fallen and every unfortunate creature murdered and burned, some even before they were dead. A Mexican whose daughters live at Beasons, and another, came into Houston's camp at Gonzales and reported on the 10th, that on the 6th day at daylight, the cavalry surrounded the fort and the infantry, with scaling ladders entered at the 4 angles of the fort, and were supported until all but seven of the Americans were killed,—these called for Santa Anna and Quarter, and were by his order immediately sacrificed. Travis, at that moment put an end to his own existence, knowing his fate if taken alive. In the stories related by the two Mexicans, there is no material difference. Mr.

McNeal (our Natchez friend) said that La Bahia, whence he has just arrived, that the Country from La Bahia to Bexar, is alive with Mexicans, that Fannin is probably surrounded, having attempted to march to the relief of Bexar, and was beat back. Our condition is very bad.—Today we finish the Constitution,—hurry through the rest of the business, and prepare for desperate efforts.

Jas. Collingsworth, Col. Carson of N. C. and D. Burnet, are nominated for the President (Provisional). Rusk, Bailey Hardiman, Potter and one of the first named will form the Cabinet. Next Congress will regulate land business.[16]

Following the Revolution, Stewart moved to the town of Montgomery, formerly seat of Montgomery County, where he practiced medicine. On March 5, 1840, Judge A. B. Shelby appointed him district attorney pro tem of the county,[17] and on May 11, 1841, President Lamar appointed him notary public.[18] He represented Montgomery County at the Constitutional Convention which convened at Austin, July 4, 1845,[19] and at the First,[20] Fourth,[21] and Fourteenth[22] Legislatures. While serving in the Fourteenth Legislature in 1874-75, his address was Danville, Montgomery County, and he represented Montgomery and Harris Counties.[23]

Toward the end of his life Dr. Stewart became almost totally deaf. His letters to Moses Austin Bryan indicate he was a profound believer in spiritualism. In a postscript to a letter dated August, 1883, he predicted that he would die in about seven years.[24] He passed away, however, in less than two years, on July 28, 1885.[25] He is buried in a marked grave in the cemetery at Montgomery. In 1936 the Commission of Control for Texas Centennial Celebrations erected a marker at the site of his former home one mile from the town of Montgomery.[26]

Mrs. Stewart died July 10, 1849, survived by five children: Charles Waters, Mary Cecelia, Lucia Annette, Medora Isabella, and Julia Arnold Stewart.

On August 28, 1851, Dr. Stewart married Mrs. Elizabeth Antoinette (Nichols) Boyd, widow of William Boyd. By an act approved February 4, 1856, the Legislature authorized Stewart to adopt Mrs. Boyd's two children, Caroline and Lucy Ann Boyd. The name Stewart was added to both of their names. By his second marriage, two children were born: Edmund Bellinger and Laura C. Stewart. The second Mrs. Stewart died in 1858.

Of the children of Dr. Stewart, Charles Waters Stewart was married to Adrianna L. Artigue Peebles; Lucia Stewart was married to Samuel D. Barclay; Mary Stewart was married to Davis M. Barclay; Medora Stewart was married to Thomas G. Griffin; and Julia A. Stewart was married to Michael H. Book.

The surviving grandchildren of Dr. Stewart in October, 1941, were: Mrs. E. B. Wilcox, Miss Reba Stewart, Miss Clare Stewart, and Mrs. Howard Fling, all of Houston; Arthur Barclay, Fort Worth; David M. Barclay, San Benito; Charles Waters Stewart, Galveston; Mrs. John Formes Barclay, Natchitoches, Louisiana; Edgar Barclay, Louisiana; Kyle Griffin, Colorado; Mrs. Frank Baldwin, Atlanta, Georgia; and Mrs. J. C. Christy, San Francisco, California.

JAMES GIBSON SWISHER
of
WASHINGTON MUNICIPALITY

*J*ames Gibson Swisher was born November 6, 1794,[1] near Franklin, Tennessee, a son of Henry and Annie (Gibson) Swisher. Swisher served in the War of 1812 as a private in Capt. David Mason's Company of Cavalry, Tennessee Militia. His services began August 18, 1813, and ended May 21, 1814. He also served as a private in Capt. John Donelson's Company of United States Mounted Rangers from September 2, 1814, to September 1, 1815.[2]

Swisher came to Texas in 1833[3] and settled at Tenoxtitlan, the site of which is in Burleson County, where he remained until in October, 1834, when he removed to Gay Hill, in the present county of Washington.[4]

In 1835 a company of volunteers was raised in Washington Municipality, of which Swisher was elected captain and Dr. G. W. Barnett, lieutenant. When they reached Gonzales, they found the Mexicans had retreated to San Antonio. They followed on and joined the main army and remained with the army during the entire campaign. When Benjamin R. Milam called for volunteers on December 5 to storm San Antonio, the company, almost to a man, volunteered, and from the 5th to the 10th were under fire.[5]

Gen. Martin Perfecto de Cos agreed to surrender on the 10th and on the following day Gen. Edward Burleson and Commissioners Maj. Robert C. Morris, Capt. Francis W. Johnson and Capt. Swisher met with Gen. Cos and his commissioners and agreed to the terms of surrender.[6]

In the elections held throughout Texas on February 1, 1836, to select delegates to the Constitutional Convention, Swisher, Dr. George W. Barnett, Jesse Grimes and Dr. Benjamin B. Goodrich were elected from Washington Municipality.[7] Swisher was seated March 1.[8] After the Convention adjourned Swisher joined the thousands who participated in the Runaway Scrape. Of this his son John M. Swisher said:

> After the adjournment of the convention at Washington, Dr. G. W. Barnett and several other members had joined the army with a view of participating in the expected battle on the Colorado. When General Houston made up his mind to retreat, he gave them permission to leave the army to seek a place of safety for their families. My father, Dr. Barnett,

Captain [Horatio] Chriesman and many other families of
the neighborhood then commenced their 'runaway scrape',
as it was called, in company. They had reached Beaumont
in Jefferson county, before they heard of the battle of San
Jacinto, when owing to the condition of their teams, they
found it impossible to return to their homes. They therefore concluded to move up to San Augustine and spend the
summer. Fortunately for them General Gaines of the United
States army having concluded to occupy Nacogdoches with
a portion of his troops, gave employment to their teams, in
transporting supplies at remunerative rates, thus enabling
them to keep down expenses.[9]

On July 3, Swisher joined Capt. William W. Hill's ranger
company,[10] from which he was honorably discharged on October 1, 1836.[11] He was a charter trustee of Union Academy
at Washington, incorporated February 4, 1840.[12] He moved
to Austin in 1846 and there died November 14, 1864. He was
married to Elizabeth Boyd who died April 27, 1875. Both are
buried in marked graves in Oakwood Cemetery, Austin.

When Swisher County, Texas, was created August 21,
1876, it was named "in honor of James G. Swisher, who
commanded a company at the storming of Bexar in 1835,
and was one of the signers of the Declaration of Texas Independence."[13]

Children of Capt. and Mrs. James G. Swisher were John
Milton, a San Jacinto veteran; James Monroe, who mar-
ried Adalaide Wells; and Annie Swisher, who married Dr.
R. N. Lane. Mrs. John R. Blocker, 212 Courtland Place, San
Antonio was one of the surviving children, in 1938, of Dr.
and Mrs. Lane.

John Milton Swisher, son of James G. Swisher, was thrice
married. He was married to Maria Simms at Washington,
Texas, May 28, 1844, by Rev. Wm. M. Tryon. Mrs. Swisher
died in 1870. Children of Mr. and Mrs. Swisher were two,
Mary and John M. Swisher, Jr.

293

In 1873 John M. Swisher was married to Nettie A. Nickerson of Ohio. Mrs. Swisher died in 1875, leaving two daughters Annie and Nellie Swisher.

On October 8, 1878, Swisher was married to Mrs. Bella French at the home of the Rev. W. H. D. Carrington. There were no children by this marriage. Swisher died March 11, 1891, and was buried in Oakwood Cemetery, Austin, where his grave is marked.

Mary Swisher was married but the name of her husband is not known to the author. Their children were Eva, who married Judge Hamilton Ward; Josephine, who married Dan Sullivan; John; and Imogen Swisher.

John M. Swisher, Jr. was married but the name of his wife is not known to the compiler. Their children were Florence, who married John S. Hoover, and Ada Swisher.

Annie Swisher married a Mr. Boone and in 1938 was residing at 1005 West Sixth Street, Los Angeles, California.

Nellie Swisher married Willis A. Keys. Her address in 1938 was Box 403, Archer City, Texas.

294

CHARLES STANFIELD TAYLOR
of
NACOGDOCHES MUNICIPALITY

Charles Stanfield Taylor was born in London, England, in 1808.[1] He immigrated to the United States in 1828 and stopped temporarily in New York City. In the same year he arrived in Nacogdoches, Texas,[2] where he established a mercantile business. On April 1, 1830, he appeared before the Ayuntamiento and stated under oath that he was "single, age 23, merchant, originally of New York, Catholic."[3] In January, 1831, he and Charles H. Sims formed a partnership under the name of Sims and Taylor. Sims sold his interest to Adolphus Sterne in February, 1831, and the name of the firm was changed to Sterne and Taylor.

In 1832, Taylor was elected a member of the Ayuntamiento of Nacogdoches[4] and in that year, also, he participated in the Battle of Nacogdoches.[5] At the First Convention of Texas which convened at San Felipe de Austin on October 1, 1832, he represented the District of Nacogdoches.[6] The Convention on October 5, named him a member of the Nacogdoches Sub-Committee of Safety and Vigilance.[7]

In 1833[8] Taylor moved to San Augustine, which had been surveyed during the spring or early summer of that year.[9] Later in the year he was elected alcalde of San Augustine and served from January 1, 1834, until the establishment of the Ayuntamiento of San Augustine, which was authorized by an act passed by the legislature of Coahuila and Texas, March 26, 1834.[10]

At this time a special decree was issued at Monclova, which was then the capital of Coahuila and Texas, naming commissioners for putting in possession of land the families who resided to the east of Austin's Colony and the inhabitants of the Department of Nacogdoches. These commissioners, without delay, should "execute the same at the expense of the persons interested, and titles heretofore legally issued are hereby confirmed."[11] On April 25, 1835, Taylor, George W. Smyth and Charles Anthony Nixon were appointed under this decree for the municipalities of San Augustine, Bevil (Jasper), and Nacogdoches, respectively.[12]

In the summer of 1834 Taylor returned to Nacogdoches, where he resided for the remainder of his life.

On October 20, 1835, the Permanent Council at San Felipe, of which R. R. Royall was president, passed a resolution requesting those vested with power to issue land titles not to issue any more after November 1, 1835, claiming that it was unfair to the soldiers of the Army of Texas on the frontier who were not in position to apply for land.[13] Taylor and some of the other land commissioners disregarded the resolution. On December 4, 1835, the General Council of the Provisional Government appointed commissioners, one of them Dr. Stephen H. Everitt, to close the offices. Everitt at Nacogdoches, December 19, 1835, wrote to Taylor:

> Sir: In conformity with the 14th Art. of the Provisional Organic Law of Texas, your duties as Commissioner for Issuing land titles are hereby suspended till farther orders from The Provisional Government. You will be pleased to hold your documents and papers generally, subject to the order of the Government and Council of Texas, taking especial care to secure them as far as possible from the danger of Fire & Ravages of our Enemy.[14]

296

Taylor, however, continued to issue titles until January 24, 1836.[15] He issued the first title August 3, 1835.[16] He, however, turned over to the *ad interim* government most of the fees he had received from those to whom land was granted. His letters show that between November 10, 1835, and February 22, 1836, he distributed from the land fees he had collected approximately $4,000 to the Committee of Vigilance and Safety of Nacogdoches and to the Army of Texas.

On February 1, 1836, Taylor, Robert Potter, Thomas J. Rusk, and John S. Roberts were elected delegates from Nacogdoches County to the Constitutional Convention.[17] Potter was seated in the Convention on March 1;[18] the other three arrived at the Convention on March 2.[19] Shortly after leaving the Convention Taylor and his family left Nacogdoches for Natchitoches, Louisiana, where he remained until the Revolution ended. While there two of his children died.[20]

On December 20, 1836, President Houston appointed Taylor chief justice of Nacogdoches County.[21] On November 13, 1838, he was nominated to the Senate of the Republic by President Houston as commissioner to run the boundary line between Texas and the United States.[22] Lamar became President, December 10, 1838, and, on December 12th, the Senate not having acted on President Houston's recommendation, the nomination was withdrawn.[23]

Taylor, on August 9, 1838, was appointed volunteer aid-de-camp on the staff of Gen. Thomas J. Rusk, his commission to expire November 14, 1838.[24] This was during the quelling of the rebellion of Mexicans and Indians under Vincente Cordova.

On March 2, 1839, Judge Taylor, although not having a license to practice law, formed a partnership with William L. Underwood under the name of Underwood and Taylor.[25] On April 12, having successfully passed an examination conducted by William L. Underwood, J. S. Mayfield, and David S. Kaufman, he was granted a license to practice law in the courts of the Republic.[26] On September 19, 1838, he was appointed district attorney of the Fifth Judicial District by President Lamar.[27] On November 29, however, his nomination was rejected by the Senate of the Congress of the Republic.[28]

On July 27, 1846, Taylor formed a law partnership with Thomas W. Blake under the name of Taylor and Blake.[29] The firm was dissolved June 8, 1847, and on June 14, the firm of Taylor & Green was formed, Taylor having as a partner Ashbell Green.[30]

Taylor was elected county treasurer of Nacogdoches County, August 5, 1850,[31] and was re-elected August 2, 1852.[32] On February 15, 1854, Gov. E. M. Pease appointed him one of two commissioners to investigate land titles in El Paso, Presidio, Kinney, Starr, Webb, Hidalgo, Cameron, and Nueces Counties.[33] This work lasted until about Oc-

297

tober 1, 1855. The other commissioner was H. H. Lane, of Bonham.

Taylor was elected chief justice of Nacogdoches County, August 6, 1860,[34] and was re-elected August 4, 1862,[35] and again on August 1, 1864.[36] He was holding that office November 1, 1865, when he died.

Taylor was married May 28, 1831, to Anna Maria Ruoff, daughter of Johann Eberhard Ruoff.[37] Mrs. Taylor was born in Esslingen, Wertenberg, Germany, March 1, 1814, and died February 8, 1873. The Commission of Control for Texas Centennial Celebrations erected a joint monument at the graves of Judge and Mrs. Taylor in Oak Grove cemetery in Nacogdoches in 1936, and a monument at the site of their former home in Nacogdoches.

Although Judge Taylor was a member of the Roman Catholic Church he was an ardent member of the Masonic Lodge.[38]

Children of Judge Charles S. and Anna Maria (Ruoff) Taylor were Evariste, born March 25, 1832, and died in Natchitoches, Louisiana, July 28, 1836; Marie Rosine, born July 21, 1833, and died in Natchitoches, Louisiana, July 28, 1836; George, born November 4, 1834; Texana, born January 12, 1836; Charles Irion, born October 15, 1837; Milam, born December 29, 1838; Julia, born June 25, 1840, married Henry Curl of Chireno, October 4, 1860, and died October 18, 1925; Lawrence S., born June 3, 1842; William, born November 13, 1843; Amelia, born April 22, 1845, and was married to William Clark, son of William Clark, Jr., a signer of the Texas Declaration of Independence; Adolphus, born March 18, 1847, and was married to Jennie Simpson; Eugene, born April 14, 1849, and was never married; and Anna Mary Taylor, who was born June 21, 1853.

Mrs. John V. Hughes, a granddaughter of Judge Charles S. Taylor, died in 1940 at 5804 Swiss Avenue, Dallas. Some of the surviving great grandchildren of Judge Taylor in 1940 were Henry C. Hughes, Mrs. Ethel H. Gannon, both of Dallas; Mrs. J. A. Green; Mrs. Russell Pettengill, Chicago; Mrs. E. N. Mather, Chicago; Miss Rosine Hughes, Dallas, and Mrs. J. C. Tennison, Dallas.

DAVID THOMAS
of
REFUGIO MUNICIPALITY[1]

*A*ccording to Goodrich, David Thomas was born in Tennessee, and from that state came to Texas. In March, 1836, he was 35 years of age.[2] This being true he was born in about 1801. He was evidently a lawyer since he was elected Attorney General of the Republic of Texas.

299

David Thomas came to Texas with "The U. S. Independent Volunteers Cavalry Company," which was organized at Nacogdoches, December 10, 1835, with Benjamin L. Lawrence as Captain; John M. Harris, First Lieutenant, and Edward Conrad, Second Lieutenant. When it was reorganized on about December 27 at Bexar as the "Mustang Company" under Francis W. Johnson and Dr. James Grant, Harris the First Lieutenant was replaced by David Thomas. After Captain Lawrence's departure from Refugio with General Houston on January 21, David Thomas succeeded to the command of the company and continued with it until about February 13. On February 1 he and Edward Conrad were chosen by the volunteers at Refugio as their representatives to the convention at Washington. Leaving Goliad about February 14, Mr. Thomas proceeded via San Felipe to Washington.[3]

On January 3, 1836, Francis W. Johnson wrote to the General Council of the Provisional Government and asked authority to head an expedition of 530 volunteers against Matamoros. He likewise requested commissions for certain men who had volunteered for the expedition. Among them were commissions for B. L. Lawrence, captain; David Thomas, first lieutenant; and John Lowary, second lieutenant.[4] The Committee of Military Affairs recommended to the General Council that the expedition be authorized and that the commissions be issued.[5]

General Houston left Washington on January 8, 1836, to confer with the officers at Refugio regarding the proposed expedition to Matamoros. He arrived at Goliad on the 14th and was at Refugio on the 20th. On January 30 he was back in Washington.[6] On February 1, while he was at Washington, he was voted upon in both Nacogdoches and Refugio Municipalities as a delegate to the Constitutional Convention. He was badly defeated in Nacogdoches but was successful in Refugio.[7]

The Municipality of Refugio was entitled to two delegates in the Convention. Two distinct elections were held in the town of Refugio. At the town voting box Houston received 44 votes; James Power, 42; and Martin Lawler, 26. Houston and Power were declared elected. The election judges were Capt. Ira Westover, Edward McDonough, and Hugh McDonald Fraser. Lewis Ayers was the secretary.[8]

The other election was held in the mission at Refugio by volunteers in the army recently arrived in Texas. The judges were Capt. William G. Cooke, Valentine Bennet, John L. Lowary, William Badgett and Samuel Wilson. The vote stood: Conrad, 119; Thomas, 91; and Bradford, 87. Conrad and Thomas were declared elected.[9]

Thomas and Conrad appeared before the election committee of the Convention and presented a petition signed by 127 soldiers requesting that Thomas and Conrad be seated. They stated that they had not been permitted to vote by the citizens of Refugio.

Upon the recommendation of the committee the Convention accepted Houston, Power, Thomas and Conrad as representatives of Refugio Municipality, and they were seated March 1.[10]

On March 17, 1836, Thomas was elected *ad interim* Attorney General of the Republic of Texas. When Thomas J. Rusk, Secretary of War, left the cabinet to join the army, Thomas was made acting Secretary of War, holding the two positions at the same time.

Thomas was mortally wounded on or about April 16, 1836, by the accidental discharge of a gun while he was a passenger on board the *Cayuga*. The exact time and place of his death has not been recorded and accounts incident to it vary. Thomas, with other members of the cabinet, was at Harrisburg, the temporary seat of government, on April 12. On the 15th, Mexican troops entered the town. President Burnet, Vice-President Zavala, Robert Potter, Secretary of the Navy, Bailey Hardeman, Secretary of the Treasury, Thomas and others boarded the steamboat *Cayuga* for Galveston. The boat anchored for the night at Lynch's, proceeding on the following morning, the 16th, for her designation.[11] Burnet disembarked at New Washington to join his family. En route to Galveston, Thomas was accidentally shot. Of the tragedy John J. Linn, who was at Galveston when the boat arrived, said:

> Quite a fatal accident occurred during the passage of the *Cayuga* to the island. A gun or pistol was carelessly discharged by some negligent person, and the ball entered the leg of Mr. David Thomas, the attorney-general, of which wound he died three days after.[12]

Linn implies that Thomas died on Galveston Island. Other evidence, however, tends to prove that he died on board the *Cayuga* and was buried near Zavala's home, across Buffalo Bayou from the San Jacinto Battlefield.

Oᴜʀ (unlikely) Fᴀᴛʜᴇʀs

The *Cayuga* was loaded with supplies and despatched on the 18th or 19th to the army wherever it might be found on Buffalo Bayou,[13] Galveston at this time consisted of but a few shacks and tents, with no medical facilities, and it has been claimed that Thomas remained aboard the *Cayuga* and arrived at the Battlefield on about April 22. From there he was taken to Zavala's home then being used by the Texans as a temporary hospital. At his death, it is claimed, he was buried on a plot of ground that later became the Zavala family cemetery. To the author it seems odd that Thomas was thus buried while the Texans who were killed or mortally wounded in battle were buried on the Battlefield.

Dixon quotes William Secrest, one of the crew of the *Cayuga*:

> We had great difficulty in stopping the flow of blood and Mr. Thomas suffered greatly while en route, as the water was rough and we passed several squalls before reaching San Jacinto, where he died.[14]

Anderson Buffington, a San Jacinto veteran, is quoted by Dixon as saying, in 1873:

> I was at San Jacinto when the ship landed with supplies. I assisted in unloading the vessel and remember that Mr. Thomas appeared to be suffering greatly. He looked pale and emaciated but did not complain. He was taken the following day to the home of Vice-President De Zavala where he died soon afterwards. Dr. [Anson] Jones attended him but the heavy loss of blood had reduced his strength and power of endurance. I do not know where he was buried as I left for my home in Montgomery County shortly after his death.[15]

Important additional evidence that Thomas died at Galveston is suggested in an official order issued at Galveston April 26, 1836, by Warren D. C. Hall, acting Secretary of War:

302

Department of War
Galveston April 26th 1836

To General Saml Houston

If you consider it inexpedient to risk an engagement with
the enemy and consider a retreat *inevitable* from the position you now occupy, you are hereby ordered to march with
the army under your command to the nearest and most convenient point to this Island giving information of the same
to this Department when transports will be sent forthwith
to cross the troops to this Island.
Warren D. C. Hall
Act. Sec. of War[16]

President Burnet appointed Thomas acting secretary
of war when Rusk entered the army, and it seems fair to
assume that he appointed Hall to succeed Thomas after
Thomas's death. If this be true, Thomas died on Galveston
Island, for it was not until April 26, after Hall's order had
been issued, that the first news from San Jacinto was received by Burnet.[17]

Believing, at that time, that Linn's version of Thomas's
death was true and assuming that he died on Galveston
Island about April 19th and that his grave could be located,
the author was instrumental in having the State Legislature appropriate funds to be used in having the remains
of General Thomas exhumed and reinterred in the State
Cemetery at Austin. A search for his grave, in Galveston,
however, proved futile.

On November 5, 1931, Miss Adina De Zavala, a granddaughter of Governor Zavala, wrote to the author and
inquired if a monument could not be erected "to David
Thomas, first Attorney General of Texas, who is buried in
the same [Zavala] cemetery." In a letter dated January 26,
1932, she wrote that she could locate General Thomas's
grave. Complying with her request, with funds previously mentioned, a monument to Thomas was erected on

the spot designated by her. This site, of course, had been pointed out to her by others.

On November 2, 1838, Headright Certificate 165 for one-third of a league was issued in the name of David Thomas, deceased, by the Board of Land Commissioners of Bastrop County.[18] This was the quantity of land a single man was entitled to receive. Capt. Jesse Billingsley was administrator of Thomas's estate.

JOHN TURNER
of
SAN PATRICIO MUNICIPALITY

304

*J*ohn Turner was born in North Carolina in about 1802 and came to Texas from Tennessee,[1] in 1834. On June 20, 1835, he received title to one league and one labor of land in McMullen and McGloin's Colony, surveyed in what is now Live Oak County.[2]

At San Patricio, on November 30, 1835, Turner wrote Capt. Philip Dimitt the following letter which Dimitt sent on to Gov. Henry Smith:

I have a few minutes ago taken some despatches from the Mexicans, which I have sent you conceiving that they contained information of importance to you.

I think from the information contained in them you will see the necessity of your assistance here; we have neither men nor means to withstand any force that may be sent against us, as the people are still divided. I therefore hope under these distressing circumstances you will send us some reinforcements with all possible despatch.

The Commandante of La Pantecian [Lipantitlan] has written a letter to us dis-annulling the authorities of this place, elected since the Battle, & closed it by inviting us to join his ranks, & if we do not, that the vengence of the Mexican army will be poured upon us; but there is still a Remnant of patriots who wish to support the Constitution, & would prefer death to slavery. Please give us all the news you can of the proceedings the army at Bexar, and elsewhere. Reports have come to us yesterday that a party of Americans & Mexicans joined and are at Revuco [Refugio] in arms for the cause of liberty. Perhaps you may have some information on this subject more correct than ours. Nothing more at present but remain.

Please not to be mistaken in our situation, we have neither men nor bread, & no place to procure some without it comes from your quarter; as there is none to be had at any price, and our men are too few to spare, to send in pursuit of it—[3]

Turner and John W. Bower, on February 1, 1836, were elected delegates from the Municipality of San Patricio to the Constitutional Convention.[4] Turner took his seat March 1.[5]

After the adjournment of the Convention Turner did not immediately join the army. He was, however, a captain in the service as early as June 14, 1836. He and Capt. John Chenoweth ranged the settlements on the Brazos, Buffalo Bayou, San Jacinto River and Galveston Bay under an order of Gen. Thomas J. Green, to procure horses and supplies for his brigade.[6]

Turner served as a member of the House of Representatives in the First Congress of the Republic from San Patricio County from October 3 to 19, 1836, when he was succeeded by John Geraghty.[7] On the following day President Houston nominated him chief justice of San Patricio County, and the Senate, on the same day, approved the nomination.[8] San Patricio County was at this time practically depopulated, its former residents temporarily scattered in other sections of the Republic.

On March 17, 1837, President Houston ordered Turner to hold an election to select a successor to Edwin Morehouse, senator from the district composed of San Patricio, Refugio and Goliad counties.[9]

Captain Turner probably moved to Houston as early as the year 1839. It is known that he was living there June 16, 1841, when he was the administrator of the estate of Robert A. Toler.[10]

On June 15, 1842, Turner and his wife, Margaret, living on the southwest corner of Smith and Rusk Streets, sold, for $100, a house adjoining theirs to Eli Williams of Fort Bend County.[11]

On August 3, 1844, Turner petitioned the county court to declare him bankrupt.[12] This, Chief Justice A. P. Thompson did August 27, 1844. The deed of conveyance and assignment to the trustees, Jesse M. Hooker, C. W. McAnelly, and R. C. Campbell, listed his property as his home on Smith Street, Houston; a house and lot in San Patricio; 320 acres of land in Fort Bend County; a small lot of farming utensils consisting of plows, hoes and carpenter tools; household and kitchen furniture.[12]

Turner died in Houston sometime between August 27, 1844, when he was declared a bankrupt, and November 2, 1848, when his widow was married to John Bradley by the Rev. Robert W. Kennan.[13] Bradley having died, Mrs. Bradley, on November 13, 1853, married William Blanton.[14]

Capt and Mrs. Turner had one child, Martha A. Turner, who was married to George Dye. Mrs. Blanton and Mr. and Mrs. Dye were living in Corpus Christi as late as May 3, 1879.[15]

EDWIN WALLER
of
BRAZORIA MUNICIPALITY

$\mathcal{E}$dwin Waller was born in Spotsylvania County, Virgin-
ia, November 4, 1800.[1] He came to Texas in 1831[2] from
Missouri. On July 20, 1831, he received title to one league
of land in Austin's Second Colony situated in what is now
Brazoria County.[3] He was a member of Lt. Henry S. Brown's
Company in the Battle of Velasco, June 26, 1832.[4] In 1835 he
was sent as a delegate from the Municipality of Columbia
(Brazoria) to the Consultation held in San Felipe de Aus-
tin,[5] and by that body was elected a member of the General
Council of the Provisional Government of Texas.[6]

In the election held throughout Texas, on February 1,
1836, to select delegates to the Constitutional Convention scheduled to meet at Washington March 1, Waller,
Asa Brigham, John S. D. Byrom, and James Collinsworth
were chosen to represent Brazoria Municipality.[7] Waller
was seated March 1.[8] On March 16, at his request, he was
discharged from further attendance on the Convention.[9]

William Fairfax Gray, on April 21, saw Waller at Beaumont, removing his and William G. Hill's negroes from
Texas. Hill with his and Waller's families had gone ahead
to Alexandria, Louisiana.[10]

Gray, on a visit to Waller's plantation on Oyster Creek
in Brazoria County, on April 5, 1837, recorded in his diary:

> Had some interesting conversation with Mrs. Waller;
> she was a Miss Dashields, daughter of Captain Dashields,
> of Northumberland, Virginia; married against her father's
> wishes. Is estranged from her father and sister, Mrs. Boy-
> sie has been six years in Texas; neither wrote nor received
> a letter from father or sister in all that time. That is bad,

but I could not but sympathize with her. Children named Hiram, Edwin, William Wharton and Juliet. They have had much trouble since they have been in the country. She is now reconciled to it, but wants to go back to Virginia to see her connections once more.

Waller returned before night. He says he once bought this place for 50 cents per acre; sold it for $1.25, and bought it back for $6; would not now take $25; works seventeen field hands, eleven of them able men. Has 1,000 acres, 275 cleared and in corn and cotton.[11]

In 1838 Judge Waller was named president of the Board of Land Commissioners for Brazoria County. In 1839 he was appointed commissioner to lay out the town of Austin, already selected as the capitol of Texas, to sell lots and to erect public buildings. En route to Austin at Damons, Fort Bend County, on May 9, he wrote President Lamar:

308

My business progresses as rapidly as I could have expected although one waggon which I expected to arrive from Houston at Columbia did not come in as I had anticipated. I started three from that place yesterday morning, which are now on the way accompanied by a number of workmen. I have found it more difficult than I anticipated to procure workmen but hope to succeed in collecting a sufficient number together before we reach our destination [Austin].

We have at length prevailed upon a gentleman, to offer himself as a candidate for Senator from our district to supply the vacancy occasioned by the death of Col. [William H.] Wharton; one in whose abilities and qualifications for filling the station we have every confidence as also in his principles, and his future course, which we believe will prove entirely satisfactory, Col. Wm. T. Austin.

We hope that the election may be held at an early a day as is possible, as there will be a greater certainty of our candidate being elected before the probable opponent Anson Jones can return or have been long returned from the United States.[12]

On October 17 President Lamar and his party visited Austin. Two miles from town they were met and escorted by most of the citizens of the place who could procure horses. The welcoming party was in charge of Col. Edward Burleson. As the city boundary line was crossed, a salute of 21 guns was fired from a six pounder by Thomas William Ward. At a selected spot Judge Waller delivered the address of welcome.

On December 9, 1839, President Lamar appointed Waller postmaster general of the Republic. The Senate, in voting on his confirmation on December 10, stood six for confirmation and six for rejection. David G. Burnet, president of the Senate, decided the issue by voting in Waller's favor.[13] On the following day Waller resigned and was succeeded on December 14 by John Rice Jones.[14]

Waller was the first mayor of Austin, having been elected January 13, 1840. This office he resigned before the completion of his term and moved to his farm in Austin County, now embraced in Waller County.

In 1840, according to Peareson, Waller participated in the Battle of Plum Creek in Caldwell County.[15]

On June 15, 1844, Waller was elected chief justice (county judge) of Austin County. He was re-elected August 2, 1852, and again August 7, 1854.

A few months before his death Waller moved to Austin to live with his daughter, Mrs. P. M. Cuney. In December, 1880, he sold his home in Waller County to W. C. Clemons. He died in Austin, January 3, 1881,[16] and his remains were placed beside those of his wife's in the Waller family cemetery in Waller County. In May, 1928, the remains of the two were exhumed and re-interred in the State Cemetery at Austin. The Commission of Control for Texas Centennial Celebration had a joint monument erected at their graves in 1936. The Commission also had a marker placed at the site of the old Waller home in Waller County.

309

The State of Texas amply honored Waller before his death. Though the act of the Legislature approved April 28, 1873, which created Waller County, did not state for whom it was named,[17] Thrall, in 1879, said it was for Edwin Waller,[18] and this is generally accepted as true.

Judge and Mrs. Waller were Methodists and Waller was a Mason. St. John's Lodge No. 12, A. F. and A. M. was organized at his home at Austin, October 11, 1839. Waller was a charter member and active worker in the Texas Veterans Association, organized at Houston, May 13-15, 1873.

Waller was married to Juliet M. de Shields, who was born in Virginia in 1801 and died May 13, 1867. Children of Judge and Mrs. Waller were Edwin; Juliet, who married F. E. Prentice, and died in July 1849, at the age of fifteen; Sarah, who married James Hillard, and died March 22, 1860, aged twenty; L. G. Waller, who died January 13, 1862, aged 25; Mary; Eva, who died February 13, 1864, aged fifteen; and Hiram B. Waller, late of Hempstead.

Col. Edwin Waller, Jr., was married to Juliet Pauline Ferguson, daughter of David Ferguson of Richmond, Texas. Children of this union were: Dora Waller, who married J. K. P. Byrn of Austin; Leonard Wharton Waller, who married Carrie M. Cooper; Edwin Waller, who married Grace Burkhart and, after her death, Mollie Florence St. John, who in 1941, was residing at San Marcos.

Mary Waller, daughter of Edwin Waller, Sr., was born November 9, 1844. She was married to P. M. Cuney. Mrs. Cuney died February 16, 1882. Miss Byrd Cuney, daughter of Mr. and Mrs. P. M. Cuney, was married to George H. Wray and in 1941 was residing in Dublin, Texas.

Hiram B. Waller, son of Edwin Waller, Sr., had a daughter, Anna, who married Dr. Ernest Thompson.

310

CLAIBORNE WEST
of
JEFFERSON MUNICIPALITY

Claiborne West was born in Tennessee in about 1800 and came to Texas from Louisiana[1] in 1831. He was elected one of the delegates from the District of Liberty to the First Convention of Texas which convened at San Felipe de Austin, October 1, 1832.[2] The Convention, on October 5, created a Central Committee of Safety and Vigilance with sub-committees for the various districts. West was named a member of the Sub-Committee for the District of Cow Bayou.[3] He represented Liberty Municipality in the Consultation held at San Felipe in 1835.[4] The Consultation created Jefferson Municipality of which, on November 14, 1835, West was sworn as a member of the General Council.[5]

When West came to Texas in 1831 the land office were closed, and it was not until May 20, 1835, that he obtained land from the Mexican Government.[6]

The number of votes cast in the election held in the Municipality of Jefferson, February 1, 1836, to elect two delegates to the Constitutional Convention, is not known. The election judge, William T. Hutton, simply notified the Convention that West and William B. Scates had been elected to represent the municipality.[7] West was seated at the Convention March 1.[8]

William Fairfax Gray, who lost no time in leaving Texas at the advance of Santa Anna, was free in his criticism of others who did likewise. On April 19, 1836, he, Nathaniel J. Dobie, and other members of a party in the Runaway Scrape were on Cow Bayou in what is now Orange County, headed for Louisiana. On that day Gray wrote in his diary:

Passed through the league of land bought of [William B.] Scates, called Pine Islands. Stopt at Shoats [Choate's] and got a dinner of milk and bread. Shoats says the Pine Islands are worth $10,000, but Scates bought it of him, and yet owes him $115 of the purchase money. His daughter, Mrs. Jackson, who is a fine looking woman, was in great wrath against Texans for bringing on the war and its consequences, and was eloquent in her vituperation against the members of the late convention, particularly her neighbor, Judge West, whom she called Sawyer West, in allusion to his early vocation, and said he ran off from Washington, after signing the Declaration of Independence, before the ink was dry, and in the panic forgot his hat and coat, and came home bareheaded. Here was a poor woman, a fugitive with three small children sick with measles. Paid for dinner 50 cents. At night we came up with Catlett and company at Williams'; only one young man at home. Got supper and corn for horses. We all stood guard to-night, each one hour, there being eight of us.[9]

312

On April 1, 1836, West was postmaster of Jefferson, the first seat of Jefferson County.[10] He was a member of Capt. Franklin Hardin's company of volunteers from July 1 to October 7, 1836.[11] He was a member of the House of Representatives from Jefferson County in the First Congress of the Republic, October 3, 1836, to September 25, 1837.[12]

West was living in Montgomery County, March 3, 1847. In 1855 he was living in Guadalupe County. In 1940 his old home on the Seguin-Gonzales highway was known as the "Denman place."[13]

West was a member of Belmont Lodge No. 131, A. F. and A. M., and the records of this defunct lodge show that he died September 10, 1866.[14] Someone who did not know the dates of his birth and death erected an expensive monument at his grave in Riverside Cemetery in Seguin.

In 1824 in Louisiana West was married to Anna Garner, daughter of Bradley and Rachel (Harmon) Garner. Mrs.

Rachel West died in Montgomery County, March 3, 1847, and in time West married Mrs. Prudence Kimble, widow of George C. Kimble.

Mrs. Prudence West died in about 1861. West's third wife was Mrs. Florinda (McCulloch) Day, widow of George W. Day. Mrs. Florinda West died May 22, 1875, and was buried between the graves of West and Day.

There were no children by the second and third marriages. Children of his first marriage were: Larkin Nash, Louisa Jane, Lucinda C. Rachel, Robert N., George C., Thomas Jefferson, David Crockett, and William C. West.

Larkin Nash West was married to Martha Conn. Their children were Milton Crockett, William Mortimer, Eugene Beverly, Florence Louisa, Walter Larkin and Jefferson Claiborne West.

Louisa Jane West was married to Thomas A. Gay. Their children were Annie West; Rosa West, who married a Mr. Scruggs and in 1940 was residing in Menard; Sarah; Lula; Kenner and Thomas A. Gay, Jr.

Lucinda C. West was married to George W. Henry in 1853. They had a son, R. A. Henry. Rachel West was married to George W. Henry in 1858, her sister Lucinda having died in 1855. Their children were Lizzie, George Washington, Henry, Millie, John C., Ernest and Jennie Henry.

Robert N. West died in infancy.

George C. West was married to Sarah Parchman. Their children were Annie, who married a Mr. Gilfoyle; Ellen; Rosa, who first married Priest Cain, and, after his death, Murray Franklin, and in 1940 was residing at Christene, Texas; Lula, who married a Mr. Ray; Dollie; Kate, who married a Mr. Gander; Alice and Bennet West.

Thomas Jefferson West was married to Katie Holland. Their surviving children, in 1940, were Thomas Jefferson West, Jr., Moore, Texas; George C. West, Fowlerton, and Mrs. Lula Kimball, Pearsall. David Crockett West was married to Nancy Trammell. Their children were Mollie and Julia West.

William C. West died while serving in the Confederate Army and is buried in Victoria, Texas.

JAMES B. WOODS
of
LIBERTY MUNICIPALITY

When interviewed at Washington, Texas, in March, 1836, James B. Woods stated that he was 34 years of age, had been born in Kentucky, and had come to Texas from his native state.[1] This being true, he was born in about 1802. He arrived in Texas in 1830.[2] But little has been recorded of his early life.

In 1834 Woods was alcalde of the jurisdiction of Liberty. In 1835 he represented Liberty Municipality at the Consultation.[3] He, A. B. Hardin, and M. B. Menard were the delegates to the Constitutional Convention.[4] Woods did not arrive at the Convention until March 6,[5] and did not sign the Declaration of Independence until March 11.[6]

After the adjournment of the Convention, Woods did not join the army until July 7 when he enlisted in Capt. Franklin Hardin's company in which he served until it was disbanded October 7, 1836.[7]

In an election held September 3, 1838, Hugh B. Johnston defeated his brother-in-law, Woods, for a seat in the House of Representatives of the Third Congress of the Republic. In a heated campaign preceding the election Woods had been accused of intemperance and had been criticized for having defended members of the Yocum families of Liberty and Jefferson Counties who were accused of being desperadoes. In a broadside dated at Liberty, July 28, 1838, Woods answered his accusers.

FELLOW CITIZENS OF THE COUNTY OF LIBERTY:

Nothing but charges the most unjust, illiberal, unfounded and false that have been and are still industriously circulating against me by designing individuals would ever have induced me to send out this address.

I have thought that I was well enough known amongst you that, whatever my faults were, they were not consealed from you—that, whatever my humble merits were, they were known to you. But whispering enmity never sleeps and saints themselves cannot avoid the poison of her aspersions.

I am a candidate for your suffrages at the next Congressional election. A relative of mine (Capt. Hugh B. Johnson, whom I take pride in saying is a gentleman) is my oponent. It is unfortunate that we should be opposed to each other, but if none except ourselves make evil of this incident, I am sure that he nor I will. I say incident because I believe we were brought out at nearly the same time by different individuals without either of us knowing that the other was or would be a candidate. For the veracity of this last fact, on my part, I pledge my word and will go to the Book upon it— that matter aside.

The main question comes up, and that is, what are the enormous crimes of which I am guilty, and which are to prevent my election.

First. It is said that I drink. To this charge I plead guilty and call upon him that is exempt from this sin to cast the first stone and vote against me.

Second. What! I am a Yocum man; why, because Mr. Yocum has so far respected my humble abilities as a lawyer to employ me generally in all his law business. Poor, pitiful and contemptible accusation. Do the circulators of such reports expect, by this mean slander, to convince my friends and fellow citizens, with whom I have always lived on terms of mutual intimacy, respect and regard, for more than ten years, that I am dishonest and faithless. No; you all know me

too well. A Yocum man! Yes, a man that belongs to the Yocum Club! And who, and what, are they that are denounced
as the Yocum Club, and my associates? Let the circulators
of this slander show their heads; let them make themselves,
visible and tangible; and then let them set up their own
meritorious acts against the gentlemen that they, for pitiful,
electioneering purposes, have thought proper to force upon
me—and how will the comparison stand. Why, the "Yocum
men" as they are called, will be found to be patriotic soldiers
with rifles in their hands, pointed at the breasts of their enemies, in the last trying effort for liberty in Texas, whilst the
fabricators of this contemptible charge were far before me
in our general retreat.

Yes, I have been guilty of the unpardonable sin of taking a
fee from Mr. Yocum; a man whom I dare say is quite as good
as some of my accusers. Horrid!!! Did Mr. Clay appear for
the traitor Aaron Burr?? Had Mr. Grundy appeared for, and
defended most of the villians in the South-West for the last
fifteen years? Is this last (Mr. Grundy) a horse thief because,
as a lawyer, he has defended horse thieves? Was this last (Mr.
Clay) a traitor because he defended the traitor Burr? If Mr.
Yocum has ever done a base act, it is unknown to me, and I
invite you fellow citizens, each and every one of you, when
a calumniator should make this charge against me to say to
him there are two sides to every case. Then say, if Woods belonged to the Yocum club; show us how, when, where, and
in what manner is he associated with Mr. Yocum?

The last, and I expect the only charge that can or will be
made against me, I should not have noticed, but that I am
compelled to leave here in a few days for my native State,
Kentucky and foul-mouthed calumny has eked out the in-
nuendo that I was about to leave permanently; that I had
sold my property for that purpose. Now I call on the base
scullion that told this, to invite the individuals to whom
I have sold to show themselves and attest the fact. That I
shall be absent during the election is true, because important business compels me. But, fellow citizens, I can never,
will never leave Texas. All the tenderest associations of my

life were formed here, and here those ties shall be severd by death. I came here as a youth, fatherless and pennyless;— many of you have become my bosom friends and associates. And now what? To abandon you? No; I shall crumble to dust in the same soil that you do.

If elected, I will serve you to the best of my humble abilities; not as a partizan, but as one who desires the general good of the county I represent and of the whole Republic.[8]

Accepted tradition among lifelong residents of Liberty County states that Woods met a tragic death, but the date is not known. Mrs. Julia D. Welder of Liberty, granddaughter of William Duncan, who knew Woods, had from her mother hearsay that Woods had been forced to kill a man named Bruxton who was reputed to be part Negro, and therefore ineligible to vote. During an election when party feeling was high, Woods and Bruxton had quarreled, and in the altercation Bruxton was killed. Woods ever afterward regretted the affair and committed suicide while duck hunting.

In 1936 the Commission of Control for Texas Centennial Celebrations erected a monument in honor of Woods in the cemetery in which he was buried about three and one-half miles south of Liberty.

Wood's wife was Mary A. White, daughter of Mathew G. and Lucy White. Mrs. Wood's sister, Martha, was the wife of Hugh Blair Johnston, who defeated Woods in 1838. Mrs. Woods died in January, 1865.

Children of Mr. and Mrs. James B. Woods were: Sam Houston, who died early in life; George B., who was killed at Richmond, Virginia, in 1862 while serving in the Confederate Army; and Margaret Woods. Margaret Woods, daughter of Mr. and Mrs. James B. Woods, was twice married. By her first husband, James Robertson, she had three children Lucy, Mary and Georgia Robertson, the two latter dying in infancy. Robertson, while serving in the Confed-

317

erate Army was wounded in the Battle of Atlanta, and died within two days. In 1870 Mrs. Robertson was married to William Jasper Smith of Orange, Texas, a widower with two children. Of this union there were two children, Maud and Vivian Smith.

Lucy Robertson, granddaughter of James B. Woods, was married to Hammond Starks of Orange. Mrs. Starks in 1940 was residing at Orange. Children of Mr. and Mrs. Starks were Vera, who married Douglas A. Pruter, and resides at Orange; Percy H., who resides at 801 Olive Street, Houston; and James Q. Starks, who resides at 807 Paschal Street, Houston.

Maud Smith, granddaughter of James B. Woods, was married to Charles O. Newcomer. Mrs. Newcomer is deceased. Mr. Newcomer resides in Silsbee, Texas. Their children were Nell and Bessie Newcomer.

Vivian Smith, granddaughter of James B. Woods, was married to Frank A. Rowland. To them were born two children, John G., who died August 31, 1899, and Bessie Smith, who married Marquis James, author of *The Raven*. Mr. and Mrs. James, in 1940, were residing in Pleasantville, New York.

LORENZO de ZAVALA
of
HARRISBURG MUNICIPALITY

*L*orenzo de Zavala was born in the village of Tecoh, near Merida, Yucatan,[1] October 3, 1789.[2] "His ancestors were Don Anastasio de Zavala, and Dona Maria Barbara Saenz, both of distinguished families"[3] of moderate means. He studied in the seminary of Ildefonso, in his native city.[4] Completing his studies in 1807 he, an ardent liberal and earnest advocate of democratic reforms, entered politics. He had served as secretary for several elective councils before May, 1814, when, as a liberal, he was arrested and sent to the castle of San Juan de Ulua, where he remained a prisoner for three years, during which he studied medicine and English.[5] When released in 1817, he returned to Yucatan. In 1821 he was elected to represent Yucatan in the Spanish Cortes in Madrid. He attended the Cortes for a short time but, learning that Mexico had declared her independence of Spain, soon returned to Yucatan. Shortly after his return, he was elected to represent Yucatan at the Congress in Mexico City.

Zavala was president of the Chamber of Deputies, October 5, 1824, when the Federal Constitution was adopted. As such he was the first to sign it. In March, 1827, running on the Federalist ticket, he was elected governor of the State of Mexico, defeating the Centralist incumbent, Gomez Pedraza, minister of war under President Victoria. A persecution of the Federalists was begun by the Army, and Zavala was forced to flee from Tlalpam, the seat of the State government. For more than a month he hid in the hills. He then went to Mexico City and cooperated with Gen. Jose Maria Lobato in directing the "Revolucion de la Acordada" which culminated in the defeat of the government troops and the election of the Federalist candidate, Vicente Guerrero.[6] By Guerrero, Zavala was placed in the new cabinet as minister of the treasury. He was permitted to retain his position as governor of Mexico by the legislature of that state. "Internal opposition in the cabinet, however, soon forced Zavala to resign his portfolio. Nor was this the end of his misfortune. The state legislature, now controlled by the Centralists, notified him that one who had been forced to resign from the President's cabinet was not qualified to hold the Governorship of the State."[7]

Zavala, deposed as governor, decided to leave Mexico: "On May 25, 1830, he sailed for New Orleans, and from there he made a tour of the United States, an account of which he gives in his book *Un Viage a los Estados Unidos*."[8]

From New York he went to Europe in connection with the business of the Galveston Bay and Texas Land Company.[9] On December 21, 1826, Joseph Vehlein, a German merchant of Mexico City, obtained an empresario contract to introduce 300 families into Texas. On December 22, 1826, David G. Burnet, a native of New Jersey, received a contract to settle 300 families. Vehlein, on November 17, 1828, was granted a second contract, this time for 100 families. On March 12, 1829, while Zavala was governor of the State of Mexico, he was granted an empresario contract to introduce 500 families into Texas. On October 16, 1830, Burnet, Vehlein and Zavala transferred their contracts to the Galveston Bay and Texas Land Company.

320

> This company consisted of trustees, directors, empresarios, and members. The members were to be responsible according to the number of shares held. According to Dey and Curtis, the empresarios were members of the company, had retained large interests in the company and would use their best efforts to promote the enterprise. The board of directors consisted of Lynde Catlin, George Griswold, John

Haggerty, Stephen Whitney, William G. Buckner, Barnet Corse and Dudley Selden. William H. Summer of Boston, Anthony Dey and George Curtis of New York were chosen as trustees and attorneys for the enterprise.[10]

...[The Galveston Bay and Texas Land Company] did all it could to place Texas before the eyes of the world. The company's policy in fact was very similar to the methods of a modern real estate firm. When anything favorable to the prospects of the company happened, it was immediately published. For instance, when Zavala sailed for Europe to obtain colonists, the company published the fact...[11]

Zavala, in Paris, used his spare time to write his most important history and historical work—his *Ensayo de las Revoluciones de Mexico*.[12]

In 1832 Zavala returned to Toluca, which had replaced Tlalpam as the capital of the State of Mexico. In February, 1833, he was again elected governor of the State.[13]

In October, 1833, President Santa Anna appointed his friend Zavala minister to France.[14]

321

By the summer of 1834 Santa Anna had definitely shown that he had no intention to continue to observe the Constitution of 1824. He had, in effect, made himself dictator, and was now cooperating with the Centralists in trying to destroy the authority of that liberal document. Zavala, always an idealist and a strong advocate of democracy, determined to resign rather than lend his support to the administration. This determination he communicated to the Mexican authorities in a letter of August 30, 1834.[15]

Zavala remained in Paris until April, 1835, when he left for New York. There he left his wife in June and set out for Texas, stopping for a short time in New Orleans. He arrived in Texas in July[16] and proceeded to purchase a home for his family.[17] Mrs. Zavala and children arrived in December, 1835.

On August 7, 1835, Zavala

published an address to the citizens of his vicinage, in which he very ably exposed the whole villany of Santa Anna's course, and encouraged his brother Texans to heroic resistance.[18]

General Cos at Matamoros on August 8, 1835, issued an order which read in part:

The commanding General has already asked of the Political Chief of the Brazos to remit to this city Senor Don Lorenzo de Zavala; for the arrest you will be guided by the orders of the Supreme Government, and if not attended to as required, you will march immediately at the risk of losing all your cavalry to complete the intended object.[19]

In writing on the causes of the Texan Revolution Bancroft said:

322

Nor can it be denied that any means were omitted by the war party to fan the flame of rebellion. The majority of the settlers were still peaceably inclined, and would have remained so but for the excitement aroused by inflammatory addresses and exaggerated representations, hard to controvert, of the dire enmity of the government. The finger of warning was pointed to the spectre of despotism and oppression, not only by their own countrymen, but by prominent Mexicans. Many of the fugitive authorities from Coahuila were among them; Lorenzo de Zavala, late governor of the state of Mexico, had fled from the tyranny of Santa Anna and sought an asylum in Texas; and Viesca, just before his fall, had addressed the Texans in such words as these: "Citizens of Texas, arouse yourselves, or sleep forever! Your dearest interest, your liberty, your property—nay, your very existence—depend upon the fickle will of your direct enemies. Your destruction is resolved upon, and nothing but that firmness and energy peculiar to true republicans can save you!"[20]

Zavala was a delegate from Harrisburg Municipality to the Consultation at San Felipe de Austin in 1835.[21] He, Andrew Briscoe and John W. Moore represented Harrisburg Municipality in the Constitutional Convention.[22] Zavala was seated March 1.[23]

William Fairfax Gray, who attended the Convention as a spectator and carefully recorded in a diary what he saw and heard, made the following entry on February 28:

> This evening a number of members arrived, among them Lorenzo de Zavala, the most interesting man in Texas—[24]

On March 9 Gray, Badgett, Ruiz, Navarro, and Zavala rented jointly a shop in Washington belonging to Samuel Heath, a carpenter. "We shall then be retired, and comparatively comfortable," wrote Gray, "and I shall enjoy the benefit of an intercourse with Zavala, whose character and attainments interest me."[25]

During the early hours of the morning of March 17, Zavala was unanimously elected *ad interim* vice president of the Republic of Texas. Following the adjournment of the Convention Zavala left for his home on Buffalo Bayou and arrived March 23, accompanied by Colonel Gray.[26]

On about April 21, Zavala, probably in a fit of anger, resigned the office of vice president.

> Persuaded that my Presence in the Cabinet at present will be of but little service & that I can better employ my time in other services of my country I beg leave to tender my resignation as Vice President of the Republic for reasons which I will explain to Congress & the Nation.[27]

Burnet, at Galveston, on April 22, replied:

> I received your note this day, resigning the office of Vice President of the Republic.
> As no specific reasons are assigned for this unexpected act, nothing more is left for me to do, than to express the

regret which I feel, in common with the gentlemen who compose the Cabinet, at the deprivation of your counsel at this interesting juncture in our affairs.[28]

Zavala nevertheless continued to serve as vice president. Following the Battle of San Jacinto, Zavala's home, just across Buffalo Bayou from the battlefield, was used as a hospital for wounded Texans, and later for wounded Mexicans.[29]

On May 27 Zavala and Bailey Hardeman were commissioned to accompany Santa Anna to Mexico to negotiate a treaty.[30] They planned to sail on the *Invincible* on June 1, but for some season the boat was delayed. On June 3, at the insistence of indignant soldiers, most of whom had but recently arrived from the United States, Santa Anna was removed from the vessel and kept a prisoner for several months.

Zavala again resigned as vice president but still continued to serve. At Quintana, on June 3 in a note addressed "To The President & members of the Cabinet Present" he said:

> Taking into consideration that the present Government of Texas has lost the moral confidence of the People and is therefore no longer able to carry into effect their measures, I have to tender my resignation as Vice President of Texas.[31]

Zavala was too ill to participate in the work of the government during September and October. The first Congress of the Republic convened for its initial session October 3, 1836, at Columbia (now West Columbia). The Constitution provided that the president and vice-president should be inaugurated on the second Monday in December, but in order that the executive and legislative branches of the government should assume their functions simultaneously, Burnet, on October 14, in a letter to Zavala, suggested that both of them resign.[32] Zavala complied with his resignation October 21.[33]

324

Lorenzo de Zavala died November 19, 1836, and was buried in the Zavala Cemetery, across Buffalo Bayou from the Battlefield and now a part of San Jacinto State Park. In 1931 the State of Texas erected a monument at his grave.

Zavala was a Roman Catholic and a member of the Ancient Free and Accepted Masons. Joel R. Poinsett, United States Minister to Mexico, denominated him a "Yorkino." Zavala was Grand Master of the new fraternity, and organized many of the subordinate lodges.[34]

When Zavalla County was created February 1, 1858, it was named in "honor of Lorenzo de Zavalla [sic] deceased, the first Vice-President of Texas."[35] Within recent years the county's name has been changed to *Zavala*.

Zavala was first married to Teresa Correa and of this union there were born three children, (1) Lorenzo, Jr., (2) Manuella and (3) a daughter who died in infancy. His wife having died, Zavala, in New York City in January, 1830, was married by Padre Varela to Emily West. There were three children of this marriage: (4) Augustin, (5) Emily and (6) Ricardo de Zavala.

(1) Lorenzo de Zavala was married to Caroline Patron.

(2) Manuella de Zavala married Prudencio Tenerio prior to March 23, 1841.

(4) Augustin de Zavala was born in New York City, January 1, 1833. He was married to Julia Tyrrell. Their children were (a) Miss Adina who resides at 141 Taylor Street, San Antonio; (b) Florence, (c) Miss Mary, who resides at 141 Taylor Street, San Antonio; (d) Zita; (e) Thomas J.; and (f) Augustin P. de Zavala, Austin.

(5) Emily de Zavala, was born in New York City, in February, 1834. She was married to Capt. Thomas Jenkins. Mrs. Jenkins died in Galveston, April 20, 1858, leaving one child, Catherine Jenkins.

(6) Ricardo de Zavala was born in New York City in 1835. He was married twice and was the father of four children,

two sons, Henry and Victor, and two daughters, whose names the author has been unable to ascertain.

Henry de Zavala, aged 65, a grandson of Lorenzo de Zavala, died at his home in Gretna, Louisiana, August 22, 1942, and was buried in the Zavala Cemetery in Harris County, Texas. He was survived by his widow, Mrs. Mary de Zavala of Gretna, Louisiana, a daughter, Mrs. J. P. Houston of Houston; a son, Lawrence de Zavala, Freeport; a brother, L. Victor de Zavala, 7713 Manchester, Houston; and a sister, Mrs. V. J. Higginbotham, Houston.

Sidney de Zavala, a grandson of Lorenzo de Zavala, was married to Emma Singleton, daughter of Spy and Eliza Singleton.

Some of the other surviving descendants of Lorenzo de Zavala are, Rosa Fay de Zavala, Elno de Zavala Martin, Joyce Erna Martin, Le Nell Vernon and Herman Vernon, Jr., Houston; and Roy De Zavala, Sheldon, Texas.

326

CHAPTER NOTES

San Felipe, Washington,
The Hall & The Document

1 Gammel, I, 982. It will be noted that Pecan Point was not a municipality. Dr. Goodrich stated that James Kerr from Jackson Municipality and John J. Linn and Juan Antonio Padilla from Victoria were elected delegates but failed to attend. Linn stated that he and Jose Maria J. Carabajal were the delegates from Victoria, but that the advance of the Mexican Army prevented their attendance. John J. Linn, *Reminiscences of Fifty Tears in Texas* (New York: D. & J. Sadlier & Co., 1883), 54, 56.

John Joseph Linn was born in Ireland, June 19, 1798, and came to Texas in 1829. He was a member of the Consultation and General Council. He and Jose M. J. Carabajal were elected delegates to the Constitutional Convention from the Municipality of Guadalupe Victoria, but neither attended. He died at Victoria, October 27, 1885.

2 Gammel, I, 994.

3 *Ibid.*, 1002.

4 *Ibid.*, 1025-1026.

5 *Ibid.*, 1035.

6 *Ibid.*, 34.

7 In San Felipe was the log cabin that Austin considered the only home he ever had in Texas. Austin to Joseph Ficklin, October 30, 1836, in Barker: Austin: III, 443.

8 Nanna Smithwick Donaldson (comp.). *The Evolution of a State or Recollections of Old Texas Days* by Noah Smithwick (Austin: Gammel Book Co., 1900), 55-57. Noah Smithwick, twenty years of age, left Hopkinsville, Kentucky, early in 1827 for Texas, to seek his fortune. At the age of 89 he dictated his reminiscences to his daughter, who in 1900 published them under the title of *The Evolution of a State*. Smithwick resided in

San Felipe from 1827 to 1831.

9 Gray, 111. William Fairfax Gray was born in Fairfax County, Virginia, November 3, 1787. On March 21, 1811, before he had reached his 24th birthday he was commissioned captain in the Sixteenth Regiment, First Brigade, Second Division of the Virginia Militia, and as such participated in the War of 1812. On May 26, 1820, he was commissioned lieutenant colonel of the Sixteenth Regiment.

Col. Gray was an active Mason, and in November, 1824, while he was master of Fredericksburg (Virginia) Lodge No. 4, General Lafayette visited the town and on a Sunday was escorted by the Lodge to the Episcopal Church. On the following day Lafayette dined at Col. Gray's home.

In 1835 two prosperous citizens of Washington, D. C., Thomas Green and Albert T. Burnley, desiring to purchase land in the lower South, employed Col. Gray to inspect land and to report on conditions in Mississippi, Louisiana, and Texas. Col. Gray kept a diary, remarkable for its accuracy, in which he recorded many of the things he saw and heard on his trip. This was published for private distribution in 1900 by his son A. C. Gray. It is a definite contribution to the history of Texas.

Col. Gray left Fort Jessup, Louisiana, January 28, 1833, and crossed the Sabine into Texas in company with Capt. Sidney Sherman and others. He was in Nacogdoches, February 1st, and there voted in the election held throughout Texas to select delegates to the Constitutional Convention. He went to Washington with the idea at first of attending the Convention as an onlooker but later decided to offer himself as secretary. He was not elected, but this did not deter him from recording many important incidents of the proceedings. Following the adjournment of the Convention he joined the Runaway Scrape and continued to Virginia. He returned to Texas in 1837 to make it his home. He was secretary of the senate of the adjourned session of the Second Congress of the Republic, April 9 to May 24, 1838. On May 13, 1840, President Lamar appointed him district attorney of the first judicial district. He died in Houston April 16, 1841, and is buried in Glenwood Cemetery.

Gray County, Texas, was named in honor of Peter W. Gray, son of William Fairfax Gray.

10 Gammel, I, 508.

11 *Ibid.,* 548.

12 *Ibid.,* 564.

13 *Ibid.*

14 On October 10, 1835, at San Felipe, Gail Borden, Jr., John P. Borden and Joseph Baker began publishing the *Telegraph and Texas Register*, the only newspaper in Texas at that time.

15 Gammel, I, 575-576

16 Joseph Urban came to Texas in 1834. He received title to one league and one labor of land, April 26, 1838. File 48, Colorado County 1st Class (MS. in General Land Office, Austin, Texas).

17 Gammel, I, 583.

18 Linn, *Reminiscences of Fifty Tears in Texas,* 112-113.

19 Gammel, I, 980-982.

20 *Ibid.,* 802-813.

21 The original deed is in the San Jacinto Museum of History, San Jacinto Monument, Texas.

22 Deed Records of Washington County (MSS. in County Clerk's Office, Brenham, Texas), A, 225-226. This instrument is without date, but, on pages 270-271, appears evidence that it was signed March 24, 1835.

23 E. W. Winkler (ed.), "Documents Relating to Municipality of Washington," in *Quarterly of the Texas State Historical Association,* X (1906), 96.

24 *Ibid.,* 99.

25 *Telegraph and Texas Register* (San Felipe), December 26, 1835

26 Gray, 107.

27 *Ibid.,* 108.

28 Gammel, I, 824-825.

29 *Ibid.,* 827-838.

30 *Ibid.,* 838.

31 *Ibid.*, 843.

32 *Ibid.*, 847-848.

33 *Ibid.*, 848.

34 *Ibid.*, 881.

35 *Ibid.*, 882.

36 Willis A. Faris was living in Vicksburg, Mississippi, as early as January, 1832. He came to Texas in December, 1834. In 1836, after the Revolution, he was appointed postmaster for the town of Brazoria. He was elected clerk pro tem of the House of Representatives of the First Congress of the Republic of Texas, October 6, 1836.

37 Gammel, I, 823.

38 Herbert Simms Kimble was born in North Carolina in 1800. He moved to Tennessee and in 1835 came to Texas. On March 1, 1836, he was elected secretary of the Constitutional Convention at Washington-on-the-Brazos. When the Convention adjourned on March 17, he set out for his home in Clarksville, Tennessee, and he never returned to Texas. He established himself in the practice of law and for many years was judge of the circuit court of the district in which Clarksville was situated. He died March 5, 1865.

39 Elisha Marshall Pease was born January 3, 1812, in Enfield, Connecticut. He came to Texas from New Orleans in 1835 and settled in Brazoria Municipality. He was elected Governor of Texas August 2, 1853, and re-elected August 5, 1855. Running as a Republican in the election held June 25, 1866, he was defeated by J. W. Throckmorton, Democrat. On July 30, 1867, General Philip Sheridan removed Gov. Throckmorton from office and named Pease his successor. Pease resigned September 30, 1869. He died August 26, 1883, and is buried in Oakwood Cemetery, Austin.

40 John Abraham Hueser, whose name has been misspelled John A. Hizer and John Abram Keiser, came to Texas in 1835 and settled in Brazoria Municipality. He resigned March 9, as doorkeeper of the Convention to meet his wife, Sophia, who had just arrived in Texas. He later joined the army and participated in

the Battle of San Jacinto, serving in Capt. Alfred H. Wyly's company. He and his wife were living in Brazoria County as late as October 5, 1844. Hueser gave his address as New Orleans when, on April 25, 1851, he sold the donation certificate for 640 acres of land he had received for having fought at San Jacinto.

41 Thomas Stovin Saul came to Texas from Louisiana in 1829. On March 28, 1831, he received title to one league in Austin's Second Colony, situated in present Washington County. In 1833 he was a delegate to the Second Convention of Texas held in San Felipe. He was orderly sergeant in Capt. John G. Swisher's Washington's Company in 1835. He died before January 21, 1840, on which date President Lamar approved an act of Congress for the relief of his heirs.

42 Isham Parmer was born in Missouri in 1813, son of Martin Parmer. On June 8, 1835, he received title to one league of land in Zavala's Colony, situated in present San Augustine County. He was a member of Capt. John M. Bradley's company at the siege of Bexar in 1835. He died near Bryan, Texas, in February, 1874.

43 F. W. Jackson, a native of England, served under Capt. Thomas H. Breece in the siege of Bexar in 1835.

331

44 Gammel, I, 826.

45 *Ibid.*, 837.

46 Gray, 123.

47 Gammel, I, 838.

48 *Ibid.*, 848.

49 Gray, 124.

50 Hubert Howe Bancroft, *History of the North Mexican States and Texas* (San Francisco: The History Co., 1889), II, 115.

51 *Ibid.*

52 Eugene C. Barker, *The Life of Stephen F. Austin.* (Dallas: Cokesbury Press, 1925), 319-320.

53 Yoakum, I, 274.
"The year 1831 found the American population of Texas still increasing. They now numbered about twenty thousand; and not withstanding the general law of April 6, 1830, prohibited

natives of the United States from immigrating, they still continued to come. They had friends and relatives in Texas, and wished to be with them. Others, attracted by the generous nature of the soil and fine climate, were induced to come in order to form homes in the new State."

54 Legally, at least, the Revolution began January 1, 1832. An act of the Legislature, approved April 21, 1874, by Gov. Richard Coke, granted pensions to "every person still living who may have served as a volunteer, or as a regular soldier, in the military service of Texas at any time between the first day of January, 1832, and the fifteenth day of October, 1836..." Gammel, VIII, 116-120.

55 Charles Adams Gulick, Jr., and Katherine Elliott (eds.), *The Papers of Mirabeau Buonaparte Lamar* (Austin: Texas State Library, 1920), I, 164.

56 Yoakum, II, 361.

57 "In the town of Washington at this time [1836] there were no public meeting places. Church houses, except Catholic, were forbidden by law, and no schoolhouses were yet built. Where could this momentous convention be held? The largest and most convenient building for such a meeting was found to be a blacksmith shop, owned by N. T. Byars, one of the few Baptists at this time, living in the town. All blacksmithing was stopped. Old plows, wagons and other disabled vehicles, machinery, tools, etc., were cleared away, crude seats were provided and the shop voluntarily turned over to this great Texas convention. And here, in this Baptist blacksmith shop, Texas declared its independence." J. B. Cranfill (ed.), *A History of Texas Baptists...by J. M. Carroll* (Dallas: Baptist Standard Publishing Co., 1923), 55-56.

58 Noah T. Byars was born in Spartanburg, District, South Carolina, May 17, 1808. He moved to Georgia in 1830 and to Texas in 1835, settling in the new town of Washington-on-the-Brazos. There he formed a partnership with Peter M. Mercer under the name of "Byars & Mercer, merchants and partners, trading in the town of Washington." He also ran a gunsmith shop and for a time repaired guns for the Texas Army. He early had a strong religious bend and was a charter member of the first Texas Baptist

Church organized in Washington in 1838. In the same year he moved to Bastrop, where he was licensed to preach. During his long life he organized and preached in many churches in Texas. He died in Brownwood, Texas, July 17, 1888, and is buried in a marked grave in Greenleaf Cemetery, Brownwood.

59 Little has been recorded of the life of Peter M. Mercer. In Headright Certificate 369 for one-third of a league of land issued to him February 20, 1838, by the Board of Land Commissioners for Washington County, it is stated that he came to Texas in the summer of 1835. The Deed Records of Washington County show that he bought and sold land in the county, having as a partner N. T. Byars. He died in Bell County in about 1847. His widow, Mrs. Celia V. Mercer, was married to W. H. Drury. On December 25, 1848, Mrs. Drury was administratrix of Mercer's estate. Mr. and Mrs. Drury were residing in Grimes County in 1853.

60 Deed Records of Washington County, A, 37.

61 Courtesy of Mr. D. Mgebroff, of Brenham, who owns the original.

62 Gray, 121.

63 Deed Records of Washington County, A, 37.

64 *Ibid.*, 360.

65 *Ibid.*, 396-397.

66 Petition of N. T. Byars, December 20, 1849, in Memorials and Petitions (MSS. in Archives, Texas State Library, Austin, Texas).

67 Comp. M. S. R.

68 Petition of N. T. Byars, December 17, 1849, in Memorials and Petitions.

69 Report of committee attached to petition.

70 "Childress, acting with Robert Hamilton, is to open negotiations with the Cabinet at Washington D. C. inviting on the part of that Cabinet a recognition of the Sovereignty and Independence of Texas and the establishment of such relations between the two Governments, as may comport with the mutual interest, the common origin, and kindred ties of their constituents."

Garrison, I, 73-74.

71 Sabin, *A Dictionary of Books Relating to America*, XXV, No. 94974, locates copies of the pamphlet in American Antiquarian Society, Boston Public Library, Boston Athenaeum, Library of Congress, and Harvard Law Library. The only copy known to be in private hands is that of Mr. Thomas W. Streeter, Morristown, New Jersey.

72 Garrison, I, 140-141.

73 *Ibid.*, 141-142.

74 *Ibid.*, 142.

75 *Ibid.*, 143.

76 *Ibid.*, 201.

77 Jim Dan Hill, *The Texas Navy* (Chicago: University of Chicago Press, 1937), 74-75.

78 Seth Shepard, son of Chauncey R. Shepard, was born in Brenham, Texas, April 23, 1847. He entered the Confederate Army, July 4, 1864, and served to the end of the war. In 1869 he began the practice of law at Brenham, subsequently moving to Galveston and still later to Dallas. In 1893 President Grover Cleveland appointed him associate justice of the Court of Appeals for the District of Columbia, which position he held until January 5, 1905, when President Theodore Roosevelt appointed him chief justice of the court. He died in Washington, December 3, 1917.

79 Several paragraphs of letter, Shepard to J. D. Campbell, in article dated Beaumont, April 4. *Galveston Daily News*, April 5, 1905. Courtesy of Andrew F. Muir.

80 W. G. Scarff, Dallas, to Adele Lubbock Looscan, Houston, October 9, 1896, in Looscan Papers (MSS. in the San Jacinto Museum of History). Courtesy of Andrew F. Muir.

81 *Journal of the Senate of Texas, Being the Regular Session of the Forty First Legislature Begun and Held at the City of Austin, January 8, 1929*, 791, 799.

82 *Dallas Morning News*, March 3, 1930.

CHAPTER NOTES

JESSE B. BADGETT

1 Badgett to Dr. Benjamin B. Goodrich. Dixon (342), in error, states that Badgett arrived in Texas early in 1829 and settled near San Antonio. "I have been unable to record" he continues, "how he passed the time until the convention...neither have I been able to secure any information regarding his career following the convention." Strangely enough, Dixon was able to fix the definite date of Badgett's birth as March 7, 1807.

2 William Badgett became a member of Capt. John Chenoweth's Company, January 14, 1836. Army Rolls (MSS. in the General Land Office, Austin), 68. He served as one of the judges at Refugio for the election of delegates to the Convention. Convention Election Returns (MSS. in Archives, Texas State Library, Austin). He entered the Alamo but left it before it fell. From November 5, 1838, to January 17, 1839, Badgett was assistant clerk of the House of Representatives. Comptroller's Civil Service Records (MSS. in Archives, Texas State Library).

That Jesse B. Badgett did not know that William had left the Alamo is reflected in Col. William Fairfax Gray's entry of March 13 in his diary:

> No intelligence yet from the Alamo. The anxiety begun to be intense. Mr. Badgett and Dr. Goodrich, members of Convention, have brothers there, and Mr. Grimes, another member, has a son there. Gray, 127-128.

3 Binkley, I, 182-183.

4 Gammel, I, 532.

5 *Ibid.*, I, 658-659.

6 *Ibid.*, 660.

7 The returns of the election held in Bexar Municipality are not among the Convention Election Returns in the Texas State Library. Ruiz and Navarro were seated in the Convention. Gray states that Seguin and Arciniega were also elected. Gray, 122.

8 Returns.

9 Convention Papers (MSS. in Archives, Texas State Library).

10 Comp. M. S. R. 321 (MS. Archives, Texas State Library).

Garrison of Bejar
February 14, 1836

This is to certify that Jesse B. Badgett has been in the Service of Texas as a volunteer from the 15th November until the present time and has discharged the duties devolving on him as such and is hereby honorably discharged from further Service giving him twenty days to return home.

J. C. Neill, Lt. Coln.
Comd. Bejar

11 The last record of him at San Antonio is dated February 17. "Received of J. B. Badgett two Bottles of wine for use in the Hospital & three lbs of powder for the use of the Garrison, all valued at three dollars 87-1/2 which the provisional Govt. will please pay to said J. B. Badgett on order."

Comp. M. S. R. 340 (MS. in Archives, Texas State Library)

336

12 Gammel, I, 824.

13 Gray, 127-128.

14 Courtesy of Dallas T. Herndon, Executive Secretary of the Arkansas History Commission, Little Rock, Arkansas.

George Washington Barnett

1 R. T. Jaynes, Walhalla, South Carolina, to the author July 17, 1943.

2 *Ibid.*,

3 In an unnumbered headright certificate for one league and one labor of land issued to Dr. Barnett, January 5, 1838, by the Washington County Board of Land Commissioners it is certified that he "emigrated to Texas on the 1st day of January, 1834." The land was surveyed in Gonzales County, February 19, 1838, by Charles Lockhart, County Surveyor of Gonzales County. File 379, Gonzales 1st Class (MS. in General Land Office, Austin).

4 For accounts of the Indian expedition see John Henry Brown, *Indian Wars and Pioneers of Texas* (St. Louis: L. B. Daniell, no date), 26. See also Yoakum, I, 352.

The names of the men of Dr. Barnett's company who served until August 28, 1835; are listed on p. 128 of the Army Rolls in the General Land Office.

5 Comp. M. S. R.

6 Dr. Barnett, on December 4, 1837, was issued Bounty Certificate 681 for 320 acres of land for having served in the army from October 8 to December 22, 1835. File 92, Gonzales Bounty (MS. in General land Office). On May 22, 1838, he received Donation Certificate No. 187 for 640 acres for having participated in the storming and capture of Bexar, December 5 to 10, 1835. File 91, Gonzales Donation (MS. in General Land Office).

7 Returns.

8 Gammel, I, 824.

9 Rena Maverick Green (ed.), *The Swisher Memoirs* (San Antonio: Sigmund Press, 1932), 50-51.

10 Comp. M. S. R.

11 Army Rolls (MS. in the General Land Office), 217. On December 18, 1837, Dr. Barnett was issued Bounty Certificate 1092 for 320 acres of land for his services in the army from July 2 to October 3, 1836. File 93, Gonzales Bounty (MS. in General Land Office, Austin).

12 Winkler, 70.

13 *Ibid.,* 112.

14 *Ibid.,* 134.

15 *Ibid.,* 182.

16 *Ibid.,* 204.

17 *Ibid.,* 230.

18 J. W. Wilbarger, *Indian Depredations in Texas* (Austin: Hutchings Printing House: 1889), 60.

Thomas Barnett

1 Inscription on the headstone at Barnett's grave.

2 Thomas Barnett, Sheriff of Livingston County, Kentucky, executed a deed to John Knight, September 10, 1821. (MSS. in the County Clerk's Office, Smithland, Kentucky), E, 133. Thomas Barnett, Sheriff of Livingston County, made a deed to William Wadlington, February 18, 1822. E, 180.

3 Some explanation is due to show why Barnett, a single man, who was ordinarily entitled to receive but one-fourth of a league of land, received one league. Under the colonization laws, three single men might combine their interests and jointly receive one league, title to be issued in the name of one of the three applicants. In English Field Notes (Span. Arch.), 87, there is an undated survey for one league of land, league 15, adjoining the David Fitzgerald Survey, for Thomas Barnett, Joseph Baker, and Joseph Stewart. It appears that in this instance, the land agent, instead of explaining the complete details of the transaction, simplified the matter by issuing title to the league in Barnett's name. Span. Arch., I, 90. The land was surveyed in Austin's First Colony, in what is now Fort Bend County.

On August 24, 1830, Barnett applied for additional land, having married in the meantime. In his petition he stated that he was a native of Kentucky, that as a single man he had received but one-third league, but that "having since acquired the new station of matrimony," he now requested an entire league. Austin recommended that the petition be granted, stating that Barnett was an early settler and a man of sterling character. Accordingly, on August 24, 1830, M. Arciniega issued him title to a league situated in what is now Washington County. Span. Arch., XXXVL, 45.

4 Barker: Minutes, XXI, 303.

5 *Ibid.*, 416.

6 *Ibid.*, XXIII, 150.

7 Gammel, I, 509.

8 *Ibid*, 565.

9 Gray, 108.

10 Gammel, I, 837.

11 Williams & Barker, I, 513.

12 *Journal of the House of Representatives of the Republic of Texas, Regular Session of the Third Congress, Nov. 5, 1838*, p. 32.

13 Harriet Smither (ed.), *Journals of the Fourth Congress of the Republic of Texas, 1839-1840*; House Journal II, unnumbered page opposite page 1.

14 Wharton, 129. On August 19, 1824, Mrs. Spencer received title to one league of land in Austin's First Colony, situated in the present Fort Bend County. (Span. Arch.), II, 492.

15 Span. Arch.

16 Barker, II, 666-667.

17 Wharton, 129.

18 *Ibid*.

STEPHEN WILLIAM BLOUNT

1 Frank Blount, San Augustine, Texas, genealogist of the Blount family, to the author, September 26, 1940. Dixon (99), and Crocket (209), in error, state that Blount was born February 3, 1808.

2 Johnson and Dixon (99-100) say that Blount was sheriff of Burke County, Georgia. Eugene C. Barker (ed.), Frank W. Johnson, *A History of Texas and Texans* (Chicago: The American Historical Society, 1914), V, 2624. According to Mrs. J. E. Hays, of Atlanta, State Historian of Georgia, in a letter to the author, October 28, 1939, the only person of this name who was sheriff of Burke County was elected January 14, 1822, when the subject of this sketch was but fourteen years old.

Dixon states that Blount served as a colonel on the staff of Governor Schley. Crocket says that he received his title of colonel while on the staff of General "Schley". Dixon (100) Crockett (209). Mrs. J. E. Hays states that two men by the name of Stephen W. Blount were residing in Burke County, Georgia, May 14, 1834, when one of them was made colonel of the Eighth Regiment, Georgia Militia. At this time, Wilson Lumpkin was Governor of Georgia and not William Schley, whose term did not begin until 1835. There was no General "Ashley" in Georgia at that time, Mrs. Hays stated.

3 Crocket, 209.

4 In Headright Certificate 49 for one-third of a league of land issued February 1, 1838, by the San Augustine County Board of Land Commissioners, it is stated that Blount came to Texas August, 1835. File 90, Jasper 1st Class (MS. in General Land Office, Austin).

5 For the election returns see the sketch of E. O. LeGrand, in this volume.

6 Gammel, I, 824.

7 Army Rolls (MSS. in General Land Office), 52.

8 James H. Walker, son of Philip Walker, to author, June 12, 1935. Dixon (99-100), in error, states that Blount participated in the Battle of San Jacinto.

9 Army Rolls (MSS. in the General Land Office), 52.

10 Crocket, 209.

11 *Ibid.*, 210.

12 *Ibid.*

13 Courtesy of Frank Blount, San Augustine.

14 Dixon (99-100), in error, states that Blount married Miss Mary Landon in 1835.

John White Bower

1 Dixon (68), states that Bower represented Goliad Municipality.

2 From the Bower Bible records sent to the author by Mrs. Thelma W. Heard, Refugio, Texas.

3 On July 15, 1835, Bower, a single man, was issued title to one-third of a league of land in the colony of McMullen and Mc-

Gloin, surveyed in what is now Atascosa County. Span. Arch.,
XLIX, 20. McMullen and McGloin were the only empresarios
who granted one-third of a league of land to a single man. In the
other colonies, he received one-fourth of a league.

In Headright Certificate 1, issued June 24, 1839, by the Refugio
County Board of Land Commissioners, for one league and one
labor of land, less the one-third league, it is stated that Bower
arrived in Texas previous to the Declaration of Independence.
File 12, Refugio 1st Class (MS. in General Land Office). Had he
arrived before May 2, 1835, it would have been so stated in the
certificate. In Brazoria, Refugio, and Bexar counties, the boards
of land commissioners stated in the headright certificates either that the applicant had arrived previous to the Declaration
of Independence or previous to May 2, 1835, the date of an act
of the Congress of Coahuila and Texas approving the revision of
the existing land laws.

4 Gammel, I, 607.

5 Consultation Papers (MSS. in the Archives of the Texas State
Library, Austin).

6 Gammel, I, 804.

7 Returns.

8 Gammel, I, 843.

9 *Ibid.*

10 *Ibid.*, 853.

11 Comp. M. S. R. 675.

12 Hobart Huson, *El Campo, the Ancient Post of Bexar and La
Bahia* (Refugio, Texas: *The Refugio Timely Remarks*, 1935), 42.

13 Becord from the Bower Bible. Courtesy of Mrs. Thelma W.
Heard, Refugio.

14 *Ibid.*

ASA BRIGHAM

1 "In closing this brief review of the life story of the *Men Who
Made Texas Free* which has been confined to the signers of the
Declaration of Texas Independence I feel that this explanation

should be made. All the early writers of Texas history and some of the latter ones include Ira [sic] Brigham as one of the signers of the Declaration of Independence and omit from the list the name of Samuel P. Carson. The original copy of that instrument in the State Library at Austin shows Samuel P. Carson was one of the signers, but it does not include the name of Ira [sic] Brigham." Dixon, p. 344.

One can but conclude that if Dixon personally examined the original document, he did so hastily. Brigham's signature on the Declaration follows that of Edwin Waller. It is omitted, however, in the purported facsimile of the Declaration published on pp. 35-42 of *The Men Who Made Texas Free*.

2 Goodrich.

3 Austin's Application Book (Span. Arch.), I, 85.

On November 30, 1830, Brigham received title to one league of land in Austin's Third Colony. Span. Arch., VII, 273. This league is on the present boundary line between Brazoria and Galveston counties.

In Headright Certificate 480 for one labor of land issued to Brigham in 1838 by the Brazoria County Board of Land Commissioners, it is merely stated that Brigham came to Texas previous to May 2, 1835. Clerks' Return Book B (MS. in General Land Office). This certificate was lost and on January 13, 1872, a duplicate, No. 27-360, was issued to his heirs. File 1443, Fannin 1st Class (MS. in General Land Office).

4 Barker: Minutes, XXIII, 215. "The best that can be made of the office [of sindico procurador] is that it called for a sort of combination of the duties of a notary and city attorney." Barker, "The Government of Austin's Colony, 1821-1831," *Southwestern Historical Quarterly*, XXI (January, 1918), 246.

5 Barker: Minutes, XXTV, 162. "The duties of the comisario were to take the census of his precinct, keep a record of the families moving into it and the places from which they came, assist tax collectors, execute the orders of his superiors, arrest disturbers of the peace and preserve public tranquility, and report idle and vicious persons to the alcalde." Barker, "The Government of Austin's Colony," *Southwestern Historical Quarterly*, XXI, 247.

342

6 Gammel, I, 503.

7 Kidd, 12.

8 *Ibid.*, 19.

9 Returns.

10 From the author's study of the San Jacinto rolls.

11 Gray, 113.

12 Gammel, I, 838.

13 *Ibid.*, 900.

14 Winkler, 33.

15 *Ibid.*, 127.

16 *Ibid.*, 211.

17 Marriage Records of Brazoria County (MSS. in County Clerk's Office, Angleton), unnumbered volume, 188.

18 Andrew Forest Muir, "Early Missionaries in Texas, With Documents Illustrative of Richard Salmon's Church Colony" in *Historical Magazine of the Protestant Episcopal Church* (New Brunswick, N. J.; Under the Auspices of the Church Historical Society, 1941), X, 219.

343

19 Charles Adams Gulick, Jr. and Katherine Elliott (eds.), *The Papers of Mirabeau Buonaparte Lamar* (Austin: Texas State Library, 1922), II, 280.

20 Probate Minutes of Brazoria County (MSS. in County Clerk's Office, Angleton), D, 118.

21 *Ibid.*, F, 338.

22 James D. Lynch, *The Bench and Bar of Texas* (St. Louis: Nixon-Jones Printing Co., 1885), 435.

ANDREW BRISCOE

1 Sketch of Briscoe written by his widow for V. O. King (MS. in the San Jacinto Museum of History, Houston). Date of birth shown in the inscription on the headstone that stood at Briscoe's grave in Mississippi.

2 Fulmore (150) states that Briscoe attended Franklin University in Kentucky, but at this time, there was neither a Franklin University nor a Franklin College in Kentucky.

3 In Headright Certificate 276 for one league and one labor of land issued February 5, 1838, by the Harrisburg County Board of Land Commissioners, it is stated that Briscoe came to Texas in 1833. File 518, Milam 1st Class (MS. in General Land Office, Austin).

4 Sketch of Briscoe written by his widow for V. O. King.

5 Adele B. Looscan, "The Old Fort at Anahuac," *Quarterly of the Texas State Historical Association* (Austin: Published by the Association, 1899), II, 23.

6 *Ibid.*

7 Footnote of Guy M. Bryan to Yoakum, reprinted in Wooten, I, 167.

8 Gammel, I, 600.

9 For the election returns of Harrisburg Municipality see the sketch of John W. Moore in this volume.

10 Gammel, I, 882-83.

11 *Ibid.*, 883.

12 Pension Papers of Lyman F. Rounds (MSS. in Archives, Texas State Library, Austin).

13 Briscoe was issued Donation Certificate 1205 for 640 acres of land, August 21, 1845, for having participated in the Battle of San Jacinto. File 263, Milam Donation (MS. in General Land Office). He received Bounty Certificate 3512 for 640 acres of land for having served in the army from November 1, 1835, to May 1, 1836. File 105, Montgomery Bounty (MS. in General Land Office).

14 Sketch of Briscoe written by his widow for V. O. King.

15 Williams & Barker, I, 514.

16 Journal of the Harrisburg Town Company and Their Board of Directors by the Company's Agent, 1839 (MS. in San Jacinto Museum of History), 2.

17 Record of Board [of] Commissioners and Election Returns

(MS. in County Clerk's Office, Houston), 213.

18 *Ibid.*

19 Sketch of Briscoe written by his widow for V. O. King.

20 Marriage Records of Harris County (MSS. in County Clerk's Office, Houston), A, 3.

21 Mrs. Adele B. Looscan, "Mrs. Mary Jane Briscoe," *Quarterly of the Texas State Historical Association*, VII, 69.

22 Probate Records of Harris County (MSS. in County Clerk's Office, Houston), H, 441.

23 Gammel, VIII, 240.

John Wheeler Bunton

1 The late Miss Brewye Bunton, genealogist of the Bunton family, to the author, May 4, 1930.

2 On April 18, 1835, Bunton, a single man, received title to one-fourth league of land in Milam's Colony, which was surveyed in what is now Bastrop County, Span. Arch., XVI, 65. In an unnumbered headright certificate issued to Bunton, January 13, 1838, for three-fourths of a league and one labor of land by the Austin County Board of Land Commissioners, it is stated that he came to Texas in 1833. File 81, Colorado 1st Class (MS. in General Land Office).

3 Comp. M. S. R. 1158.

4 Army Rolls (MS. in General Land Office), 23. On March 11, 1853, Bunton was issued Bounty Certificate 1244 for 320 acres of land for participation in the storming of Bexar. File 243, Bastrop County (MS. in General Land Office).

5 Yoakum, I, 337.

6 Returns. For the number of votes received by the candidates in Mina Municipality see the sketch of Robert M. Coleman in this volume.

7 Gammel, I, 824.

8 Comp. M. S. R. 141. It is stated that Bunton served in the army from March 28 to May 12, 1836.

9 On February 8, 1853, Bunton was issued Donation Certificate 484 for 640 acres of land for having participated in the Battle of San Jacinto. File 1278, Milam Donation (MS. in General Land Office).

10 *Journals of the House of Representatives of the Republic of Texas, First Congress—First Session* (Houston: Printed at the office of *The Telegraph and Texas Register*, 1838), 3.

11 Miss Brewye Bunton to the author, May 4, 1930.

12 Bunton was not seated until November 19, 1838. *Journal of the House of Representatives of the Republic of Texas, Regular Session of the Third Congress, No. 5, 1838*, 63.

13 Miss Brewye Bunton to the author, May 4, 1930.

14 *Ibid.*

JOHN SMITH DAVENPORT BYROM

1 Goodrich. Dixon (104) states that Byrom was born September 24, 1798. S. B. Byrom, Byromville, Georgia, genealogist of the Byrom family, who supplied much of this sketch, including Byrom's full name, states that the Bible records do not show the date of his birth.

2 S. B. Byrom stated that Byrom came to Texas in 1830. In Headright Certificate 24 for one league and one labor of land, issued in Byrom's name and delivered to his assignee, Anson Jones, in 1838, by the Brazoria County Board of Land Commissioners, it is merely stated that Byrom arrived in Texas previous to May 2, 1835. File 191, Goliad 1st Class (MS. in General Land Office).

3 Charles Adams Gulick, Jr. and Katherine Elliott (eds.), *The Papers of Mirabeau Buonaparte Lamar* (Austin: Texas State Library, 1920), I, 104.

4 Gammel, I, 508.

5 *Ibid.*, 590.

6 Returns. For the number of votes received by the candidates in Brazoria Municipality in the elections held February 1, 1836, see the sketch of Asa Brigham in this volume.

7 Gammel, I, 824.

8 Kidd, 12.

9 The will is on file in the office of the County Clerk at Angleton, Brazoria County.

10 Marriage Records of Brazoria County (MSS. in County Clerk's Office, Angleton), unnumbered volume, 85-86.

11 *Ibid.*, 162.

MATHEW CALDWELL

1 Dixon (81), without quoting his authority, states that Caldwell was born March 8, 1798.

2 On February 20, 1831, Caldwell was issued title to one league of land in DeWitt's Colony, situated in the present county of Lavaca. Span. Arch., XII, 315. In an unnumbered headright certificate it is shown that when Caldwell appeared before the Gonzales County Board of Land Commissioners, April 25, 1838, to apply for one labor of land due him, he stated that he came to Texas in 1832. File 355, Gonzales 1st Class (MS. in the General Land Office). This is an error, as the grant in DeWitt's Colony indicates.

3 Gammel, I, 605.

4 *Ibid.*, 726.

5 Returns. For the number of votes received by the candidates in Gonzales Municipality, see the sketch of John Fisher in this volume.

6 Gammel, I, 824. Fulmore (71-72) in 1915 and Dixon (81-84) in 1924, in error, state that Caldwell came to Texas in 1833, settled in what is now Sabine County and represented Sabine Municipality in the Constitutional Convention.

7 Gammel, I, 839.

8 Winkler, 126.

9 *Ibid.*, 136.

10 Brown, II, 177.

11 *Ibid.*, 180.

12 *Ibid.*, 223.

13 Yoakum, II, 364-365.

14 Thrall, 520.

15 Gammel, III, 53.

16 Thrall, 649.

17 Marriage Records of Washington County (MSS. in the County Clerk's Office, Brenham, Texas).

SAMUEL PRICE CARSON

1 *Biographical Directory of the American Congress, 1774-1927* (Washington: United States Government Printing Office, 1928), 791.

2 "Col. John Carson was a man of education, who, so tradition has it, left his native Ireland to escape his family's desire that he become an Episcopal rector. A man of means and an iron will, he soon became a leader in that portion of Burke County, which now is in McDowell County, and represented Burke in the State General Assembly for many years.

"Coming to America in about 1769, he is said to have first lived at the Yancey place, then at a home on Catawba River and finally building his great house on Buck Creek for his bride Rachael, a daughter of the prominent 'Hunting John' McDowell, who owned much land in the upper Catawba valley, known as Pleasant Gardens. His bride brought the name 'Pleasant Gardens' with her for her new home and it clung to the community. She died several years after the marriage, and he married the second time." From: A sketch by J. B. Hicklin of Asheville, North Carolina, written January 4, 1940, and published shortly afterward in a newspaper. The sketch was sent to the author February 15, 1940, by Dr. J. A. Sinclair of Asheville, whose mother was a niece of Carson. The name of the newspaper was not given. Children of John Carson by his first marriage were: Jason, Joseph M., Charles, John, James, Rebecca and Sallie; by his second were: Samuel P., William, George, Logan and Matilda. Carson's home, Pleasant Gardens, located four miles west of Marion, served as first courthouse of McDowell County, after the War

Between the States as an exclusive girls' school, and later as an inn. Somewhat modernized, it is now (1940) owned by A. L. Finley, of Marion.

3 John Preston Arthur, *Western North Carolina, a History (from 1730 to 1913)*, (Asheville: Edward Buncombe Chapter, D. A. R., 1914), 360.

4 *Ibid.*, 363.

5 *Ibid.*

6 *Ibid.*, 360.

7 *Ibid.*, 364.

8 Deed Records of Miller County, Arkansas (MSS. in County Clerk's Office, Texarkana), A, 2.

9 *Ibid.*, 8-9. Also recorded in Deed Records of Lafayette County, Arkansas (MSS. in County Clerk's Office, Lewisville), B, 167-69.

10 Deed Records of Lafayette County, B, 172.

11 *Star and North Carolina Gazette* (Raleigh), March 10, 1835. Courtesy of Samuel E. Asbury, College Station, Texas.

12 For election returns of Pecan Point and Vicinity see the sketch of Richard Ellis in this volume.

13 Gammel, I, 881.

14 Gray, 129.

15 Binkley, I, 507.

16 Gray stated that Burnet received a majority of seven votes. Gray, 132.

17 Garrison, I, 75-76.

18 Binkley, I, 573.

19 *Ibid.*, 702-03.

20 Garrison, I, 101.

21 *Ibid.*, 145-147.

22 Deed Records of Lafayette County, Arkansas, B.

23 "Replying to your letter of December 10th relative to burial place of Samuel Price Carson, you are advised that we have

inquired from every known authority in Hot Springs in the premises, and are unable to locate any record of Mr. Carson's place of interment. There was, we are informed, a number of years ago a Government cemetery at Hot Springs. The ground on which this cemetery was located was needed for the construction of the post office, and in 1888 the bodies were removed to other cemeteries in the city, but inquiry at each has failed to locate any record of removal of the remains of Mr. Carson."—Captain J. F. Hamer, Adjutant Medical Administration Corps, Hot Springs National Park, to author, December 17, 1935.

"When your father and I were in Hot Springs, Arkansas, he tried to find out where Uncle Sam was buried but we could find nothing satisfactory."—Mrs. M. C. Sinclair to Dr. James A. Sinclair, February 9, 1940.

24 Probate Record Book of Lafayette County, Arkansas (MS. in County Clerk's Office, Lewisville), B, 111-13. The will was filed for record, February 15, 1839. Letters testamentary were issued to Hamilton the next day.

25 Headright Certificate 4/86 was issued in Carson's name, August 26, 1856, by Stephen Crosby, Commissioner of the General Land Office, in compliance with "An act for...the heirs of Samuel P. Carson, approved August 25, 1856." File 1594, Milam 1st Class (MS. in General Land Office).

26 Gammel, VIII, 1076.

GEORGE CAMPBELL CHILDRESS

1 *The Southwestern Historical Quarterly* (Austin: The Texas State Historical Association, 1928), XXXI, 131-132.

2 Greer cites J. Catron, Nashville, to Dr. Ashbel Smith, Galveston, November 20, 1841, Ashbel Smith Papers (MSS. in University of Texas library).

3 Greer cites Clayton, *History of Davidson County, Tennessee*, 97.

4 *Ibid.*, 238.

5 The donation was made by H. K. W. Hill of Nashville, to whom the thanks of the Constitutional Convention were extended March 7, 1836. Gammel, I, 849.

6 Charles Adams Gulick, Jr. and Katherine Elliott (eds.), *The Papers of Mirabeau Buonaparte Lamar* (Austin: Texas State Library, 1920), X, 253-257.

7 The original letter is owned by the New York Historical Society, 170 Central Park West, New York City. It is printed through the courtesy of Alexander J. Wall, Director of the Society.

The folded letter is addressed: "John C. McLemore, Nashville, Tennessee," with lines run through the last two names and the name "Pontotoc" substituted for them. It is postmarked "New York, Dec. 7" and "Nashville, T., Jan. 1." The inference is that McLemore was not in Nashville when the letter was received there and that it was forwarded to Pontotoc.

While Swartwout was looked upon with suspicion by some prior to that time, it was not until 1839 that it became known that he had appropriated more than a million dollars of public funds to his own use. He was Collector of the Port of New York, the most lucrative public office in President Andrew Jackson's gift. Despite the warnings of Van Buren, who distrusted Swartwout's reputation for speculation, Jackson continued him in office, and Van Buren as president followed suit. On November 20, 1837, President Houston nominated Swartwout to the Senate of the Republic as agent to purchase ships for the navy of Texas. The Senate, however, on the following day, requested him to withdraw the nomination. See Winkler, I, 89. Swartwout's name was withdrawn on December 1. *Ibid.*, 92.

8 From Memphis, Tennessee, December 7, 1835, Micajah Autry wrote to his wife:

"I have taken passage in the steamboat *Pacific* and shall leave in an hour or two...I have met in the same boat a number of acquaintances from Nashville and the District, bound for Texas, among whom are George C. Childress and his brother [James B.] Childress thinks the fighting will be over before we get there, and speaks cheeringly of the prospects..."

From Natchitoches, Louisiana, on December 13, 1835, he

wrote:

"About 20 minutes ago I landed at this place safely after considerable peril. About 20 men from Tennessee formed our squad
at Memphis, and all landed safely at the mouth of Red River.
Major Eaton and lady were on board the *Pacific*, to whom I suppose I was favourably introduced by Mr. Childress—." Adele B.
Looscan, "Micajah Autry, a Soldier of the Alamo," *The Quarterly
of the Texas State Historical Association* (Austin: Published by
the Association, 1911), XIV, 317-318.

9 On January 12, 1836, Childress registered in the land application book of his uncle, Sterling C. Robertson, pending the
re-opening of the land office of the colony which had been
closed by order of the Consultation.

10 Z. N. Morrell, *Flowers and Fruits in the Wilderness* (Dallas:
W. G. Scarff & Co., 4th edition, 1886), 41.

11 Gammel, I, 98-09.

12 Judge George W. Tyler, son of Orville T. Tyler, one of Robertson's colonists, in writing of the empresario's land office, said:

"In order, probably, to place his land office more nearly in the
center of his colony, Robertson established the village of Sarahville de Viesca further up the river on the western heights
overlooking the great falls of the Brazos a few miles south of the
present town of Marlin. The village was laid out some time in
the summer of 1834 and the land office was placed there about
October 1 in the same year. Here resided the land commissioner, William H. Steele, who issued titles to the settlers, and
Moses Cummings, the 'principal and scientific surveyor,' who
ran out the land selected by the colonists. Here, too, were kept
the maps, field notes, proofs of immigration and records which,
collectively, were denominated the 'archives' of the colony.—
The place was abandoned in 1836—." Charles W. Ramsdell (ed.),
George W. Tyler, *The History of Bell County* (San Antonio: The
Naylor Co., 1936), 10.

The village was named in honor of Sarah, the mother of
Sterling C. Robertson, and Jose Maria Viesca, first governor of
Coahuila and Texas. The name was changed to Milam Decem-

ber 27, 1835, in honor of Benjamin B. Milam who had lost his life on December 7 at the storming of San Antonio.

13 Register Book, Applicants for Land in Robertson Colony (MS. in General Land Office), 18. Fulmore in 1915 (106) and Dixon (49-52) in 1924 stated that Childress came to Texas in 1832. Fulmore made a serious mistake in saying that Childress had never married and Dixon follows with the statement: "Never having married he left no family." Fulmore says Childress died in 1840 and Dixon makes the same statement.

14 Morrell, *Flowers and Fruits*, 44.

15 Returns.

16 Gammel, I, 824.

17 *Ibid.*, 825-826.

18 *Ibid.*, 890.

19 Garrison, I, 74.

20 *Ibid.*, 84.

21 *Ibid.*, 99.

22 Barker: Austin, III, 391.

23 Garrison, I, 91-92.

24 Headright Book in the County Clerk's Office in Nacogdoches. He was issued Headlight Certificate 72, dated February 1, 1836, which reads as follows:

"This is to certify that George G. Childress has appeared before the Board of Land Commissioners for the County of Nacogdoches and proved according to law that he arrived in this Republic January A. D. Eighteen Hundred and Thirty-six and that he is a married man and entitled under the 23rd section of the land law to one league and labor of land." File 11, Goliad First Class Headright (MS. in General Land Office).

The following appears in the Headright Book but not in the certificate: "He was granted the land because he 'rendered much service to the country by his acts.'"

25 Miss Harriet Hall Dowe to the author, December 20, 1939.

26 File 11, Goliad First Class Headright (MS. in the General Land Office).

353

27 The original letter is in the Archives of the Texas State Library, Austin.

28 Ashbel Smith Papers (MSS. in University of Texas Library).

29 Gammel, VIII, 1076.

30 Miss Harriet Hall Dowe to the author, December 20, 1939.

31 *Ibid.*

WILLIAM CLARK, JR.

1 Dixon (111), in error, states that Clark was born in Virginia. Clark told Dr. Benjamin B. Goodrich at the Convention that he was born in North Carolina. Colonel Gray, who was especially interested in those born in Virginia, listed Gaines, Goodrich, Houston and Mottley as haying been born in his native state, but he fails to list Clark. Gray, 121-22.

2 Dixon (111), in error, states that Clark was born in 1778. The date, April 14, 1798, is taken from the old tombstone that stood at Clark's grave.

354

3 Dixon (112), in error, states that Clark came to Texas from Louisiana, where he engaged in farming and merchandising.

4 Dixon, in error, states that Clark came to Texas in 1829. *Ibid.* That he came in 1835 is proved by the following document:

Certificate No. 96

Republic of Texas, Sabine County

Board of Land Commissioners

Feby Session, 1838

Thursday, the Fourth Day of the Month

The Board of Land Commissioners, met agreeable to law.—Present: John Boyd, President; Martin D. White and John H. McRae, Assistant Commissioners, do certify that "William Clark Jr. appeared, took and subscribed to the oath prescribed by law, as a resident citizen of Texas; M. D. White & E. M. Collins appeared as witnesses, who after being duly sworn upon their oaths, that the said William Clark Jr. was a resident citizen of Texas at the date of the Declaration of Independence, and that he had continued to be so to this day, and that he was a married man at the time and the head of a family; the said William Clark emigrated to Texas in the year 1835 which entitles him to receive one League & Labor of land in said Republic.

> Jno. Boyd, President
> John H. McRae, Asst Commissioner
> M. D. White, Asst Commissioner
>
> *Attest* William H. Harris, Clerk

Clark transferred the headright to Matthew Cartwright of San Antonio, April 1, 1850. File 630, Nacogdoches 1st Class (MS. in General Land Office, Austin).

5 Gammel, I, 994.

6 Returns.

7 Gammel, I, 824.

8 *Journal of the House of Representatives of the Republic of Texas, Called Session of September 25, 1837, and Regular Session commencing November 6, 1837,* 21.

9 R. B. Blake, Nacogdoches, to the author, October 3, 1938.

10 Inscription on the old headstone that stood at his grave.

11 Unfortunately, it is stated in the inscription on the monument that Clark was born in Virginia.

12 R. B. Blake, Nacogdoches, to the author.

Robert M. Coleman

1 Goodrich.

2 On February 1, 1835, Coleman was issued title to 24 labors of land in Robertson's Colony situated in what is now Lee County on the Yegua. Span. Arch., IXV, 459.

In Headright Certificate 258 for one labor of land issued in Coleman's name, but delivered to his heirs, August 16, 1838, by the Bastrop County Board of Land Commissioners, it is certified that Coleman came to Texas in 1832. File 1594, Milam 1st Class (MS. in General Land Office).

3 For accounts of the Indian expedition see John Henry Brown, *Indian Wars and Pioneers of Texas* (St. Louis: L. E. Daniell, no date), 26. See also Yoakum, I, 352.

In Comp. M. S. R. 7508 it is certified that Coleman served as captain of rangers from June 12 to August 28, 1835, at $75 per month.

4 Brown, I, 422.

5 Returns.

6 Gammel, I, 824.

7 Comp. M. S. R. 7509 (MS. in Archives, Texas State Library). Donation Certificate 128 for 640 acres of land was issued in Coleman's name October 21, 1848, due him for having participated in the Battle of San Jacinto. File 684, Milam Donation (MS. in General Land Office). Bounty Certificate 470 for 1280 acres was issued in his name October 21, 1848, due him for having served in the army for a period of one year and for having died in the service. File 682, Milam Bounty (MS. in General Land Office).

8 Gray, 210.

9 *Ibid.*, 211.

10 On petition of Mrs. Elizabeth Coleman, widow of Robert M. Coleman, Andrew Churchill was appointed administrator of Colonel Coleman's estate at the August, 1837, term of the probate court of Brazoria County.

11 "Captain Robert M. Coleman was a gallant soldier, but an impetuous man, governed too much by passion. His tirade against General Houston, after having served on his staff at San Jacinto, was as unseemly as unjust. He was drowned in 1837, while bathing at the mouth of the Brazos. His death was a great loss to the frontier, for despite his faults, he was a most valuable man, and none realized it more than General Houston. The death of his widow, an excellent lady, and his heroic son Albert (a boy of fourteen), and the captivity of a son of five years by Indians early in 1839 clothes his memory and that of his family with a melancholy interest. That this illusion is void of prejudice or unkindness is evidenced by the fact that he who pens this note, more than twenty years after his death, named the

356

county of Coleman in his honor." Brown, II, 129.

12 Albert Wilson McClellan, genealogist of the Coleman family, to the author, June 16, 1941.

JAMES COLLINSWORTH

1 Goodrich.

2 Fulmore, 195. Fulmore misspells the name James T. *Collingsworth*.

3 The following is from a letter written at Washington, D. C., November 14, 1939, by Edward G. Kemp, assistant to the Attorney General, and addressed to Senator Tom Connally:

The records of this Department indicate that a James Collingsworth was given a recess appointment as United States Attorney for the Western District of Tennessee on April 30, 1829. This appointment was received by the Senate and was confirmed on February 16, 1830. It also appears that Mr. Collingsworth received a confirmation for an additional appointment on February 27, 1834—.

4 In a letter addressed to President Burnet May 13, 1836, by Collinsworth he stated that he had been in Texas for about fifteen months. The letter is published in full in Binkley, II, 669-670.

Collinsworth was issued Headright Certificate 83, January 25 1838 for one-third of a league of land by the Brazoria County Board of Land Commissioners. File 909, Fannin 1st Class (MS. in the General Land Office, Austin).

5 Charles Adams Gulick, Jr. and Katherine Elliott (eds.), *The Papers of Mirabeau Buonaparte Lamar* (Austin: Texas State Library, 1921), I, 233-235.

6 Barker: III, 99-100.

7 Gulick and Elliott, *The Papers of Mirabeau Buonaparte Lamar*, I, 600.

8 Consultation Papers (MSS. in Archives, Texas State Library). Binkley, I, 189-190.

9 For the election returns of Brazoria municipality see the

sketch of Asa Brigham in this volume.

10 Gammel, I, 824.

11 *Ibid.*, 843.

12 Charles Adams Gulick, Jr. and Katherine Elliott (eds.), *The Papers of Mirabeau Buonaparte Lamar*, IV, 259-260.

13 Printed through the courtesy of the late Gen. Andrew J. Houston.

14 Comp. M. S. R. 5699.

15 A donation certificate for 640 acres of land was issued in Collinsworth's name, due him for having participated in the battle of San Jacinto. This was lost and a duplicate, 655, was issued January 3, 1855. File 516, Fannin Donation (MS. in the General Land Office, Austin).

16 Binkley, II, 632-633.

17 *Ibid.*, I, 507.

18 *Ibid.*, II, 671.

19 Binkley, II, 669-671.

20 Garrison, I, 89-90.

21 *Ibid.*, 91.

22 *Ibid.*, 126.

23 Winkler, 16.

24 *Ibid.*, 24.

25 *Ibid.*, 10.

26 *Ibid.*

27 Gray, 212.

28 Kidd, 36.

29 Anson Jones, *Memoranda and Official Correspondence Relating to the Republic of Texas, Its History and Annexation* (New York: D. Appleton & Co., 1859), 28.

30 Yoakum, II, 250.

31 Barker, III, 472-473.

32 Wharton, 86.

33 Kidd, 12.

34 Yoakum, II, 72. Fulmore (195) in 1915 refers to James Collinsworth as "James T. Collingsworth," and Dixon (115) made the same mistake in 1924.

35 Gammel, VIII, 1076.

EDWARD CONRAD

1 Dixon (119), in error, gave the name as Edwin.

2 John Conrad, in 1803, was a publisher in Philadelphia. In 1811 he was a bookseller at 205 High Street. On May 30, 1812, unable to pay his debts, he made an assignment to Samuel F. Bradford and John Morgan, and removed from Philadelphia. He returned to Philadelphia and entered politics. In 1837 he was elected alderman. The city directory of 1837 shows him living at 167 Callowhill Street. In 1841 he was listed: "John Conrad, alderman, 208 North Third Street; house, 40 Wood Street." The Philadelphia *Public Ledger*, of December 8, 1851, announced:

Death of Alderman Conrad. Alderman John Conrad, well known to most of our citizens as an old and respected resident and magistrate, died at his residence, Sixth Street, above Vine, yesterday about noon, after an illness of two weeks. Mr. Conrad has been in public and official life for many years, and at the time of his death was alderman of the Second Ward of the Northern Liberties.

On the next day, the same paper carried the item:

Died on Sunday morning, the 7th inst. John Conrad, Esq., in the 75th year of his age. The friends of the family are respectfully invited to attend his funeral from his late residence, No. 181 North Sixth Street, north of Vine Street this (Tuesday) afternoon, the 9th inst., at 1-1/2 o'clock, without further notice.

Philadelphia Deed Book, GWR XVIII, 576; lc XXII, 38. Philadelphia city directory, 1803, 1811, 1841.

John Conrad had at least two other sons, John and Robert Taylor Conrad. John died during the Seminole Campaign, as evidenced by an obituary in *Poulson's American Daily Advertiser*, August 25, 1838:

> Died on the 10th inst. in camp on James Island, Fla., in the 31st year of his age, Lieutenant John Conrad, of the 61st Regiment, U. S. Infantry, eldest son of John Conrad, Esq., of this city.

Robert Taylor Conrad (June 10, 1810-June 27, 1858) was a journalist, jurist and dramatist. He was admitted to the bar in 1831, but soon turned to journalism and literature. From 1831 to 1834 he was associated with the *Daily Commercial Intelligence*. In his spare time he wrote plays and verses. His first play, "Conrad, King of Naples" (later changed to "Jack Cade") was produced at the Arch Street Theatre by James E. Murdoch, January 17, 1832, and at Forest Theatre, New York, May 24, 1841. The success of this play made Conrad a literary figure. In 1843 he was the chairman of the committee which selected Edgar Allen Poe's "The Gold Bug" as the test story submitted to the *Dallas Magazine*. In 1836 Conrad was appointed judge of the Court of Criminal Sessions. On June 1, 1854, with the support of the Whig and Know-Nothing parties, he was elected the first mayor of greater Philadelphia. At the conclusion of his term in 1856 he was reappointed to the quarter sessions and served for one year. Dumas Malone (ed.), *Dictionary of American Biography* (New York: Charles Scribners' Sons, 1933), IV, 355-56.

A letter to Stephen F. Austin, dated at Philadelphia, April 12, 1836, shows that Robert Taylor Conrad was also interested in Texas:

> Sir, having a brother engaged in the cause of Texas, I myself feel a deep interest in its progress and an anxious desire to promote, by any means in my power, its success. For that purpose, I am desirous of lending my feeble aid to excite, in it favour, the sympathies of our public, and to secure it, as well as the advantage of a recognition by Congress, as more direct and effectual aid, by collections, etc. This has caused, and I hope will excuse, this intrusion upon you. I

would have called upon and consulted you during your stay in the City, but was myself absent. I have succeeded in enlisting the press of this city in favour of popular movements and have issued a call for a meeting preparatory to a general town meeting. I should like to have your views in relation to the proper course to be adopted and the measures most likely to prove serviceable to the cause—if any such are within the scope of your power. Should you return to Phil I will be happy to wait on you—if not, I would be gratified to learn if any, and what, of course, will be calculated to promote the cause of Texas...

The brother referred to is Edward Conrad—a member of the Texan Convention and one of the Committee to draw up the Declaration.

Barker: Austin, 1926, III, 331.

3 Dixon states without quoting his authority that Conrad was born February 22, 1810. Considering that Dixon's sketch is at variance with the recorded facts of Conrad's life, it is doubtful that this can be accepted. Since Conrad had not reached his 26th birthday at the time of his death, and since his brother Robert Taylor was born June 10, 1810, it is probable that April, 1811, is a close approximation.

361

4 Binkley, I, 215-216. Harbert Davenport, Brownsville, Texas, to the author, October 4, 1939.

5 Austin's Application Book (MS. in Span. Arch., General Land Office), II, 101. Dixon (121), in error, states that Conrad came to Texas in 1829.

6 For the election returns of Refugio Municipality see the sketch of David Thomas in this volume.

7 J. H. Kuykendall (ed.), "Reminiscences of Early Texans," *Quarterly of the Texas State Historical Association* (Austin: Published by the Association, 1904), VII, 57.

8 Gammel I, 824.

9 Yoakum II, 486.

10 In his petition for a veteran's pension, Burke, on December 15, 1870, wrote:

"He [Burke] was sent on recruiting service to report at Galveston, which he did, and was to be supplied transportation from there to New Orleans, but was ordered on special service by the Hon. Robt. Potter, Secy, of the Navy, to take charge of the brig *Pocket*, then a prize at Galveston. He had charge of her until the news of the victory of San Jacinto, when he went on board the *Yellowstone* up to the army." Pension Papers (MSS. in Archives, Texas State Library).

11 Courtesy of the late Gen. Andrew Jackson Houston.

12 Binkley, II, 675-676.

13 Army Rolls (MSS. in General Land Office), 135. The name is given as Edwin, but there is no doubt that it referred to Edward Conrad.

14 *Ibid.*, 90, shows that Conrad died July 13.

15 Gray, 211.

362

WILLIAM CARROL CRAWFORD

1 Crawford signed his name to the Declaration of Independence as Carrol and not Carroll.

2 Mrs. Rhoda E. Crawford Moore, daughter of the Reverend Mr. Crawford, to the author, April 16, 1938.

3 In Headright Certificate 69 issued to Crawford, February 1, 1838, for one league and one labor by the Board of Land Commissioners for Shelby County it is stated that he came to Texas in 1835. File 110, Shelby 1st Class (MS. in General Land Office.)

4 On December 8, 1837, Mr. Watkins was issued Bounty Certificate 844 for 640 acres of land for having served in the army from April 9 to September 8, 1836. File 36, Shelby Bounty (MS. in General Land Office).

5 Returns.

6 Gammel, I, 824.

7 Domestic Correspondence, Archives, Texas State Library. Courtesy of Miss Harriet Smither, Archivist.

8 Courtesy of Miss Smither.

9 Courtesy of Miss Winnie Allen, Archivist, Library of the University of Texas, Austin.

RICHARD ELLIS

1 From the inscription at the old headstone that stood at the original grave of Judge Ellis.

2 Thomas M. Owen, *History of Alabama and Dictionary of Alabama Biography*, III, 536-537.

3 Barker, II, 1183.

4 *Ibid.*, 1266.

5 *Ibid.*, 1586.

6 *Ibid.*, 1678.

7 *Ibid.*, II, 3.

8 *Ibid.*, 421.

363

9 "This is to certify that Richard Ellis appeared before the Board of Commissioners for the County of Red River and proved according to law that he arrived in the Country 22nd Febr. 1834 that he is a married man and is Entitled to One League and One Labor of Land..." File 9, Red River 1st Class (MS. in the General Land Office, Austin).

This corrects Fulmore and Dixon who said that Ellis came to Texas in, or before, the year 1825. Fulmore, 107; Dixon, 44.

10 A. W. Nevill, *The History of Lamar County* (Paris, Texas: The North Texas Publishing Co., 1937), 7.

11 Dallas T. Herndon, Executive Secretary, Department of Archives and History, Arkansas History Commission, Little Rock, to the author, October 26, 1939.

12 Neville, *The History of Lamar County*, 10.

13 *Ibid.*

14 Dallas T. Herndon to the author, February 6, 1940.

15 *Ibid.*

16 *Ibid.*

17 Gammel, I, 532.

18 Binkley, I, 231.

19 Gammel, I, 981.

20 Returns.

21 Gammel, I, 824.

22 *Ibid.*, 825.

23 Winkler, 10.

24 *Ibid.*, 70.

25 *Ibid.*, 112.

26 *Ibid.*, 134.

27 Gammel, VIII, 454.

28 Thrall, 658.

29 Gray, 201.

364

STEPHEN HENDRICKSON EVERITT

1 Full name supplied by Mrs. Thomas W. Causey of Kirbyville, Texas, June 10, 1936.

2 Goodrich.

3 Census of Bevil Municipality. Sent to the author by Mr. R. B. Blake, Nacogdoches, Texas. Dixon, without quoting his authority, fixes the date of Dr. Everitt's birth as November 26, 1807. It is doubtful if this can be accepted as a fact since Dixon misspells Everitt's name and shows him as having died in Jasper County, Texas, in 1849. Dixon, 301-302.

4 Span. Arch., XXII, 203. Everitt failed to claim the one labor of land due him from the Republic of Texas as an augmentation to his headright.

5 Gammel, I, 541-542.

6 *Ibid.*, 614.

7 *Ibid.*, 677.

8 Binkley, I, 513-514.

9 *Ibid.*

10 *Ibid.*, II, 631.

11 Returns.

12 Gammel, I, 824.

13 Winkler, 10.

14 *Ibid.*, 70.

15 *Ibid.*, 112.

16 *Ibid.*, 134.

17 *Ibid.*, 182.

18 *Ibid.*

19 Houston Wade, *Masonic Dictionary, Republic of Texas* (La Grange, Texas: *La Grange Journal*, 1935), 38.

20 An editorial in the Houston Banner in 1837 is accredited to "Dr." S. H. Everitt. Charles Adams Gulick, Jr. and Katherine Elliott (eds.), *The Papers of Mirabeau Buonaparte Lamar* (Austin: Texas State Library, 1922), II, 8.

21 The following confidential letter was written by Dr. Everitt at Nacogdoches, August 16, 1838, and addressed to Lamar at Houston:

> In conformity with my former intention I visited this place to see how the wind blew. On my arrival here I was astounded with the news of the death of Grayson, and that by his own hand—from what I can learn I have no doubt but the conscientious feeling that he would be Eternally & disgracefully beaten has been the Cause of this sudden termination of his Career—poor Human nature! Who would have thought it!
>
> His demise has settled the question beyond a doubt, he would have made a miserable run if he had lived.
>
> They are out against Horton the Bitterest possible style, he will run however, he will get a large vote in my District. Jasper and Jefferson will send men favorably disposed towards you & who will support your measures...
>
> Houston and Rusk have had some misunderstanding as I

learn from some of the soldiers—they dislike each other, and the volunteers dislike both. They die politically, a natural Death—neither Your particular friend (in my opinion) they will both pretend to be so. Houston was undoubtedly in favor of Grayson. He will now be warmly in favor of you.

We have had a Regular Kick up among the Mexicans they declaring in favor of the Constitution of 24—the thing is over—and I think better of Texas than Ever. She is safe beyond a Doubt—1,000 men were got together in about 4 days are eager for fight. You Will Have the power of carrying any measure You may desire in congress if I may Judge from the complexion of the Candidates here. The people look with confidence to the time when you shall take the Chair—Satisfied that you will correct all Evils & abuses.

May God Prosper you in all things.

Gulick and Elliott, *The Papers of Mirabeau Buonaparte Lamar*, II 203-204.

22 Deed Records of Jefferson County, Texas (MSS. in the County Clerk's Office, Beaumont), L, 69-70.

23 Anson Jones, *Memoranda and Official Correspondence Relating to the Republic of Texas, Its History and Annexation* (New York: D Appleton and Co., 1859), 270.

24 Probate Records of Jasper County, Texas (MSS. in the County Clerk's Office, Jasper). Courtesy of Mr. Walter P. Smith and Mr. E. T. Seale of Jasper, who spent hours finding the date. Most of the early records of Jasper County were destroyed in a courthouse fire.

25 Deed Records of Jefferson County, Texas (MSS. in the County Clerk's Office, Beaumont), L, 69-70.

JOHN FISHER

1 Mrs. Sophie G. B. Fisher, Washington, D. C., to Mr. L. T. Christian, Jr., Richmond, Virginia. Courtesy of Mr. Christian.

Dixon (277-281), in error, stated that John Fisher was born in Albemarle County, Virginia, March 8, 1800, and came to Texas in 1829. He, however, makes no attempt to state when and where Fisher died, leaving him in 1836 "at Columbia where he was one of the agents of the Allen Brothers in their campaign to have the capital of the Republic located at Houston."

James Fisher was born in Dumfries, Scotland, in 1770. He came to America in 1794, settled in Richmond, Virginia, and married Margaret Nimmo, also a native of Scotland. He died in Richmond in October, 1844. -Mrs. Fisher to Mr. Christian.

2 Binkley, I, 499-500.

3 Austin's Application Book (Span. Arch.), II, 99.

4 Barker, III, 233-234.

5 Returns.

6 Gammel, I, 824.

7 Gray, 167.

8 Applications, Bonds, Oaths, Resignations, in the Archives of the Texas State Library. Sent through the courtesy of Miss Harriet Smither, Archivist.

9 File 29, Brazoria First Class (MS. General Land Office, Austin).

10 Governor's Papers (MSS. in Archives, Texas State Library). Courtesy of Miss Harriet Smither, Archivist.

11 Courtesy of Wilmer L. Hall, State Librarian, Richmond, Virginia, March 9, 1940.

12 Following is the inscription on the granite slabs at the grave of Mr. Fisher: "Sacred to the memory of John Fisher—born in Richmond, Va., Jan. 18, 1800; died Aug. 14, 1865. He giveth His beloved sleep."

13 Following is the inscription on the granite slab at the grave of Mrs. Fisher: "Sacred to the memory of Margaret C. Fisher, beloved wife of John Fisher—born in Richmond, Va., Sept. 16, 1810; died March 22, 1879. Whereas I was blind now I see."

14 Records of Hollywood Cemetery (MSS. in Cemetery Office, Richmond, Virginia), D, 56. Courtesy of Mr. T. L. Christian, Jr., Richmond.

OUR (unlikely) FATHERS

SAMUEL RHOADS FISHER

1 Inscription on the headstone at Fisher's grave. Dixon (273), in error, says that S. Rhoads Fisher was born October 22, 1795.

Fisher, on December 2, 1830, received title to one league of land in Austin's Third Colony, situated in what is now Matagorda County. Span. Arch. (MSS. in General Land Office, Austin), VII, 309. This was all the land Austin was permitted to let him have. Fisher then appealed to the Governor at Saltillo for an augmentation of ten leagues. This was denied him, but on October 29, 1832, as S. *Rhoades* Fisher, he was issued title to two leagues which were also surveyed in Austin's Third Colony in the present County of Matagorda. Span. Arch. (MSS. in General Land Office), VIII, 653. On August 10, 1835, Samuel R. Fisher received title to one league of land in Zavala's Colony, surveyed in the present counties of Hardin and Tyler. Span. Arch., XXIII, 877.

In addition to the above land, Fisher, on February 5, 1838, received Headright Certificate 155 for one labor of land from the Harrisburg County Board of Land Commissioners. File 1277, Bexar 1st Class (MS. in General Land Office).

2 Barker, II, 462-465.

3 *Ibid.*, 583-584.

4 Binkley, I, 185-186.

5 *Ibid.*, BFE. Also see Gammel, I, 670.

6 Returns.

7 Gammel, I, 847.

8 *Ibid.*, 853.

9 Winkler, 15.

10 *Ibid.*, 17.

11 *Ibid.*, 74-75.

12 *Ibid.*, 80.

13 *Ibid.*, 81.

14 *Ibid.*, 81-82.

15 *Ibid.*, 82.

16 *Ibid.*, 91.

17 District Court Records (MSS. in District Clerk's Office, Bay City, Matagorda County, Texas).

18 Tombstone inscription.

19 Gammel, VIII, 1076.

JAMES GAINES

1 Richard and his brother James were sons of William Henry and Isabella (Pendleton) Gaines. Edmund Pendleton Gaines was the son of James Gaines.

Edmund Pendleton was born in Culpeper County, Virginia, March 20, 1777 and died in New Orleans, June 6, 1849.

Gaines was early taken by his father to North Carolina. He studied law for a time, but in 1799 entered the United States Army as an ensign, and from 1801 to 1803 was employed in the making of a topographical survey from Nashville to Natchez for the location of a military road. He gradually rose to the rank of brigadier general. R. T. Green, *Genealogical and Historical Notes on Culpeper County, Virginia*, I, 96. *The Century Cyclopedia of Names* (New York: The Century Co., 1914). *The New International Encyclopedia*, Second Edition, Vol. IX.

369

2 Goodrich. Fulmore (75) and Dixon (303) state that James and Edmund Pendleton Gaines were brothers.

3 R. B. Blake (ed.), *Unpublished Selected Letters and Papers of Judge Charles S. Taylor*, I, 11.

On February 13, 1830, in applying to Commissioner J. A. Padilla for land, Gaines stated that his family consisted of five persons, that he was an American, and, that he had emigrated to Texas in 1812. On April 3, 1830, title to one league of land was issued to him which was surveyed in what is now in Sabine County adjoining a tract of land owned by his son, John G. Gaines. Spanish Archives (MSS. in General Land Office, Austin), XXXVIII, 782.

In Headright Certificate 484 issued to Gaines, March 31, 1838, for one labor of land by the Sabine County Board of Land Commissioners, it is stated that he was a married man and had arrived in Texas in 1812.

The certificate was endorsed on the back April 10, 1838, by Gaines to Susan Jackson and her heirs and was acknowledged by Francis T. Gaines, Chief Justice of Sabine County. File 4, Sabine 1st Class (MS. in General Land Office).

4 Yoakum, I, 133.

5 *Ibid.*, 200.

6 Nacogdoches Archives (MSS. in Archives, Texas State Library, Austin).

7 Transcripts of Nacogdoches Archives, XXXV, 259. *Inventory of County Archives, No. 202, Sabine County* (San Antonio: Works Progress Administration), 7.

8 Gammel, I, 668.

9 *The Texas Almanac for 1858* (Galveston: Richardson and Company), 7.

10 Returns.

11 Gammel, I, 824.

12 *Ibid.*, 826.

13 Binkley, I, 551.

14 Winkler, 48-49.

15 *Ibid.*, 134.

16 *Ibid.*, 182.

17 *Ibid.*, 204.

18 *Ibid.*, 204.

19 Gammel, VIII, 1078.

20 John Norris et al. vs. A. Yancy, Case No. 2206, Nacogdoches County District Court Records (MS. in District Clerk's Office, Nacogdoches). Courtesy of Mr. R. B. Blake, Nacogdoches.

21 W. O. Liston, 613 North First Street, Harlingen, to the author August 12, 1940.

CHAPTER NOTES

THOMAS JEFFERSON GAZLEY

1 Courtesy of Mrs. Kate Gazley Nagle, Ft. Worth, genealogist of the Gazley family.

2 "He probably graduated from the College of Medicine of Maryland, afterwards to become the Medical Department of the University of Maryland." Dr. P. I. Nixon, San Antonio, to the author, August 9, 1942.

3 On March 1, 1831, Dr. Gazley received title to one league of land in Austin's Second Colony situated on Spring Creek in what is now Bastrop County. Span. Arch. (MSS. in General Land Office, Austin), III, 194.

In Headright Certificate 105 issued to Dr. Gazley, February 3, 1838, for one labor of land by the Harrisburg County Board of Land Commissioners it is stated that he arrived in Texas in 1831. File 435, Bastrop 1st Class (MSS. in the General Land Office). This, however, was a mistake. Dr. Gazley was practicing medicine in Texas in 1829.

4 Barker: Minutes, XXI, 411-412.

5 *Ibid.*, XXII, 78.

6 *Ibid.*, 86.

7 Gammel, I, 495.

8 *Constitution, or Form of Government of the State of Teas Made in General Convention, in the Town of San Felipe de Austin, in the month of April, 1833*, 13. The pamphlet was printed at the office of the *Commercial Bulletin*, New Orleans, in 1833. A photostatic copy was given the author by Samuel E. Asbury, College Station, Texas.

9 Comp. M. S. R. 907.

10 Barker, 161.

11 *Ibid.*, 162-163.

12 Returns.

13 Gammel, I, 824.

14 *Ibid.*, 901.

15 The following is from a letter written by R. H. Walker in 1859 but not published in the *Texas Almanac* until 1868:

Halifax County, North Carolina
October 1, 1859

Gentlemen: I have been furnished recently with a number of your ALMANAC for the present Year, (1859) which far excels anything of the kind I have ever seen. In looking over its pages, however, I see stated what I have seen before, namely, an official report of the rank and file of men and officers that took part in the battle of San Jacinto, which, I must beg leave to state, is not exactly correct for I see omitted the names of several brave and meritorious men: Nicholas M. Bain, who took Colonel Almonte prisoner; Turner Barnes, Joseph Weeks, Doctor Gazley, etc. I had the names of many that I do not see named who fought by my side, and, least of all my own, and would never have noticed the report only to correct in part the statements that have been so often made as official.

372

Noel Moses Baine, shown in Walker's letter as "Nicholas M. Bain" is listed on the official rolls as printed in 1836, as "V. M. Bain" and not omitted as Walker thought.

Brown in the San Jacinto rolls published in his history evidently had Walker's letter before him when he added the names of Turner Barnes, Joseph Weeks and Dr. T. J. Gazley to the rolls. Brown, II, 33-38. Wortham when he wrote his history most likely followed Brown in also listing Barnes, Weeks and Gazley. Louis J. Wortham, *A History of Texas* (Ft. Worth: Wortham-Molyneaux Co., 1924), III, 442-448.

The compiler of this volume cannot, of course, assert that Dr. Gazley, Captain Barnes and Weeks did not participate in the Battle of San Jacinto, but he does say that after a most exhaustive search he has been unable to procure official information that would justify the addition of their names to the San Jacinto rolls.

16 *Journal of the House of Representatives of the Republic of Texas. Called Session of September 25, 1837, and Regular Session Commencing November 6, 1837* (Houston: *National Banner* Of-

fice, 1838), 4.

17 Dixon (96) states that Dr. Gazley "served several terms as County Judge of Colorado County. His home in Columbus was noted for its hospitality...The descendants of Thomas J. Gazley have been unable to give the date of his death though it is known that he died in Colorado County previous to 1880." Dr. Gazley was at no time County Judge of Colorado County. In fact he was never a resident of that county.

18 Kidd, 17.

19 *Ibid.*, 69.

20 *Ibid.*, 19.

BENJAMIN BRIGGS GOODRICH

1 Although the roster of students is not known, this college was definitely the College of Medicine of Maryland, afterwards to become the Medical Department of the University of Maryland. Dr. P. I. Nixon, San Antonio, to the author August 9, 1942.

2 E. L. Blair, *Early History of Grimes County*, 102.

Mrs. Marie B. Owen, Director of the Department of Archives and History, Montgomery, Alabama, wrote to the author on October 26, 1939, that Dr. Goodrich served as a member of the House of Representatives from Jackson County, Alabama, in 1832.

3 On July 26, 1835, Dr. Goodrich received title to one league of land in Vehlein's Colony situated in the present County of Walker. Span. Arch. (MSS. in General Land Office, Austin), XX, 695.

In Headright Certificate 72 issued to Dr. Goodrich, February 2, 1838, for one labor of land by the Montgomery County Board of Land Commissioners, it is certified that he arrived in Texas April 30, 1834. File 72, Montgomery 1st Class (MS. in General Land Office).

4 Deed Records of Washington County (MSS. in County Clerk's Office, Brenham, Texas), C, 232.

5 Gammel, I, 824.

6 Yoakum, II, 512-513.

7 Gray, 107.

8 Amelia Williams, "A Critical Study of the Siege of the Alamo," printed in the *Southwestern Historical Quarterly* (Austin: The Texas State Historical Association, 1934), XXXVII, 262-263.

9 Courtesy of the late Gen. A. J. Houston, La Porte, Texas.

Jesse Grimes

1 Date of birth as shown on the old headstone at his grave.

2 On April 6, 1831, Grimes received title to one league of land in Austin's Second Colony situated in the present Grimes County Spanish Archives (MSS. in General Land Office, Austin), IV, 758. In Headright Certificate 388 issued to him June 8, 1838, for one labor of land by Montgomery County Board of Land Commissioners, it is certified that he came to Texas in 1827. In the file containing the certificate there is a document signed with an X by Mrs. Rosanna Grimes, widow of Jesse Grimes. File 258, Robertson, 1st Class (MS. in General Land Office).

3 Barker in *Southwestern Historical Quarterly*, XXI, 408.

4 *Ibid.*, XXIII, 214.

5 *Ibid.*, XXIV, 162.

6 Gammel, I, 497.

7 *Ibid.*, 503.

8 *Ibid.*, 519.

9 *Ibid.*, 544.

10 Returns.

11 Gammel, I, 824.

12 Binkley, II, 640.

13 Army Rolls (MSS. in General Land Office), 197-198.

14 Charles Adams Gulick, Jr. and Katherine Elliott (eds.), *The Papers of Mirabeau Buonaparte Lamar* (Austin: Texas State Li-

brary, 1922), II, 395-396.

15 Winkler, 10.

16 Elizabeth Le Noir Jennett, *Biographical Directory of the Texan Conventions and Congresses, 1832-1845* (Published by the State of Texas, 1941), 33.

17 *Journal of the House of Representatives of the Seventh Congress of the Republic of Texas,* 3.

18 Winkler, *Secret Journals of the Senate, Republic of Texas,* 3.

19 *Ibid.,* 304.

20 *Journals of the Senate, First Legislature of the State of Texas,* 4.

21 *Journals of the Senate of the State of Texas, Second Legislature,* 3.

22 *Journals of the Senate of the State of Texas, Third Session,* 3.

23 *Journals of the Senate of the Fourth Legislature of the State of Texas,* 4.

24 *Journal of the Senate of the State of Texas, Sixth Legislature,* 3.

25 *Journals of the Senate of the State of Texas, Seventh Biennial Session,* 4.

26 *Journal of the Senate of Texas, Eighth Legislature,* 3.

27 Gammel, 1356.

28 Thrall, 666.

29 As shown on the headstone at their graves.

ROBERT HAMILTON

1 Goodrich. In one paragraph Patrick Hamilton Baskerville stated that the date of Robert Hamilton's birth was unknown, but later in the same paragraph he set the date as October 17, 1780. Patrick Hamilton Baskerville, *The Hamiltons of Burnside, North Carolina* (Richmond, Virginia: William Ellis Jones, Inc., 1916), 88-89.

Dixon (295) without citing his authority set the date as March 24, 1783, and said that Hamilton came to Texas in 1828.

2 Baskerville, *The Hamiltons of Burnside, North Carolina*, 85-86.

3 File 75, Red River 1st Class (MS. in General Land Office). Following is a copy of Headright Certificate 484 in the file:

This is to Certify that Robert Hamilton appeared before the Board of Commissioners for the County of Red River and proved according to law that he arrived in this country on the 15th day of December 1834 and being by the board considered a single man and entitled to one-third of a league of land...

4 Baskerville, *The Hamiltons of Burnside, North Carolina*, 88-89.

5 Gammel, I, 824.

6 *Ibid.*, 838.

7 *Ibid.*, 881.

8 See the sketch of Samuel P. Carson in this volume.

9 For additional information regarding this territory see the sketch of Richard Ellis in this volume.

10 Garrison, I, 73-74.

11 *Ibid.*, 74.

12 *Ibid.*, 84-85.

Following are copies of two letters the original of which were shown the author in Washington, D. C. in 1936 by Mr. Hunter Miller, Historical Advisor to the State Department:

Washington City
May 21, 1836
Hon. John Forsyth
Secretary of State, U. S. of America
Sir:

The undersigned have the honor to herewith accompany the Commission which has been conferred upon them by the Republic of Texas. It is the wish and object of the Government we represent to enter as early as possible into the most friendly relation with the United States of America.

Will you be so good as to indicate the earliest hour at which the undersigned can have a personal interview with you in their official capacity. With sentiments of the highest consideration and respect we are,

Geo. C. Childress
Robt. Hamilton.

On May 25, they wrote from Washington to the president:

Sir:

We have the honor to state that last night we received dispatches from the Government of Texas, containing an official account of the battle of San Jacinto; and the capture of the President of the Republic of Mexico, his staff and principal officers, and respectfully ask to be informed whether you wish to make any use or reference to them in your communication responding to the call of the Senate.

With the greatest respect, Sir, we have the honor to be your obedient servants,

Robert Hamilton
George C. Childress

13 Garrison, I, 96-97.

14 *Ibid.*, 103.

15 *Ibid.*, 145-147.

16 Winkler, 34.

17 Binkley, II, 1085.

18 Original will is in the office of the county clerk of Hempstead County, at Hope, Arkansas, and copies in the office of the county clerk of Lafayette County at Lewisville, Arkansas, and in the office of the clerk of Red River County at Clarksville, Texas.

19 Probate Records of Red River County, Texas (MS. in County Clerk's Office, Clarksville), B, 151.

20 Miscellaneous Records, County Court, Probate Court; Bonds & Marriage Certificates, Lafayette County, Arkansas, Vol. B., pp. 31 and 32, County Clerk's office, Lewisville, Arkansas.

21 John M. Corey, City Historian of Saratoga Springs, wrote to the author December 12, 1939, that he had been unable to locate the grave of Robert Hamilton. He stated that the Pavillion Hotel, where Hamilton died, burned in October, 1843. The present City Hall stands on the site of the hotel.

BAILEY HARDEMAN

1 Mrs. Ethel N. Bassett, Washington, D. C., genealogist of the Hardeman family, to the author, June 23, 1943. Goodrich. Fulmore (109), in 1915, stated that Hardeman was born February 28 1795.

2 W. M. Matthews, "Thomas Jones Hardeman," *The Bolivar* (Hardeman County, Tennessee), *Bulletin*, April 23, 1943, p. 1.

3 *Ibid.*

4 W. M. Matthews.

5 Mrs. Bassett.

6 W. M. Matthews. Fulmore mistakenly said the county was named for the father, Thomas Hardeman. Fulmore (109).

7 Mrs. Bassett.

8 Adjutant General A. S. Adams to United States Senator Tom Connally, March 5, 1940. Letter in possession of the author.

9 In his sketch of William P. Hardeman, son of Thomas J. Hardeman, Brown wrote:

His father reached Texas with his family in 1835, just at the time when the colonists were preparing for unequal war with Mexico. Burleson, Milam, Frank Johnson, and others, had determined to capture the garrison at San Antonio. Their followers were the frontier hunters and almost their only weapons were hunter's rifle. Artillery was especially needed, and W. P. Hardeman, then but nineteen years old, accompanied his uncle, Bailey Hardeman, and a few neighbors to Dimmits landing, below the mouth of the Lavaca river, and procured an eighteen pound cannon, which had been brought on a schooner from Matagorda Pass. On the march the force was increased to seventy-five men, among them were twenty men known as the Mobile Grays. Marching rapidly with this piece of artillery to San Antonio, the news of the approaching reinforcement reached Gen. Cos in advance and precipitated his surrender, which occurred before the artillery arrived.

John Henry Brown, *Indian Wars and Pioneers of Texas*, (St. Louis: Nixon-Jones Printing Co., date not shown), 397.

10 Gammel, I, 599.

11 Returns. For the number of votes each candidate received in Matagorda Municipality see the sketch of S. Rhoads Fisher in this volume.

12 Gammel, I, 824.

13 *Ibid.*, 826.

14 Gray, 132.

15 Binkley, II, 573.

16 Louis J. Wortham, *A History of Texas from Wilderness to Commonwealth* (Ft. Worth: Wortham-Molyneaux, 1924), II, 330.

17 Binkley, II, 709-712.

18 *Ibid.*, 1048-1049.

19 Probate Records of Matagorda County (MS., County Clerk's Office, Bay City, Texas). Courtesy of Rev. Paul E. Engle, Bay City.

Headright Certificate 128 for one league and one labor of land was issued January 18, 1838, in the name of Bailey Hardeman, but delivered to his heirs, by the Board of Land Commissioners for Matagorda County. File 551, Bastrop 1st Class (MS., General Land Office, Austin).

20 Through error, the inscription states that Hardeman died October 12, 1836.

21 Thomas Jones Hardeman was born January 31, 1788, and died January 15, 1854. In 1850 he was Grand Master of the Grand Lodge of Texas. *Proceedings of the Special Communications of the M.W. Grand Lodge of Texas, A. D. 1926-A. L. 5926.* p. 327.

22 Gammel, IV, 963.

23 Marriage Records of Williamson County, Tennessee. Cour-

tesy of Mrs. Ethel N. Bassett.

24 Marriage Records of Matagorda County (MSS. in County Clerk's Office, Bay City, Texas).

Augustine Blackburn Hardin

1 From the Hardin family records sent to the author August 5, 1936, by Mrs. Robert W. Humphreys, Liberty, Texas. Fulmore (111) in 1915 and Dixon (289) in 1924, in error, stated that Hardin was born in 1798.

2 The author has a photostatic copy of the bond of office which Hardin made on April 26, 1824.

3 Gammel, IV, 932.

4 Hardin received title to one league of land from Commissioner J. F. Madero, May 11, 1831, which was surveyed in what is now Liberty County. Spanish Archives (MSS. in General Land Office, Austin), XXXVIII, 896. In Headright Certificate 89 for one-half of a league of land issued to Hardin, February 1, 1838, it is stated that he came to Texas in 1825. File 136, Liberty 1st Class (MS. in General Land Office).

5 Barker.

6 Fulmore (111) and Dixon (208) in error, state that Hardin was a member of the Second Convention of Texas in 1833.

7 Gammel, I, 497.

8 *Ibid.*, 544.

9 Returns.

10 Gammel, I, 838.

11 Gray, 166-167.

12 Fulmore (111) in 1915 and Dixon (289) in 1924, in error, stated that Hardin died July 27, 1871.

13 File 697. Robertson Second Class (MS. in General Land Office. Austin).

14 *Ibid.*

380

15 *Ibid.*

16 Comp. M. S. R., unnumbered. Hardin was issued Bounty Certificate 6094 for 320 acres of land January 11, 1839, for having served in the army, from July 7 to October 7, 1836. File 6, Liberty Bounty (MS. in General Land Office, Austin).

17 File 1223, Veterans Donations (MS. in General Land Office, Austin).

SAMUEL HOUSTON

1 Unless otherwise noted, all dates dealing with Houston's United States Army Service are from Francis B. Heitman, *Historical Register and Dictionary of the United States Army, 1789-1903*, I, 545. Quoted by Williams & Barker, II, 1.

2 George Creel, *Sam Houston, Colossus in Buckskin* (New York: Cosmopolitan Book Corp., 1928), 22-25.

3 *Ibid.*, 26.

4 *Ibid.*, 28.

5 *Biographical Directory of the American Congress, 1774-1927* (Washington: U. S. Government Printing Office, 1928), 1117.

6 Williams & Barker, IV, 9.

7 James, 75. When, on November 30, 1833, Houston filed suit for divorce in Nacogdoches, he said in his petition: "That on the 18th day of January in the year of our Lord 1820 he intermarried with Miss Eliza H. Allen of Sumner County in said last mentioned state. That on the 15th day of April next thereafter a separation took place..." Marquis James fixed the date of the marriage as January 22, 1829. James had evidently examined the court records of Sumner County, while General Houston probably relied on his memory. A copy of the divorce proceeding is in the Samuel E. Asbury Papers (MSS. in University of Texas Library). Cited from Williams & Barker, I, 277-79.

8 James, 127.

9 Williams & Barker, I, 230-231.

10 James, 186.

11 On January 9, 1833, Houston received title to one league of land in Austin's Third Colony, stating in his petition "my status is that of a married man." Span. Arch., XVIII, 315.

On May 5, 1835, Houston was issued title to one labor and 836,291 sq. varas of land in Burnet's Colony, stating in his petition: "I have come without family."

12 William Carey Crane, *Life and Select Literary Remains of Sam Houston of Texas* (Philadelphia: J. B. Lippincott Co., 1884), 46-47.

13 Gammel, I.

14 *Ibid.*, 553.

15 Williams & Barker, I, 343-344.

16 *Ibid.*

17 Returns.

18 *Ibid.*

19 The following letter appeared in the *Red River Herald* and was reprinted in the *Mississippi Free Trader*, of Natchez, Mississippi, March 25, 1836:

In order to correct a report which has gone abroad in the United States, respecting the volunteers of Texas refusing to serve under General Houston, we take pleasure in giving to the public, the following extract of a letter to a gentleman of this place, from one in Texas, dated Nacogdoches, Feb. 18, who has the means of knowing the truth:

With some surprise, I have understood that a report is now in circulation, that the volunteers from the United States, lately stationed at the mission at Refugio, had refused to submit to the command of General Houston. The report is utterly without foundation. The troops marched under the orders of Gen. Houston, from Goliad to Refugio. And upon the arrival of Mr. Johnson, upon the second evening after their encampment, bearing the resolutions passed by the council, or a part of them. Gen. Houston returned to St. Phillippe on the night succeeding, for the purpose of reporting to the Gover-

nor, as the only officer he could recognize. No doubt can be entertained, but that a great portion of the volunteers would immediately disband, had they known of the departure of their General. This General Houston wished to avoid, as he would not countenance insubordination in any form, or under any circumstances. He therefore left the post at night, and without their knowledge of the time he would leave.

20 Winkler, 101.

21 Gammel, I, 844.

22 Gray, 125.

23 Comp. M. S. R.

24 File 1134, Nacogdoches 1st Class (MS. in General Land Office, Austin).

25 The *Natchitoches Gazette*, of June 18, 1836, carried the following item:

General Sam Houston, Commander-in-Chief of the Texian Army, arrived in this town in the *Caspian*, and has taken lodging at Cook and Porter's hotel.

26 Harriet Smither (ed.), *Journals of the Fourth Congress of the Republic of Texas, 1889-1840*. The House Journal, unnumbered page opposite page 1.

27 *Journals of the House of Representatives of the Republic of Texas, Fifth Congress, First Session*, 94.

28 Williams & Barker, II, 330-331.

29 *Biographical Directory of the American Congress, 1774-1927* (Washington: United States Government Printing Office, 1928), 1117.

30 Crane, 599-610.

31 Gammel, I, 270-271.

32 Thrall, 670.

33 Williams & Barker, I, 297. On April 21, 1835, at Nacogdoches, John M. Dor issued Houston a certificate of character:

This is to certify that the foreigner Samuel Pablo Houston is a man of good moral character and industrious, loving the constitution and the laws of the country, a bachelor without family and generally known as a good man.

Nacogdoches Archives (MSS. in Archives, Texas State Library).

34 George J. Burleson (comp.), *The Life and Writings of Rufus C. Burleson*, D. D., LL. D. (Mrs. Georgia J. Burleson, 1901), 165.

35 Houston vs. Starr, tried in May, 1849. Nacogdoches County District Court Records (MSS. in District Clerk's Office, Nacogdoches), file 2188. Courtesy of B. B. Blake, Nacogdoches.

36 Houston was a resident of city of Houston on October 5, 1841, when he sold a block of land in Nacogdoches to Eve Helena Sterne. Deed Records of Nacogdoches County (MSS. in County Clerk's Office, Nacogdoches), G, 137.

37 Gen. Andrew Jackson Houston to author, October 16, 1936.

38 "Gen. Houston has removed to Independence, in Washington County." *Houston Telegraph*, November 4, 1853.

39 File 135, Liberty Bounty (MS. in General Land Office).

40 File 162, Montgomery Donation (MS. in General Land Office).

41 File 1134, Nacogdoches 1st Class (MS. in General Land Office).

42 Houston Wade, *Masonic Dictionary* (La Grange: La Grange Journal, 1937), 44.

43 Kidd, 19.

44 Crane, 253-254.

WILLIAM DEMETRIS LACEY

1 The descendants of William Demetris Lacey now spell the name *Lacy*.

2 Goodrich.

3 On March 1, 1831, title to one-fourth of a league of land in Austin's Second Colony, situated in what is now Fayette Coun-

ty, was issued in the name of Wm. B. Lacy. Span. Arch. (MSS. in General Land Office, Austin), III, 474. On January 9, 1838, Lacey, having married in 1832, received Headright Certificate 112 for three-fourths of one league and one labor of land from the Matagorda County Board of Land Commissioners. In the certificate the name was spelled *Lacy*. The certificate was lost and a duplicate was issued August 14, 1845. This was also lost and on October 20, 1857, Certificate 130, was issued. In the file containing the certificate there is a letter dated July 12, 1866, and signed, with a mark, by Mrs. Sally Lacy, widow of W. D. *Lacy*. File 1128 Fannin 1st Class (MS. in General Land Office). Although Certificate 112 was lost a record of it was made in Book A, Clerk's Return (MS. in General Land Office). It shows that when Lacey applied for the land he stated that he had arrived in Texas in 1831.

4 Comp. M. S. R. 415 (MS. in Archives, Texas State Library).

Colorado
January 26, 1836

Rec'd of William D. Lacey twelve saddles at fourteen dollars each—for the use of the Texas Legion of Cavalry.

Thomas R. Jackson,
Quarter Master

Headquarters, Burnam's
January 25, 1836

To Wm D. Lacy:

Sir you will please deliver to Jesse Burnam one of the saddles you have made for the government, in place of the one he has furnished to the troops under my command.

Your obt servant,
W. B. Travis,
Lt. Col. Comdt.

5 Gammel, I, 479.

6 *Ibid.*, 757.

7 Returns.

8 Gammel, I, 825.

9 Comp. M. S. R., 1350 (MS. in Archives of the Texas State Library):

This will certify that William D. Lacey joined my company as a volunteer on the eighth of July and served until September 17, 1836 and that he had served under Colonel Morgan at Galveston from April 18 to May 12.

George Sutherland.

On January 21, 1841, Wm. D. Lacey was issued Bounty Certificate 9752 for 320 acres of land for having served in the army from April 18 to September 16, 1836. File 9, Matagorda Bounty (MS. in General Land Office).

10 File 954, Robertson 1st Class (MS. in General Land Office).

Albert Hamilton Latimer

386

1 From the inscription on the headstone at Latimer's grave. Dr. Goodrich erroneously stated that Latimer was born in about 1809.

2 Albert H. Latimer, Jr., The Emigration of the Latimers (MS. in possession in 1935 of Judge J. M. Deaver, El Paso).

3 In Headright Certificate 2 issued to A. H. Latimer, January 31, 1838, by the Red River County Board of Land Commissioners for one league and one labor of land it is stated that he had arrived in Texas, December 3, 1833. File 43, Red River 1st Class (MS. in General Land Office).

4 Pat B. Clark, The History of Clarksville and Old Red River County (Dallas: Mathis, Van Nort & Co., 1937), 108.

5 Gammel, I, 982.

6 Returns.

7 It appears that from the situation of the settlers on Red River that it has heretofore been almost impossible to impart to them the true situation of our Country. The citizen delegates of Pecan

Point have represented to your Committee that their population extends along the bank of the Red River for nearly 300 miles. That though there was an order for two persons to represent that community, yet then; having been subsequently one order for five another one for six members of this Convention. That the order for five members having come to hand acted upon it and certificate of election for them presented to your Committee, who reported favorably to their being read and having come to hand, it is believed by a majority of your Committee that the inhabitants of Red River are entitled to at least six members."

Binkley, I, 348-349.

8 Gammel, I, 838.

9 *Ibid.*, 881.

10 *Ibid.*, 1431-1432

11 A copy of this unpublished sketch was sent to the author by Judge J. H. Deaver, El Paso.

12 Latimer's name appears on an original muster roll of Captain Becknell's Company owned in 1940 by Judge J. M. Deaver of El Paso. Latimer was issued Bounty Certificate 4498 for 320 acres of land December 4, 1838, for having served in the army from July 14 to October 14, 1836. File 27, Red River Bounty (MS. in General Land Office).

13 Gammel, I, 1366.

14 *Ibid.*, 1431-1432.

15 *Ibid.*, 1464.

16 "The business district of the town of La Grange was a two-story log house, the lower story a store and the upper a courtroom. There the records were kept. Texas held court at La Grange, and Miller County, Arkansas, held court at Jonesboro. When a tax collector from Miller County, appeared at La Grange demanding taxes, a mob gathered, and he was chased out of town.

"In latter years the courthouse was used as a stable by 'Gunboat' Latimer, a grandson of James Latimer. The name of the town was changed to Madras, and a settlement by that name is

387

still in Red River County, but it is not now a post office."

MS. sent to the author by Judge J. M. Deaver, El Paso, January 5, 1935.

17 *Journals of the House of Representatives of the Republic of Texas Fifth Congress, First Session*, 4.

18 Elizabeth Le Noir Jennett, *Biographical Directory of the Texan Conventions and Congresses, 1832-1845* (Published by the State of Texas, 1941), 33.

19 Oran M. Roberts, "The Political Legislative, and Judicial History of Texas for Its Fifty Years of Statehood, 1845-1895," Wooten, II, 8.

20 *Journals of the Senate of the State of Texas, Third Session*, 3.

21 Wooten, II, 167-168.

22 *Ibid.*, 185.

23 Judge J. M. Deaver, El Paso, to the author, March 12, 1940.

24 *Biographical Souvenir of the State of Texas* (Chicago: F. A. Battey & Co., 1889), 508-509.

388

EDWIN OSWALD LEGRAND

1 Crocket, 207.

2 In 1936, the Commission of Control for Texas Centennial Celebrations erected a monument at the grave of LeGrand. On it, through error, it was inscribed that LeGrand was born in 1801.

3 LeGrand appeared before the San Augustine County Board of Land Commissioners in 1838 and under oath stated that he had first arrived in Texas in 1834. Clerk's Returns (MS. in the General Land Office, Austin). As a single man, he was issued Headright Certificate 268 for one third of a league of land. Files 425-426, Robertson 1st Class (MSS. in the General Land Office). He received no land from the Mexican government.

4 LeGrand did not apply for the land due him for his army service until July 9, 1860, when he signed the following affidavit

at San Augustine before S. W. Blount, a justice of the peace:

> Before me the undersigned authority appeared Edwin O. LeGrand who states that he entered Bexar between the 5th and 10th of December 1835, and actually assisted in the reduction of that place, and remained there until the surrender of General Cos, and was honorably discharged from the services and that he served three (3) months in Capt. Wm. Kimbro's Company in Texas and that he has not received any bounty warrant for either of said services.

File 420, Court of Claims Papers. (MSS. in the General Land Office).

On August 2, 1860, LeGrand was issued Donation Certificate 831 for 640 acres of land for having participated in the Storming and Capture of Bexar. File 501, Nacogdoches Donation (MS. in the General Land Office). On August 22, 1860, he received Bounty Certificate 283 for 320 acres of land for having served in the army in 1835 for a period of three months, enlistment period not shown. File 1042, Fannin Bounty (MS. in the General Land Office).

5 Gammel, I, 993-994.

6 Returns.

7 LeGrand's name appears on p. 39 of the San Jacinto rolls in the General Land Office. On December 18, 1858, James A. Chaffin, who served with him in the battle, deposed: "E. O. Legrand joined Captain Wm. Kimbro's Company at Groos on the Brassos River a short time before the Battle, and fought as a soldier in said battle." File 420, Court of Claims (MS. in General Land Office, Austin).

Inasmuch as but one donation certificate was issued to a soldier, LeGrand did not receive one for his participation at San Jacinto. On August 2, 1860, he received Bounty Certificate 284 for 320 acres of land for having served in the army from March 15 to June 15, 1836. File 1507, Bexar Bounty (MS. in General Land Office).

8 Winkler, 107.

9 Charles Adams Gulick, Jr. and Katherine Elliott (eds.), *The*

Papers of Mirabeau Buonaparte Lamar (Austin: Texas State Library, 1922), II, 443.

Samuel Augustus Maverick

1 From the inscription on the headstone at his grave. Dixon (266), in error, states that Maverick was born July 28, 1803.

2 Marjory L. Jones, Yale University, to author, November 15, 1939.

3 Rena Maverick Green (ed.), *Memoirs of Mary A. Maverick* (San Antonio: The Alamo Printing Co., 1921), 128. Sketch of Samuel A. Maverick by Dr. George Cupples.

4 Statement by Maverick in the *Journal of the House of Representatives, The State of Texas, Fifth Legislature*, 51.

Dr. Benjamin B. Goodrich was mistaken in stating that Maverick emigrated to Texas from South Carolina.

5 Yoakum, II, 24-25.

On May 21, 1838, Maverick was issued Donation Certificate 877 for 640 acres of land for having participated in the storming and capture of Bexar, December 5 to 10, 1835. File 877, Bexar Bounty (MS. in the General Land Office, Austin).

On December 19, 1846, he was issued Bounty Certificate 165 for 320 acres of land for three months' army service, period of service not shown. File 976, Bexar County (MS. in General Land Office).

Maverick on March 2, 1838, was issued Headright Certificate 293 for one league and one labor of land by the Bexar County Board of Land Commissioners. File 924, Bexar 1st Class (MS. in General Land Office).

6 Gammel, I, 847.

7 Gray, 122.

8 Amelia Williams, "A Critical Study of the Siege of the Alamo and of the Personnel of its Defenders" in *The Southwestern Historical Quarterly*, XXXVII (1934), 31.

9 In a letter written by Maverick at Port Cavallo, Matagorda County, July 3, 1847, to Captain S. M. Howe, San Antonio, he said among other things: "I must add that I have a desire to reside in this particular spot [near the Alamo]. A foolish prejudice, no doubt, as I was almost a solitary escapee from the Alamo massacre having been sent by those unfortunate men only four days before the Mexican advance appeared, as their representative in the convention which declared independence." Green, *Memoirs of Mary A. Maverick*, 134.

10 Gammel, I, 847.

11 *Ibid.*, 853.

12 Green, *Memoirs of Mary A. Maverick*, 53.

13 *Ibid.*, 60.

14 Manuscript Sketch of Dr. Shields Booker by Dr. P. I. Nixon, of San Antonio.

15 Anderson Hutchinson in his diary, stated the number as 55. E. W. Winkler (ed.), "The Bexar and Dawson Prisoners," *Quarterly of the Texas State Historical Association*, XIII (1910), 295. Yoakum places the number at 53. Yoakum, II, 363.

16 Green, *Memoirs of Mary A. Maverick*, 76.

17 *Journals of the House of Representatives of the Seventh Congress of the Republic of Texas*, 12.

18 *Journals of the House of Representatives of the Eighth Congress of the Republic of Texas*, 4.

19 Green, *Memoirs of Mary A. Maverick*, 96.

20 *Journals of the Extra Session of the House of Representatives of the Fourth Legislature*, 9.

21 *Journal of the House of Representatives, The State of Texas, Fifth Legislature*, 5.

22 *Journal of the Senate, The State of Texas, Sixth Legislature*, 4.

23 E. R. Lindley (ed.), *Members of the Legislature of the State of Texas, 1846 to 1939* (Published by the State of Texas in 1939), 27.

24 *Ibid.*, 35.

25 *Ibid.*, 42.

26 O. M. Roberts, "The Political, Legislative, and Judicial History of Texas for its Fifty Years of Statehood, 1845-1895." Wooten, II, 107, 110, 111.

27 Railroad Papers, Reports, Inspections (MSS. in Archives, Texas State Library). Courtesy of Andrew F. Muir.

28 Inscription on the monument at Maverick's grave.

29 Gammel, IV, 251.

30 Thrall, 681.

31 D. Appleton-Century Co., New York, to the author, March 4, 1940.

Collin McKinney

1 From the inscription on the headstone at his grave. Fulmore, in error, states that McKinney was born in 1776. Fulmore, 73.

2 Younger Scott McKinney, son of Collin McKinney, in *Biographical Souvenir of the State of Texas* (Chicago: P. A. Battey & Co., 1889), 556-557.

3 Order for Election, precinct at Columbus,
  filed at my office this 20th day of July, 1835.
  B. C. Fowler, Clerk

To the Judge of Miller Cty Court:
To the Honorable Judge of the county of Miller your humble petitioners respectfully present that we are without a precinct in this township for holding elections manifestly to the inconvenience of our neighbourhood (to-wit: the neighbourhood of the Spanish Bluffs and Esqr. McKinneys) we furthermore beg leave of your honor to designate a place in this township for holding elections for the above obvious reasons we would suggest Mr. Godly's grocery, near the residence of Mr. Charles Colloms, as a convenient place, we in duty bound will ever pray.

John H. Dyer   George Collom
Blakesley McKinney   Ebenezer Frazier

Chapter Notes

John T. Smith	Charles Collom
Nathaniel D. Ellis	Jas. D. Smith
Collin McKinney	

The original document in January, 1940, was owned by Mr. George Travis Wright, Paris, Texas, and is used with his permission. It was also printed in Pat B. Clark, *The History of Clarksville and Old Red River County* (Dallas: Mathis, Van Nort & Co., 1937), 82-83.

4 Returns.

5 Gammel, I, 824.

6 William Becknell was seated October 3, 1836, in the House of Representatives of the First Congress of the Republic. His election was successfully contested, however, by McKinney who was seated October 10. *Journals of the House of Representatives of the Republic of Texas, First Congress—First Session*, 39.

7 *Journal of the House of Representatives of the Republic of Texas, Second Congress—Adjourned Session*, 3.

8 The Fourth Congress convened November 11, 1839, and McKinney was not seated until December 13, 1839. Harriet Smither (ed.), *Journals of the Fourth Congress of the Republic of Texas, 1839-1840. The House Journal*, 173.

9 In vetoing the bill Houston said:

Gentlemen:—I have under consideration the bill to organize the county of Colon on Red River. By reference to its locality, it will be perceived that it includes within its limits a part of the territory on that river which is now in dispute between Texas and the United States.

The peculiar circumstances of our diplomatic relations respecting the territory in question, are too well known to the honorable congress to require on the present occasion, any detailed remarks relative thereto.

To persevere in the organization of that county while such a state of things exists, regardless of the repeated remonstrance of such acts on the part of Texas by the United States, it is believed would render more complicated the boundary question, and have a tendency to procrastinate the final adjustment of the difficulty which now unhappily exists between the two governments on the subject.

Influenced by these considerations, the Executive is constrained to return this act to the honorable house of representatives without his signatures.

Williams and Barker, II, 235-236.

10 Brown, in 1887, in writing about the first settlers in Collin County said:

A portion of the history of Collin county, in its first settlement, is so closely allied to that of Dallas that I condense a few of the facts. In the same month that John Neely Bryan camped at Dallas (November, 1841), Dr. William E. Throckmorton, from Fannin County, with his family, settled on Throckmorton creek, near the present town of Melissa...In January, 1842 he was joined by Pleasant Wilson, Edmund Dodd, Wm. B. Garnett, Garrett Fitzgerald, and Littleton Bottan.—In February, 1843 McGarrah, Wilcox, Helms, Harlan, Blankenship and Rice were engaged in building at the former's (McGarrah) place, afterward called Buckner, and for a short time after the creation of Collin County in 1846, the county seat...

In 1843—but few settlers ventured into Collin.—In 1844, among others the old patriarch, Collin McKinney, with his sons William and Scott, and widowed daughters, from Red River county.

John Henry Brown, *History of Dallas County, From 1837 to 1887.* (Dallas: Milligan Cornet & Farnham, Printers, 1887).

11 Gammel, II, 1350-1351.

The Act specifies that John McGara [McGarrah], J. C. M. Hodge, Thomas Batton [Bottan], Ashley McKinney, and Pleasant Wilson:

...be and they are hereby appointed commissioners, whose duty it shall be to find the centre of said county, and select two places within three miles of said centre, (having due respect to donations that may be offered by individuals,) for a townsite for the use of the county; the commissioners shall then proceed to hold an election, and the place receiving the greatest number of votes shall be the county seat, and the place so elected, shall be known and called by the name of Buckner...

12 *Ibid.*, III, 112.

13 Thrall, 655.

14 Brown, II, 541.

15 Genealogical information courtesy of Mrs. W. C. Bryant of Anna, Texas, September 2, 1938.

MICHEL BRANAMOUR MENARD

1 Fulmore (85) in 1915 and Dixon (283) in 1924 spelled the name *Michael Branaman Menard.*

2 From the inscription on the headstone at Menard's grave. Dixon (283), in error, states that Menard was born December 5, 1803.

3 In the Book of Foreigners Settled at Nacogdoches, (MS. in Nacogdoches Archives, Texas State Library), he is listed: "Michael Menard—Oath taken December 3, 1829, before Jose Ygnacio Ybarvo. Came from Province of Canada to Nacogdoches three days ago. Catholic. Age 25, merchant, single."

4 In Headright Certificate 251 for one labor of land issued to Menard March 29, 1838, by the Liberty County Board of Land Commissioners it is certified that he arrived in Texas in 1832. File 93, Liberty 1st Class (MS. in General Land Office).

Menard, on June 5, 1835, received title to one league of land in Vehlein's Colony, situated in what is now San Jacinto County. Span. Arch.

5 Returns. For the number of votes each candidate received in Liberty Municipality see the sketch of Augustine B. Hardin in this volume.

6 Gammel, I, 838.

7 Gray, 135.

8 Winkler, 25.

9 Gammel, I, 1130-1131.

10 *Journals of the House of Representatives of the Republic of Texas, Fifth Congress—First Session*, 95.

11 Houston Wade, *Masonic Dictionary, Republic of Texas* (La Grange: La Grange Journal, 1935), 50.

12 Gammel, IV, 931.

WILLIAM MENEFEE

1 From the inscription on the headstone that stood at his grave in Fayette County, Texas. Dixon (229), in error, says that Menefee was born March 28, 1796.

2 On November 24, 1830, Menefee was issued title to one league of land in Austin's Third Colony, situated in what is now Jackson County. Span. Arch. (MSS. in General Land Office), VII, 245. On March 2, 1838, Menefee received Headright No. 91 for one labor of land from the Colorado County Board of Land Commissioners. File 368, Bexar 1st Class (MS. in General Land Office).

3 John S. Menefee, "Early Jackson County History," *Jackson County Clarion*, Texana, Texas, May 20, 1880.

4 Gammel, I, 479.

5 Brown, I, 228. Menefee's same is not attached to the Constitution of 1833. *Constitution or Form of Government of the State of Texas, Made in General Convention, in the Town of San Felipe de Austin, in the month of April, 1833* (New Orleans: Printed at the office of *The Commercial Bulletin*, 1833), 13. Nor is Menefee listed in Elizabeth LeNoir Jennett, *Biographical Directory of the Texan Conventions and Congresses, 1833-1845* (Published by the State of Texas, 1941), 17. Brown, however, secured the names of the delegates from James Kerr, who was a delegate.

6 Gammel, I, 544.

7 *Ibid.*, 637.

8 Gammel, I, 1034-1035.

9 *Ibid.*, 757.

10 Returns. For the number of votes received by each candidate in Colorado Municipality see the sketch of William D. Lacey in this volume.

11 Gammel, I, 825.

12 On April 20, 1836, Gray recorded in his diary:

Left Williams' at 7 o'clock; $1. As we approached the Neches, we found there was great uncertainty about crossing the river. The boats were said to have been taken from all the ferries and carried down to the lower bluff. Thither we bent our way, passing great numbers of fugitives, men, women and children, black and white, with all the accustomed marks of dismay. Arrived about noon at lower bluff...

The report of the Mexicans being on Cow Creek is not credited here. It is believed to have been circulated by Rains, McLaughlin, etc. There are many families here waiting to be ferried across the bay, a distance of seven or eight miles, and put on the United States shore. There are at last 1,000 fugitives here, among them Menifee, A. B. Hardin, Smith, [Smyth], John Fisher, all members of the convention.

Gray, 166-167.

13 Winkler, 34.

14 *Ibid.*, 190.

15 *Ibid.*, 194.

16 Ernest William Winkler, "The Seat of Government of Texas," *The Quarterly of the Texas State Historical Association* (Austin: Published; by the Association, 1907), X, 215-217.

17 *Journal of the House of Representatives, Republic of Texas, Called Session of September 25, 1837, And Regular Session, Commencing November 6, 1837*, 21.

18 *Journal of the House of Representatives of the Republic of Texas, Regular Session of the Third Congress, Nov. 5, 1838*, 3.

19 Harriet Smither, (ed.), *Journals of the Fourth Congress of*

the Republic of Texas, 1830-1840, Vol. II, House Journal, unnumbered page opposite page 1.

20 *Journal of the House of Representatives of the Republic of Texas, Fifth Congress, First Session*, 3.

21 *Journal of the House of Representatives of the Republic of Texas Ninth Congress*, 4.

22 Elizabeth Le Noir Jennett, *Biographical Directory of the Texan Conventions and Congresses, 1832-1845*. (Published by the State of Texas, 1941), 137-138.

JOHN W. MOORE

1 Goodrich.

2 Moore received title to one league of land in Austin's Second Colony, April 28, 1831. The land was surveyed in what are now Wharton and Fort Bend Counties. Span. Archives (MSS. in General Land Office), V, 1158. In Headright Certificate 507 issued April 21, 1838, by the Harrisburg County Board of Land Commissioners, it is certified that Moore came to Texas in 1830. File 614, Bexar 1st Class (MS. in General Land Office.)

3 Barker, Minutes, XXIV, 162.

4 Gammel, I, 510.

5 *Ibid.*, 567.

6 *Ibid.*, 725.

7 *Ibid.*, 728.

8 Returns.

9 *Ibid.*

10 Gammel, I, 848.

11 *Ibid.*, 883.

12 Moore received the following order:

War Dept., March 17, 1836 - To Captn John W. Moore

Sir, You are hereby authorised & commanded to call out & immediately organise two thirds of the Militia of the Municipality of Harrisburg of ninety days service & report yourself to this Dept. so soon as organised— all communications directed to me at Harrisburg—By order of the President.

THOMAS J. RUSK
Secretary of War

Binkley, I, 512.

13 *Journals of the House of Representatives of the Republic of Texas, First Congress—First Session* (Houston: Published at the office of *The Telegraph and Texas Register*, 1838), 3.

14 *Ibid.*, 41.

15 Record of Board of Commissioners and Election Returns, A. Briscoe, C. J., Jan. 30, 1837, to June 26, 1866 (MS. in Probate Department, County Clerk's Office, Houston, Harris County).

16 Following is a copy of a letter written by Sheriff Moore to President Lamar, March 10, 1839:

Oweing the suspension of issues from the treasury of the Republic for some time past—and my pecuniary embarrassments, occasioned by the great expense of keeping prisoners confined in the common jail of the county—I am under the necessity of asking of your aid, in your official capacity, provided it is within your power to extend it—by ordering a portion at least of any funds in the treasury subject to the order of your Excellency.

I am ready at any time you will appoint to call on your Excellency—exhibit my claims & situation and receive your Excellency's answer.

Charles Adams Gulick, Jr. and Katherine Elliott, (eds.) *The Papers of Mirabeau Buonaparte Lamar*, (Austin: Texas State Library, 1922), II, 489.

17 Minutes of the Houston City Council (MSS. in City Secretary's Office, Houston), A, 1. Courtesy of Andrew F. Muir.

18 Marriage Records of Harris County (MSS. in County Clerk's Office, Houston), A, 96.

19 Probate Records of Harris County (MSS. in County Clerk's Office, Houston), G, 280.

20 Courtesy of Andrew F. Muir, Houston.

Our (unlikely) Fathers

Junius William Mottley

1 Goodrich. Dixon (198) without quoting his authority states that Dr. Mottley was born April 9, 1812. Mrs. Charles F. Norton, Librarian of Transylvania College, wrote to the author, January 3, 1940, that the records of the college do not give the date of Mottley's birth.

2 Headright Certificate 235 for one-third of a league of land, the amount due a single man, was issued in Dr. Mottley's name, but delivered to his heirs, February 22, 1838, by the Milam County Board of Land Commissioners. File 1157, Milam 1st Class (MS. in General Land Office, Austin.)

3 E. Polk Johnson, *A History of Kentucky and Kentuckians...* (Chicago: The Lewis Publishing Co., 1912), II, 1146.

4 Comp. M. S. R.

5 Returns.

6 Gray, 114.

7 *Ibid.*, 116.

8 Gammel, I, 824.

9 Bounty Certificate 3704 for 1920 acres of land was issued in Dr. Mottley's name June 5, 1838, due him for having served in the army from March 1 to April 21, 1836, and for having been killed while in the service. File 613, Milam Bounty (MS. in General Land Office, Austin.) He had, of course, entered the army prior to March 1, but this was not stated in the certificate. This was perhaps thought unnecessary since his heirs received the maximum amount of bounty land a soldier was entitled to receive. Donation Certificate 259 for 640 acres of land was issued in his name May 30, 1838, due him for having participated in the Battle of San Jacinto. File 149, Travis Donation (MS. in General Land Office).

10 Deed Records of Travis County, (MSS. in County Clerk's Office, Austin), B, 32.

11 Gammel, VIII, 1076.

CHAPTER NOTES

JOSE ANTONIO BALDOMERO NAVARRO

1 Frederick C. Chabot, *With the Makers of San Antonio* (San Antonio: Artes Graficas, 1937), 202.

2 *Ibid.*

3 Charles Adams Gulick, Jr. and Katherine Elliott (eds.) *The Papers of Mirabeau Buonaparte Lamar* (Austin: Texas State Library, 1923), III, 597-598.

4 J. De Cordova. *Texas: Her Resources and Her Public Men* (Philadelphia: First Edition, E. Crozet, 1858), 147.

5 Fulmore, 113.

6 Span. Arch., XLII, 97.

7 *Ibid.*, LVIII, 176.

8 De Cordova, *Texas: Her Resources and Her Public Men*, 148.

9 Fulmore, 113.

10 De Cordova, *Texas: Her Resources and Her Public Men*, 148-149.

11 *Ibid.*, 149.

12 Gammel, I, 982.

13 Gray, 122.

14 Returns.

15 Gammel, I, 824.

16 Gray, 127.

17 *Ibid.*, 180.

18 *Journal of the House of Representatives, Republic of Texas, Regular Session of the Third Congress, Nov. 5, 1838*, 7.

19 Harriet Smither (ed.), *Journals of the Fourth Congress of the Republic of Texas, 1839-1840*. The House Journal, 6.

20 Following is a copy of a petition sent to General Houston in behalf of Navarro, December 11, 1844:

Republic of Texas, Washington County
To his Excellency, Genl Sam Houston

Our (unlikely) Fathers

The petition of the undersigned, lately prisoners of war in Mexico, would respectfully represent that they have reason to believe, from information acquired while in prison, that it is in the power of your Excellency to procure the release of their unfortunate fellow countryman, Antonio Navarro.

Your petitioners are aware that the influence of your Excellency's character with General Santa Anna would be sufficient to bend the will of that despot. Your magnanimity towards him in his own final restoration to liberty having given you claims upon his gratitude which even his heart cannot resist.

Your petitioners, therefore, request, that you will write to General Santa Anna soliciting, as a personal favor, to yourself, that he will return to his country and to the bosom of his family the unhappy, long-suffering and brave and constant Antonio Navarro.

John Hoffer	David Allen
John R. Baker	G. N. Harris
William Kaigler	Francis Hughes
Peter Menard Maxwell	John Johnson
James Calvert	James R. Nealy
Claudius Buster	Wm. Mallon
F. S. Thomson	J. G. W. Pierson

Copy sent to the author by Mr. Houston Wade.

21 "There is one remarkable coincidence in the life of Navarro which I will here relate, being as curious as it is true. It is the following coincidence of dates. He left Austin to go to the comp of the Santa Fe expedition on the 18th June, 1841. After being made prisoner at Laguna Colorado, he left San Miguel del Valdo for Mexico on the 18th of October, 1841. After his arrival in Mexico, he was tried by courtmartial, and was sentenced to death on the 18th May, 1842. After the sentence was annulled by the Supreme Court-Martial, he was conducted to San Juan de Ulloa, having left the Acordada on the 18th October, 1843. On the 18th of December, 1844, he was taken out from San Juan de Ulloa, and allowed to remain a prisoner on parole in Vera Cruz. When he

CHAPTER NOTES

escaped from Vera Cruz, coming by way of Havana, he arrived at New Orleans on the 18th January, 1845. And lastly on the 18 February, 1845, he had the pleasure of embracing his wife and children at San Geronimo, near Seguin." De Cordova, *Texas: Her Resources and Her Public Men*, 153;

22 Oran M. Roberts, "The Political Legislative, and Judicial History of Texas for its Fifty Years of Statehood, 1845-1895." Dudley G. Wooten, *A Comprehensive History of Texas* (Dallas: William G. Scarff, 1898), II, 8.

23 *Journals of the Senate, First Legislature, State of Texas*, 4.

24 *Journals of the Senate, Second Legislature, State of Texas*, 4.

25 Gammel, II, 132-133.

26 Thrall, 686.

27 Fulmore, 113.

28 Houston Wade, *Masonic Dictionary of the Republic of Texas* (La Grange, Texas: *La Grange Journal*, 1935), 53.

MARTIN PARMER

1 Bible record of the Parmer family. Courtesy of Mrs. J. W. Terry, Navasota, March 4, 1936.

2 Yoakum, I, 247.

3 Copy sent to author by Judge J. M. Deaver, of El Paso, February 10, 1940.

4 Adjutant General A. S. Adams to United States Senator Tom Connally, March 5, 1940. Letter in possession of the author.

5 Louis Houck, *History of Missouri*, III, 157. Courtesy of Floyd Shoemaker, Secretary of the State Historical Society of Missouri, Columbia, November 17, 1939.

6 Courtesy of Mr. Shoemaker.

7 *The History of Clay and Platte Counties, Missouri*. Courtesy of Mr. Shoemaker.

8 Courtesy of Mr. Shoemaker.

9 Brown, I, 136.

10 *Senate Journal, Third General Assembly, Missouri, Special Session* (1836), 9.

11 *Ibid.,* 13.

12 Chichester Chaplin had married Emily Panner, daughter of Martin Parmer. Foote was mistaken in stating that Chaplin was a son-in-law of Haden Edwards. Henry Stuart Foote, *Texas and The Texans* (Philadelphia: Thomas Cowperthwait & Co., 1841), I, 229. Yoakum (239), probably following Foote, made the same mistake.

13 Foote, *Texas and The Texans*, I, 233.

14 Yoakum, I, 244.

15 And the Court being sworn in took their seats.

It was determined by the Court that martial Law shall be enforced in the town, and every American be compelled to bear arms, or be put under arrest, and fined according to the pleasure of the Court. This law shall be in force until ordered by the Court.

"ORDER TO THE SERGEANT OF THE GUARD"

You are commanded to bring forthwith every American in the village and compel him to bear arms—if he refuses, put him under arrest.

Martin Palmer [sic]
Col. Commander in Chief
Sergeant of the Guard.

Barker, *Austin*, Vol. II, Part II, 1515-1522.

16 *Ibid.,* 1519.

17 The following is from the verdict rendered in the case of Norris:

We, the Court Martial, find Samuel Norris late Alcalda of the District of Nacogdoches, worthy of death, but in consideration of his ignorance, and the influence of infamous advisors over him sentence him to be deprived of the office of Alcalda of said District, and forever incapable of holding any office, trust, honor or profit, in the said District and in case of his resuming or attempting to resume its functions, that his punishment of death shall be inflicted on him.— And that he be forever incapable of holding any office of trust, honor or profit within the said District.—

Martin Palmer [sic]
Col. Commandant Nacogdoches

Ibid., 1522.

18 *Ibid.*, 1558.

19 Order for the Arrest of Martin Palmer

The Political Chief of Texas, to the Military Commander of Texas.

The Citizen Alcalde of the town of San Felipe de Austin in a communication of the 16th inst. informs me that Martin Palmer, a citizen of the U. S. of North America, and one of the principal lenders of the outbreak in the Village of Nacogdoches toward the end of 1826, passed through that town on the 10th inst. with a passport from the Mexican Consul at New Orleans, on his way to the new town of Gonzales. As the communication of his Excellency the Commanding General Inspector of these States, which your Lordship has been pleased to transmit to me yesterday alludes to that man, and also to the entry by land of his son, Isom Palmer, to join him, and considering that he may attempt to disturb good order and public peace in this Department, I have thought it to be my duty to suggest to your Lordship the expediency of arresting both these men. I will on my part give orders to the Commissioner of the Supreme Government to the Town of Gonzales to call upon the assistance of the Empresario and Commissary of Police, in order to secure the persons of these individuals, and to deliver them to the scouting party, which I hope your Lordship will send there with your instructions on this subject.

God and Liberty. Bexar, April 26, 1831

Ramon Musquiz, Chieftancy of the Dept of Bexar

OUR (unlikely) FATHERS

Nacogdoches Archives (MSS. in Archives, Texas State Library), LVII, 100. Courtesy of Mr. R. B. Blake, Nacogdoches.

20 Gammel, I, 532.

21 Yoakum, I, 247.

Martin Partner was only one of the extraordinary characters that appeared in Texas about that time. His life had been a thrilling romance. He was born in Virginia, in 1775. At twenty years of age he emigrated to Tennessee, where he married Miss Sarah Hardwick. He was engaged for sometime in superintending the works of Montgomery Bell, of Dickson County. But his ambition was not satisfied. In 1818 he emigrated to Missouri, and settled fifty miles above the highest county formed in the then territory—surrounded by the Sioux, Iowa, and the Osage Indians. He gave fifty dollars for a bear dog, and by the chase kept such supplies of meat as drew the Indians around him. One of them, called *Two Heart* (from the fact that he had killed a white man and eaten his heart,) came to partake of his bounty, when he spread before him a large quantity of meat, and, standing over him with a drawn knife [Parmer] forced him to eat till it ultimately killed him!

Parmer had numerous and fearful fights with the savages, but at last acquired an influence over them, which induced the government at Washington to appoint him an Indian agent. He was elected colonel of the militia, and then a member of the convention to form a state constitution. It was shortly after taking a seat in this body, that, two of the members getting into a fight, he interfered in behalf of one of the parties, announcing himself as the "Ringtailed Panther," by which name he afterwards was known in the west. After serving two or three terms in the Missouri legislature, Parmer emigrated to Texas, and settled near Mound prairie [now near Alto in Cherokee County]. It is said he fired the first gun of the Fredonian war.

Among the numerous stories told of him, it is related upon good authority, that when his bear dog died, he sent fifty miles for a clergyman to attend the funeral, which he actu-

406

ally did—supposing it to be one of Colonel Parmer's family! His son [Thomas], from whom the above account is obtained, says he heard the sermon.

22 Gammel, I, 532.

23 *Ibid.*, 534.

24 *Ibid.*, I, 663.

25 Returns. For the number of votes received by the candidates in San Augustine Municipality see the sketch of E. O. Le Grand in this volume.

26 Gammel, I, 824.

27 Gammel, I, 900-901.

28 Gray, 131-135.

29 Winkler, 135.

30 *Ibid.*, 175.

31 Fulmore (90) states that Parmer died in 1837. Thrall (597) says Parmer died soon after the revolution. Dixon (153) states that Parmer died in 1857.

407

Mrs. J. W. Terry, Navasota, Texas, on March 4, 1936, wrote to the author: "As to the date of his [Parmer's] death; the family Bible of his daughter Matilda Palmer [Morris] now owned by her daughter Mrs. A. E. Nation, carries the following entry—'Colonel Martin Parmer Died March 2nd A. D. 1850.'"

32 Gammel, VIII, 1078.

33 Barker: *Austin*, Vol. II, Part II, 1554-1555.

34 Nacogdoches Archives (MSS. in Archives, Texas State Library), LXXXIX. Courtesy of R. B. Blake, Nacogdoches.

SYDNEY O. PENINGTON

1 Dixon (193-195) lists Penington as *Sidney Oswald Penington*, says he same to Texas in 1832 and thinks he died in about 1859.

2 Penington to Dr. Benjamin Goodrich.

3 In Headright Certificate 167 for one-third of a league of land issued March 14, 1838, by the Shelby County Board of Land Commissioners in Penington's name, but delivered to William Watson, administrator of his estate, it is certified that Penington was "an emigrant of the year Eighteen hundred and Thirty four." File 220, Shelby 1st Class (MS. in General Land Office, Austin).

4 Comp. M. S. R.

5 On December 16, 1853, Donation Certificate 647 for 640 acres of land was issued in Penington's name, but delivered to his heirs, due him for having participated in the storming and capture of Bexar, December 5 to 10, 1835. File 245, Houston County Donation (MS. in General Land Office). On December 16, 1853, Bounty Certificate 1835 for 320 acres of land was issued in Penington's name, due him for having served in the army for a period of three months in 1835. File 290, Houston County Bounty (MS. in General Land Office).

6 Gammel, I, 994.

7 Returns.

8 Gammel, I, 824.

9 Army Rolls (MS. in General Land Office), 124. Following are copies of Comptroller's Military Service Records:

Harrisburg
4th May 1836
Rec'd of Sydney O. Penington a rifle for the use of the Volunteers of my Company valued at eighteen dollars.

Rec'd by Me
James Chessher, Capt.

Victoria
June 22, 1836
This may certify that Sydney O. Penington furnished Lewis Wells of Company one grey mule valued at sixty dollars and one double barrelled shot gun valued at forty dollars for the purposes of forwarden letters from the army to San Augustine.   Jas Chessher, Capt.

(MSS. in Archives, Texas State Library).

10 Army Rolls (MSS. in General Land Office), 199.

11 *Ibid.*, 51.

12 Elizabeth Le Noir Jennett, *Biographical Directory of the Texan Conventions and Congresses, 1832-1845* (Published by the State of Texas. 1941), 23.

13 Letter Book of the Department of State (MS. in the Texas State Library, Austin), II, 51.

14 The inscription on the monument has the following mistakes in it. The name is spelled *Pennington*; he is shown as having participated in the Battle of San Jacinto, and as having died in 1838.

15 The records in this case, called to the attention of the writer by Mrs. Walter M. Burgess, Dallas, are in File 698 in the office of the District Clerk, Center, Shelby County, Texas.

16 Frank H. Bassett, County Clerk of Christian County, Kentucky, wrote to the author December 20, 1939, that a Jacob Pennington and his wife, Mary, were living on Pond River in Christian County, Kentucky, in 1820 on land patented to them August 10, 1819.

17 The original will was filed at Shelbyville and was destroyed when the courthouse of Shelby County burned. A copy of it was recorded in Book of Wills (MS. in County Clerk's Office, San Augustine), I, 553.

18 Domestic Correspondence (MSS. in Archives, Texas State Library). Binkley copies the letter but, in error, he has the signature as *Pennington*. Binkley, II, 683.

ROBERT POTTER

1 Potter's brilliance and spectacular career attracted many biographers. None of them attempted to fix the exact date of his birth except Dixon (220), who, in error, set it at January 8, 1800.

Capt. Randal Jacobs, Assistant Chief of the Bureau of Navigation, Navy Department, Washington, D. C., on November 10, 1939, furnished United States Senator Tom Connally with the naval record of Potter, which Senator Connally forwarded to the author. In his letter of transmittal, Captain Jacobs wrote: "No specific place of birth has been found. All encyclopedia sketches give Granville County, and in his oath of allegiance he states that he is of Granville County. His letter of acceptance states 'I shall be sixteen years of age in June next.' This was written on 28 March, 1815.

On the monument at the grave of Robert Potter it is stated that he was born in 1800 and died March 3, 1842.

2 Joseph Blount Cheshire, *Nonnulla, Memories, Stories, Traditions, More or Less Authentic* (Chapel Hill: The University of North Carolina Press, 1930), 64.

3 Capt. Randall Jacobs to Senator Tom Connally, November 10, 1939.

4 Cheshire, *Nonnulla*, 64.

5 Robert Watson Winston, "Robert Potter: Tar Heel and Texas Dare devil," *The South Atlantic Quarterly*, April, 1930. A copy of the *Quarterly* was sent to the author by Mr. Samuel E. Asbury, College Station, Texas.

6 Cheshire, *Nonnulla*, 76.

7 Robert Watson Winston, in *The South Atlantic Quarterly*, April, 1930.

8 Cheshire, *Nonnulla*, 79-80.

9 In Headright Certificate for one league and one labor of land, the amount due a married man living with his wife, issued to Potter March 14, 1838, by the Red River County Board of Land Commissioners, it is certified that he arrived in Texas, July 1, 1835. File 287, Red River 1st Class (MS. in the General Land Office, Austin).

10 Unpublished Austin Papers (MSS. in the Archives, University of Texas Library, Austin), Series 3. Courtesy of R. B. Blake, Nacogdoches.

11 Gammel, I, 608.

12 Binkley, I, 151.

13 Gammel, I, 611.

14 Returns. For the number of votes each candidate in Nacogdoches Municipality received see the sketch of Thomas J. Rusk in this volume. Incidentally, Potter received three votes more than did John K. Allen, who with his brother, A. C., later founded the City of Houston.

15 Gray, 89-90.

16 Gammel, I, 824.

17 *Ibid.*, 847.

18 Binkley, II, 641.

19 Army Rolls (MSS. in General Land Office), 41. Page was issued Donation Certificate 698 for 640 acres of land, December 18, 1838, for having been detailed to guard the baggage at the camp opposite Harrisburg, April 21, 1836.

20 The History of Harriet A. Ames during the early days of Texas. Written by herself at the age of eighty-three. 20-21. (MS. in the Library of the University of Texas).

21 *Ibid.*, 20-21.

22 *Ibid.*, 25. The marriage of Potter and Mrs. Page having been declared invalid by the Supreme Court of Texas, the author has refrained from referring to the lady as Mrs. Potter.

411

23 Minutes of the 11th District Court (MSS. in District Clerk's Office, Houston), B, 280. The original papers in the case, including Page's petition, have been lost. Courtesy of Andrew F. Muir, Houston, Texas.

24 Winkler, 182.

25 *Ibid.*, 204.

26 The History of Harriet A. Ames, 45-53.

27 Gammel, VIII, 1076.

28 Lewis vs. Ames in 44 *Texas Reports*, 319-351. All facts relative to the case against William P. Rose, Preston Rose, Scott, Peters, Perkins, Miller, Williams, Smith, Jones and Fuller are from this source.

OUR (unlikely) FATHERS

JAMES POWER

1 Inscription on the monument at Power's grave, Mount Calvary Cemetery, Refugio.

2 Mary Virginia Henderson, "Minor Empresario Contracts for the Colonization of Texas, 1825-1834," in *The Southwestern Historical Quarterly* (Austin: The Texas State Historical Association, 1929), XXXII, 10-12.

3 Gammel, I, 130.

4 *Ibid.*, 223.

5 Henderson, "Minor Empresario Contracts," 10-12.

6 Span. Arch., XVII, 14, 119, 162.

7 Binkley, I, 581.

8 Gammel, I, 581.

9 Binkley, I, 298.

10 Gammel, I, 674.

11 Returns.

12 *Ibid.*

13 Gammel, I, 824.

14 Courtesy of Hobart Huson, Refugio.

15 William E. Walker was seated after election unsuccessfully contested by Elkanah Brush; Power named in a special election to succeed Walker. Elizabeth LeNoir Jennett, *Biographical Directory of the Texan Conventions and Congresses, 1882-1845* (Printed by the State of Texas, 1939), 25-26.

16 Oran M. Roberts, "The Political, Legislative and Judicial History of Texas for its Fifty Years of Statehood, 1845-1895," in Wooten, II, 8.

17 Inscription on monument at Power's grave.

Chapter Notes

John S. Roberts

1 From the inscription that was on the old headstone that stood at Roberts' grave. This corrects Dixon (249) who stated that Roberts was born in 1795. Dixon (249) also states that Roberts participated in the Battle of New Orleans, January 8, 1815. Maj. Gen. E. S. Adams, Adjutant General of the United States, on September 7, 1939, wrote to the author that the War Department had no record of Roberts' having served in the War of 1812.

2 Unpublished sketch of Roberts by R. B. Blake, Nacogdoches. Roberts received title to one league of land in Zavala's Colony, situated in the present county of Chambers, January 12, 1835. (Span. Arch. MS. in General Land Office, Austin), XXXIV, 95. He was issued Headright Certificate 421 for one labor of land March 19, 1838, by the Nacogdoches County Board of Land Commissioners. File 1013, Nacogdoches 1st Class (MS. in General Land Office).

In the Certificate of Character issued to Roberts October 7, 1834, Luis Prosela, successively First Regidor and Alcalde, it is stated: "Is married, was married in the Holy Mother Church in this town."

3 From the official report of Gen. Edward Burleson, printed in Brown, I, 417-426.

4 Roberts was issued Bounty Certificate 904 for 320 acres of land, July 29, 1852, for having served in the army for a period of three months in the year 1835. File 423, Nacogdoches Bounty (MS. in the General Land Office). On July 8, 1851, he received Donation Certificate 350 for 640 acres of land for having participated in the storming and capture of Bexar, December 5 to 10, 1835. File 350, Nacogdoches Donation (MS. in the General Land Office).

5 Span. Arch., XXXIV, 95. The grant was made to Roberts through Samuel M. Williams, Francis W. Johnson and Robert Peebles by Commissioner Radford Berry. This was cancelled by the Texas government.

6 Eugene C. Barker, "Land Speculations as a cause of the Texas

Revolution" in *The Quarterly of the Texas State Historical Association* (1907), X, 76-95.

7 Returns. For the number of votes received by the various candidates in Nacogdoches Municipality see the sketch of Thomas J. Rusk in this volume.

8 Barker: *Austin*, Vol. II, Part II, 1519.

9 Williams & Barker, II, 307.

10 Courtesy of R. B. Blake.

11 Wade, 55.

12 Gammel, VIII, 1076.

13 *Ibid.*, II, 37-38.

Sterling Clack Robertson

1 Fulmore, 47.

2 John Henry Brown, *Indian Wars and Pioneers of Texas* (St. Louis: Nixon-Jones Printing Co.), 392.

3 Fulmore, 47.

4 Charles W. Ramsdell (ed.), *The History of Bell County*, by George W. Tyler (San Antonio: The Naylor Co., 1936), 3.

5 Mary Virginia Henderson, "Minor Empresario Contracts for the Colonization of Texas, 1825-1834," *The Southwestern Historical Quarterly*, XXXI (1928), 319.

6 Fulmore, 49-50.

7 Gammel, I, 241-242.

8 Following is a copy of the order sent to Steele:

Viesca, Nov. 27, 1835
To William H. Steele

In compliance with an ordinance passed by the chosen Delegates of all Texas in general convention assembled on the 14th. inst. to take charge of all the archives belonging to the different land offices in the Department of Brazos and deposit the same in safe places secure from the ravages of fire or the devastation of enemies, and directed to us as commissioners to carry the same into effect, we require of you forthwith to deliver over to us, all the books, documents, and papers, contained in the land offices now under your charge at this place.

With due consideration, we are, respectfully &c,

> Robt. Peebles
> C. C. Dyer

Binkley, I, 149-150.

9 The answer of Steele:

Commission of Colonization
for the Nashville Colony
November 27, 1835
To Messrs Peebles & Dyer

Gentlemen:

I received your communication dated Viesca Novr. 27, 1835, in which you as the Commissioners of the Delegates of Texas in Convention assembled, require of me to deliver to you forthwith all the Books, documents &c belonging to the Archives of this Colony now under my charge, and in answer to which I must say that the authority under which I now discharge the duty of Commissioner of the state of Coahuila & Texas and that of the General Government of Mexico, that when the People of Texas elected a consultation they delegated to them no power whatever to Legislate, they were elected alone to advise the people of their condition, and if possible to advise measures to sustain that law and the Constitution our Fellow Citizens are in arms, and in conclusion I am forced to say that I cannot recognise in said consultation or any person acting under their authority any right whatever to demand or receive of me the Archives of this Colony under my charge.

Ibid., I, 150.

10 Gammel, I, 947.

11 *Ibid.*, 677.

415

12 Binkley, I, 218.

13 Returns. For the number of votes received by the various candidates in Milam Municipality see the sketch of George C. Childress in this volume.

14 At Washington, Texas, on March 5, 1836, General Houston addressed the following order to Robertson:

Sir—You will proceed forthwith to the United States and are hereby authorized to raise such number of Troops as may be in your power for the service of Texas for two years or during the present war—in the event of a company or Regiment being raised the men shall have the power of electing their own officers who will report their command to the Head Quarters of the Army of Texas without delay.

That this order was probably countermanded is evidenced by the fact that on December 22, 1845, Bounty Certificate No. 10043 for 640 acres of land was issued in his name, but delivered to his son, due him for having served in the army from April 20 to September 20, 1836. File 496, Milam Bounty (MS. in General Land Office). On May 1, 1846, Donation Certificate 7 for 640 acres of land was issued in Robertson's name, due him "for having been detailed to guard the encampment near Harrisburg, April 21, 1836." File 494, Milam Donation (MS. in General Land Office).

15 *Richmond Enquirer*, June 12, 1836.

16 Gammel, I, 1398.

17 Thrall, 691.

18 Gammel, I, 1445.

JOSE FRANCISCO RUIZ

1 Record of San Fernando Church, San Antonio. See Frederick C. Chabot, *With The Makers of San Antonio* (San Antonio: Artes Graficas, 1937), 198.

2 Charles Adams Gulick, Jr. and Katherine Elliott (eds.), *The Papers of Mirabeau Buonaparte Lamar* (Austin: Texas State Library, 1924), III, 597.

3 Courtesy of Dr. G. E. Castaneda, Latin-American Librarian, Library of the University of Texas, Austin, January 8, 1940.

4 "The suppression of the Fredonian rebellion took a large Mexican force to Texas in the spring of 1827, and General Bustamente was preparing for a campaign of extermination when peace overtures came from all the marauding tribes. On May 13, after conferring with Austin, Bustamente signed a treaty with the principal Karankawa chief, Antonito. This renewed the treaty of September, 1824; fixed the eastern range of the Indians at the Lavaca River; pledged Antonito to bring all the Karankawas and Cokes into the peace or to abandon them to their fate in war with the colonists; and allowed Austin to keep as a hostage a Karankawa woman and some children who had been captured, until convinced of the good faith of the Indians. At the same time a delegation of Wacos and Tahuacanos assured Colonel Francisco Ruiz at Nacogdoches of their desire for peace, and he seems to have accompanied them to San Antonio, where Bustamente concluded a treaty with them and also with the Comanches." Eugene C. Barker, *The Life of Stephen F. Austin* (Dallas: Cokesbury Press, 1925), 166.

5 Louis J. Wortham, *A History of Texas*...(Ft. Worth; Wortham-Molyneaux Co., 1924, I, 361-362.

6 Barker, *The Life of Stephen F. Austin*, 339-340.

7 *Ibid.*, 401.

8 Span. Arch., XXIX, 29.

9 *Ibid.*, XXX, 205.

10 Barker: *Austin Papers*, III, 470.

11 The report of the election held by the civilians of Bexar is not in the Convention Election Returns in the Archives of the Texas State Library. William Fairfax Gray, who attended the Convention as a spectator and recorded in a dairy what he saw and heard there, stated that Ruiz, Navarro, Arciniega, and Seguin were the delegates chosen by Bexar Municipality. Gray, 122.

12 The memorial is copied in full in the sketch of Jesse B. Badgett in this volume. The original is in the Archives of the Texas State Library. Austin.

13 Gammel, I, 824.

14 Frederick C. Chabot, *With The Makers of San Antonio*, 200.

Following is the account of the burning of the martyrs of the Alamo as related by Francisco Ruiz, Jr., translated by J. H. Quintero, and printed on pages 80-81 of the *Texas Almanac*, Galveston, of 1860.

Francisco Ruiz, the alcalde of San Antonio, gives some important additional details. He says:

On the 6th March (1836) at 3 a.m., General Santa Anna at the head of 4,000 men advanced against the Alamo. The infantry, artillery and cavalry had formed about 1,000 varas from the walls of the same fortress. The Mexican army charged and were twice repulsed by the deadly fire of Travis' artillery, which resembled a constant thunder. At the third charge to Toluca battalion commenced to scale the walls and suffered severely. Out of 830 men only 130 were left live.

When the Mexican army entered the walls, I with the political chief, Don Ramon Musquiz and other members of the corporation, accompanied by the curate, Don Refugio de la Garza, who by Santa Anna's orders had assembled during the night at a temporary fortification on Protero Street, with the object of attending the wounded, etc. As soon as the storming commenced we crossed the bridge on Commerce street, with this object in view and about 100 yards from the same a party of Mexican dragoons fired upon us and compelled us to fall back on the river and the place we occupied before. Half an hour had elapsed when Santa Anna sent one of his aides-de-camp with an order for us to come before him. He directed me to call on some of the neighbors to come with carts to carry the (Mexican) dead to the cemetery and to accompany him, as he was desirous to have Col. Travis, Bowie, and Crockett shown to him.

On the north battery of the fortress convent, lay the lifeless body of Col. Travis on the gun carriage, shot only through the forehead. Towards the west, and in a small fort opposite the city, we found the body of Col. Crockett. Col. Bowie was

418

found dead in his bed in one of the rooms on the south side.

Santa Anna, after all the Mexican bodies had been taken out, ordered wood to be brought to burn the bodies of the Texans. He sent a company of dragoons with me to bring wood and dry branches from the neighboring forests. About three o'clock in the afternoon of March 6, we laid the wood and dry branches upon which a pile of dead bodies were placed, more wood was piled on them and another pile of bodies was brought and in this manner they were all arranged in layers. Kindling wood was distributed through the pile and about 5 o'clock in the evening it was lighted.

The dead Mexicans of Santa Anna were taken to the graveyard, but not having sufficient room for them, I ordered some to be thrown into the river, which was done on the same day.

The gallantry of the few Texans who defended the Alamo was really wondered at by the Mexican army. Even the generals were astonished at their vigorous resistance and how dearly victory was bought.

The generals, who under Santa Anna participated in the storming of the Alamo, were Juan Amador, Castrillon, Ramirez y Sesma and Andrade.

The men (Texans) burnt were one hundred and eighty-two. I was an eyewitness, for as Alcalde of San Antonio, I was, with some of the neighbors, collecting the dead bodies and placing them on the funeral pyre.

15 Chabot, *With the Makers of San Antonio*, 199.

16 The Commission of Control for Texas Centennial Celebrations in 1936 appropriated funds with which to erect a monument to the memory of Francisco Ruiz. The monument was erected in the Ruiz family cemetery twelve miles south of San Antonio, where descendants of Colonel Ruiz said he was buried. It has since been established that he was buried in San Fernando Church, now the Cathedral of the Archdiocese of San Antonio.

17 Dixon, 317-318.

18 Marriage Records, Mission Purisima Concepcion, San An-

tonio.

19 Chabot, *With The Makers of San Antonio*, 199-200.

20 Miss Anita A. Ruiz, El Paso, to the author, September 6, 1941.

THOMAS JEFFERSON RUSK

1 Monument at the grave of General Rusk, Oak Grove Cemetery, Nacogdoches. Dr. Benjamin B. Goodrich erroneously listed Rusk as twenty-nine years of age in March, 1836, when as a matter of fact he was about 32.

2 *The Texas Almanac* for 1858, 105-109. The Almanac was "Prepared, Printed and Published by Richardson & Co., at the 'News' Office," Galveston, in 1857.

3 On November 5, 1835, Rusk received title to one league of land in Burnet's Colony situated in what is now Cherokee County. The title was issued by Commissioner George A. Nixon. Span. Arch., XXIII, 1015.

The following was copied from Headright Certificate 214 issued to Rusk February 8, 1838: "This is to certify that Thos. J. Rusk has appeared before the Board of Land Commissioners for the County of Nacogdoches, and proved according to law he arrived in this Republic, Feby...A.D. Eighteen hundred and thirty five and that he is a married man and [since he has received one league] is entitled to one labor of land..." File 7311, Nacogdoches, 1st Class (MS. in General Land Office).

4 Yoakum, II, 17.

5 Gammel, I, 646.

6 *Ibid.*, 647.

7 Rusk in his letter to Judge Taylor said:

I am by force of circumstances, over which I have no control, thrown into a responsible position. You are apprized that I have been appointed by the General Council to proceed east of the Trinity to forward on recruits to the theatre of war. In the same resolutions which appointed me, I am fully

authorized to make any contract for the purpose of support-
ing these troops and if necessary press articles into service
receipting for them by a resolution of that council, since the
fall of San. Antonio. I am requested to enroll volunteers and
regulars for the service. I have unfortunately seen a disposition throughout the country to procrastinate the time of
mustering a respectable force in the field until spring. We
are at war with an enemy whose success heretofore has been
entirely owing to the celerity of his movements. Many persons are now in our town and many more will arrive in a few
days from the U. S. I have no means of mustering them into
service for the want of provisions. I am not willing that the
country should suffer by any neglect of mine, and you as
well as all others must at once perceive the consequence to
our cause by the return to the U. S. of men who have volunteered themselves in our cause. I have therefore, although
an unpleasant office, felt myself under the necessity of calling on you to furnish we with One Thousand Dollars of the
publick funds in your hands to enable me to muster these
men into service.

The powers granted me are ample and will protect you in
this disposing of publick funds to sustain the country.

R. B. Blake (ed.) Selected Letters and Papers of Judge Charles
S. Taylor, (MS.) I, 88. Courtesy of R. B. Blake, Nacogdoches.

8 Gray, 90-91.

9 *Ibid.*, 91.

10 Binkley, I, 378-379.

11 Returns.

12 Gammel, I, 838.

13 Gray, 132.

14 Yoakum, II, 117.

15 On December 9, 1837, Rusk was issued Bounty Certificate
880 for 320 acres of land for having served in the army from October 8, 1835, to February 25, 1836. File 327, Nacogdoches Bounty
(MS. in General Land Office, Austin). On December 9, 1837, he
received Bounty Certificate 879 for 640 acres for his services

from May 4 to November 4, 1836. File 359, Nacogdoches Bounty (MS. in General Land Office). He received Donation Certificate 2 for 640 acres of land May 15, 1838, for having participated in the Battle of San Jacinto. File 291, Fannin Donation (MS. in General Land Office).

16 *Journal of the House of Representatives of the Republic of Texas Called Session of September 26, 1887, and Regular Session, Commencing November 6, 1837, 4.*

17 Rusk to Lamar, August 24, 1838. Charles Adams Gulick, Jr. and Katherine Elliott (eds.), *The Papers of Mirabeau Buonaparte Lamar* (Austin: Texas State Library, 1922), II, 207.

18 Hugh McLeod to Ashbel Smith. (MS. in the Ashbel Smith Papers, University of Texas Library). Used by Lois Poster Blount, "A Brief Study of Thomas J. Rusk," *The Southwestern Historical Quarterly* (Austin: The Texas Historical Association, 1931), XXXIV, 282.

19 *Ibid.*

20 Yoakum, II, 268-269.

21 *Journals of the Senate of the Seventh Congress of the Republic of Texas,* 133.

22 Oran M. Roberts, "The Political, Legislative, and Judicial History of Texas For Its Fifty Years of Statehood, 1845-1895," Dudley G. Wooten, (ed.), *A Comprehensive History of Texas, 1686-1897.* (Dallas: William G. Scarff, 1898), II, 8.

23 *Journals of the Senate of the First Legislature of the State of Texas,* 22.

24 Lois Foster Blount, "A Brief Study of Thomas J. Rusk," *The Southwestern Historical Quarterly* (Austin: The Texas Historical Association. (1931), XXXIV, 285.

25 *Biographical Directory of The American Congress, 1774-1927.* (Washington: Government Printing Office, 1928), 1485.

26 Kidd, 19.

27 *Ibid.*

28 Gammel, II, 859.

29 Thrall, 692.

30 Blount, *The Southwestern Historical Quarterly*, XXXIV, 189.

WILLIAM BENNETT SCATES

1 Dr. Goodrich shows that in March, 1836, Scates was thirty years of age. Had this been true Scates would have been born in about 1806. Dr. Goodrich's records have proved remarkably accurate but, as was to be expected, there were a few discrepancies between the ages shown by him and the actual ages. The mistakes could have been made by Goodrich, the printer, or someone else.

Dixon (311-314), coincidentally, states that Scates was born October 24, 1806. He adds, however, "I have been able to locate a number of citizens who knew Mr. Scates, but they have been unable to furnish me the date of his death or any reliable data regarding his family, other than that recorded above."

There is an error, also, in the inscription on the monument at the grave of Scates in the State Cemetery at Austin. It is stated that he was born January 26, 1802.

423

2 *The Texas Almanac for 1873* (Galveston W. & D. Richardson & Co., 1874), 73.

3 Courtesy of Mrs. W. R. Martin, Electra, Texas, granddaughter of William B. Scates and genealogist of the Scates family.

4 Returns. The number of votes east in the election held in the municipality of Jefferson February 1, 1836, to select two delegates to the Constitutional Convention are not known. The election judge, William T. Hutton, simply reported to the Convention that Claiborne West and William B. Scates had been elected to represent the municipality.

A headright certificate for one league and one labor of land was issued to Scates in 1838 by the Board of Land Commissioners for Washington County. This was lost and on March 29, 1849, he was issued a duplicate certificate by George W. Smyth, Commissioner of the General Land Office. Hie 837, Milam 1st Class (MS. in General Land Office. Austin).

5 Gammel, I, 824.

6 The following resolution was adopted by the Convention March 3:

Resolved that a committee of five be appointed to devise & report to the Convention a suitable flag for the Republic of Texas

And the question being taken thereon was decided in the affirmative; whereupon the President appointed Messrs. Gazley, Scates, Zavala, Robertson and Barnett of Austin, and

On motion of Mr. Houston, the President was added to said committee.

Gammel, I, 841.

The flag evidently proposed by Mr. de Zavala, was adopted on March 10. On March 12 the following resolution was adopted:

On motion of Mr. Scates, the Rainbow and six points sinking below was added to the flag of Mr. Zavala accepted on Friday last.

424 *Ibid.*, 889.

7 Army Rolls (MS. in General Land Office), 39.

8 On October 24, 1846, Scates was issued Donation Certificate 49 for 649 acres of land for having participated in the Battle of San Jacinto. File 695, Travis Bounty (MS. in General Land Office, Austin).

9 Army Rolls (MS. in General Land Office) Scates on January 18, 1838, was issued Bounty Certificate 1928 for 320 acres of land for having served in the army from March 20 to June 5, 1836. File Bounty (MS. in General Land Office).

10 William Fairfax Gray returned to Texas in 1837 and on March 27 of that year at the town of Washington he wrote in his diary:

Arrived at Washington at 3 o'clock. Found a considerable increase in building; in March, 1836 there were only about ten families here, now thirty, and several houses building. Put up at S. R. Roberts', who is now a Justice of the Peace, and called Squire Roberts. Saw Dr. Smith, who was very polite, and took me to his house. Saw Scates, who is married to the

Doctor's daughter, but did not marry until after their return from the runaway scrape.

GEORGE WASHINGTON SMYTH

1 "The Autobiography of George W. Smyth," with introductory note by Winnie Allen in *Southwestern Historical Quarterly*, XXXVI (1933), 200.

2 *Ibid.*, 201. This corrects Dixon (124) who said Smyth arrived in Texas in 1828.

That Smyth arrived in 1830 is also stated in Headright Certificate 248 for one labor of land issued to him March 3, 1838, by the Jasper County Board of Land Commissioners. File 41, Jasper 1st Class (MS. in the General Land Office, Austin).

Smyth, on May 6, 1835, received title to one league in Zavala's colony, situated in the present Jasper County. Span. Arch., XXII, 503.

3 "The Autobiography of George W. Smyth," 203.

4 *Ibid.*, 206.

5 *Ibid.*, 207.

6 *Ibid.*, 212.

7 *Ibid.*, 213.

The following is from a letter written by John P. Borden, Commissioner of the General Land Office, to Hon. Robert Potter, Chairman of the Committee of Public Lands:

The Commissioners, Charles S. Taylor and G. W. Smyth, issued three hundred and thirty-three titles, one hundred and fifty of which bear date after the closing of the Land Offices. The lands included by these titles, Viz:—under Taylor and Smyth, are situated (so far as I can judge from the vagueness of description) in almost every county east of the Trinity river; the greater portion, however, appears to be in Harrison, Red River and Jefferson counties."

Appendix to the *Journals of the House of Representatives of the Fifth Congress*, 353 E.

8 Gammel, I, 589.

9 Returns. The number of votes cast in the election in Jasper Municipality is not known. The election judges, Joseph Mott, Barney G. Lowe, Hannibal Good and John Miller, simply notified the Convention that George W. Smyth and Stephen H. Everitt had been elected to represent the municipality.

10 Gammel, I, 824.

11 William Fairfax Gray, returning to his home in the United States on April 20, 1836, recorded in his diary:

The report of the Mexicans being on Cow Creek is not credited here. It is believed to have been circulated by Rains, McLaughlin, etc. There are many families here waiting to be ferried across the bay, a distance of seven or eight miles, and put on the United States shore. There are at least 1,000 fugitives here, among them Menifee, A. B. Hardin, Smith [sic], John Fisher, all members of convention.

Gray, 166-167.

426

12 Winkler, 135.

13 *Ibid.*, 184.

14 *Journals of the Extra Session of the House of Representatives of the Ninth Congress*, 4.

15 Oran M. Roberts, "The Political, Legislative, and Judicial History of Texas for Its Fifty Years of Statehood, 1845-1895," Wooten, II, 8.

16 J. T. Robison, *Report of the Commissioners of the General Land Office, 1918-1920* (Austin: General Land Office, 1920), 2.

17 Oran M. Roberts said of the nomination:

The prominent candidates were William C. Young, of Red River County...and O. M. Roberts of Shelby County. A vote nearly approaching two-thirds of the whole convention was soon exhibited in favor of O. M. Roberts, but George W. Smith [sic] of Jasper County, was nominated on the second day. He was not present and had never been spoken of publicly as a Candidate tor Congress...[He was] an intelligent and much respected citizen of the republic and state. He was elected.

Wooten, II, 31-32.

18 *Biographical Directory of the American Congress, 1774-1927* (Washington: United States Government Printing Office, 1928), 1546.

ELIJAH STAPP

1 Goodrich.

2 Barker: *Austin*, Vol. II, Part II, 1271.

3 Ethel Zivley Rather, "De Witt's Colony" in *The Quarterly of the Texas State Historical Association* (Austin: Published by the Association. 1905), VIII, 166.

In Headright Certificate 24 for one labor of land it is certified that Stapp appeared before the Board of Land Commissioners for Jackson County on January 19, 1839, and under oath stated that he came to Texas in 1830. File 111, Goliad 1st Class (MS. in the General Land Office, Austin). This corrects Dixon who states that Stapp arrived in Texas in 1825. Dixon, 223. 427

4 Span. Arch., XXII, 409.

5 Gammel, I, 631.

6 *Ibid.*, 950.

7 Returns.

8 Gammel, I, 824.

9 In the letter Stapp said:

...having been informed that J. J. Linn is now in Harrisburg taken there as a Spy for the enemy;—and my having been acquainted with Linn 5 or six years and having had several conversations with him on the political situation of our country I have ever found him the warm friend to the cause of Texas, (to wit) at the first meeting of the precinct of Lavaca before the taking of La Bahia J. Linn addressed us a letter entreating us not to be deceived in Santana's movements against Texas, that the sale of the public lands (Viz), 300 League & 400 Leagues was not the prime cause. But that Centralism was his object, the yoke of tyranny we must wear or be driven out of the Country; again he furnished horses for young men to wride in the service last fall. It is also well known that he rendered considerable service last fall in the army he was also in the attack made on Lepantaclon [Lipantitlan] and acted not only brave but as a warm friend to his country.

Binkley, II, 613.

10 *Ibid.*, 613-614.

11 Winkler, *Manuscript Letters and Documents of Early Texians, 1821-1845* (Austin: The Steck Co., 1937), 191.

12 I. T. Taylor, *The Cavalcade of Jackson County* (San Antonio: The Naylor Company, 1938), 434. Dixon, quoting Neal Rainey, said that Stapp died in 1872. Dixon, 225.

428

Dr. Charles Bellinger Stewart

1 Courtesy of Mrs. Howard W. Fling, Houston, genealogist of the Stewart family.

2 Charles B. Stewart to Moses Austin Bryan, May 17, 1876. Texas Veterans Association Papers (MSS. in Archives, The University of Texas Library, Austin).

3 On May 17, 1831, Stewart received title to one-fourth of a league in Austin's Second Colony, and the land was located in what is now Fort Bend County. Span. Arch. (MSS. in General Land Office, Austin), IV, 1478. In Headright Certificate 221, issued to Stewart by the Montgomery County Board of Land Commissioners, February 19, 1838, it is stated that he came to Texas in 1830. File 14, Liberty 1st Class (MS. in General Land Office).

4 Pension Papers (MSS. in Archives, Texas State Library, Austin).

5 Gammel, I, 497.

6 Original commission in possession of Mrs. Howard W. Fling, October, 1940.

7 Yoakum, I, 340-341.

8 The original document is in possession of Mrs. Howard W. Fling.

9 Barker explained the function of this body:

The Committees of Safety and correspondence of the various municipalities had ordered an election of delegates to attend a convention or consultation, to be held at San Felipe beginning October 15, 1835.

Before the election could be held it became evident that war was inevitable. During the latter half of September the San Felipe committee, with Austin—who had just returned from his Mexican prison—as chairman, assumed general direction of affairs. Austin, however, felt that this committee lacked authority, and in order to make it representative he urged each of the other committees to send to San Felipe one member to form a "permanent counsel" until the meeting of the consultation. Only Matagorda and Liberty responded, but on October 11, the council organized itself by electing R. R. Royal president and appointing C. B. Stewart Secretary. It numbered five members. In the meantime delegates to the consultation had been elected, but hostilities had also begun, and when the day of assembly came it was found that so many delegates were away with the army that a quorum could not be obtained. Those present therefore adjourned until November 1, and upon invitation of the permanent council a number of them united with that body.

Eugene C. Barker (ed.), "Journals of the Permanent Council," *The Quarterly of the Texas State Historical Association* (1904), VII, 251.

10 Gammel, I, 497.

11 *Ibid.*, 795.

12 *Ibid.*, 801.

13 Gray, 108.

14 Gammel, I, 824.

429

15 Deed Record of Washington County (MSS. in County Clerk's Office, Brenham), A-1, 240-44.

16 *Mississippi Free-Trader* (Natchez), April 1, 1836.

17 Original commission in possession of Mrs. Howard W. Fling.

18 Winkler, 205.

19 Oran M. Roberts, "The Political, Legislative, and Judicial History of Texas for Its Fifty Tears of Statehood, 1845-1895" in Wooten, II, 8.

20 Lindley, 4.

21 *Ibid.*, 15.

22 *Ibid.*, 85.

23 *Ibid.*

24 Texas Veterans Association Papers (MSS. in Archives, The University of Texas Library).

25 From the inscription on the monument at his grave.

26 Through error, it was stated on the marker that Stewart was a member of the Consultation in 1835 and that he was the first secretary of state.

JAMES GIBSON SWISHER

1 Inscription on the headstone at Captain Swisher's grave. Fulmore in 1915 refers to Swisher as John G. Swisher; says he was born in 1795 and died in 1869. Dixon (213), in 1924, makes the same mistakes regarding Swisher's birth and death. Mrs. J. R. Blocker says that her grandfather, James G. Swisher, was born in 1794 and died in 1862. Rena Maverick Green (ed.), *The Swisher Memoirs By Col. John M. Swisher* (San Antonio: The Sigmund Press, Inc., 1932), 5.

2 The Secretary of War to United States Senator Tom Connally, November 14, 1939. The letter is in possession of the author of this volume.

3 In Headright Certificate 264 issued to Swisher February 1, 1838, for one league and one labor of land by the Board of Land Commissioners for Washington County it is certified that he arrived in Texas in 1833. File 14, Gonzales 1st Class (MS. in the General Land Office).

4 Rena Maverick Green (ed.), *The Swisher Memoirs*, 7-8.

5 On May 15, 1839, Swisher was issued Donation Certificate 885 for 640 acres of land for having participated in the storming and capture of Bexar, December 5 to 10, 1835. File 66, San Patricio Donation (MS. in General Land Office).

6 Brown, I, 824-426.

7 Jess Hass, election judge of the municipality, reported to the convention on March 1 that Grimes, Dr. Barnett, Dr. Goodrich and Swisher had been elected to represent Washington Municipality. The number of votes received was not stated. Returns.

8 Gammel, I, 824.

9 Rena Maverick Green (ed.), *The Swisher Memoirs*, 50-51.

10 Army Rolls (MS. in the General Land Office).

11 Swisher was issued Bounty Certificate 9138 on May 15, 1839, for 320 acres of land for having served in the army from July 3 to October 3, 1836. File 154, Fannin Bounty (MS. in the General Land Office).

12 Gammel, II 418-419.

13 *Ibid.*, VIII, 1076.

CHARLES STANFIELD TAYLOR

1 Goodrich.

2 When Taylor, on April 11, 1833, applied for land in Austin's Colony, he stated he had been a resident of Texas for five years. Austin's Application Book (MS. in the General Land Office, Austin), II, 2. Commissioner George W. Smyth issued Taylor title to one league of land which was surveyed "South of Soda Lake." Span. Arch. (MSS. in the General Land Office), XXIX,

323. On June 11, 1838, Taylor was issued Headright Certificate 593 for one labor of land by the Nacogdoches County Board of Land Commissioners. File 706, Nacogdoches 1st Class (MS. in the General Land Office).

3 Transcripts of Nacogdoches Archives (MSS. in the University of Texas Library, Austin), XXXII.

4 From an unpublished sketch of Taylor by R. B. Blake, Nacogdoches.

5 *Ibid.*

6 Gammel, I, 480.

7 *Ibid.*, 496..

8 Brown (I, 227-229), in error, states that Taylor was a member of the Second Convention of Texas in 1833.

9 Unpublished sketch of Charles Stanfield Taylor by R. B. Blake.

10 *Ibid.*

11 Gammel, I, 357-362.

12 R. B. Blake, Selected Papers of Judge Charles S. Taylor (Mimeographed in three volumes) I, 34.

13 *Ibid.*, I, 67-68.

14 *Ibid.*, 86.

15 *Ibid.*, 108.

16 *Ibid.*, 110.

The following is from a letter written by John P. Borden, Commissioner of the General Land Office, to Hon. Robert Potter, Chairman of Committee of Public Lands:

> The Commissioners, Charles S. Taylor and G. W. Smyth, issued three hundred and thirty-three titles, one hundred and fifty of which bear date after the closing of the Land Offices. The lands included by these titles, Viz:—under Taylor and Smyth, are situated (so far as I can judge from the vagueness of description) in almost every county east of the Trinity river, the greater portion, however, appears to be in Harrison Red River and Jefferson Counties.

Appendix to the *Journals of the House of Representatives of the Fifth Congress*, 353.

17 Returns. For the number of votes received by each of the candidates in Nacogdoches County see the sketch of Thomas J. Rusk in this volume.

18 Gammel, I, 824.

19 *Ibid.*, 838.

20 Blake, Selected Papers of Judge Charles S. Taylor, I, 101.

21 Winkler, 1911, 34.

22 *Ibid.*, 113.

23 *Ibid.*, 116..

24 Blake, Selected Papers of Judge Charles S. Taylor, I, 122.

25 *Ibid.*, I, 123.

26 *Ibid.*, 125.

27 *Ibid.*, 127.

28 Winkler, 144.

29 Blake, Selected Papers of Judge Charles S. Taylor, I, 172.

30 *Ibid.*, 189.

31 *Ibid.*, II, 36.

32 *Ibid.*, 67.

33 *Ibid.*, 89.

34 *Ibid.*, III, 28.

35 *Ibid.*, 97.

36 *Ibid.*, 125.

37 At Nacogdoches December 21, 1835 Judge Taylor wrote:

I this day solemnly promise, for in consideration of the respect due my wife, never again during my life to drink either wine or spirituous liquors of any kind.—We were married on the 28 (Saturday) of May, 1831, at Nacogdoches, by Padre Bias de Leon.

Blake, Selected Papers of Judge Charles S. Taylor, III, 129.

38 He was a member of Milam Lodge No. 40, A. F. and A. M.,

in 1837, and a charter member of the Grand Lodge of Texas, organized at Houston, December 20, 1837. Kidd, 19.

DAVID THOMAS

1 Dixon (320) said of Thomas:

He came to Texas early in 1835 and settled in the southwest, identifying himself with the settlers in the Hewitson-Power Colony in the Municipality of Refugio.

When General Houston was sent to Goliad and Refugio by Governor Smith to investigate the situation and, if favorable, to assume command of Johnson's and Grant's troops rendezvousing at Refugio, Mr. Thomas met him and extended to him many courtesies and he and Mr. James Power were instrumental in having Refugio, endorse him as a delegate to the convention which had been called to meet at Old Washington. Mr. Thomas was elected from Goliad to this convention and Mr. James Power and Edwin [Edward] Conrad were ejected from Refugio.

Dixon was mistaken. Thomas was not elected from Goliad Municipality and was not instrumental in having Refugio endorse General Houston.

2 Goodrich.

3 Harbert Davenport, Brownsville, Texas, to the author, February 26, 1940. Davenport gives as references a letter from Captain Lawrence to the General Council, State Papers; and Timothy Pickering Jones, Pension Papers, Archives, Texas State Library.

4 Binkley, I, 268-269.

5 Gammel, I, 729-730.

6 Williams & Barker, I, 343-344.

7 Returns.

8 *Ibid.*

9 *Ibid.*

10 Gammel, I, 824.

11 Gray, 161.

12 John J. Linn, *Reminiscences of Fifty Years in Texas* (New York: D. & J. Sadlier & Co., 1883), 261.

13 *Ibid.*, 261.

14 Dixon, 321.

15 *Ibid.*, Buffington's home was at that time in San Augustine Municipality. He did not move to Montgomery County until 1842.

16 Yoakum, II, 153.

17 *The Texas Almanac for 1869* (Galveston), 58-59.

18 File 433, Travis County First Class Headright Certificate (MS., in General Land Office, Austin.)

JOHN TURNER

1 Goodrich. Dixon (329-332), without citing authority, fixes December 4, 1802, as the precise date of Turner's birth. Since there are inaccuracies in Dixon's sketch, stating, for example, that Turner died in 1840, the date of birth set by him cannot be accepted.

2 Span. Arch., LX, 77. McMullen and McGloin were the only empresarios who granted married colonists one league and one labor of land.

3 Binkley, I, 155-156.

4 Returns. For the number of votes received by each of the candidates in San Patricio Municipality see the sketch of John W. Bower in this volume.

5 Gammel, I, 824.

6 Charles Adams Gulick, Jr. and Katherine Elliott (eds.), *The Papers of Mirabeau Buonaparte Lamar* (Austin: Texas State Library, 1922), I, 410.

7 *Journals of the House of Representatives of the Republic of Texas, First Congress—First Session* (Houston: Printed at the

office of *The Telegraph and Texas Register*, 1838), 75.

8 Winkler, 34.

9 Williams & Barker, II, 70.

10 On June 16, 1841, Turner sold at auction in Houston Donation Certificate 1124 for 640 acres of land issued in the name of
Robert A. Toler, who was killed at Goliad, March 27, 1836. Deed
Records of Harris County (MSS. in County Clerk's Office, Houston), H, 385.

11 *Ibid.*, I, 429. On February 21, 1853, Mrs. Margaret Bradley,
widow of John Turner, sold to Thomas Jefferson Ewing, the
Turner home on lots 3, 4 and 5, of block 88. This house, with
modifications, served as the Ewing home until the deaths of
Ewing in 1870 and of Mrs. Ewing in 1873, when it was sold to
George H. Hermann. The building stood until the City of Houston began to prepare the present civic center in 1928. Courtesy
of Andrew P. Muir, great-grandson of Thomas J. Ewing.

12 *Ibid.*, J, 2. Probate Records of Harris County (MSS. in County Clerk's Office, Houston), F, 483.

13 Marriage Records of Harris County (MSS. in County Clerk's
Office, Houston), B, 117. On December 4, 1849, Mrs. Bradley
sold to Stephen S. Tompkins a part of lot 2 in Block 88 in Houston. She could not write and signed the deed with a mark. Deed
Records of Harris County, N, 313.

14 Marriage Records of Harris County, B, 483.

15 Deed Records of Live Oak County (MSS. in County Clerk's
Office, George West, Texas), F, 90.

E D W I N W A L L E R

1 Courtesy of Mrs. George H. Wray of Dublin, Texas, genealogist of the Waller family. Dixon (338), in error, states that Waller
was born March 16, 1800.

2 The records of the Texas Veterans Association for the year
1874 show that he was "74; nativity, Virginia; emigrated in 1831;
in battle of Velasco in 1832 and in campaign of 1835, and member

of convention in March. 1836." D. W. C. Baker, *A Texas Scrap-Book* (New York: A. S. Barnes and Co., 1875), 617.

3 Span. Arch., VIII, 453. On February 1, 1838, Waller was issued Headright Certificate 63 for one labor of land by the Brazoria County Board of Land Commissioners. File 962, Milam 1st Class (MS. in the General Land Office).

4 Charles Adams Gulick, Jr. and Katherine Elliott (eds.), *The Papers of Mirabeau Buonaparte Lamar* (Austin: Texas State Library, 1921), I, 105.

5 Gammel, I, 508.

6 *Ibid.*, 544.

7 Returns. For the number of votes received by each of the candidates in Brazoria Municipality see the sketch of Asa Brigham in this volume.

8 Gammel, I, 824.

9 *Ibid.*, 900.

10 Gray, 169-170.

11 *Ibid.*, 227-228.

12 Gulick and Elliott, *The Papers of Mirabeau Buonaparte Lamar*, II, 568.

13 Winkler, 146-147.

14 *Ibid.*, 159.

15 P. E. Peareson (ed.) "Reminiscences of Judge Edwin Waller," *The Quarterly of the Texas State Historical Association* (Austin: Published by the Association, 1901), IV, 51.

16 Correcting Dixon (341) who states that Waller died on his farm in Austin County in 1883.

17 Gammel, VII, 501.

18 Thrall, 702.

CLAIBORNE WEST

1 Goodrich. Dixon (334) who lost all trace of West after the year 1837, nevertheless was able to set November 24, 1800, as the

exact date of his birth.

2 Gammel, I, 480. Dixon (334) was mistaken in stating that West was a member of the Second Convention of Texas in 1833.

3 Gammel, I, 496.

4 *Ibid.*, 509.

5 *Ibid.*, 547.

6 On May 20, 1835, West was issued title to one league of land in Zavala's Colony, situated in the present Orange County. Span. Arch. (MSS. in the General Land Office, Austin), XXII, 455. West did not apply for the one labor of land due him from the Republic of Texas.

Following is a copy of the certificate of character issued to West:

> I, William Hardin, Judge of the first instance for the Jurisdiction of Liberty, do hereby certify that the Honorable Claiborne West is a man of Family consisting of his wife and four children, and that he is a man of good morals and industrious habits, a good citizen and friendly to the Laws and Religion of the Country. Given at the instance of the party interested.

> Span. Arch. (MSS. in the General Land Office).

7 Returns.

8 Gammel, I, 824

9 Gray, 166.

10 Binkley, II, 628.

11 Army Rolls (MSS. in the General Land Office).

12 *Journals of the House of Representatives of the Republic of Texas, First Congress—First Session* (Houston: Printed at the office of *The Telegraph and Texas Register*, 1838), 3.

13 Courtesy of Mrs. Weinert, Seguin, Texas.

14 Wade, 61.

CHAPTER NOTES

JAMES B. WOODS

1 Goodrich. Dixon who had lost all trace of Woods after the adjournment of the Convention on March 17, 1836, closed his sketch of him by saying: "The above record of Mr. Woods' early life is all the information I have been able to secure of his career. If he has descendants in Texas I have been unable to locate them, though I have labored assiduously to do so." Dixon (324-328), however, was able to fix the date of Woods's birth as January 21, 1802, in Mercer County, Kentucky.

2 On March 21, 1831, Commissioner J. F. Madero issued Woods title to one lot situated in the town of Liberty. Span. Arch. (MSS. in the General Land Office, Austin), XLIV, 122. On April 9, 1835, he received title to one league in Vehlein's Colony, situated in the present Liberty County. *Ibid*, XX, 355. In Headright Certificate 262 for one labor of land issued to him April 12, 1838, by the Liberty County Board of Land Commissioners it is certified that he came to Texas in 1830.

439

3 Gammel, 520.

4 Returns. For the number of votes received on February 1, 1836, by the candidates in Liberty Municipality, see the sketch of Augustine Blackburn Hardin in this volume.

5 Gammel, I, 848.

6 *Ibid.*, 883.

7 Army Rolls (MSS. in the General Land Office, Austin.)

8 Original in William B. Duncan Papers (MSS. in San Jacinto Museum of History). Courtesy of the owner, Mrs. Julia D. Welder, of Liberty.

LORENZO DE ZAVALA

1 W. S. Cleaves, "Lorenzo De Zavala in Texas," in *Southwestern Historical Quarterly* (Austin: The Texas State Historical Association. 1933). XXXVI, 29.

Appletons', usually accurate, states that Zavala was born in

Merida, Yucatan. James Grant Wilson and John Fiske (eds.),
Appletons' Cyclopaedia of American Biography (New York: D.
Appleton and Co., 1889), VI, 657. Dixon (139), in error, says that
Zavala was born in Spain.

2 Appletons' and most biographers of Zavala fix his birth as
October 3, 1788. Miss Adina De Zavala, genealogist of the Zavala
family in Texas, wrote the author February 12, 1932, that Lorenzo
de Zavala was born October 3, 1789.

3 "Lorenzo de Zavala" (A Free Translation From Sosa), C. W.
Raines, *Year Book For Texas* (Austin: Gammel Statesman Publishing Co., 1903), II, 29.

4 Appletons', VI, 657. "He attended the clerical boarding-school
of the Franciscans in Merida. Here he received instructions in
Latin, morals, theology, and classical philosophy." Cleaves, "Lorenzo de Zavala in Texas," 30.

5 Appletons', VI. 657.

6 Cleaves, "Lorenzo de Zavala in Texas," 31.

7 *Ibid.*, 32.

8 *Ibid.*

9 Cleaves, "Lorenzo de Zavala in Texas," 32.

10 Mary Virginia Henderson, "Minor Empresario Contracts
for the Colonization of Texas, 1825-1834," *The Southwestern Historical Quarterly* (1928), XXXI, 306.

11 Henderson, "Minor Empresario Contracts for the Colonization of Texas," 306-307.

12 Cleaves, "Lorenzo de Zavala in Texas," 32.

13 *Ibid.*

14 *Ibid.*, 33.

15 *Ibid.*

16 *Ibid.*

17 In Headright Certificate 187 for one league and one labor
of land issued in Zavala's name February 5, 1838, by the Harrisburg County Board of Land Commissioners it is stated that
be arrived in Texas in 1835. File 30-1/2, Lamar 1st Class (MS. in

General Land Office, Austin).

Philip Singleton, in 1828-29, had I settled on the north side of Buffalo Bayou nearly opposite the Arthur McCormick league of land. He built a small log house, afterwards covered with planks. This place was bought by Zavala, and it was his first home in Texas. —Dermot H. Hardy and Ingham S. Roberts (eds.), *Historical Review of South-East Texas* (Chicago: The Lewis Publishing Co., 1910).

"Zavala only owns one labor of land here...The house is small, one large room, three small bed closets and a porch, kitchen, etc." —Gray, 155

18 Henry Stuart Foote, *Texas And The Texans* (Philadelphia: Thomas, Cowperthwait & Co., 1841), II, 81.

19 *Texas Republican* (Columbia), August 19, 1835.

20 Hubert Howe Bancroft, *History of the North Mexican States and Texas* (San Francisco: The History Co., 1889), II, 158.

21 Gammel, I, 508.

22 Returns. For the number of votes received by each of the candidates in Harrisburg Municipality, February 1, 1836, see the sketch of John W. Moore in this volume.

23 Gammel, I, 824.

24 Gray, 120.

25 *Ibid.*, 127.

26 *Ibid.*, 144.

On April 3, 1836, General Houston in a letter to Thomas J. Rusk, Secretary of War, said:

"Mr. Zavala has arrived and reported for duty. I am glad of it. He informed me that I should have the pleasure of seeing you; and indeed it would give me pleasure to do so." Yoakum, II, 490.

Of this Yoakum said: "On the 2d of April, Colonel Zavala joined the camp, bringing the information that a visit might be expected from Colonel Rusk, the secretary of war." *Ibid.*, 116.

Yoakum, it appears, thought Houston referred to Vice-President Zavala, but such was not the case. He alluded to Governor Zavala's son, Lorenzo, Jr., who later participated in the Battle of

San Jacinto.

27 Binkley, II, 641-642.

28 *Ibid.*, 642-643.

29 M. B. Lamar, Secretary of War, at Velasco, on May 19, 1836, wrote to James Morgan, Commander of Galveston:

> Genl. Zavala is here and complains that he is put to considerable inconvenience in consequence of his house being made use of as a hospital for the sick and wounded prisoners. You will please therefore, upon receipts of this to order the *Cayuga* to proceed immediately to the residence of Gen. Zavala; with instructions to bring the sick and wounded to Galveston. This order has reference to the prisoners solely, but should any of the sick or wounded Texians request to come in the *Cayuga*, you will instruct Capt. [William P.] Harris to bring them, otherwise you will give orders to have arrangements made for their comfort in the neighborhood of Genl. Zavala.

Binkley, II, 693.

30 Binkley, II, 709-712.

31 *Ibid.*, 744.

32 *Ibid.*, II, 1066.

33 Brown, II, 105.

34 Foote, *Texas and Texans*, II, 73.

35 Gammel, IV, 960.